Edgar Degas

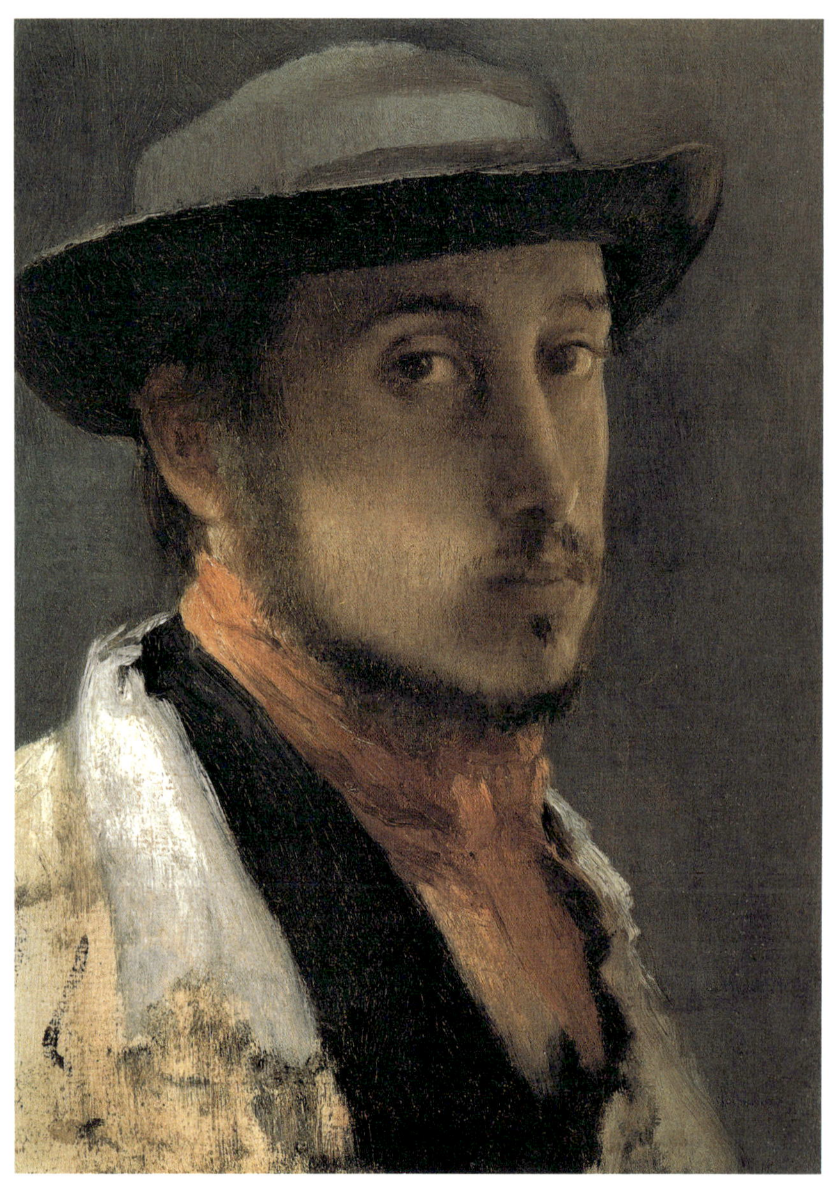

Self-Portrait, c. 1857–58. Oil on paper mounted on canvas,
26 × 19.1 cm (10¼ × 7½ in.). Sterling and Francine Clark Art Institute,
Williamstown, Massachusetts

Edgar Degas
Drawings and Pastels

Christopher Lloyd

With 238 illustrations

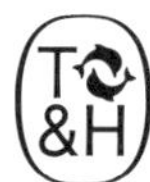

For Dora, Frederick, Henry, Mela, Poppy and Sohan …

Publisher's Note: All works are by Edgar Degas and are on paper
unless otherwise stated. Measurements are height before width.

First paperback edition 2017
Reprinted 2023

First published in the United Kingdom in 2014 by
Thames & Hudson Ltd, 181A High Holborn, London WC1V 7QX

Edgar Degas: Drawings and Pastels © 2014 Thames & Hudson Ltd, London
Text © 2014 Christopher Lloyd

British Library Cataloguing-in-Publication Data
A catalogue record for this book is available from the British Library

ISBN 978-0-500-29341-6

Printed and bound in China by C&C Offset Printing Co. Ltd

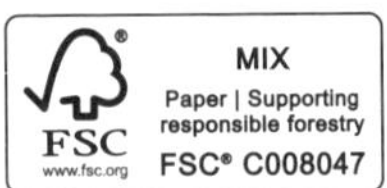

Contents

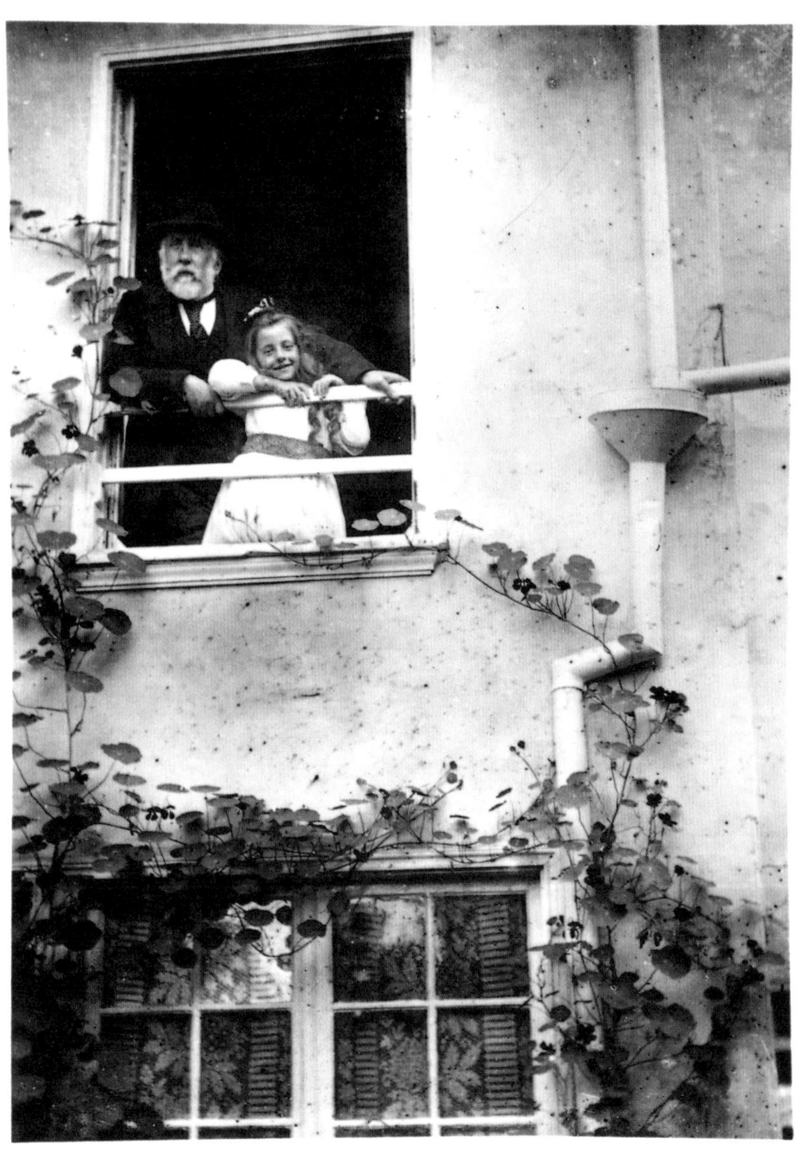

1. Degas with his niece at Saint-Valéry-sur-Somme,
c. 1900. Photo by René Degas.
Bibliothèque Nationale, Paris

Introduction

'Draw a lot. Oh! The beauty of drawing!'

(Degas, Notebook 23, p. 45, used between 1868 and 1872)

Edgar Degas was one of the outstanding draughtsmen of the nineteenth century. More than that, he falls into that rare category of artists – Leonardo da Vinci, Dürer, Raphael, Michelangelo, Rubens, Rembrandt, Watteau – of whom it can be said that every mark they make on paper is worthy of consideration. None of Degas's contemporaries – not even Manet, Pissarro, Gauguin or Cézanne – drew as compulsively or as rigorously as Degas.

Although Degas was recognized as a formidable draughtsman during his lifetime and exhibited numerous pastels and works on paper at several of the Impressionist exhibitions held between 1874 and 1886, the full extent of his commitment to drawing only became apparent on his death in 1917. The four sales of the artist's studio contents held at the Galerie Georges Petit between May 1918 and July 1919 revealed more than a thousand drawings in all media. Even then, no reckoning was made of Degas's known Notebooks, thirty-two of which were included in a summary inventory of the studio but excluded from the sale. In addition, dealers such as Paul Durand-Ruel and Ambroise Vollard had begun to sell works on paper by Degas while he was still alive and collectors – at first friends of the artist – to show them on their walls.

Degas was born on 19 July 1834 in the centre of Paris. His father, who referred to himself as Auguste De Gas, had been born in Naples and his mother, Célestine Musson, in New Orleans. The family into which Degas was born was prosperous: on the father's side from banking and on the mother's from cotton. It was also cultured. These connections created an extended family that was to play an important part in Degas's life. His mother died when the artist was aged thirteen and subsequently he developed a closer relationship with his father.

The young Degas underwent a traditional schooling as a boarder in
Paris at the Lycée Louis-le-Grand from 1845 to 1853 and embarked on
studying the law, but without much conviction. If the father hoped that
his eldest son would follow him into the family bank, it did not happen.
Instead, it seems that Auguste De Gas was content for Edgar to become
an artist and indeed he himself may have positively encouraged this
since art was one of his own interests. But, if he gave encouragement at
the outset of Degas's career, he may have been surprised by the course
of its development and the nature of its ultimate success. Starting as a
traditionalist producing history paintings, portraits and genre scenes in
a realist style during the 1860s, by the 1870s Degas was associated by
virtue of his style and treatment of contemporary subject matter with
the avant-garde, holding a prominent position within Impressionism.
However, even by the time of the final Impressionist exhibition in 1886
Degas preferred not to align himself any longer with a single group of
artists. He eschewed the scientific approach of the Neo-Impressionists
and abhorred the escapism of the Symbolists – movements that both
followed upon Impressionism. And he remained distant from the Nabis
and Fauves artists who might be said to have benefited from the technical
advances made by the Impressionists. Rather, Degas defended his
independence fiercely and this was to remain his stance for the rest of
his long life. Indeed, the care taken by the artist from the 1880s onwards
to remain independent and to preserve his individuality is a measure
of his importance as an artist. For it is within the privacy of his studio
that Degas was most able to deploy his creative resources and it is as a
result of his single-mindedness that he was able to experiment without
fear of failure.

Degas's life spans the second half of the nineteenth century and
extends well into the first quarter of the twentieth, which witnessed
some of the most dramatic developments in European art. Throughout
this period Degas sought to safeguard those values of art that he
particularly cherished not by being overly protective of them, but rather
by challenging or even subverting them. 'Art is vice', he once said, 'you
don't marry it legitimately, you ravish it.' Only in recent years has it been
acknowledged that Degas's work serves as a vital link between Jean-
Auguste-Dominique Ingres and Eugène Delacroix on the one hand and
Pablo Picasso and Henri Matisse on the other. As such he stands at the
threshold of modern art.

Degas drew constantly throughout his working life. What began in
the 1850s and 1860s as an act of self-discipline exercising mind and eye
became from the 1870s onwards an emotional necessity, to the degree
that drawings, as opposed to paintings, came to form the basis of his

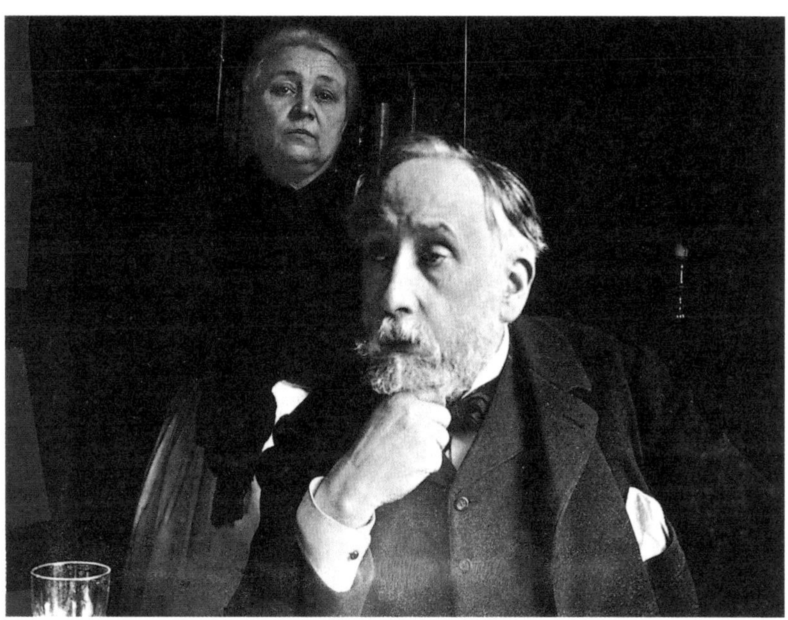

2. *Self-portrait with Zoë Closier, c.* 1895.
Gelatin silver print, 18.2 × 24.2 cm (7⅛ × 9½ in.).
Bibliothèque Nationale, Paris

art. For Degas drawings were, in the final analysis, made by instinct whereas a painting was an artificial construct. While at the outset Degas saw drawing as the means to an end in the evolution of a painting, by the middle of his career it had become an end in itself. From the 1870s pastels and mixed-media works, as well as many of the drawings made on coloured papers, possess an autonomy challenging the status of paintings, which from the 1890s were far fewer in number. This emphasis is a reversal of the traditional hierarchy whereby drawing was subservient to painting and is a good example of the revolutionary nature of Degas's art. The scale of many of Degas's works on paper, the choice of medium, the degree of finish and the method of presentation within elaborate frames introduced a note of rivalry between paintings and drawings to the extent that they could be seen as interchangeable.

The sheer volume and variety of the works on paper by Degas, in addition to the emphasis he placed on the act of drawing itself, enables his life and the evolution of his style to be told through an examination of his drawings and pastels alone, which is one of the purposes of this book. As a draughtsman embarking on a career in mid-nineteenth-century France, Degas was heir to a well-established tradition. That tradition was enshrined in the Académie Royale de Peinture et de Sculpture, which was founded in 1648 and quickly established long-lasting parameters for artistic practice in France. Reconstructed as the Académie des Beaux-Arts after the Revolution of 1789, it set standards, codified principles, organized exhibitions and competitions, administered awards, orchestrated criticism and protected reputations.

The mouthpiece of the Académie in the nineteenth century was the Ecole des Beaux-Arts. Teaching at the Ecole was standardized and was intended to produce artists who would undertake narrative paintings (often on a large scale) based on historical, religious or mythological subjects for inclusion at the annual exhibitions of the Paris Salon. Other subjects such as landscapes, portraits, or genre scenes, although accepted, did not have the same kudos. Following acceptance at the Ecole, students progressed from copying engravings after works of art to making copies after three-dimensional objects and finally to working from live models. Proficiency in drawing was regarded as the basis of art as a whole: it inculcated manual skills and implied moral rectitude. The teaching was done by leading Salon artists of the day, who also opened their own studios for teaching and were not always diligent in their attendance at the Ecole. Some basic reforms to the Ecole's teaching made in 1863 lifted several of the restrictions and introduced greater flexibility by encouraging students to work outside the studio more, but its status was not as yet severely undermined by these changes. The essential criticism of the Ecole remained; namely, it produced able draughtsmen, but did little to develop artistic imagination or encourage artists to engage with everyday life.

Degas was all too aware of the practices of the Ecole des Beaux-Arts when he decided to become an artist, but he was never in thrall to it even after he enrolled there in 1855. He certainly made copies after earlier works of art and he also often used pencil for the purpose as opposed to the softer media that he soon came to prefer. Yet during the three years (1856–59) that he spent visiting Italy on his own volition as part of his training, he distanced himself from the Villa Medici in Rome, which was run by the Académie des Beaux-Arts. Nonetheless, he formed friendships with artists who were enrolled there and availed himself of the opportunity to draw from live models. Degas became an artist in spite of the system rather than because of it and to that extent he could be described as self-taught.

By nature standoffish, Degas carefully selected for himself those artists from whom he could learn most. Among these were Ingres and

Delacroix who represented the polarities of French art – the former honouring the classical tradition and the latter epitomizing Romanticism. He also sought out other artists such as Jean-Baptiste-Camille Corot, Gustave Courbet and Honoré Daumier whose styles assisted him in developing his own. Later in life Degas obtained works by these artists, as well as those by old masters and his immediate contemporaries, for his collection, which was displayed in his house in the Rue Victor-Massé in Paris. The collection was dispersed in three sales held in March and November 1918 in parallel with the sales of his studio contents. The diversity and wide-range of those artists who engaged Degas's attention indicates his determination to break free from any formal training and to pursue his own course of action. Many other Impressionists shared this outlook, which is why in 1874 they formed the co-operative known as the Société Anonyme des Artistes, Peintres, Sculpteurs, Graveurs, etc. to present the first Impressionist exhibition. However, few of the artists who participated in the eight Impressionist exhibitions remained as true to their own principles as Degas.

Degas's earliest drawings lie within the bounds of convention. He favours pencil and black chalk with highlights in white body-colour or washes of various hues. Sometimes the paper is prepared with a coloured wash or is tinted. Pen and ink is reserved for landscapes and caricature. Pure watercolour is occasionally used for landscapes or vignettes. The point of the brush is sometimes preferred to the pen. Pastel makes an early appearance; red chalk is rarely seen. But nothing is straightforward in Degas and even by the end of the 1860s he is introducing all kinds of variations and combinations by mixing media and trying out different supports: paper, card, board, silk, canvas. The speed with which he develops as a draughtsman is astonishing and a hint of things to come is found in the repetition of figures on the same sheet often seen from different, sometimes exploratory, viewpoints. Looking at these drawings of the late 1860s is like the rumble of an approaching thunderstorm.

The 1870s sees an increase in Degas's technical skills as his preference for the softer media grows in accordance with his concern to depict scenes from contemporary life. Black chalk and charcoal are deployed more on their own, now frequently with highlights in gouache or pastel. Gradually pastel takes over as Degas's principal medium and he begins to explore its possibilities on its own in fully worked up compositions, sometimes drawn over monotypes acting as a dark background and thereby reinforcing the intensity of the colours. *Essence* (oil paint diluted with turpentine) applied with a brush was equally important. It allowed for greater spontaneity and freedom of line, as well as a deeper chiaroscuro, particularly when used on tinted papers.

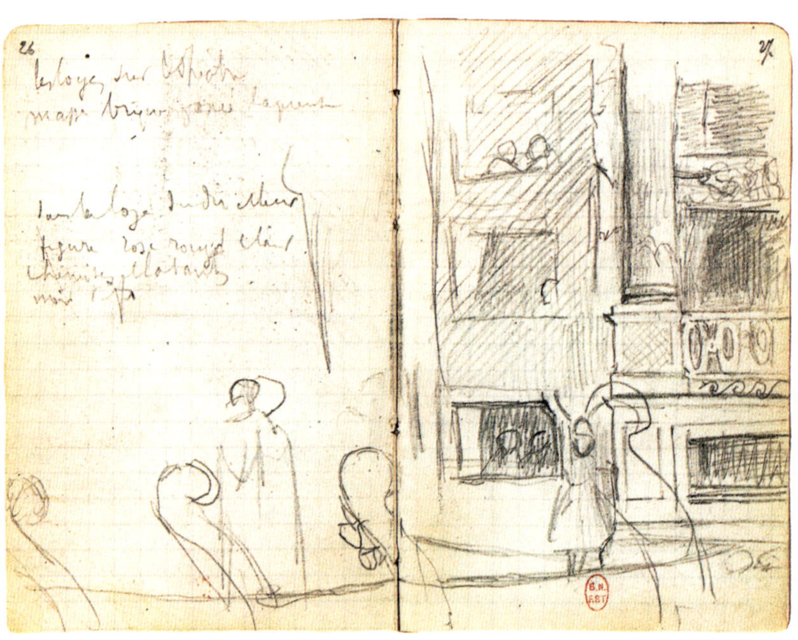

3. *View of a Theatre Stage, Orchestra Pit and Boxes,*
Notebook 24, pp. 26–27, 1868–73. Pencil on paper
with blue squaring, 11.7 × 7.9 cm (4⅝ × 3⅛ in.).
Bibliothèque Nationale, Paris

Some indication of Degas's progress as a draughtsman is apparent
from his Notebooks, of which thirty-eight in all have survived. These
date from the mid-1850s to the mid-1880s when he was less inclined to
search for new motifs or incorporate authentic material in his pictures.
The Notebooks are a rare survival in terms of avant-garde painting
of the late nineteenth century. The sketchbooks of Manet, Pissarro,
Gauguin and Cézanne have for the most part been dismembered and can
be reconstituted only with difficulty. In the case of Degas, notebooks
(as opposed to sketchbooks) is the appropriate term for this material
because the information in them is so extraordinarily detailed and varied,
including appointments, addresses, travelogues, notes on works of art,
references to literature, ideas for pictures, lists of people he has met
or performances he has attended, accounts and theoretical statements
about art. There are, of course, also many drawings and in all media.
These are equally diverse, ranging from doodles and caricatures to
copies, individual studies from life and compositional sketches [3 and
4]. Above all, the Notebooks are essentially private, like a diary, and

therefore revealing as regards Degas's personality (with its occasional scatological overtones), his working methods and his artistic aspirations. There is a general chronological sequence to the Notebooks, but the internal evidence shows that they were used both consecutively and simultaneously, sometimes randomly and sometimes consistently. The earlier Notebooks of the late 1850s were drawn in regularly and in quick succession, but from the early 1860s the periods that each Notebook was in use became more extensive. Overall, the Notebooks provide a context for Degas's art by revealing his thought processes and sometimes anticipating those dazzlingly powerful and beautiful drawings and pastels that he made on single sheets of paper.

An important shift occurs in Degas's approach to drawing at the beginning of the 1880s. The preference for black chalk, charcoal and pastel is fully established, but the artist now withdraws more into his studio, partly as a result of the deterioration of his eyesight due to a progressive retinal disease, which caused him to suffer from photophobia and increasingly blurred vision from as early as the late 1860s. There is a greater reliance on models summoned by him and on his own memory,

4. *Studies of a Woman Holding a Child, a Man Wearing a Hat, and Horses*, Notebook 12, pp. 74–75, 1858–59. Brown ink with wash, 14.5 × 9.8 cm (5¾ × 3⅞ in.). Bibliothèque Nationale, Paris

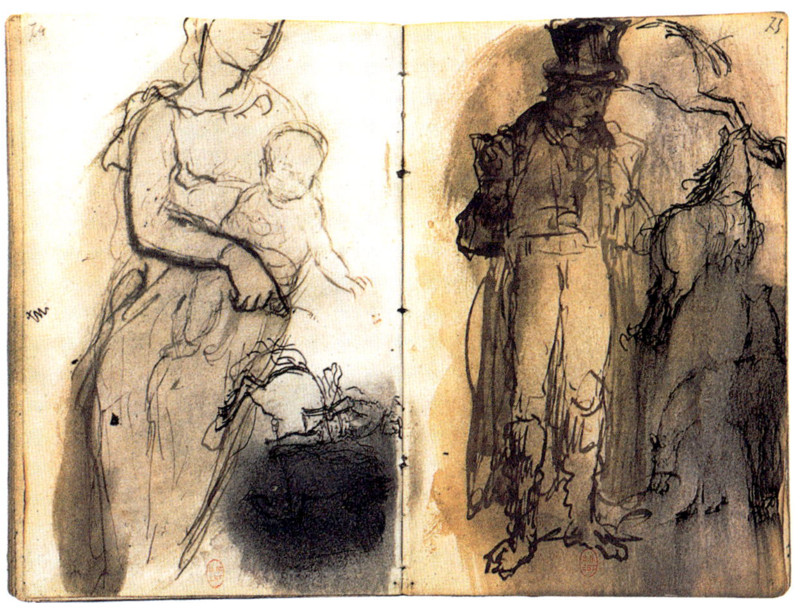

which he had carefully trained for the purpose, as opposed to direct observation of the social scene. The subject matter – dancers, singers, milliners, jockeys, laundresses, women at their toilette – remains fixed, but more emphasis is placed on smaller groupings such as pairs of figures or single figures seen from oblique or steep angles. Degas explores horizontal compositions in the form of friezes involving complicated patterns and overlapping forms with figures seen in relief. More and more, as he moves through the final decades of his life, Degas strives to create a synthesis in his compositions, as opposed to accumulating a whole range of visual data that is then carefully fitted together to make a convincing whole. However broadly handled the drawings are and however many times the outlines are redrawn, the figure is always subject to close analysis resulting from several years practice. This ruthless examination undertaken with a relentless unforgiving gaze continues unabated in the studio. Degas's ability to squeeze so much from a single motif is unrivalled. Female bathers get in and out of bath tubs, sponge or dry themselves, or are waited on by maids; ballet dancers raise their arms, adjust clothing, exercise, rest or fidget; horses turn and twist or shy away; and jockeys tip their caps, flick their whips or raise themselves in the stirrups.

Although he returned to landscape as a subject during the early 1890s, Degas remained the supreme draughtsman of the human form in the late nineteenth century. His favourite subjects – ballet dancers and the female nude – recur again and again; the horses and jockeys less often at the end. Such drawings were not necessarily intended to be seen in series, but they were certainly produced in sequences aided by the use of tracing paper and frequent redrawing. As his eyesight worsened and physical infirmity advanced, Degas's drawing reaches a plateau until it ceases around 1912 when he left the Rue Victor-Massé. Experience proved to be everything in the final years of activity. There is a frantic concern to keep drawing as the inky darkness gathers around him: outlines are blurred, distances misjudged, faces dissolve, arms flail. The charcoal drawings become messengers of the night while the pastels in Degas's own words become 'orgies of colour'. In these late works it is as though Degas is desperately trying to reclaim his vision through the act of constantly drawing, just as Beethoven hammered on his forte piano more and more loudly to test his hearing or repeated chords in his symphonies in the hope of hearing at least one of them.

One of the chief characteristics of Degas as artist is his constant search for perfection, which led in turn to his proclivity for experiment. This was not limited to drawing, but extended to printmaking, sculpture and photography. He could never leave anything alone and often reversed his decisions and made frequent revisions. The surprising feature about Degas's drawings is how early he began his search for originality. He had introduced *essence* by the end of the 1860s and many drawings were made on coloured or tinted papers during the 1870s. Even more significant was the decision during the mid-1870s to allow monotype prints to be the starting point for drawings by adding colour in pastel and gouache to the dark ground. The increasing interest in pastel led to Degas researching into the different types of fixative available so that the surfaces could be protected. Later, during the 1880s and 1890s, when he introduced tracing paper as an intermediary in the creation of his drawings and pastels, he required stronger supports. He therefore began to lay sheets of paper (including tracing paper) on different kinds of card, board, or even linen and canvas.

A more extraordinary development occurs in the handling of Degas's pastels dating from the mid-1880s onwards, which was his habit of enlarging the surface of the work by adding on strips of paper sometimes as many as five or seven times. Rubens in the seventeenth century often did the same with his canvases, as though there was no physical limit to the boundaries of a composition. The enlarging of Degas's pastels occurred not because of an initial misjudgment, but out of necessity as the compositions grew in an almost organic way. The physical nature of the creative process invests the whole work, therefore, with a kinetic energy of its own.

Degas's complex and prolix working methods mean that everything he produced has to be carefully and meticulously examined in order to be properly appreciated. Nothing is ever what it seems in a work by this artist and the same might be said of his personality. For an unmarried man with simple habits Degas was full of contradictions. Radical in art he was conservative in politics; sociable on one day but reclusive on another; encouraging and condemning in equal measure; charming and witty when he wanted to be, but increasingly acerbic and excoriating with advancing age. He was a notable raconteur famous for his aphorisms and often wounding *mots*. People listened intently to his admirations and his detractions: everyone approached him with trepidation. Numerous statements about art, past masters and his contemporaries abound, many of them recorded by those who knew him or whose parents had known him – among them Walter Sickert, Ambroise Vollard, Georges Jeanniot, Daniel Halévy, Ernest Rouart, George Moore and William Rothenstein.

One of the most moving recollections of a visit to see Degas at 37 Rue Victor-Massé is given by the poet and critic Paul Valéry who knew the artist during his final years.

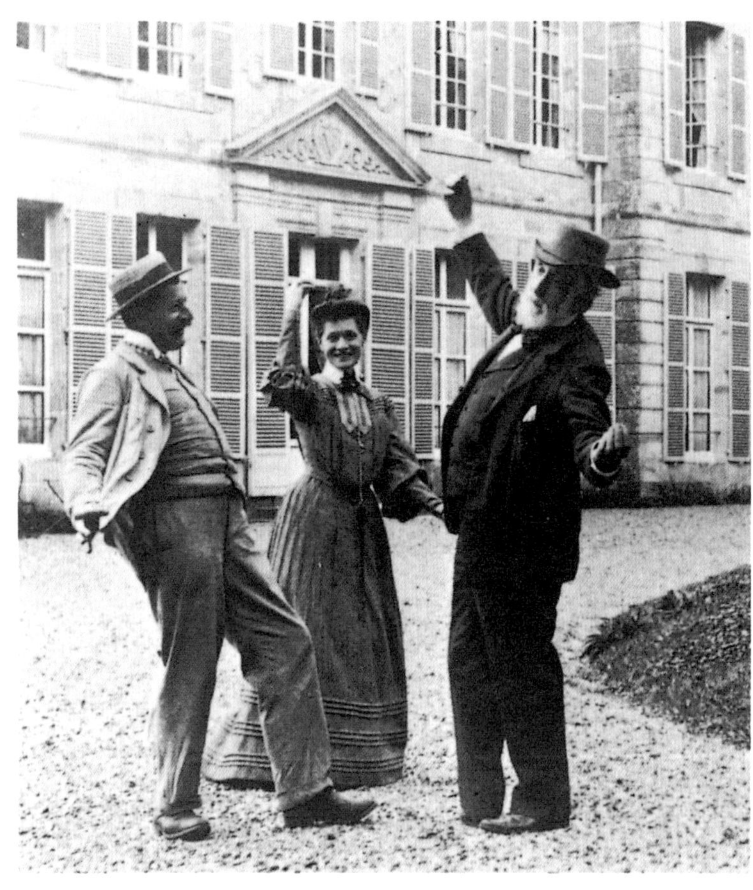

5. Degas with Monsieur and Madame Fourchy
at Ménil-Hubert (Orne), *c.* 1895. Hortense Fourchy was
the daughter of Degas's school friend Paul Valpinçon.
Bibliothèque Nationale, Paris

Going into the studio, I would find him shuffling about in slippers,
dressed like a pauper, his trousers hanging, never buttoned. A door
standing wide open exposed all the most inward and private places
in his apartment.

And yet this was a man who could be a dandy, whose manners,
when he chose, were of the most natural distinction, a man who
spent his evenings in the wings at the Opéra, a frequent visitor
in the paddock at Longchamp, an intensely acute observer of the
human form, a cruel connoisseur of all the shapes and attitudes of
women, an expert judge of the finest horses, the most intelligent,
the most demanding, the most merciless draughtsman in the
world…And on top of that he was a witty guest whose *mot*, in its
careful selection of facts, its lordly abuse of any sense of fairness,
was always fatal…

Drawing was not only the central tenet of Degas's art, it was also
essential to his existence. As Valéry again says,

The sheer labour of Drawing had become a passion and a
discipline to him, the object of a *mystique* and an ethic all-
sufficient in themselves, a supreme preoccupation which abolished
all other matters, a source of endless problems in precision which
released him from any other form of inquiry. He was and wishes to
be a specialist, of a kind that can rise to a sort of universality.

No doubt influenced by Degas, Valéry also had views on the type of
activity that drawing represented.

I know of no art which calls for the use of more intelligence than
that of drawing. Whether it be a question of conjuring from the
whole complex of what is seen, the one pencil stroke that is right,
of summarising a structure, of not letting one's hand wander, of
deciphering and mentally formulating before putting down; or
whether the moment be dominated by creation, the controlling
idea growing richer and clearer with what it becomes on paper and
under one's eyes; every mental faculty finds its function in the task,
which no less forcibly reveals the personality the artist may have.

The importance of Degas's drawings was widely acknowledged
during his lifetime by artists, dealers and critics. Having quickly mastered
established practices at the outset he soon recognized that drawing had
a far greater potential than just being part of a summary process. The
art of drawing, Degas soon realized, could denote a more serious artistic
intent and harbour far wider creative ambitions.

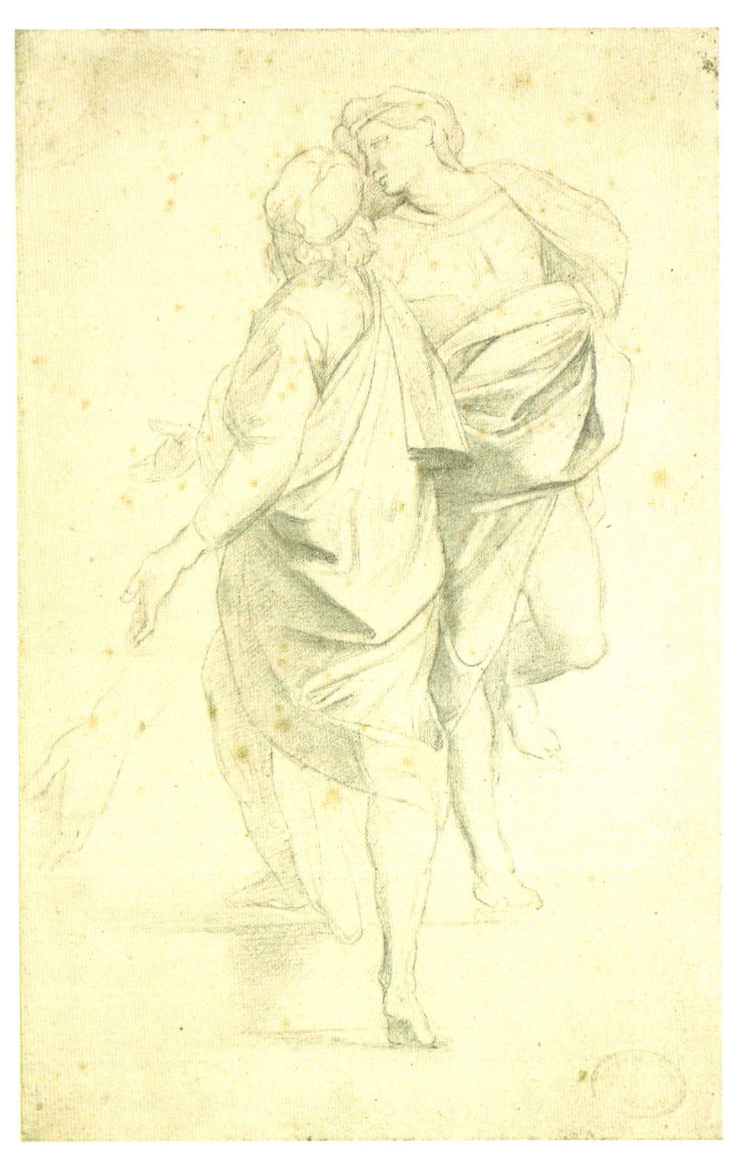

6. *Copy after Raphael (School of Athens), c.* 1853.
Pencil, 23 × 15 cm (9 × 5⅞ in.).
Ashmolean Museum, Oxford

CHAPTER ONE

Beginnings 1853–1855

'Study line, draw lots of lines, either from memory or from nature.'

(Ingres to Degas in 1855, from Paul Valéry, *Degas Danse Dessin*, 1938)

The earliest drawings made by Degas offer no real clue as to his future achievements. He was approaching his twentieth birthday when he made the final decision to become an artist. Even though the documentary evidence is meagre, it seems that he started out on his chosen career with his family's blessing following his education at the Lycée Louis-le-Grand. At this prestigious school in the 5th arrondissement of Paris he had received a solid grounding in the language and literature of the ancient world and French classical literature.

Degas may also have discovered a penchant for art at the Lycée where, among others, the respected painter Léon Cogniet taught drawing. Indeed, when Degas enrolled as a copyist at the Musée du Louvre on 7 April 1853 and in the Cabinet des Estampes at the Bibliothèque Nationale (formerly Impériale) two days later – the first references to Degas as an aspiring artist – he cites Félix Barrias, one of Cogniet's pupils, as his current drawing master. However, when he registers on 6 April 1855 as a student at the Ecole des Beaux-Arts, it is on the recommendation of Louis Lamothe, who had been taught by Hippolyte Flandrin, a former pupil of Ingres. Clearly, at the outset Degas opts, in principle at least, to take the accepted path to artistic success. Attendance at the Ecole presented him with the possibility of winning the coveted Prix de Rome, which was awarded each year to the most gifted history painter and was acknowledged to be the best way of gaining public recognition as an artist. What is significant, however, is that Degas seems to have been careful to distance himself from the Ecole even while paying lip service to its orthodoxies. This he could do partly because he was a young man of private means, but also partly because he was fiercely independent-minded. His time at the Ecole

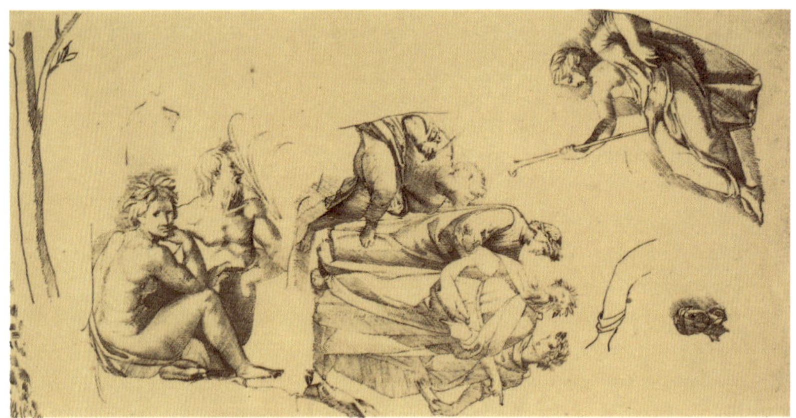

7. Copies after Raphael from Prints by
Marcantonio Raimondi, c. 1853.
Pen and ink, 15.2 × 31.2 cm (6 × 12¼ in.).
Fogg Museum, Cambridge, Massachusetts

shows how he could be part of the system while also operating outside it. Such dualities frequently occur throughout the artist's life.

The teaching system that Degas was exposed to at the Ecole began with a rigorous exercise in copying works principally from the antique and the Renaissance, as well as from works by the most admired artists of the French school, such as Nicolas Poussin – examples of all of which could be seen in the Musée du Louvre. Prints, facsimiles, casts and original paintings were the sources from which such copies were made. The purpose was to encourage students to become conversant with the highest achievements in the history of art through a careful analysis of style and technique.

Degas began by copying prints in pen and ink, pencil or chalk, concentrating on outlines and shading by cross-hatching before studying sculpture and paintings from life. For these exercises he used single sheets of paper and his Notebooks. Even though these copies are understandably tentative in execution, they do, nonetheless, reveal a remarkably sophisticated awareness of stylistic distinctions: the rhythmical elegance of Raphael [6, 11], the brittleness of Mantegna [8, 12] or the *sfumato* of Leonardo da Vinci [see 25]. Whether using pen, pencil or chalk Degas is extremely adroit at establishing the outlines that he may later have redrawn or accentuated by applying greater pressure. Shading (sometimes diffused by rubbing with a tool called a stump) helps to build up the figure's sense of form or the fall and texture of garments. Similarly, Degas is careful to emphasize the three-dimensional quality of sculpture: for example, the carving of the marble in the Borghese Gladiator [9] is implied by the rippling musculature and silhouetted shadows suggest the low relief of the Parthenon Frieze [10]. Degas's facility with each of the media that he was given to use is also impressive at this early stage: the fluidity of the pen, the pithiness of the pencil and the softness of the chalk. He may be feeling his way, but already his drawings are purposeful and articulate.

The emphasis in this preliminary training for the student was on intense observation and strict manual control, but it had limitations as it encouraged young artists in the development of a superior drawing technique only, as opposed to aiming for spontaneous expression. In short, to reproduce a work of art was considered to be more important than creating one.

Degas stands out because he was not preoccupied with imitation alone, but with exploring the pictorial possibilities inherent within the works he was copying. Significantly, like Paul Cézanne, Degas continued to make copies well beyond his student years (over 600 are known in all) as he recognized copying in itself to be a creative exercise that assisted his artistic imagination. From the start, rarely are his copies slavish and more often they are commentaries or improvisations on the original. For this reason, echoes of many of his copies dating from this early stage in his career can be found in later works: for instance, the figures on the steps of Raphael's *School of Athens* [6] in the numerous dancers depicted on stage or in the rehearsal rooms, the Roman soldier from Mantegna's *Crucifixion* [8] in the commanding poses of the dancing masters in the ballet pictures, or the horsemen from the Parthenon Frieze [10] in the horseracing compositions. These links are hardly likely to have been consciously made by Degas so many years later as direct quotations, but they do show how at one remove he was able to integrate the art of the past with his own. The quality and manner of execution of these copies reveals not only the excitement that Degas felt towards performing the task, but also the pleasure he took in learning from the work of his illustrious predecessors. Even so, two general interests of Degas that would absorb him for the rest of his life are nascent: the dynamics of movement and the exploration of multiple viewpoints. Both of these aspects are combined in his copy of the Borghese Gladiator [9].

Copies made by Degas, therefore, reveal him to be an artist of the greatest intelligence in seeking out the potential of a work of art rather than simply observing it passively as though learning by rote. Amusingly, he said, 'The masters must be copied again and again, and only after having given every indication of being a good copyist can you reasonably be given leave to draw a radish from nature.'

The role played by Louis Lamothe in Degas's early life was limited but salutary. When Lamothe went south to his home town of Lyon to assist his own master, Hippolyte Flandrin, Degas visited them during the summer of 1855 before going on to spend September in Provence. Flandrin was painting fresoes in the church of Saint-Martin-d'Ainay that Degas was able to observe at first hand, but he also continued to make copies at the Ecole des Beaux-Arts in Lyon and at museums in both Lyon and further south in Provence.

Whether inspired by Flandrin's connection with the painter or not, Degas's interest in Ingres was now aroused and this was to prove to be one of the defining moments in his life. Later, in 1858, the artist's father, Auguste, ruefully remarked in a letter how relieved he was that his son had abandoned 'that flaccid and banal draughtsmanship à la Flandrin and Lamothe' and chosen instead to follow his own path. 'Your drawing is strong, the tone of your colour is correct…You have a great destiny before you, do not be discouraged, do not trouble your mind. By peaceful but steady, unrelenting work follow this furrow that you have opened for yourself. It is yours, it is no one else's.'

A first meeting with Ingres occurred early in 1855 through his school friend, Paul Valpinçon, whose father was an important collector. Degas made copies of several works shown by Ingres at the Exposition Universelle held in May–June 1855 [14]. Ingres soon became a mentor. He was not only a consummate painter of historical, mythological and religious pictures, as well as portraits, but also a brilliant draughtsman and spokesman for art. By nature conformist and predictable, he was considered single-minded and perfectionist. The clarity of his neoclassical compositions in oil and the precision of his drawings, particularly his famous portrait drawings, were for Degas admirable demonstrations of what Ingres himself referred to as 'the probity of art'. It is hardly surprising, therefore, that when Degas embarked on what was possibly intended to be his first history painting, *King Candaules's Wife*, Ingres was uppermost in his thoughts as regards both the pose of the principal figure and the refined setting full of archaeological details. The project, however, was never completed.

Degas had great veneration for Ingres both as an artist and as a man. Later he collected his paintings and drawings even though overall the direct influence of the older master on his own work was periodic and not sustained. One of the most vivid vignettes of the elderly Degas is his daily visit in 1911 to see an exhibition of Ingres's work when he could hardly see the works but was allowed 'to touch them and run his hands over them' in an act of affectionate homage.

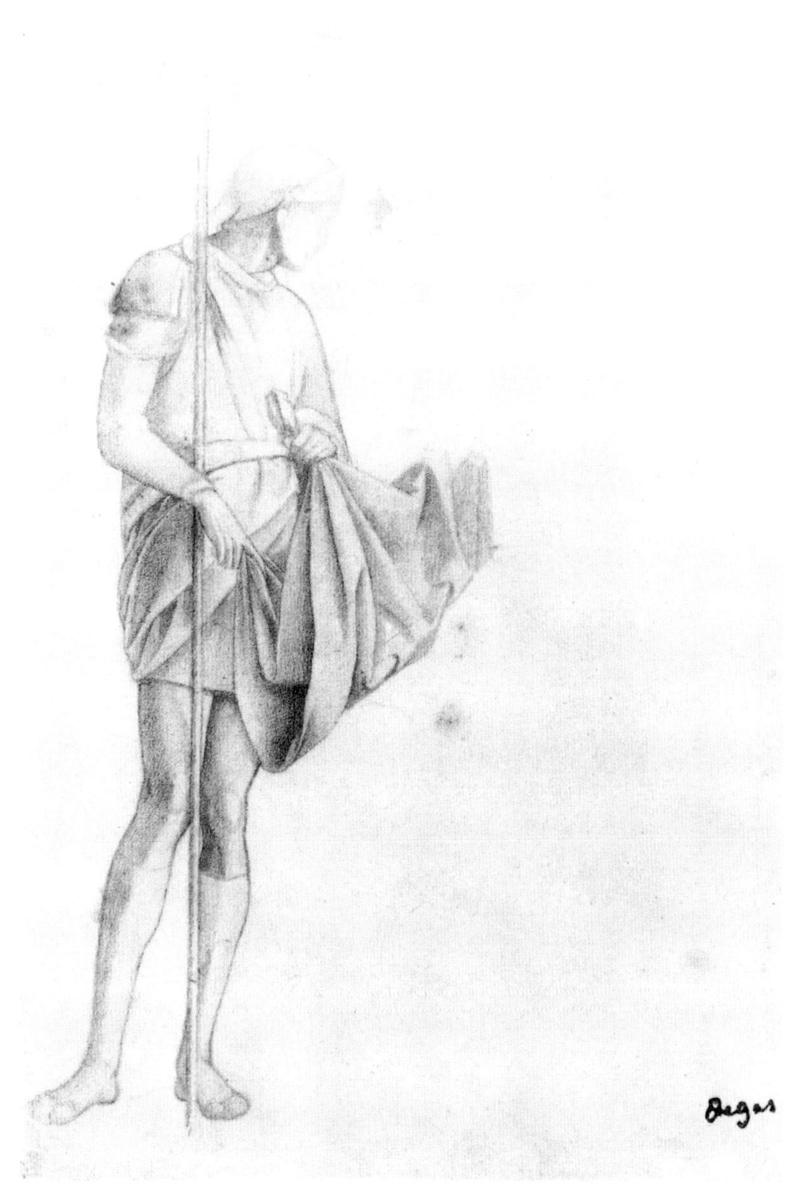

8. *Copy after Mantegna (Crucifixion)*, c. 1853–55.
Pencil and black chalk, 30.8 × 21.6 cm (12⅛ × 8½ in.).
Sterling and Francine Clark Art Institute,
Williamstown, Massachusetts

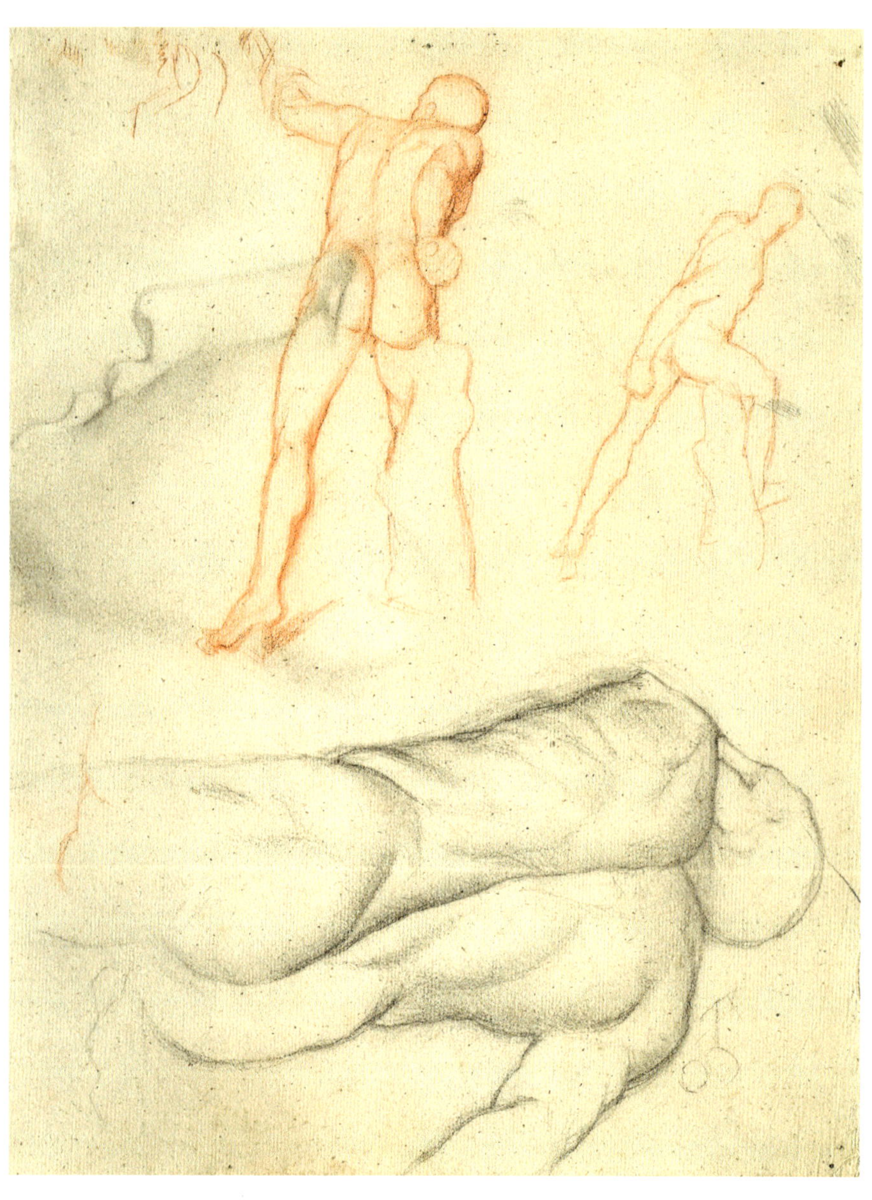

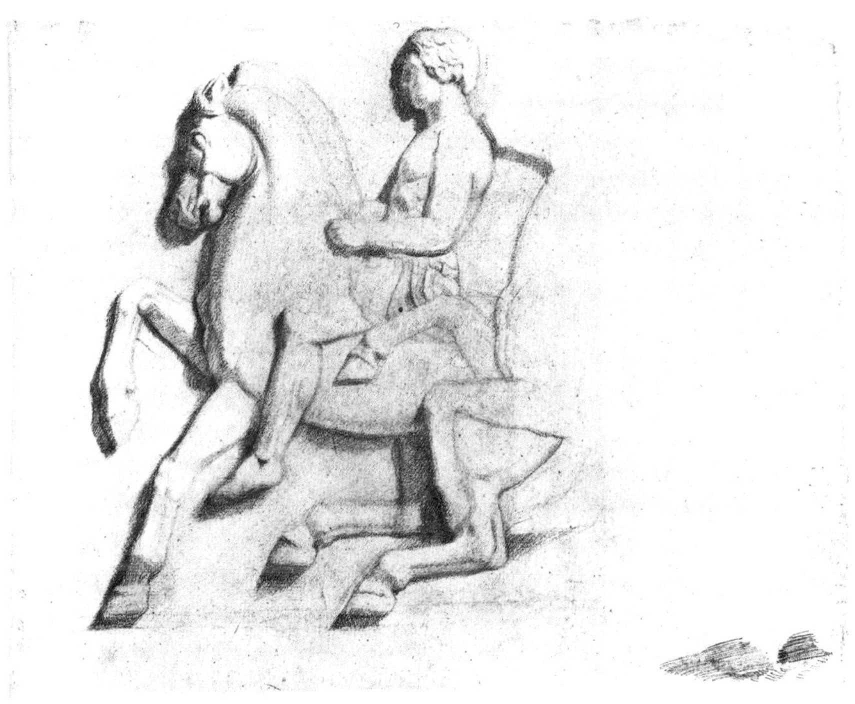

OPPOSITE
9. *Copy after the Borghese Gladiator*, c. 1854–56.
Black and red chalk, 31.3 × 24.2 cm (12⅛ × 9½ in.).
Sterling and Francine Clark Art Institute,
Williamstown, Massachusetts

ABOVE
10. *Copy after the Parthenon Frieze*, c. 1853–55.
Pencil, 23.5 × 30.2 cm (9¼ × 11⅞ in.).
Kunsthalle Bremen

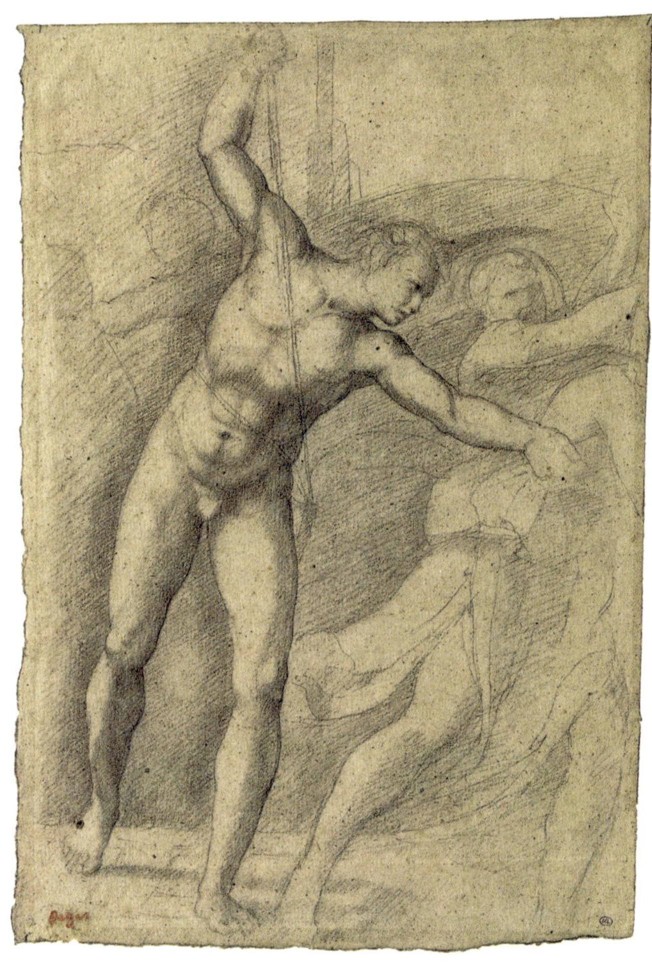

11. *Copy after Marcantonio Raimondi (Massacre
of the Innocents after Raphael)*, c. 1854–56.
Black chalk, 40.8 × 28.3 cm (16 × 11⅛ in.).
Musée d'Orsay, Paris

12. *Copy after Mantegna (Pallas Expelling the Vices
from the Garden of Virtue)*, c. 1855.
Pencil, 29.1 × 20.2 cm (11⅛ × 8 in.).
Ashmolean Museum, Oxford

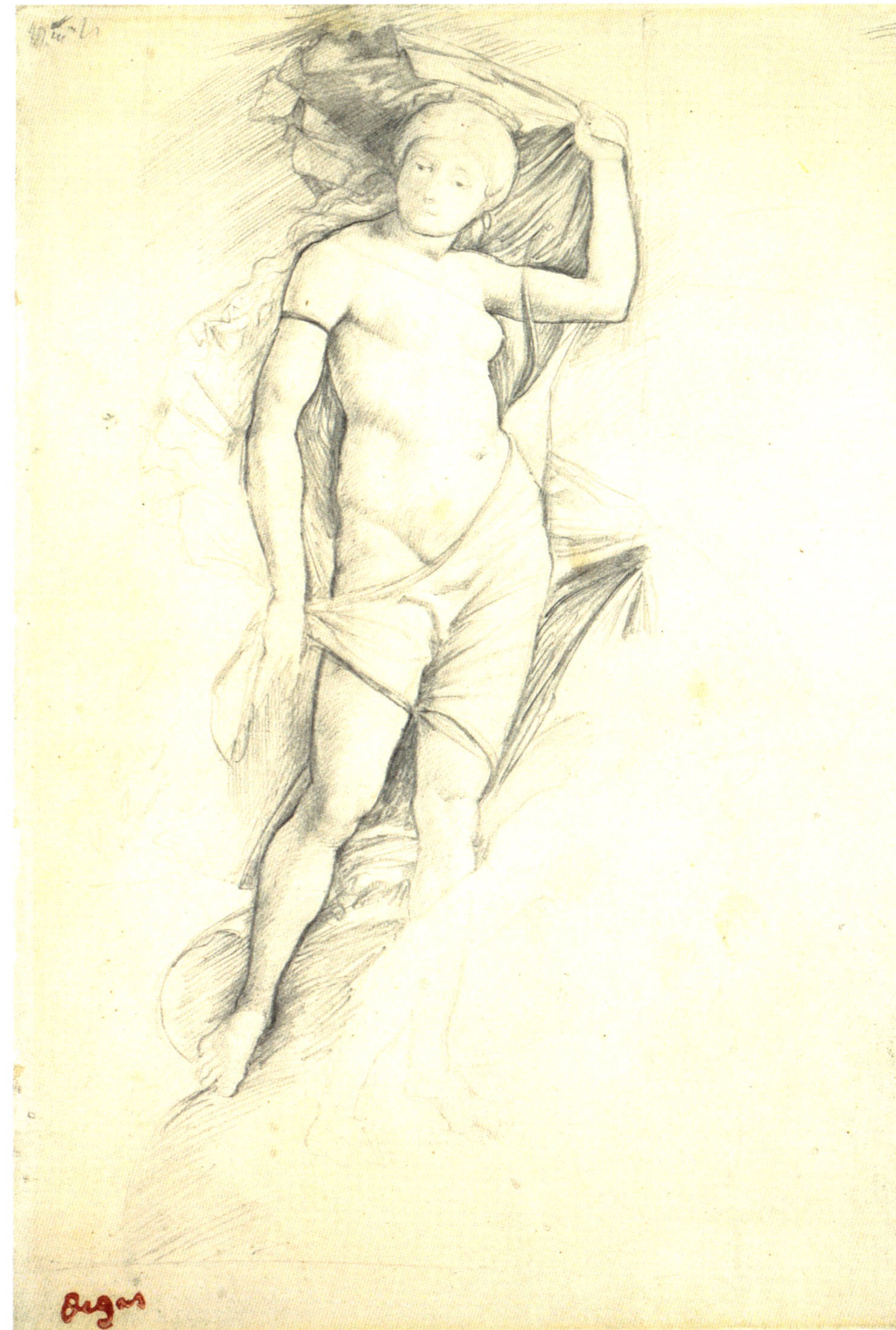

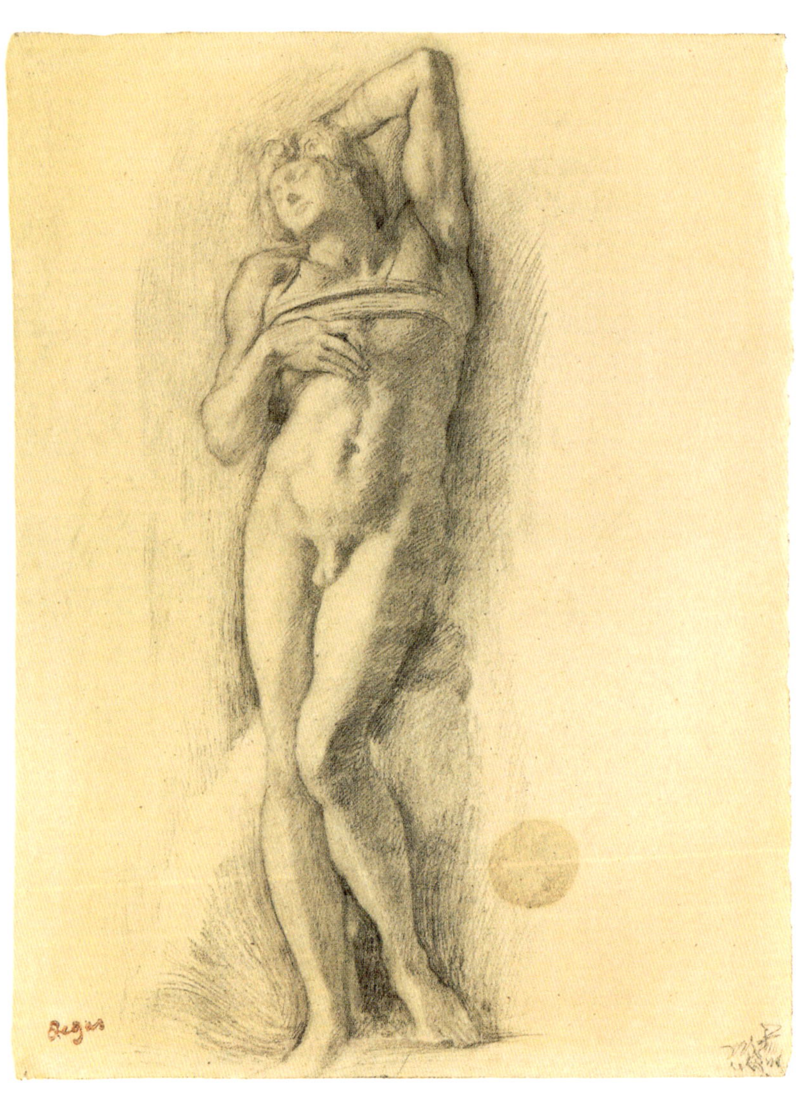

13. *Copy after Michelangelo
(Bound Slave)*, c. 1855. Pencil,
33 × 25 cm (13 × 9⅞ in.).
Private collection

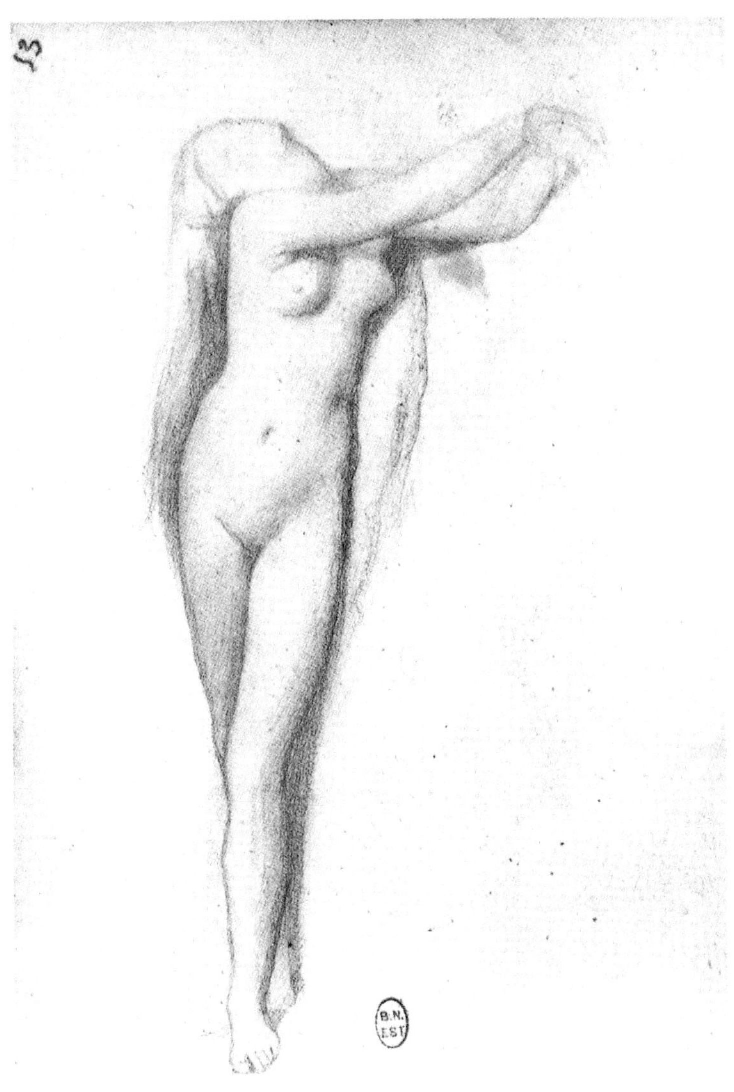

14. *Copy after Ingres (Roger Freeing Angelica)*,
Notebook 2, p. 53, 1855.
Pencil, 15.2 × 10.4 cm (6 × 4⅛ in.).
Bibliothèque Nationale, Paris

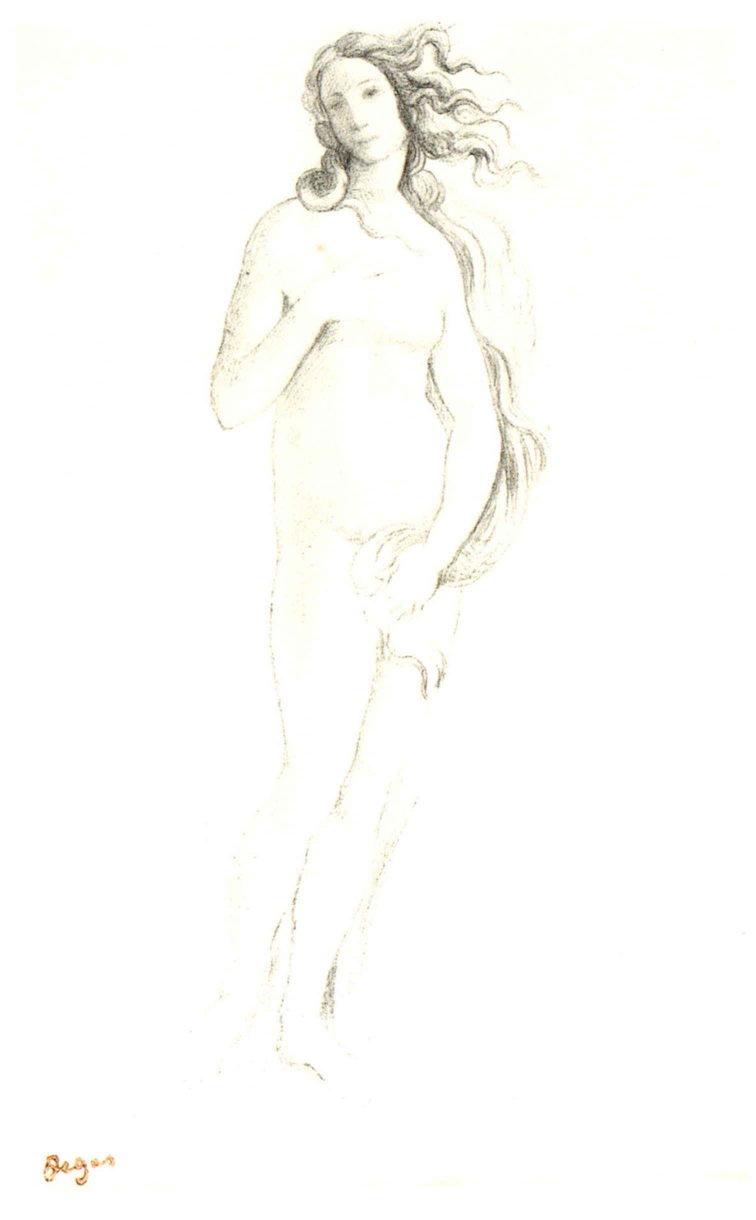

15. *Copy after Botticelli (The Birth of Venus)*, 1858–59.
Pencil, 29 × 21 cm (11⅛ × 8¼ in.).
Private collection

CHAPTER TWO

Italy 1856–1859

'If one wants to travel alone one must visit areas full of life or else full of works of art.'

(Degas, Notebook 11, p. 65, used between 1857 and 1858)

The three years that Degas spent in Italy enabled him to combine family matters with the advancement of his art. It was a heady combination that added considerably to Degas's impetus to become a successful artist. Most of the portraits he made either in oil or as drawings during this early stage of his career are of members of his family. It is as though working within the family circle gave him extra confidence both personally – he never married – and artistically. Throughout his life he only ever made portraits of his family or of close friends and he never took commissions.

Degas's grandfather, René Hilaire Degas, was a grain merchant born in Orléans. He fled France during the Revolution and eventually established himself as a banker in Naples trading under the name of Degas, Padri e Figli. Three of his sons, Edouard, Achille and Henri, remained with him in Naples, while the fourth, the artist's father, Auguste, was dispatched to France in 1825 to run a French branch of the bank. The main family residence in Naples was the Baroque Palazzo Pignatelli di Monteleone, but in summer they retired to a villa at San Rocco di Capodimonte overlooking the Bay of Naples. Hilaire Degas formed a collection of Neapolitan paintings and had a considerable library: he was a cultivated and beneficent patriarch.

Degas's arrival in Naples in July 1856 was timely since his grandfather was aged eighty-six and lived for only two more years. He enjoyed his grandfather's company and meeting the rest of the family – aunts, uncles, cousins – of whom he later painted several portraits. Each of his aunts made good marriages: Rosa to Giuseppe Morbilli, Duke of Sant'Angelo a Frosolone; Laura to a political activist, Gennaro Bellelli; and Stefania to Gioacchino Primicile, Marchese di Cicerale and Duke of Montejasi. They and their progeny came into Degas's life at irregular intervals and usually on such occasions he liked to paint or draw them.

While travelling in Italy Degas spent some of his time with the Bellelli family in Florence, where they were living in exile from Naples for political reasons. The family comprised Gennaro and Laura and their two children, Giovanna and Giulia. On arriving in Florence in 1858 Degas first thought of doing a double portrait of his cousins alone, but he then decided to include their mother before embarking on a more ambitious composition involving the whole family. Degas was gambling on the success of *The Bellelli Family* [16], as the painting came to be known, as a way of establishing his reputation as a painter of realist portraiture. He therefore prepared very carefully, making numerous studies for each of the figures in a variety of media [20–23], as well as several compositional drawings ending with an elaborate pastel. The individual studies are essentially isolated portraits, but they also concentrate on other aspects, such as expression, pose and clothes. They are achieved with great intensity of observation and remarkable deliberation as though Degas is desperate not to make a mistake in front of his family. What is certain is that Degas was becoming much bolder in technical matters. Pencil and black chalk are used sometimes in combination; body colour and touches of pastel are introduced for heightening and in one memorable study [23] he tries *essence*. Furthermore, he introduces tinted papers and tracing paper into the procedure.

The preparatory drawings for *The Bellelli Family* show how fearless the artist was in breaking the rules. Delays meant that the picture could not be completed in Florence and he may not have even begun it there, although he returned for a brief visit in 1860. Ultimately, all the preparatory material travelled back with Degas to Paris where, however, the picture remained unfinished until 1867, when it was most probably exhibited in the Salon of that year.

As it was conceived while Degas was in Italy, *The Bellelli Family* is surely to be considered an early masterpiece of those years, but it is not perhaps the type of picture with which he intended to make his debut and there is plenty of evidence to show that he had more appropriate historical subjects in mind for that purpose. Yet *The Bellelli Family* is brilliantly done. Set in an apartment in Florence, Degas skilfully captures the family's predicament. The lack of engagement between the figures, the awkward poses and the atmosphere of passive aggression reveal their personal difficulties while living in exile. Laura shields Giovanna, Giulia sits precariously on her chair and Gennaro is seen only in profile with his back to the viewer. The tension is heightened by the way in which

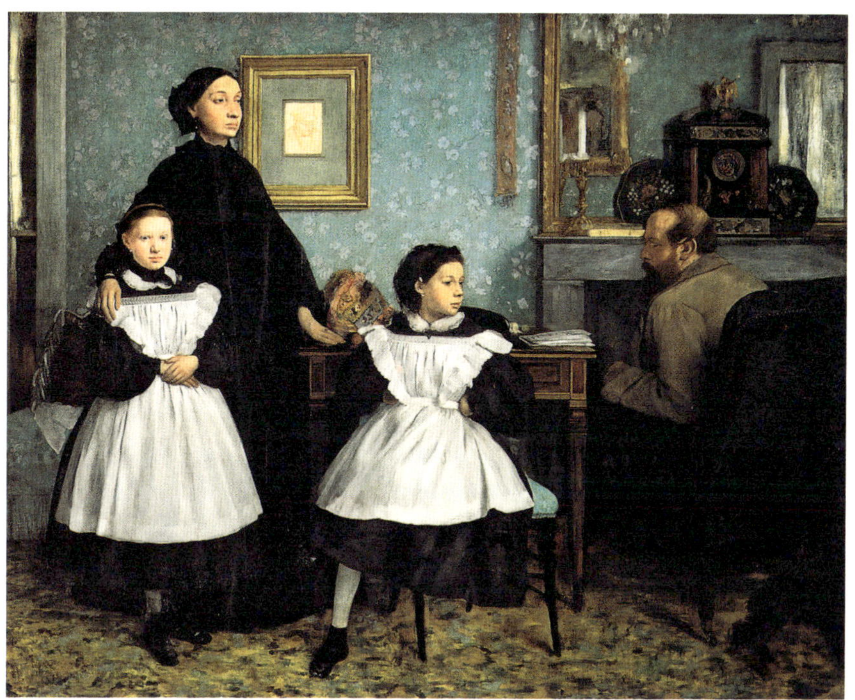

16. *The Bellelli Family*, 1858–67.
Oil on canvas, 200 × 250 cm (78¼ × 98⅜ in.).
Musée d'Orsay, Paris

the figures are set against a background of rigid geometric shapes. On
the wall behind is the ghost of Laura's father, Hilaire, in the form of a
framed red-chalk drawing.

Degas also depicted his brothers and sisters during the mid-1850s:
Achille, Thérèse [18], Marguerite and René [17]. Thérèse married her
cousin Edmondo Morbilli and Marguerite an architect, Henri Fèvre,
before emigrating with him to Buenos Aires. The lives of Achille and
René were not straightforward, forcing Degas at times to distance
himself from them, particularly after the death of their father, Auguste,
in 1874 when the family bank began to make losses, which also affected
Degas's own financial situation. A point of reference for all the brothers,
however, lies with their mother, Célestine Musson, who died in Paris
in 1847. The Mussons were successful cotton traders in New Orleans,
but they had strong links with France where René met his cousin Estelle
Musson while her mother was taking refuge with her two daughters
from the American Civil War. René persuaded Achille to set up a

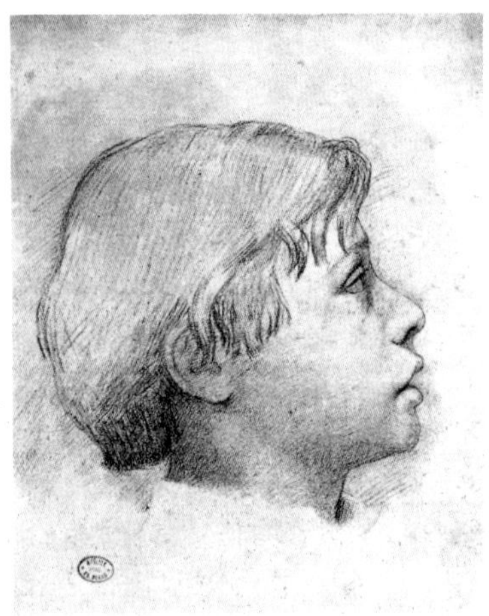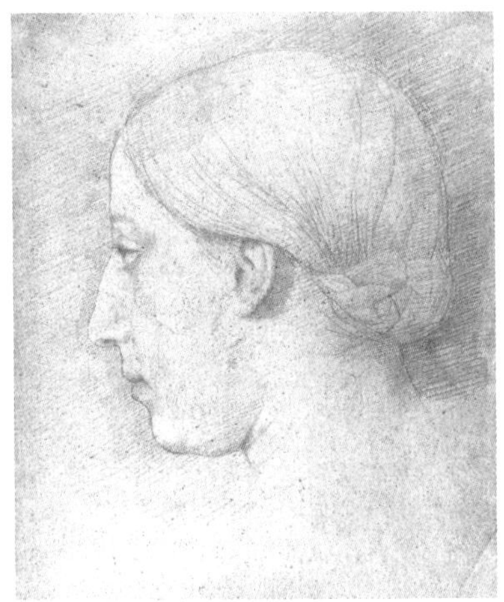

ABOVE LEFT 17. *René Degas, c.* 1855. Black chalk, 34.6 × 28 cm (13⅝ × 11 in.).
The Art Institute of Chicago
ABOVE RIGHT 18. *Thérèse Degas, c.* 1855–56. Pencil, 28.5 × 23.6 cm (11¼ × 9¼ in.).
Fitzwilliam Museum, Cambridge

wine importing business in New Orleans. This was short-lived, but it
provided Degas with an excuse to travel to America in 1872–73 to visit
his mother's family. While there he painted *The Cotton Office* [19],
which includes portraits of Achille and René and is in many respects an
American equivalent of *The Bellelli Family*.

Family reasons, therefore, were undoubtedly one of the main
attractions of Italy for Degas, but it was certainly not the only one. He
was also keen to continue his exploration of the rich artistic legacy of
the peninsula in all its manifestations, as well as to meet other artists
pursuing the same aims. Now he was no longer limited to copying from
prints, casts or facsimiles. All Italy lay before him and he spent long
periods in Naples, Rome and Florence, with shorter periods in Viterbo,
Orvieto, Perugia, Spello, Arezzo, Siena, Pisa and Genoa. Although
encouraged to travel to Venice, he did not do so. In all the places Degas
went to he copied intensely in the museums, churches, palaces and
private collections. Some were copies of whole works of art; others were
partial. Objects dating from antiquity frequently appear, but works by
Giotto, Uccello, Signorelli, Botticelli [15], Gozzoli [24], Leonardo da
Vinci [25], Pintoricchio, Raphael and Michelangelo received special
attention, among many others. The Baroque seems not to have had such
an appeal. Exposure to all this art seen *in situ* dramatically widened
Degas's terms of reference.

Another artist who was furiously busy making copies in Italy at this time was Gustave Moreau. Eight years older than Degas, they met most probably in 1858 and were given permission to attend life-drawing sessions at the Villa Medici in Rome by the Director, Jean Victor Schnetz, although neither artist was officially affiliated to this important outpost of the French Académie des Beaux-Arts. Moreau was intelligent, well read and a passionate music lover. Later, his treatment of subject matter would become increasingly exotic and other-worldly, which prompted several wounding barbs from Degas ('He wants to make us believe the Gods wore watch chains…'), but in Italy he acted as a mentor to the younger man, providing him with a stimulus that other friends – Elie Delaunay, Joseph Tourny, Joseph Henner – could not. Moreau, for instance, encouraged Degas to think more seriously about colour and to pay closer attention to works by Venetian painters such as Giovanni Bellini, Giorgione and Titian, even if he decided not to travel to Venice itself. Together they made drawings from life at the Villa Medici in the evenings. On these occasions Degas began to make much stronger studies of nude models – male and female – carefully set in challenging

19. *The Cotton Office, New Orleans*, 1873.
Oil on canvas, 73 × 92 cm (28¼ × 36¼ in.).
Musée des Beaux-Arts, Pau

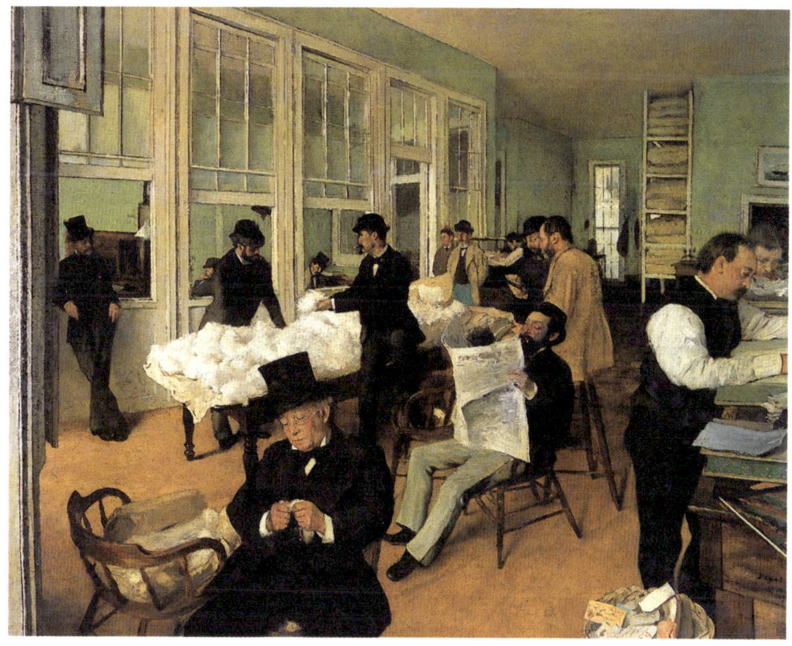

poses [26]. These and other drawings done from models reveal a much more fluent handling of the pencil, with wonderfully supple outlines, a greater range of shading and more frequent accenting [27, 28].

Degas was rapidly becoming an accomplished artist and naturally his thoughts were turning towards ideas for compositions that he could develop into finished paintings for exhibition. In his Notebooks he explores such subjects as *Dante and Virgil*, *Hero and Leander*, *David and Goliath*, *Leda and the Swan,* or scenes from Homer. He returns again and again to record compositional ideas, to make studies of individual figures and even to advance them to the point of making oil sketches. This though is Degas thinking aloud with a tendency to be over-elaborate in the preparatory stages, a problem that he will overcome in later life.

One idea for a painting was developed further than the others. This was the religious subject of St John the Baptist and the Angel. The drawings for this picture, which was never completed, are the most eloquent that Degas made in Italy [29, 30]. In them he moves beyond studies from the model to figures that are more fully characterized. The implied sense of movement in the advancing, youthful St John the Baptist and the Angel blowing a trumpet are more animated forms of the still, silent, firmly grounded models absorbed in their own thoughts that Degas drew at the Villa Medici.

The full flavour of Degas's three years in Italy is found in his Notebooks. The pages are densely crowded with images and notations sometimes made in a frenzy with pen and ink and watercolour in addition to pencil. There is more than a hint of eclecticism in the choice of works he copies, but there is a new element in the way Degas records what he observes in Italy – the landscape and the scenes from everyday life. For these Degas prefers watercolour, suggesting that he is beginning to come under the influence of Delacroix [31, 32].

The Notebooks that Degas filled in Italy between 1856 and 1859 and again in 1860 contain more than drawings. They are also full of the artist's written observations, forming a private travelogue:

> 10 o'clock in the evening. I leave for Orvieto – moonlight. I can
> make out the landscape and the mountains. Superb terrain –
> Montefiascone – mountains – daybreak. Fog over the plain – we
> descend into Orvieto – the Cathedral appears above the fog – we
> climb up the steps, real eagle's nest…Sublime Cathedral. I am quite
> startled – façade so rich and so tasteful. The mosaics too fresh –
> one so dreadfully decadent – I recognize the sculptures – I go in and
> run to Luca Signorelli.

It always seems that there must be, in the most beautiful
monuments, this mixture of tastes...I don't know what to
say – I am in a dream which I don't know how to recall
(Notebook 11, pp. 55–58).

A similar enthusiasm is recorded for the church of San Francesco
in Assisi:

I feel remorse for having seen so many beautiful things already –
I am going to leave. Everything breathes an atmosphere of prayer.
Everything is beautiful, the details, the whole. I would rather do
nothing than do a rough sketch without having looked at anything.
My memories will do better (Notebook 11, p. 78).

While going by boat to Naples in 1860 he watches the shoreline
and the sea:

The Pontine Marshes stretch out reddish-brown, behind them
the Apennines with their snow-capped peaks...Far away on the
horizon, a line of small lateen-sailed boats like a flight of seagulls,
in tone and in shape...The foam which marks the ship's wake is like
that of a woman washing in running water, layered in little steps.
Beneath the foam it looks like bubbling snow: the intervals have a
greenish-blue depth which makes one giddy (Notebook 18, pp. 111
and 111A).

And on arriving in Naples:

Through the mass of green oaks patches of the sea were visible.
I have never seen a green so powerful and so sober at the same time,
nor a grey sea and sky so pink and clear-looking. It was perfectly
suited to an epic poem. I will never forget this pearly grey and
powerful dark green of the trees (Notebook 19, pp. 15–16).

Italy opened Degas's eyes to the world, which he knew to be rich in
possibilities. The question now was how to translate his powerful
feelings for what he saw into art.

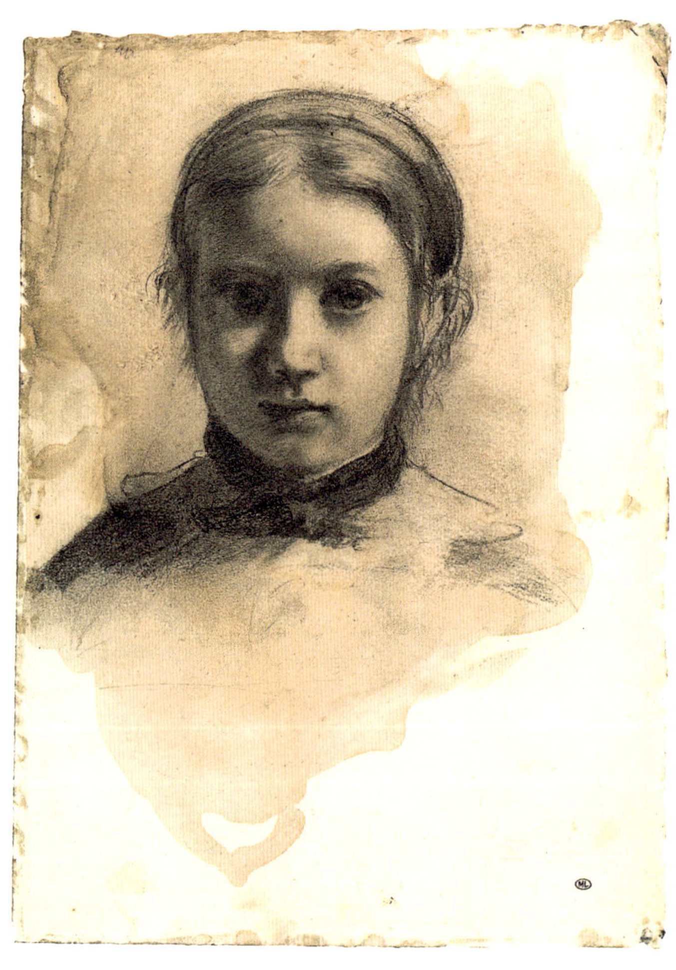

20. *Giovanna Bellelli*, 1858–59.
Black chalk with stump and wash on pink paper,
32.6 × 23.8 cm (12⅞ × 9⅜ in.).
Musée d'Orsay, Paris

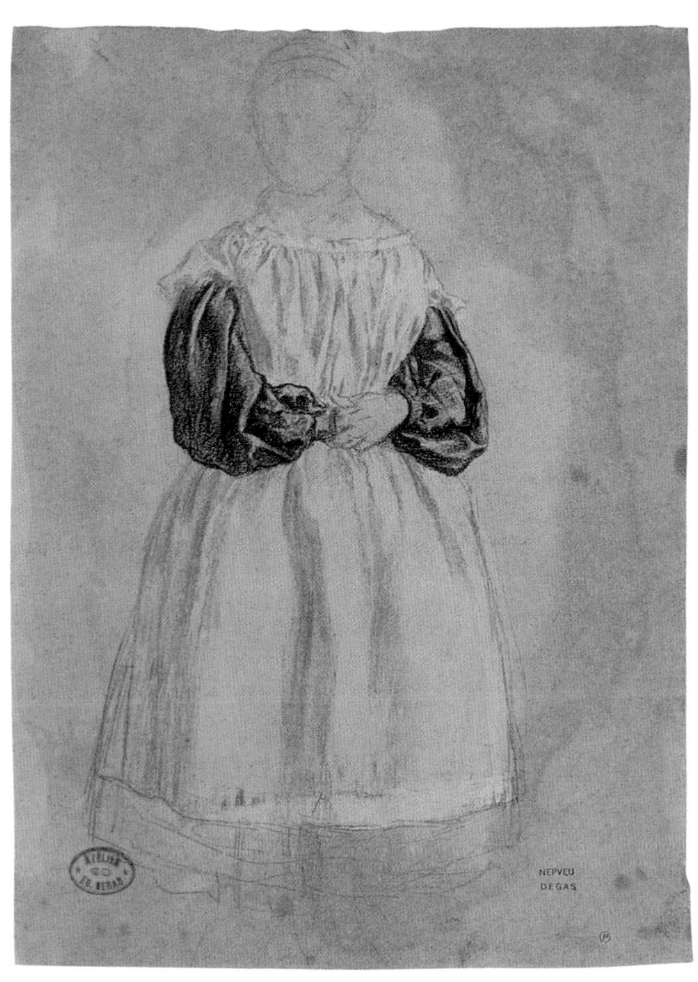

21. *Study of Giovanna Bellelli's Dress*, 1858–59.
Pencil, black chalk heightened with bodycolour on blue paper,
29.5 × 21.8 cm (11⅝ × 8⅝ in.).
Prat Collection, Paris

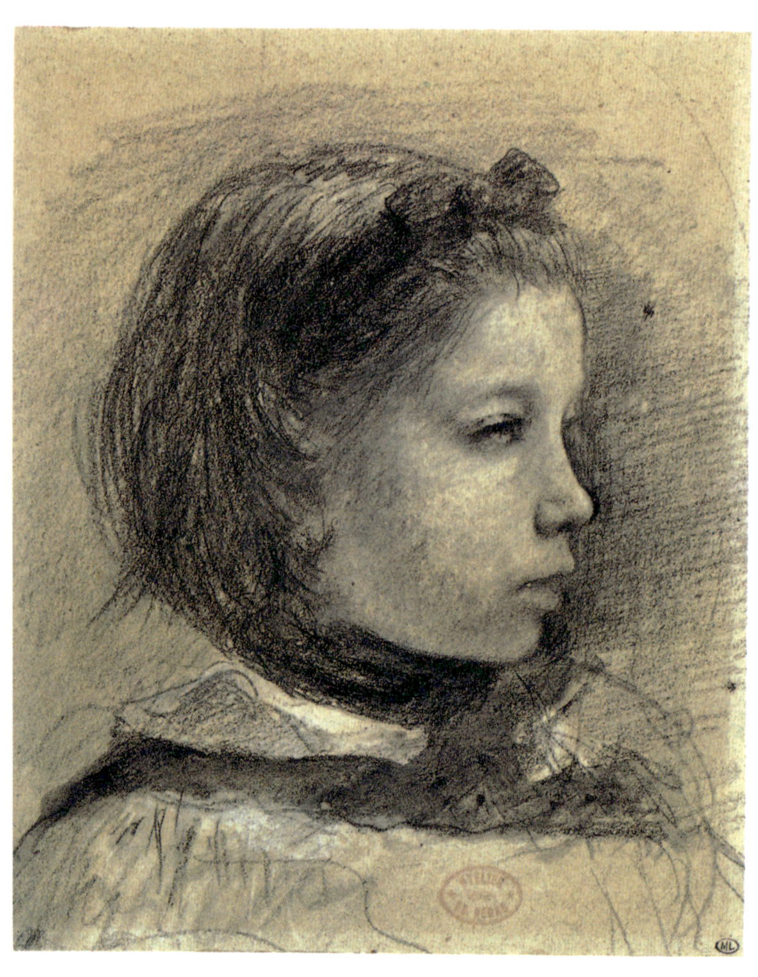

ABOVE
22. *Giulia Bellelli*, 1858–59.
Pencil, black chalk with wash heightened with
bodycolour, 23.4 × 19.6 cm (9¼ × 7¾ in.).
Musée d'Orsay, Paris

OPPOSITE
23. *Giulia Bellelli*, 1858–59.
Essence over pencil on buff paper, 36.2 × 24.77 cm (14¼ × 9¼ in.).
Dumbarton Oaks, Washington, DC

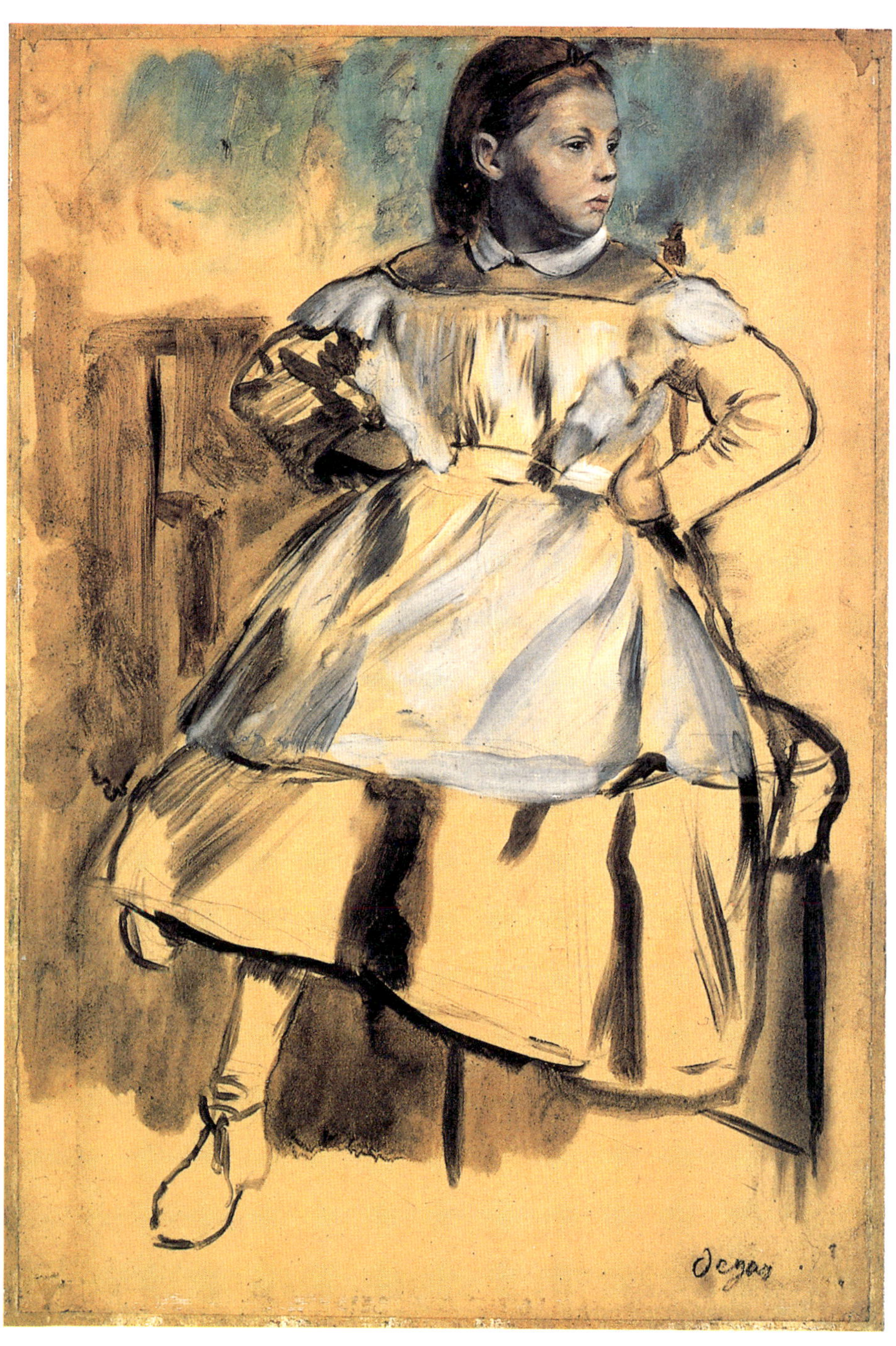

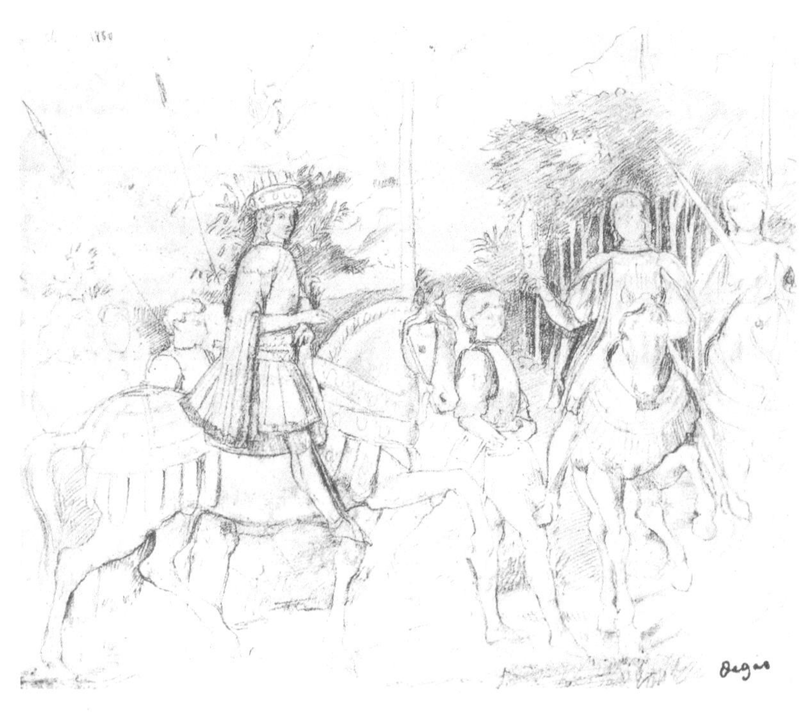

24. *Copy after Gozzoli (The Journey of the Magi)*, 1859–60.
Pencil, 25.9 × 30.4 cm (10¼ × 12 in.).
Fogg Museum, Cambridge, Massachusetts

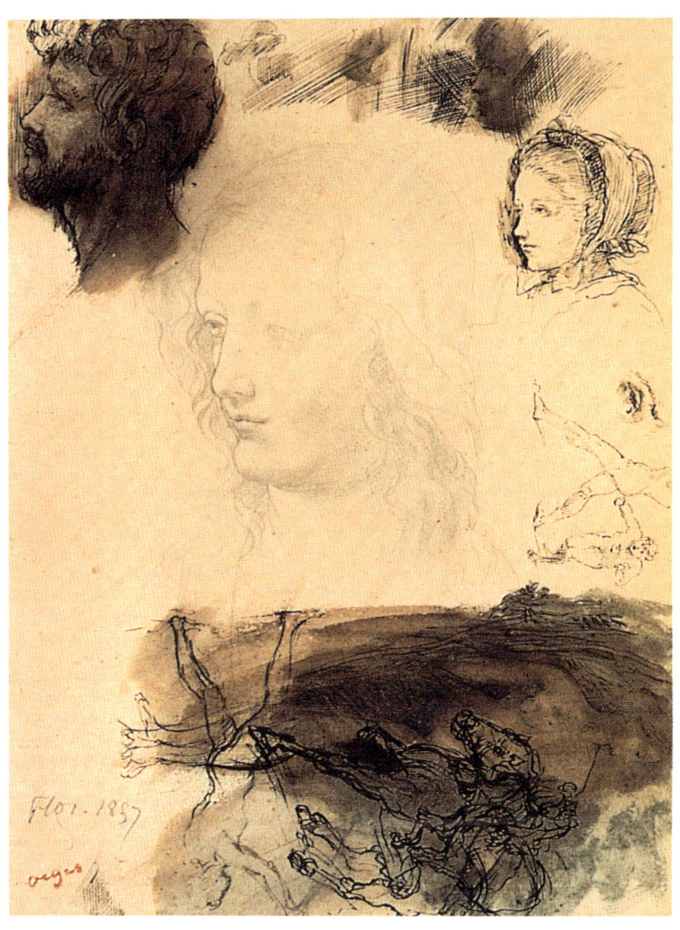

25. *Sheet of Studies including a Copy after a Drawing from the Studio of Leonardo da Vinci (Head of a Woman)*, 1858–59.
Pencil, pen and ink with washes on pink paper,
30.5 × 23.5 cm (12 × 9¼ in.).
Cleveland Museum of Art

26. *Study of a Standing Female Nude*, c. 1856–58.
Pencil, 29.1 × 21.8 cm (11½ × 8⅝ in.).
Sterling and Francine Clark Art Institute, Williamstown,
Massachusetts

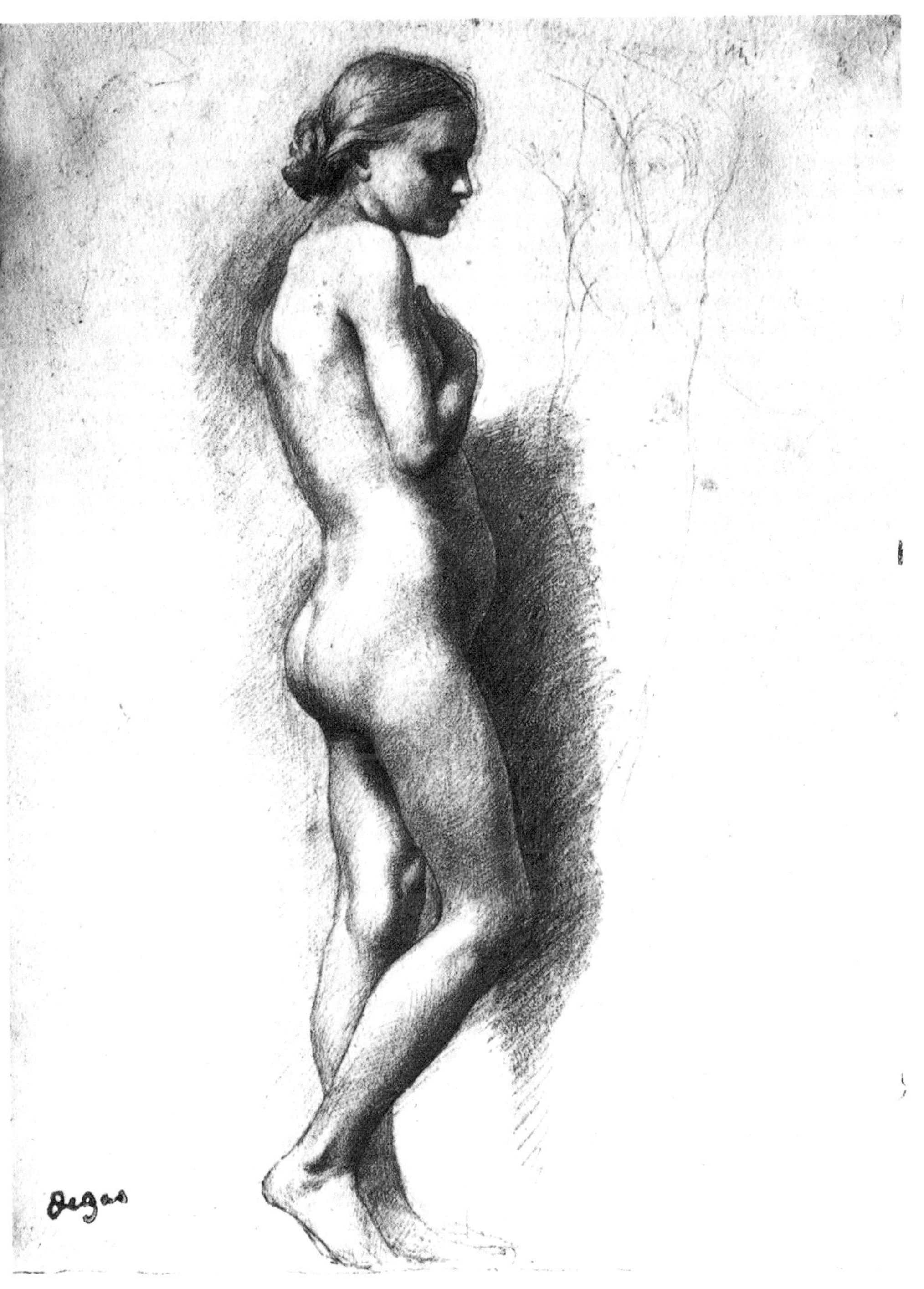

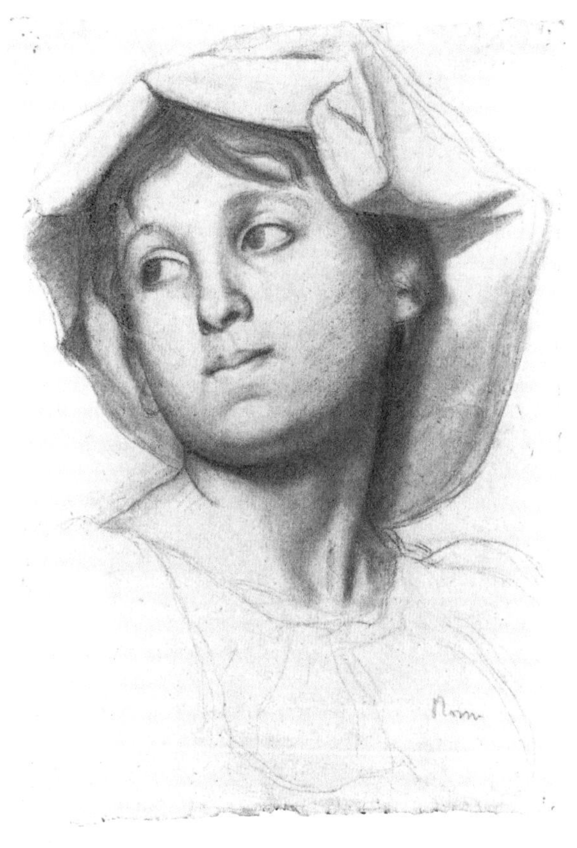

ABOVE
27. *Head of a Young Roman Woman*, c. 1857.
Black chalk and charcoal, 38.8 × 26.7 cm (15¼ × 10½ in.).
Baltimore Museum of Art

OPPOSITE
28. *Two Studies of the Head of a Man*, c. 1856–57.
Pencil heightened with bodycolour on red/brown paper,
44.8 × 22.6 cm (17⅝ × 8⅞ in.). Sterling and Francine Clark
Art Institute, Williamstown, Massachusetts

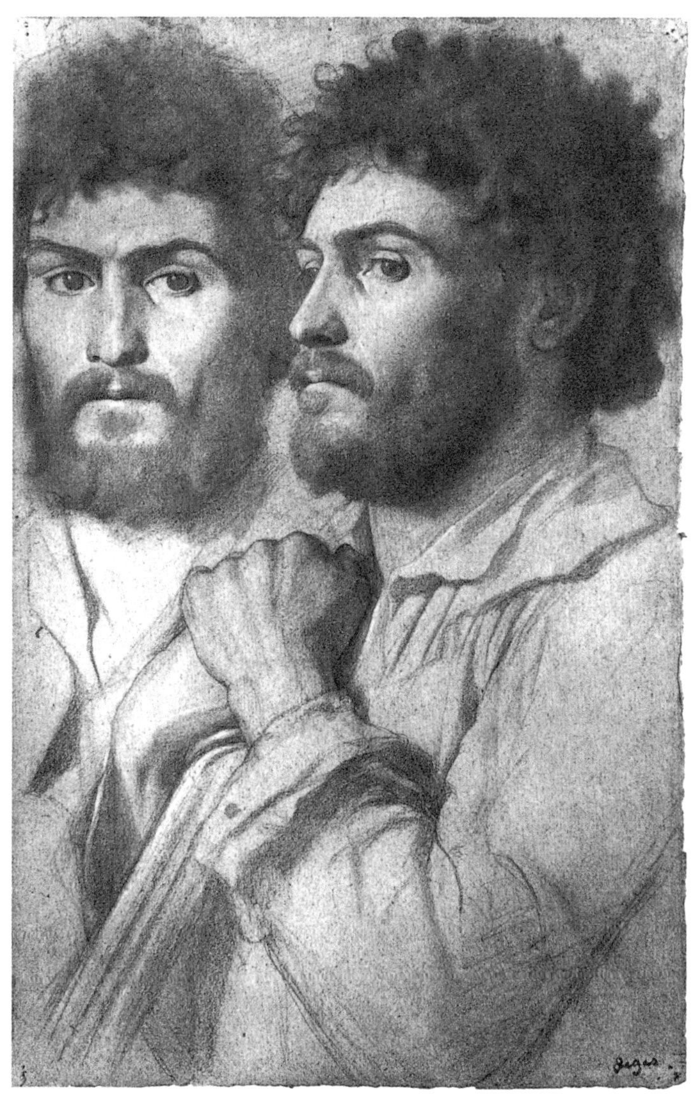

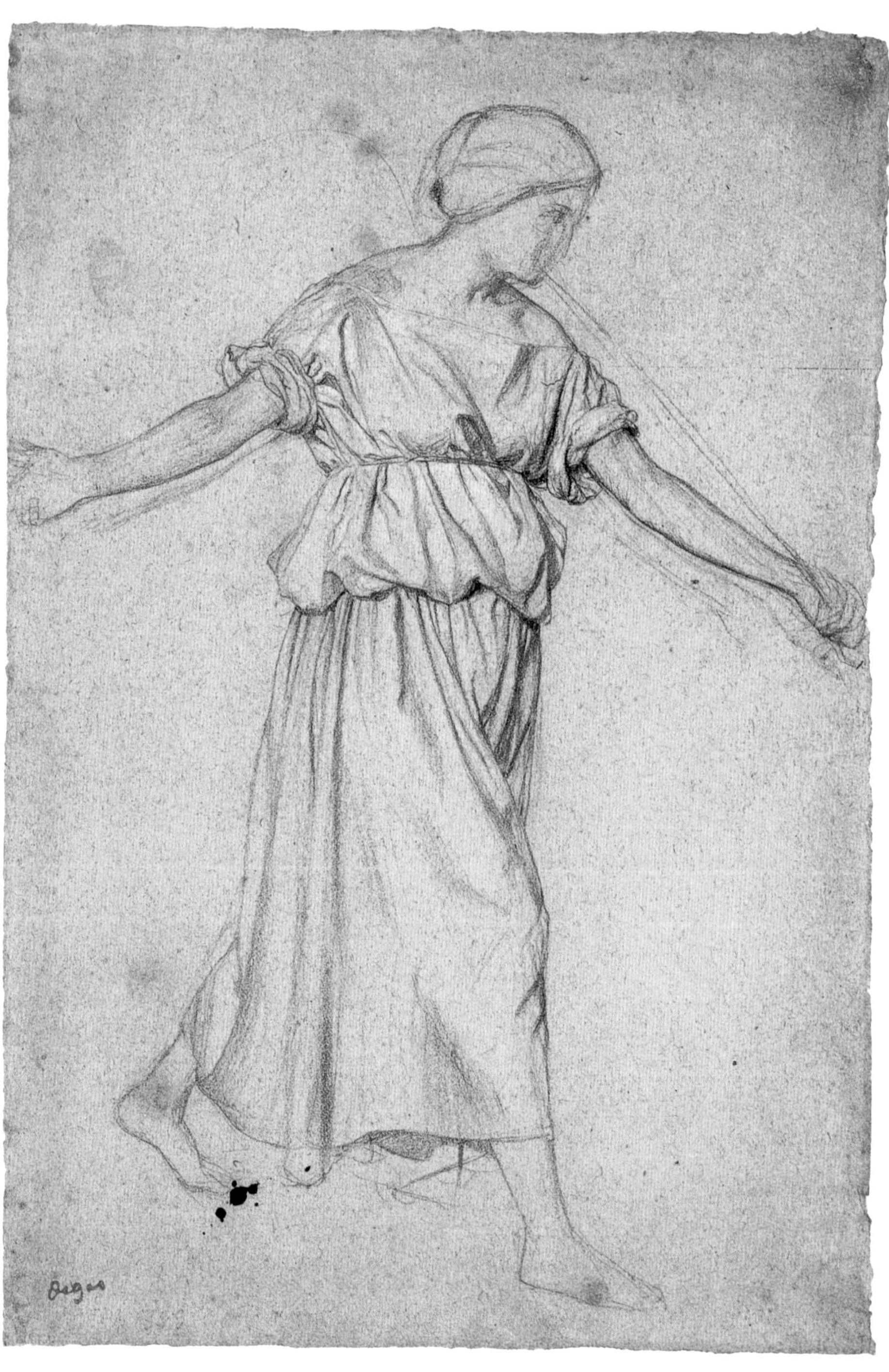

48   *Italy 1856–1859*

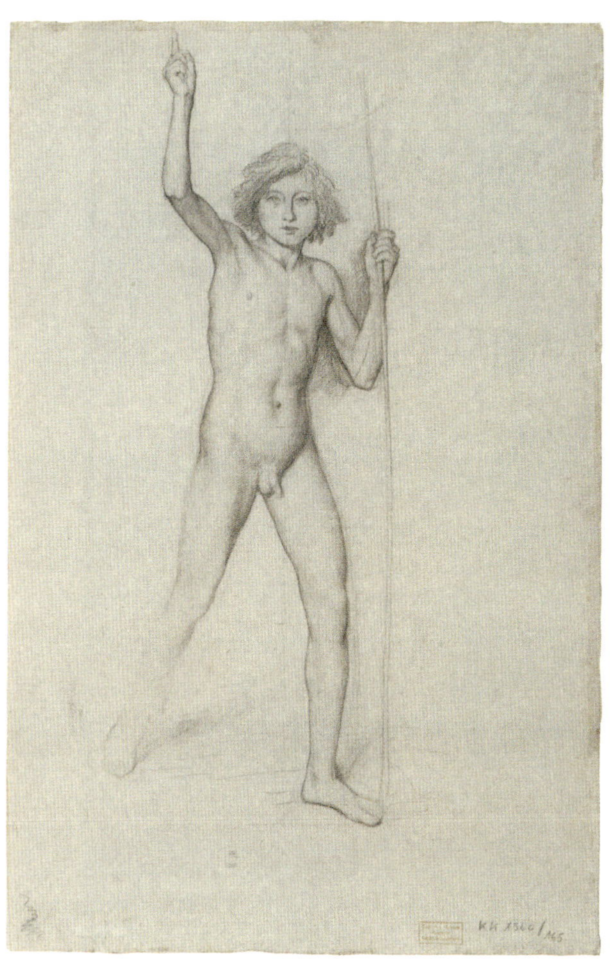

OPPOSITE

29. *Study for 'St John the Baptist and the Angel'*, 1857.
Pencil heightened with bodycolour on pink paper,
42 × 28.5 cm (16½ × 11¼ in.).
Kunsthalle Bremen

ABOVE

30. *Study for 'St John the Baptist and the Angel'*, 1857.
Pencil, 44.5 × 29 cm (17½ × 11⅜ in.), squared.
Von der Heydt Museum, Wuppertal

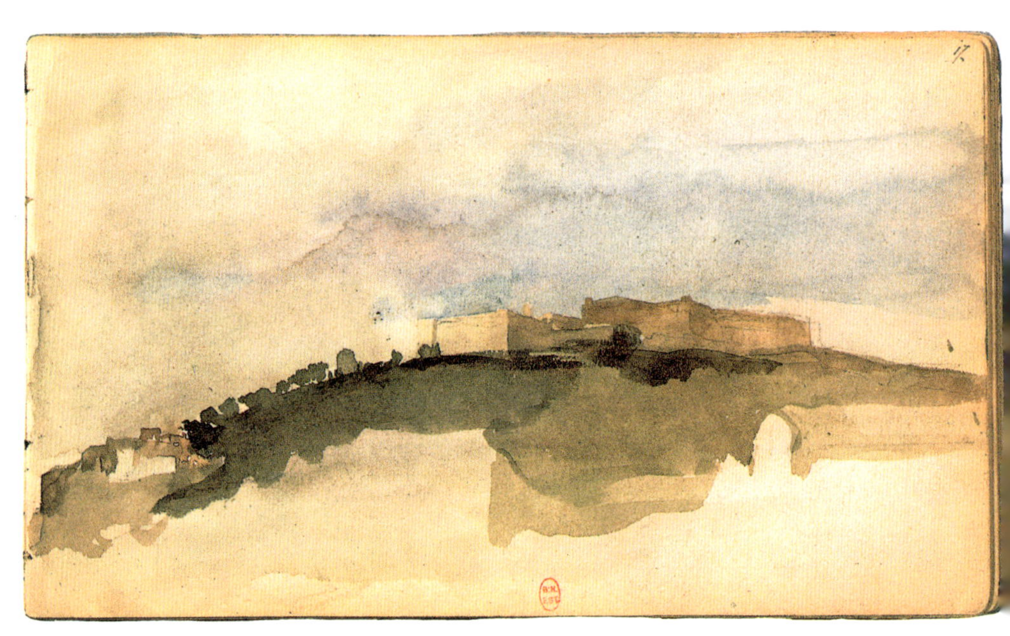

31. *Castello Sant'Elmo*, Notebook 19, p. 17, 1860.
Watercolour, 12.5 × 21.5 cm (4⅞ × 8½ in.).
Bibliothèque Nationale, Paris

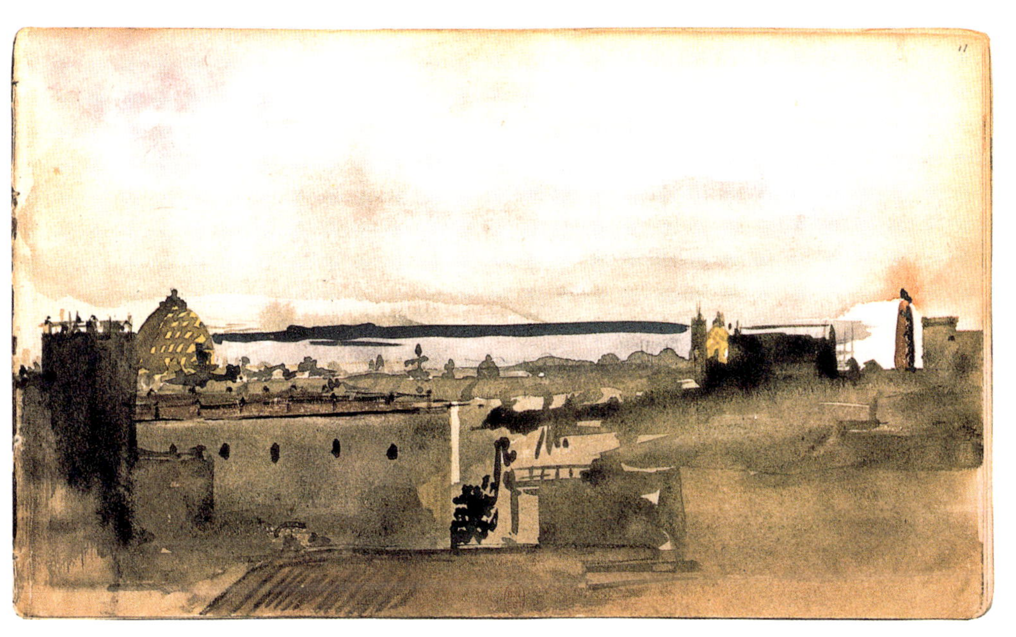

32. *View of Naples*, Notebook 19, p. 11, 1860.
Watercolour, 12.5 × 21.5 cm (4⅞ × 8½ in.).
Bibliothèque Nationale, Paris

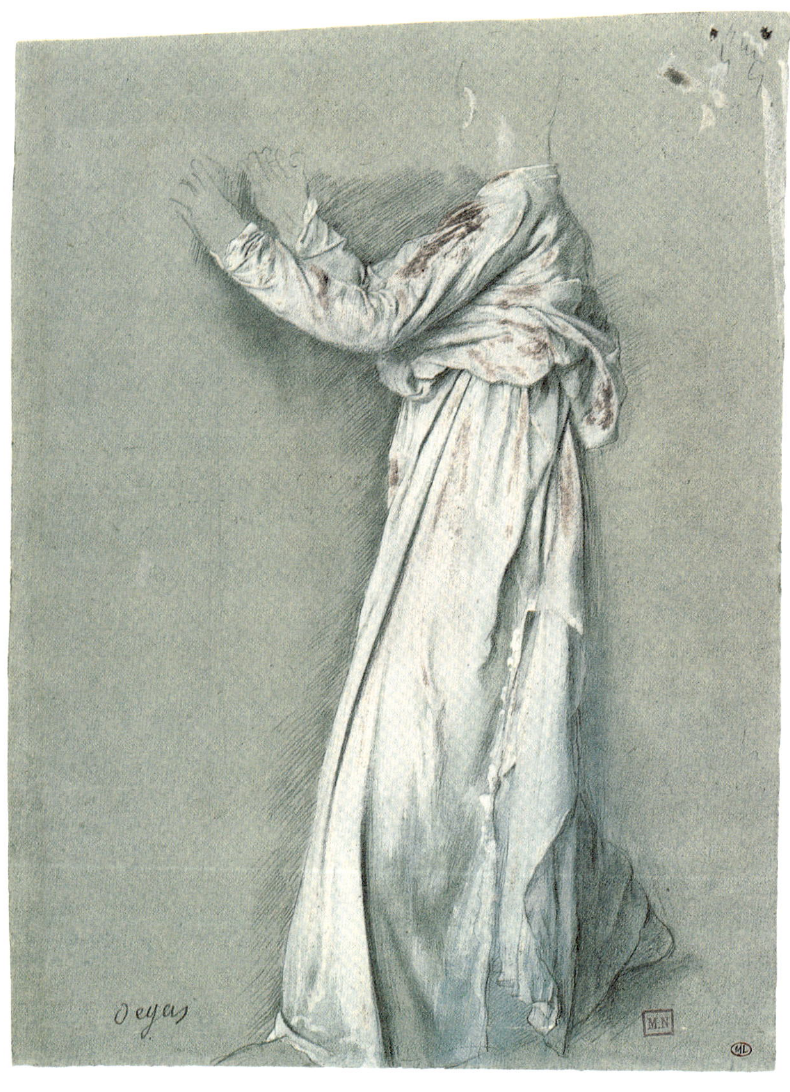

33. *Drapery Study for Standing Figure, c.* 1860–61.
Pencil and watercolour heightened with bodycolour
on blue paper, 29.1 × 21.9 cm (11½ × 8⅝ in.).
Musée d'Orsay, Paris

CHAPTER THREE

History Paintings 1860–1865

'There are people who are always talking about the masters…They don't understand them, they use them and they dishonour them. The secret is to follow the advice given by the masters in their work by doing something other than what they have done.'

(Degas in Georges Jeanniot, *Memories of Degas*, 1933)

On returning to Paris Degas set about becoming a successful painter. The programme of training that he had put himself through and his experiences in Italy now needed to be applied to specific tasks. History painting was still highly and widely regarded as the best way to establish a reputation, particularly if such a picture was well received at a Salon exhibition. At the beginning of the 1860s Degas saw this as the right path to follow, and in the space of only five years, with intense effort, he produced five major large-scale paintings: *Alexander and Bucephalus* (c. 1859–60), *The Daughter of Jephthah* (c. 1859–61), *Young Spartans Exercising* (c. 1860), *Semiramis Building Babylon* (c. 1860–61) and *Scene of War in the Middle Ages* (1865). Of these only *Scene of War in the Middle Ages* was actually shown in the Salon. Yet, even though these bold attempts at history painting seem not to have met with outright success, Degas was immensely proud of them. And two of these pictures – *Young Spartans Exercising* and *Scene of War in the Middle Ages* – remained in his studio for the rest of his life. Indeed, Degas contemplated including *Young Spartans Exercising* in the fifth Impressionist exhibition of 1880, but, although it is listed in the catalogue, it does not in the end seem to have been shown. It is with these history pictures that Degas endeavoured to prove himself and the effort he put into them shows how determined he was. A great deal was at stake after his deep and continuing engagement with copying and his frequent drawing from the model, but what needed to be tested now was his imagination.

Degas's choice of becoming a history painter was inspired in part by the examples of Ingres and Delacroix and in part by his own literary interests. The influence of Delacroix was a comparatively new departure for Degas and almost certainly encouraged by Moreau, although it was

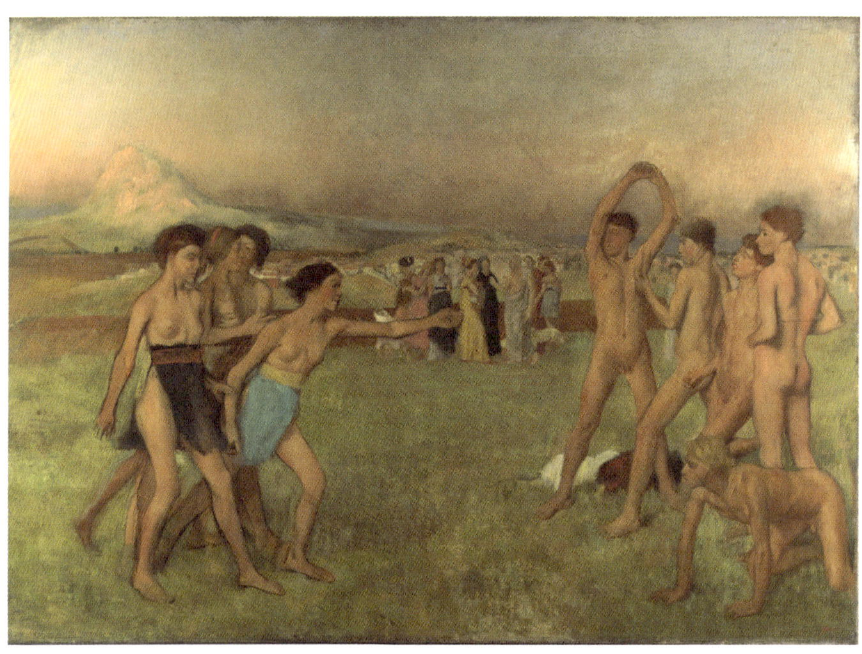

34. *Young Spartans Exercising*, *c.* 1860, reworked until 1880.
Oil on canvas, 109.5 × 155 cm (43⅛ × 61 in.).
National Gallery, London

a situation regarded with some alarm by his father whose taste was less
variable. Degas would no doubt have been aware of the retrospective
exhibition of Delacroix's work mounted, like that of Ingres, at the
Exposition Universelle in 1855, but the Notebooks reveal that he also
examined Delacroix's work with mounting interest in Paris at the
beginning of the 1860s. Furthermore, the great artist died in 1863,
triggering fresh appraisals of his contribution to French painting.

Ingres and Delacroix can be seen as opposites and the fundamental
differences in their art – one neoclassical and the other a romantic – are
equally apparent in their differing personalities. Ingres was conformist
and doctrinaire; Delacroix a rebel and enigmatic. Ingres was concise and
aphoristic; Delacroix open-hearted and reflective. Both drew regularly
and purposefully, but where Ingres sought perfection in the purity of his
pencil line, Delacroix relished variety in his preference for the liquidity
of ink and softer, more pliable media. In these respects Ingres can be
seen as the heir to Raphael and Delacroix to Rubens. Where Ingres drew
delicately but with precision ('like a fly walking on a sheet of paper'),

Delacroix preferred to rely upon chance or the 'random accidents of life'. Ingres plotted his pictures carefully, fitting the pieces together like a jigsaw puzzle, whereas Delacroix relied upon spontaneity. He once said, 'If you have not sufficient skill to make a sketch of a man throwing himself out of a window, in the time that it takes him to fall from the fourth floor to the ground, you will never be capable of producing great *machines*.' For Ingres, therefore, drawing was almost an act of contrition, but for Delacroix it was a celebration.

This sudden veneration for Delacroix felt by Degas did not mean that Ingres was cast aside. The opposite is the case, since he had the capacity to absorb both influences, however divergent in style or approach, and to refer to one or other if and when required. As a result, throughout Degas's life there were moments when Ingres was uppermost in his mind and others when Delacroix was paramount. Of the two, Degas had met Ingres personally, but Delacroix he seems only to have glimpsed from afar 'pressed for time, and hurrying'. What mattered to Degas was the integrity of both Ingres and Delacroix as artists, so apparent in their working procedures and in their ultimate intentions. Regarding Degas's ambitious programme of history paintings at the start of the 1860s, there could be no better exemplars than Ingres and Delacroix. The careful preparatory process for each of these paintings emulates Ingres, whereas the dynamism of the compositions and the treatment of colour betoken Delacroix.

Young Spartans Exercising [34] is an evocation of ancient Greece. The foreground is filled by opposing groups of young girls and boys. The girls appear to be taunting the boys who adopt defensive poses. At the centre of the composition in the middle distance is a group of women surrounding an old man who is identifiable as Lycurgus, who drew up the laws of Sparta. The city lies beyond, dominated at the left by the rock from which malformed Spartan infants were thrown. Degas's imagination was undoubtedly sparked by accounts of Sparta in sources of various dates ranging from Plutarch in antiquity to the eighteenth century, but primarily this rare subject presented him with the opportunity to demonstrate his mastery in depicting the nude. The composition as a whole, however, gave him some difficulty. He abandoned his first full-scale attempt (now in The Art Institute of Chicago) when it was quite advanced and more or less began again. And even the finished version now in the National Gallery in London was subject to changes at later dates since Degas kept the picture close to hand in his studio.

Common to both versions were the groups of young girls and boys in the foreground and it is for these figures that Degas made at least sixteen surviving studies, although it is not always easy to ascertain exactly at which stage of the preparatory process each was made. When he had settled the final composition Degas transferred several of the drawings to the surface of the picture by tracing, but this did not prevent him from making further changes on the canvas itself, where some parts remain unresolved. The drawings for the principal figures were made from posed models and are superbly executed, although occasionally tentative in places. The clear outlines are often strengthened and the modelling restrained. *Youth with Arms Raised* [40] accords with the corresponding figure in the abandoned version in Chicago; *Young Spartan Girl* [41] shares features in common with both compositions.

Semiramis Building Babylon [35] is a recreation of one of the greatest civilizations of the ancient world. It is romantic in conception, but presented in a neoclassical guise. Degas was not alone in seeking to recapture the magnificence of fallen empires: Rossini's opera *Semiramis* was performed in Paris while Degas was working on this picture at the same time as Flaubert was conjuring up Carthage in his novel *Salammbô* (1862). He may also have known about the Assyrian artefacts recently found by archaeologists, some of which were on view in the Musée du Louvre. Degas settles for a frieze-like composition reminiscent of works by Piero della Francesca, with statuesque figures that come closer to Puvis de Chavannes than to Ingres and a degree of exoticism that is comparable with Moreau. The composition is surprisingly static with Semiramis, who has just arrived by chariot, attended by her retinue. She is standing on the terrace of her palace overlooking the city of Babylon, which is being constructed on both banks of the river Euphrates. Behind on the right are the palace gardens.

Degas made numerous studies for this picture for which he had to widen his terms of reference considerably. It was not just a question of working out the poses of the figures or their interrelationships, but also historical details of the costumes and accessories, as well as the appearance of the city itself. The intellectual content of the painting was as important as its artistic basis. Intimations of Degas's interest in developing this subject as a painting occur in the Notebooks, leading to several detailed compositional studies on separate pieces of paper followed by oil sketches and, in the final moments before actually starting the painting, by a pastel. He then makes studies (many of which he rejected) for the figures from posed models first observed in the nude and then clothed, before concentrating on specifics such as coiffure or personal attributes [33, 42–45]. As with *The Bellelli Family* [see 16], Degas takes a great interest in the clothes and accessories, working on such aspects in immense detail. One of the outstanding and

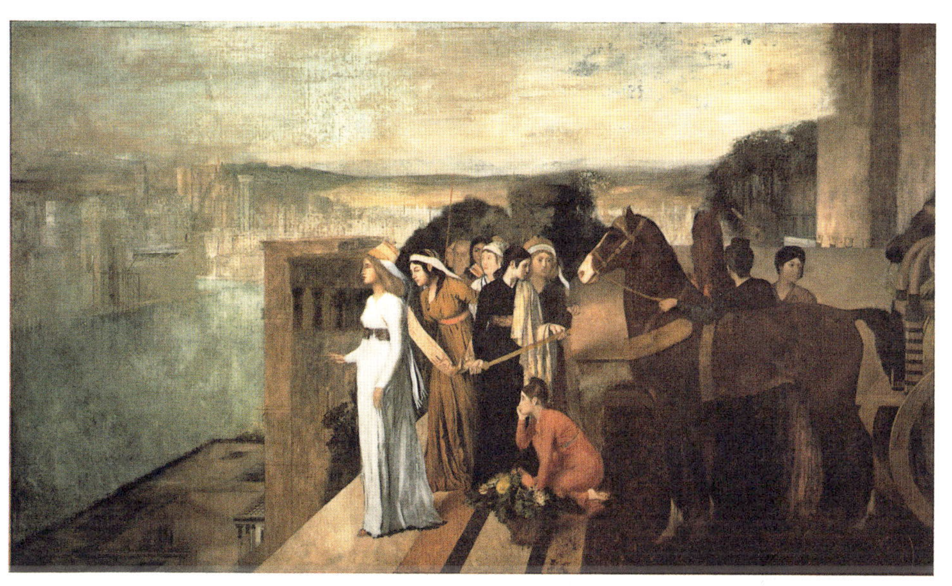

35. *Semiramis Building Babylon*, *c.* 1860–61.
Oil on canvas, 151.5 × 258 cm (59⅝ × 101⅝ in.).
Musée d'Orsay, Paris

more finished drawings in this group is of the horse with its powerful
musculature and glossy coat [37].

The Daughter of Jephthah [36] is a biblical story from the Book of
Judges. A mercenary, Jephthah, is prevailed upon by the Israelites to lead
their country in war against the Ammonites. Before the battle he makes
a vow that if victorious he will sacrifice 'the first creature that comes
out of the door of my house to meet me when I return'. But, after his
victory 'who should come out to meet him with tambourines and dances
but his daughter, and she an only child'. The subject was popular with
French painters during the seventeenth and eighteenth centuries and
subsequently with writers. Degas shows Jephthah on horseback in the
centre foreground with his sword over his shoulder surrounded by his
soldiers with their prisoners and trophies. Dominating the background
before a bucolic setting Jephthah's daughter and her attendants advance
to greet him extending their arms in welcome and unaware of the vow
he has made: they act like a Greek chorus, but their movements are
more like a corps de ballet. Jephthah himself averts his eyes in disbelief

36. *The Daughter of Jephthah*, c. 1859–61.
Oil on canvas, 195.5 × 298.5 cm (77 × 117½ in.).
Smith College, Northampton, Massachusetts

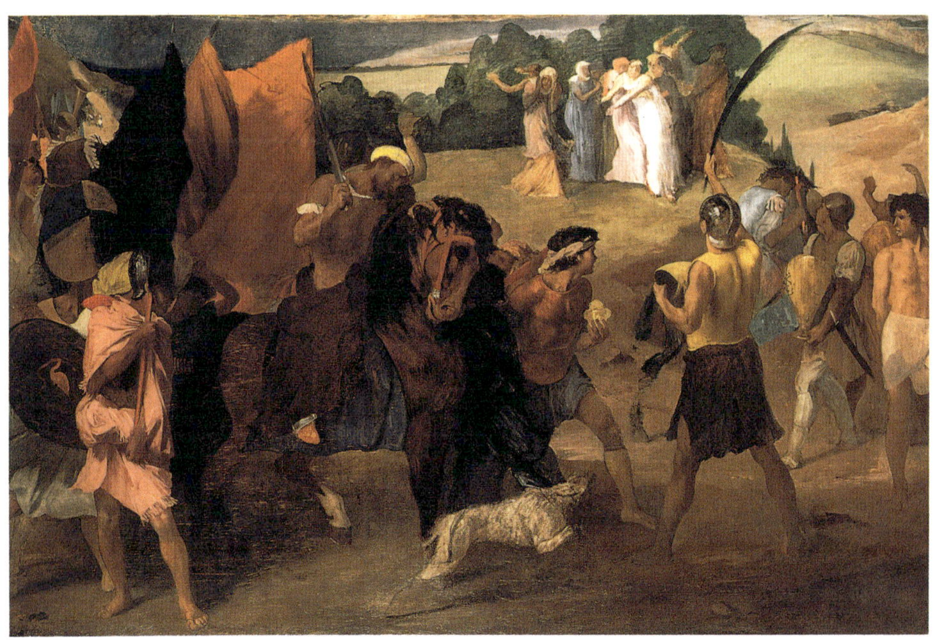

and bows his head overcome by the horror of the situation, which his daughter later stoically accepts, allowing herself to be sacrificed.

Where the composition of *Semiramis Building Babylon* is static and reposeful, *The Daughter of Jephthah* is extremely agitated and full of expression. The emotional tenor of the picture, its spirited rhythms and its intense colours reveal the impact of Delacroix on Degas, whose extensive commentary on the picture in his Notebooks (14, 14A, 15, 16) refers not only to Delacroix but also to Mantegna and Veronese ('Look for Mantegna's spirit and love of Veronese's colouring', he writes).

The drawings for *The Daughter of Jephthah* in the Notebooks [38] are concerned primarily with the evolution of this complicated composition, although ideas for individual poses, particularly Jephthah's, do occur. The use of the brush suggests the taut internal rhythms that Degas wanted to emphasize. From the mêlée presented by these compositional studies he isolates individual figures and clarifies their poses in the painting – a process that forces him to make final decisions.

Of the history paintings *The Daughter of Jephthah* is the largest in size in the group, but the most compelling is *Scene of War in the Middle Ages* [39], for which there seems to be no specific literary source. A later title given to the picture, *The Miseries of the City of Orléans*, led to much speculation as to whether Degas was painting an imaginary historical scene set during the Hundred Years' War or a political allegory prompted by family circumstances. After all, his father had been born in the city of Orléans and his mother had originally come from New Orleans in Louisiana, where her family was still based. Indeed, atrocities committed in New Orleans in 1862 during the American Civil War had caused members of the family to move to France, where they became exiles for a short period. The theory is that *Scene of War in the Middle Ages* could be an allegory based on events in New Orleans associated with the American Civil War but transferred to the Middle Ages. If this is indeed the case, Degas, characteristically, left no clue as to his intentions. What is irrefutable, however, is that the scene depicted is one of undeniable violence with horrible crimes inflicted on women. It is a subject worthy of Goya's series of prints *The Disasters of War* of which Degas owned a copy of the edition issued in 1863. The painting is executed in *essence* on several pieces of paper mounted on canvas. The matt appearance of the surface resembles fresco painting and caused confusion from the start, in so far as the Salon catalogue of 1865 described the work as a 'pastel'.

As with all his other history paintings, Degas prepared every aspect with the greatest care probably over a considerable period. The concept of the painting is not dissimilar from works by Puvis de Chavannes,

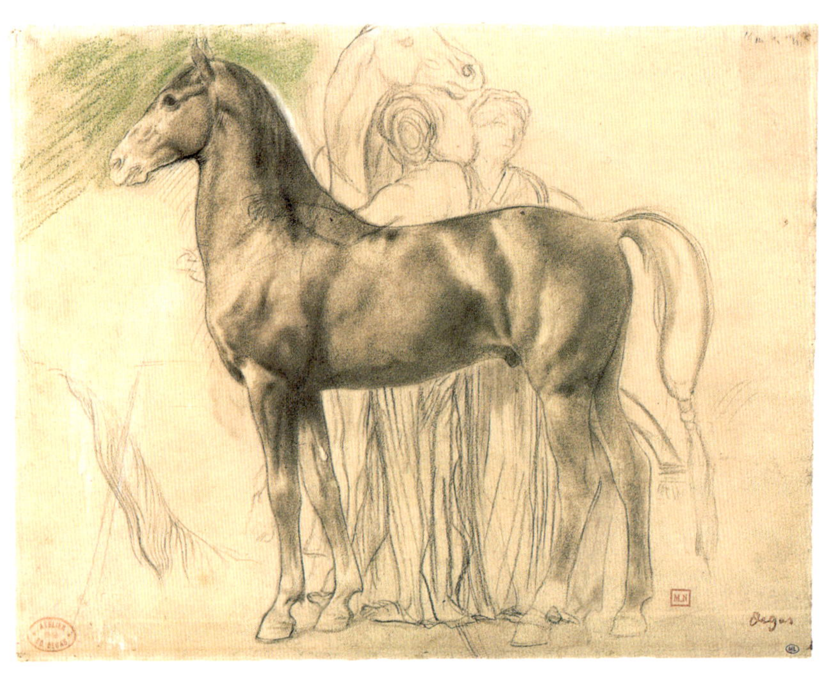

37. *Study of a Horse with Figures*, c. 1860–61.
Pencil, black chalk and pastel, 26.8 × 34.7 cm (10½ × 13⅝ in.).
Musée d'Orsay, Paris

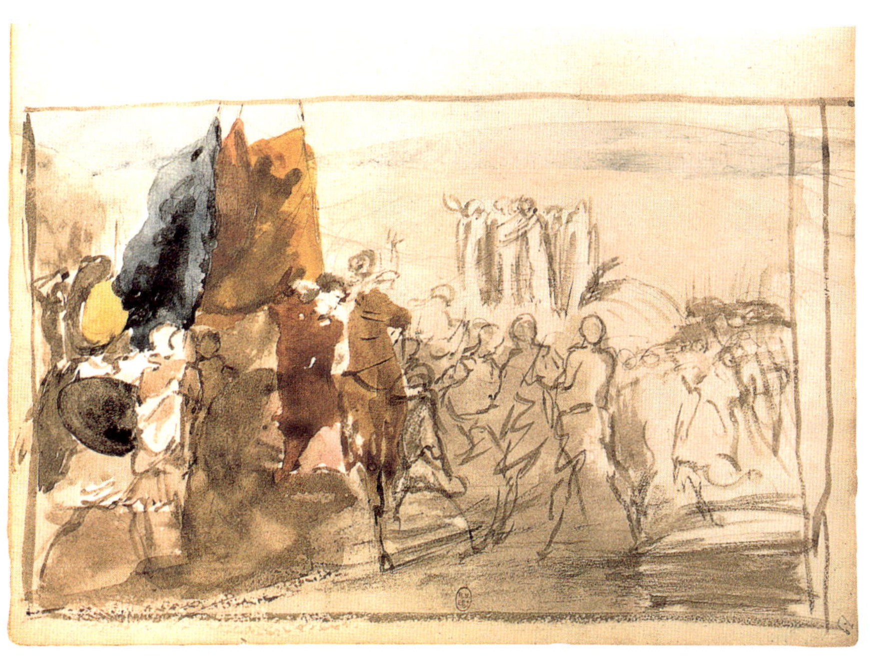

38. *Compositional Study for 'The Daughter of Jephthah'*,
Notebook 18, p. 79, *c.* 1859–61.
Watercolour, 19.2 × 25.4 cm (7½ × 10 in.).
Bibliothèque Nationale, Paris

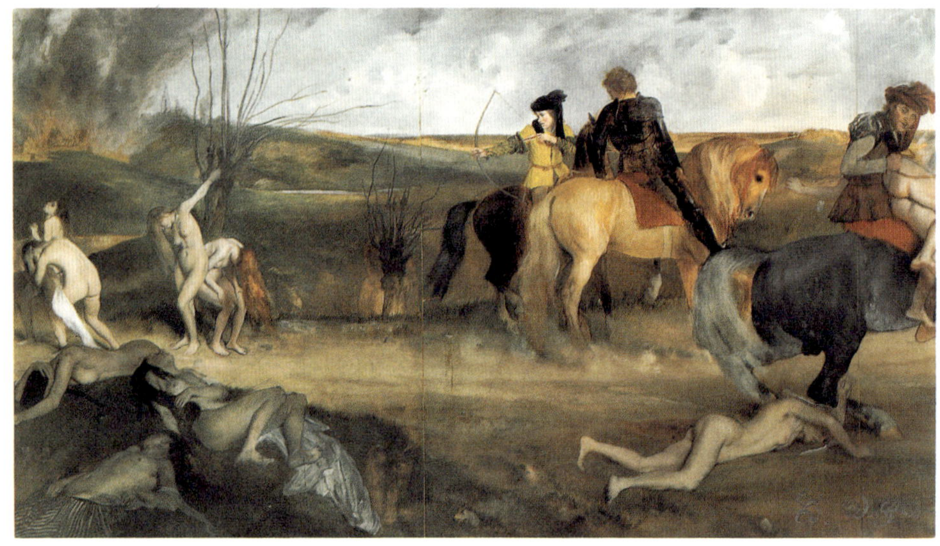

39. *Scene of War in the Middle Ages*, 1865.
Essence on paper mounted on canvas, 83.5 × 148.5 cm
(33⅞ × 57½ in.). Musée d'Orsay, Paris

who had himself exhibited an allegory entitled *War* at the Salon of
1861, but the inspiration clearly comes from Delacroix and in a lesser
vein from Moreau. Degas is not afraid to show the drama almost in
close-up against a background where the land has been laid waste. Men
on horseback ride out of the composition to the right where one has
captured a woman and pulled her on to his horse. The other women
have either been raped, tortured or are wounded. Three lie prostrate
on the ground on the left while one on the right is trampled by a horse:
all of these are in shadow in the immediate foreground. Fully lit in the
middle distance on the left two women are attempting to run away,
but are being shot at by the mounted archer. Two other women are
shackled to a tree. It amounts to a remarkable scene of carnage with an
underlying threnody inspired in part by Renaissance paintings of the
Crucifixion, the Expulsion from the Garden of Eden or the Martyrdom
of St Sebastian. Of Delacroix's pictures only *The Death of Sardanapalus*
(1844) is comparable in its horrific subject matter.

Even more revealing than the finished painting is the series of
drawings Degas made in preparation. Unlike some of the other
history paintings (*Semiramis Building Babylon* or *The Daughter
of Jephthah*), there are no indications in the Notebooks that *Scene*

of War in the Middle Ages had a long gestation period. There is only
a single compositional drawing, which is in an awkward, perhaps
deliberately primitive, style that has only general similarities to the
finished work. But there is instead a long series of powerful studies made
from posed models, which demonstrates for the first time Degas's real
potential [46–53]. Made in pencil or black chalk, the handling of the
contours and the delicacy of the shading reveal a growing confidence
in the treatment of the female nude – a subject with which Degas was
to become closely associated from the mid-1880s onwards. Most of the
studies were incorporated into the finished composition and there were
few changes of mind. One of the finest of the rejected studies is *Female
Nude Seated on the Ground* [46], which is a powerful, monumental
image of despair that anticipates the women in Paul Gauguin's late
canvases or even work by the twentieth-century sculptor Käthe Kollwitz.
Ironically, the models for the male horsemen were female.

Another aspect of these drawings when they are seen as a group is
the number of different viewpoints that break the bounds of academic
teaching. For the first time, it seems, Degas is realizing that within
such a traditional subject as the female nude there exists the possibility
of novelty or innovation. It is no surprise, therefore, that echoes of
several of these studies are found in contexts that later became Degas's
principal themes – the ballet and the female bather. Also, by drawing a
whole sequence of studies based on what was ostensibly a single subject
was tantamount to creating a series. It is possible that while Degas
was preparing his history paintings this possibility arose in his mind.
Subsequently, beginning in the 1880s, he tended to work more regularly
in series to the extent that the practice eventually became one of the
defining aspects of his *oeuvre*. Similarly, the habit of thinking out and
testing each part of a painting in advance with such deliberation never
left him. Whatever degree of spontaneity his finished works might appear
to have had is belied by his working processes. As Degas later declared
to the Irish novelist and critic George Moore, 'I assure you no art was
ever less spontaneous than mine. What I do is the result of reflection and
study of the great masters; of inspiration, spontaneity, temperament –
temperament is the word – I know nothing.'

Scene of War in the Middle Ages may in one sense be a
straightforward history painting, but in another it led to a quickening
of Degas's creative urges. It shows him standing at the threshold of the
contemporary world, which from this moment onwards would become
the sole focus of his attention.

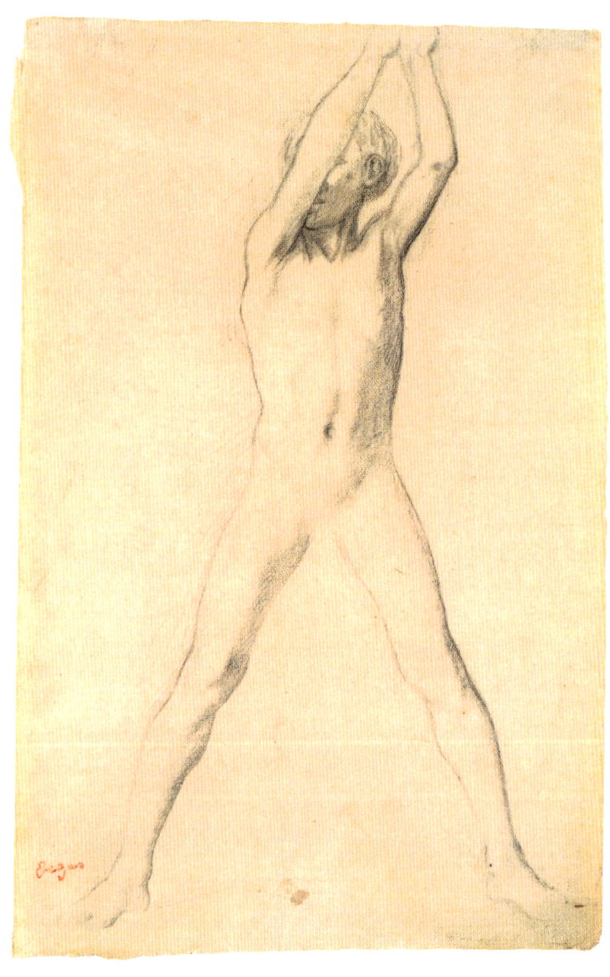

40. *Youth with Arms Raised, c. 1860.*
Black chalk over pencil on beige paper, 31.7 × 19.4 cm (12½ × 7⅝ in.).
Metropolitan Museum of Art, New York

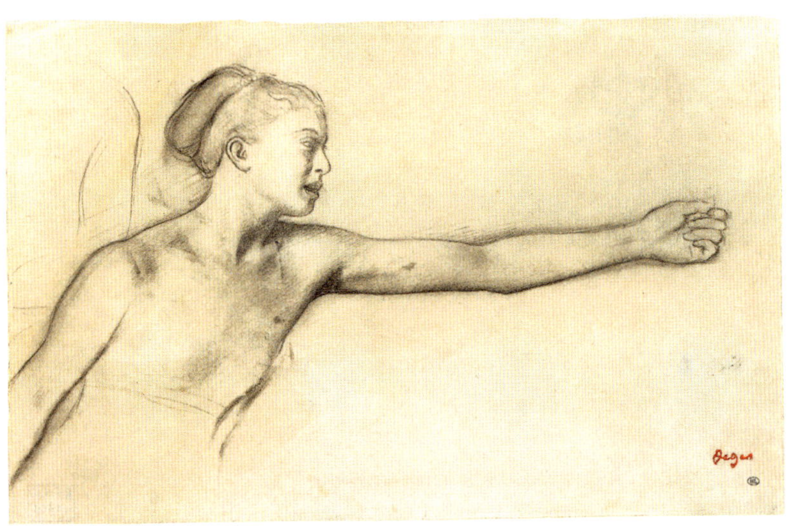

41. *Young Spartan Girl*, *c.* 1860.
Pencil, 28 × 38 cm (11 × 15 in.).
Musée d'Orsay, Paris

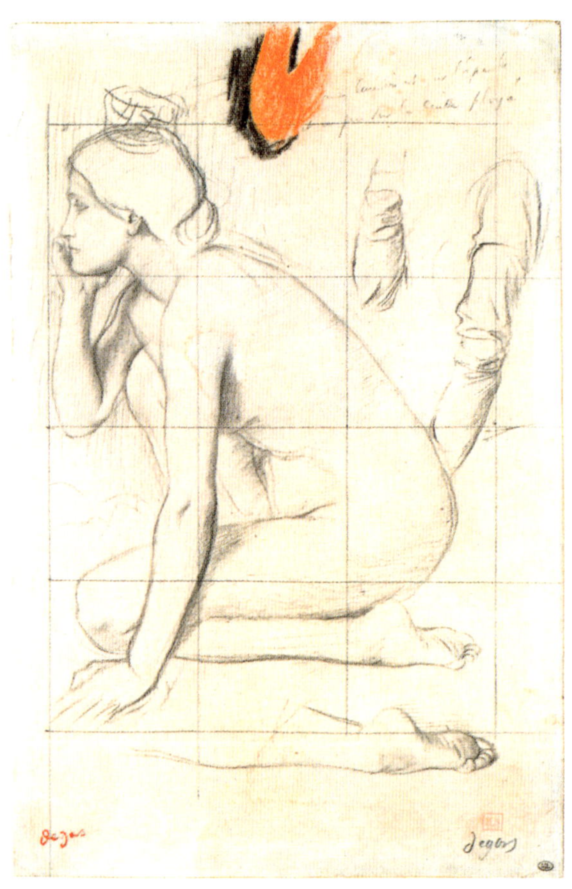

42. *Kneeling Female Figure*, c. 1860–61.
Black chalk and pastel, 34.1 × 22.4 cm (13⅜ × 8½ in.), squared.
Musée d'Orsay, Paris

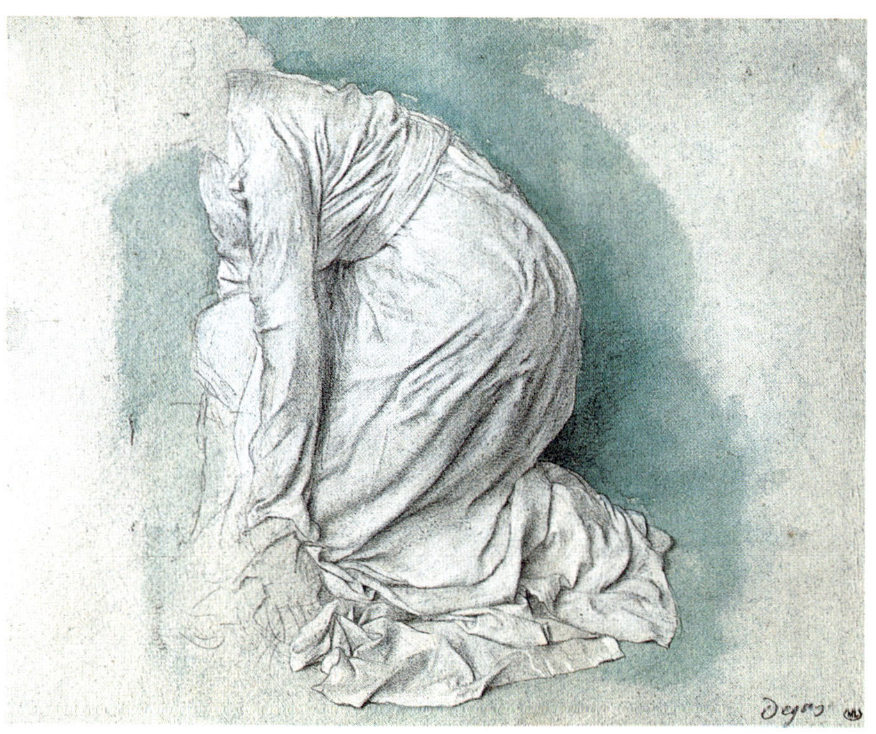

43. *Drapery Study for Kneeling Figure*, c. 1860–61.
Pencil, watercolour heightened with bodycolour on
grey-blue paper, 24.4 × 31.1 cm (9⅝ × 12¼ in.).
Musée d'Orsay, Paris

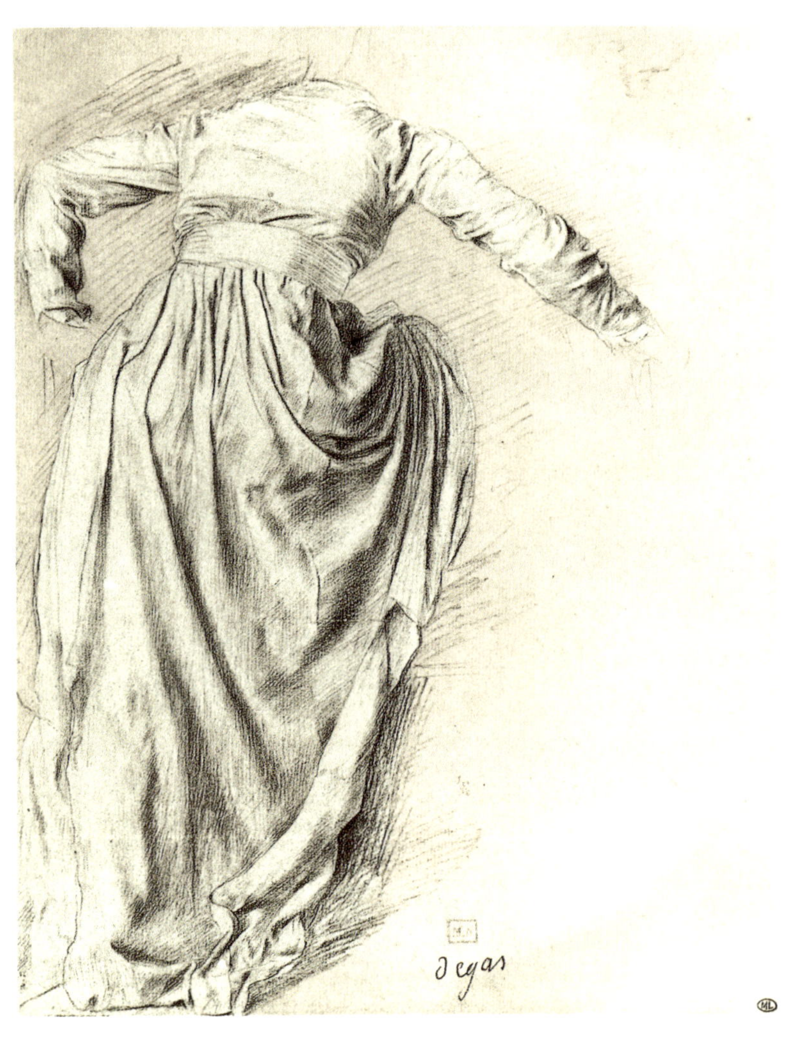

44. *Woman Mounting a Chariot, c.* 1860–61.
Pencil, 30.4 × 22.6 cm (12 × 8⅞ in.).
Musée d'Orsay, Paris

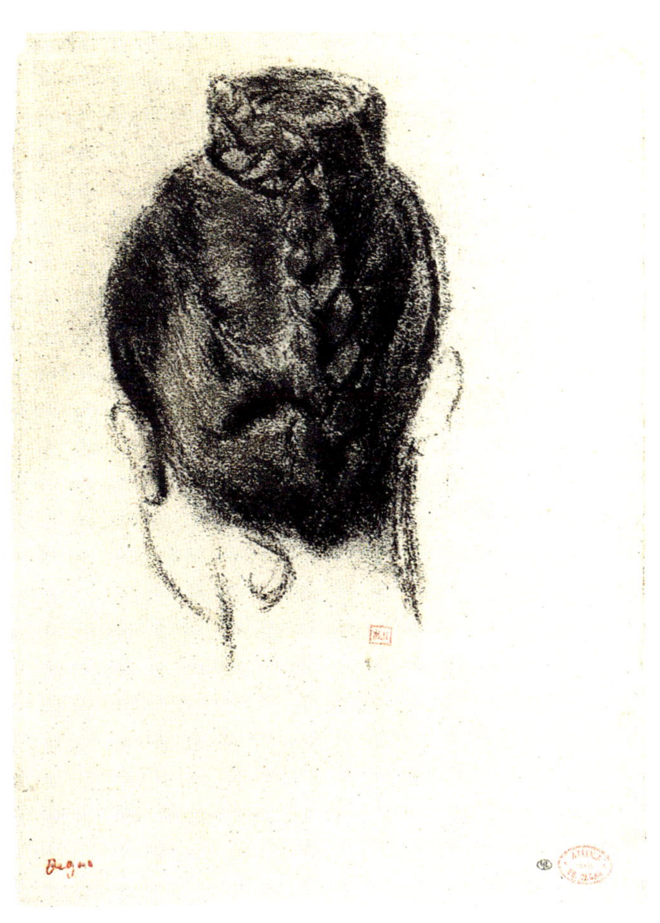

45. *Study of a Woman's Hair*, c. 1860–61.
Black chalk, 32.9 × 24.6 cm (13 × 9¾ in.).
Musée d'Orsay, Paris

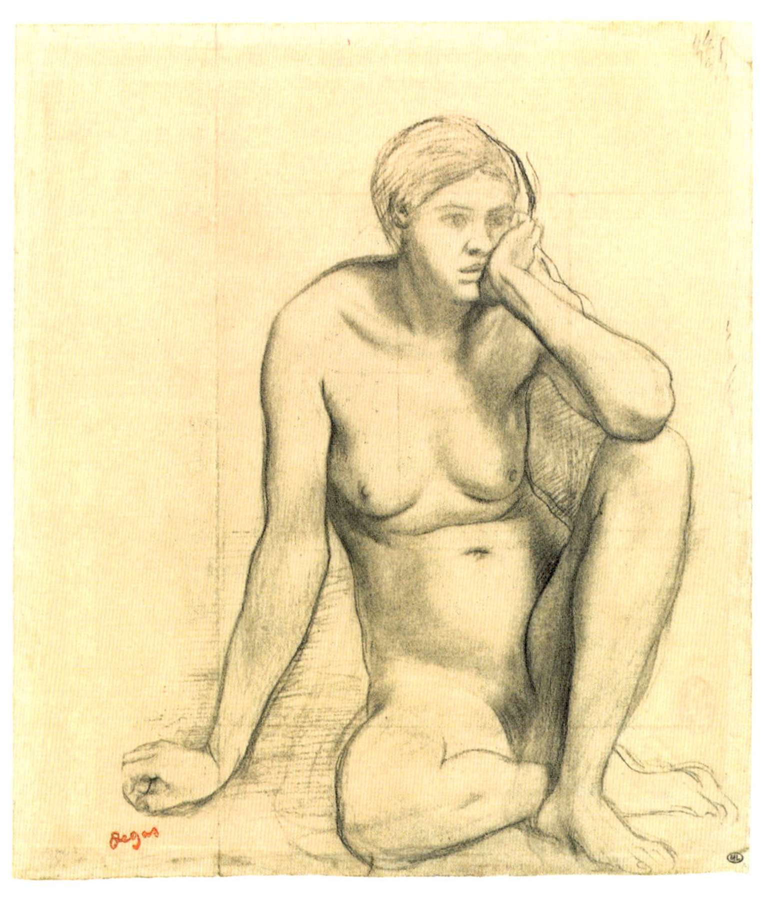

46. *Female Nude Seated on the Ground*, 1865.
Black chalk on beige paper, 31.3 × 27.6 cm (12½ × 10⅞ in.), squared.
Musée d'Orsay, Paris

47. *Female Nude Standing*, 1865.
Black chalk, 37.3 × 19.7 cm (14⅝ × 7¼ in.).
Musée d'Orsay, Paris

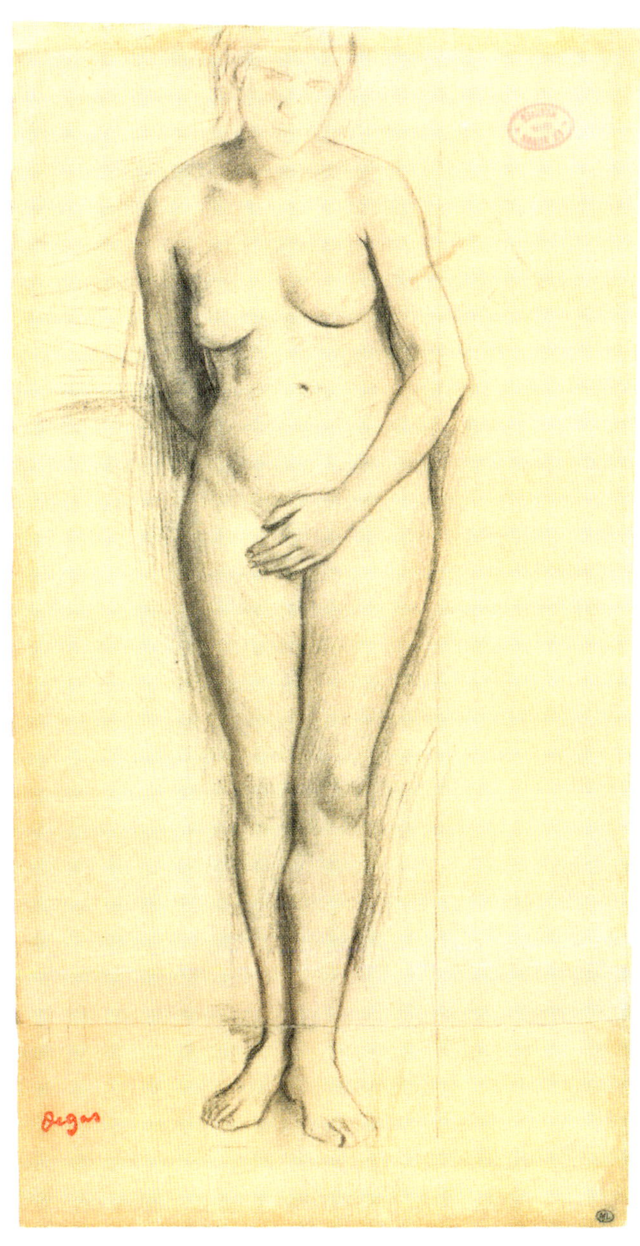

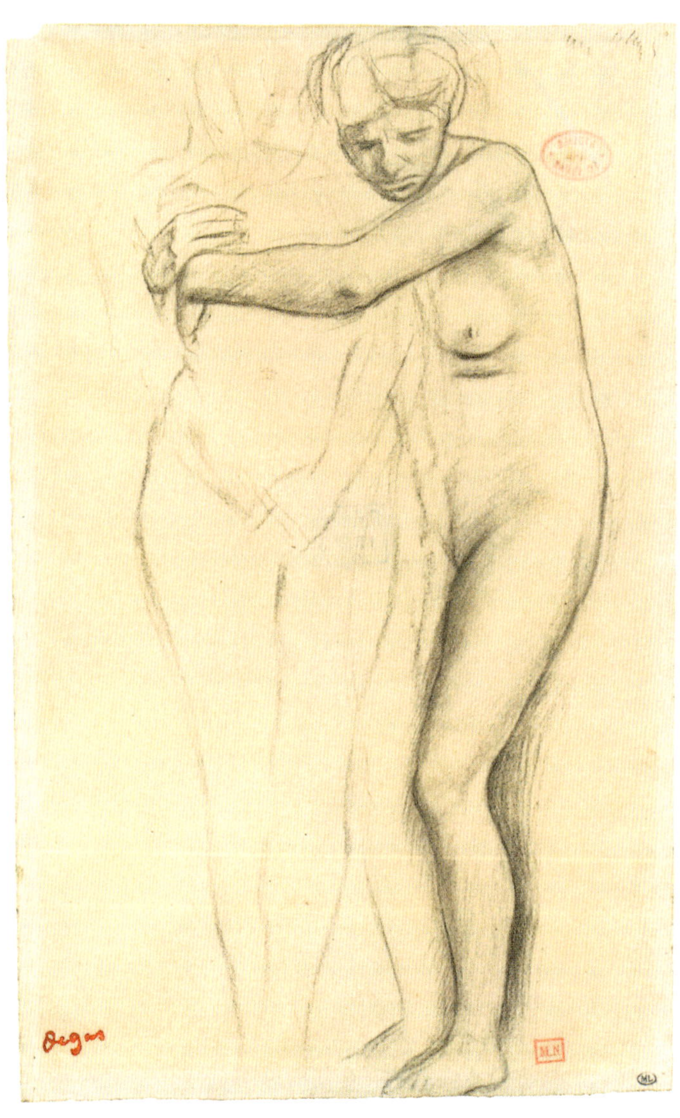

48. *Two Female Nudes Standing Embracing*, 1865.
Black chalk, 31.6 × 19.7 cm (12½ × 7¾ in.).
Musée d'Orsay, Paris

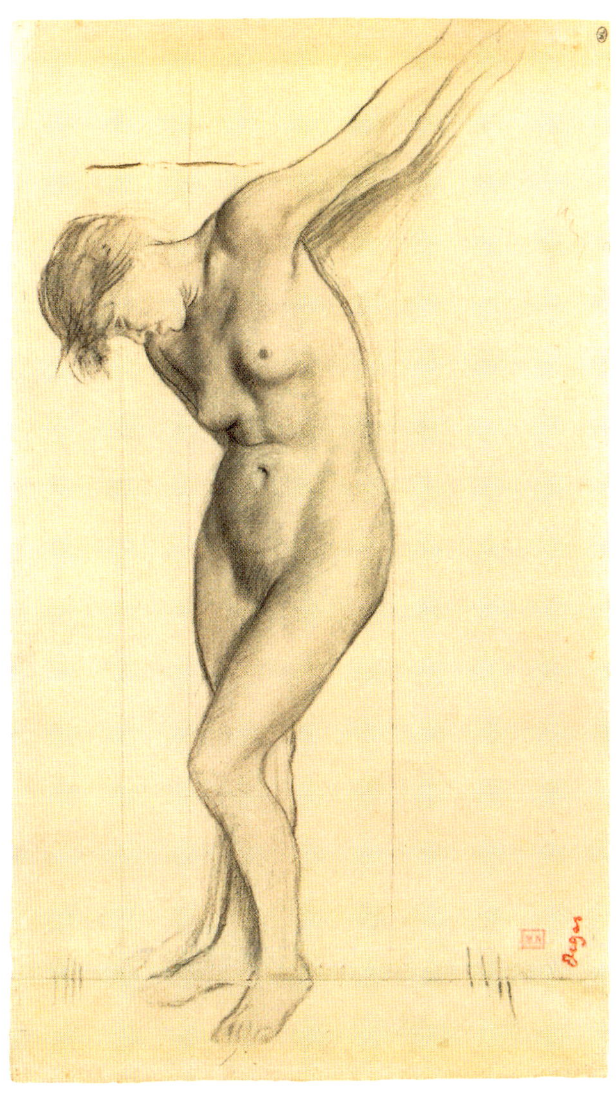

49. *Female Nude Standing with Arm Raised*, 1865.
Black chalk, 39.3 × 22.5 cm (7⅝ × 14 in.).
Musée d'Orsay, Paris

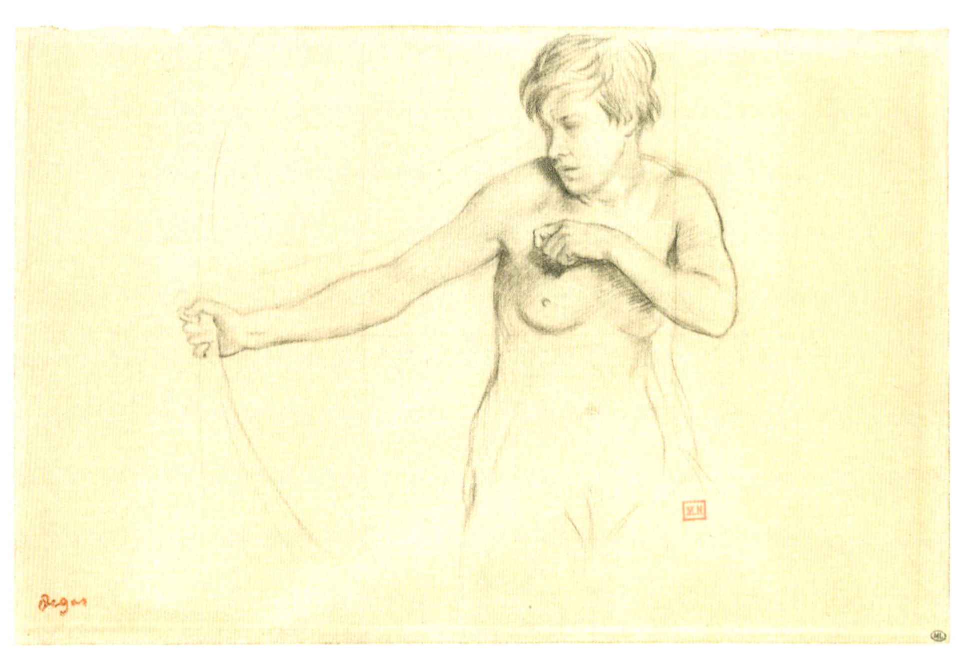

50. *Study of an Archer*, 1865.
Black chalk, 22.9 × 35.7 cm (9 × 14 in.).
Musée d'Orsay, Paris

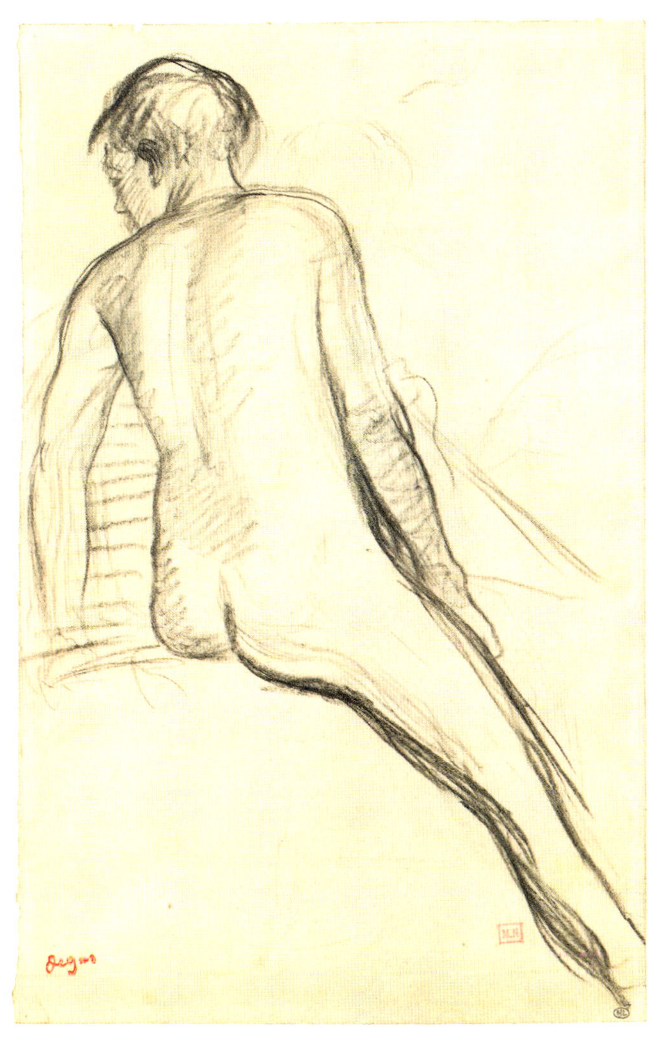

51. *Study of a Nude Rider*, 1865.
Black chalk, 36.3 × 22.8 cm (14¼ × 9 in.).
Musée d'Orsay, Paris

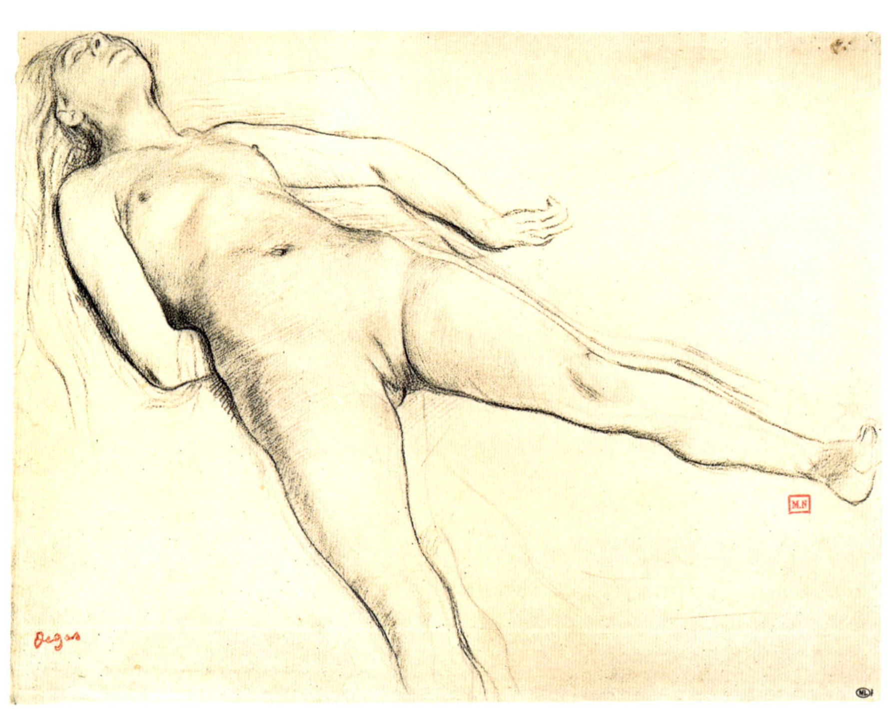

52. *Female Nude on her Back*, 1865.
Black chalk, 26.5 × 35.1 cm (10½ × 13¾ in.).
Musée d'Orsay, Paris

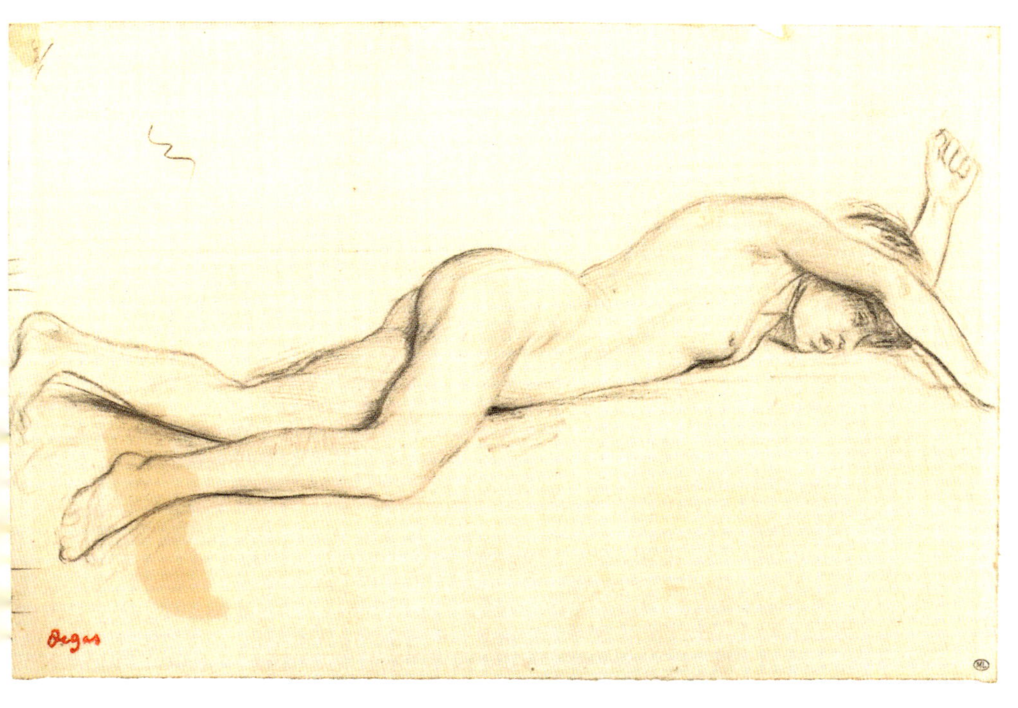

53. *Female Nude Lying on her Stomach*, 1865.
Black chalk, 22.8 × 35.6 cm (9 × 14 in.).
Musée d'Orsay, Paris

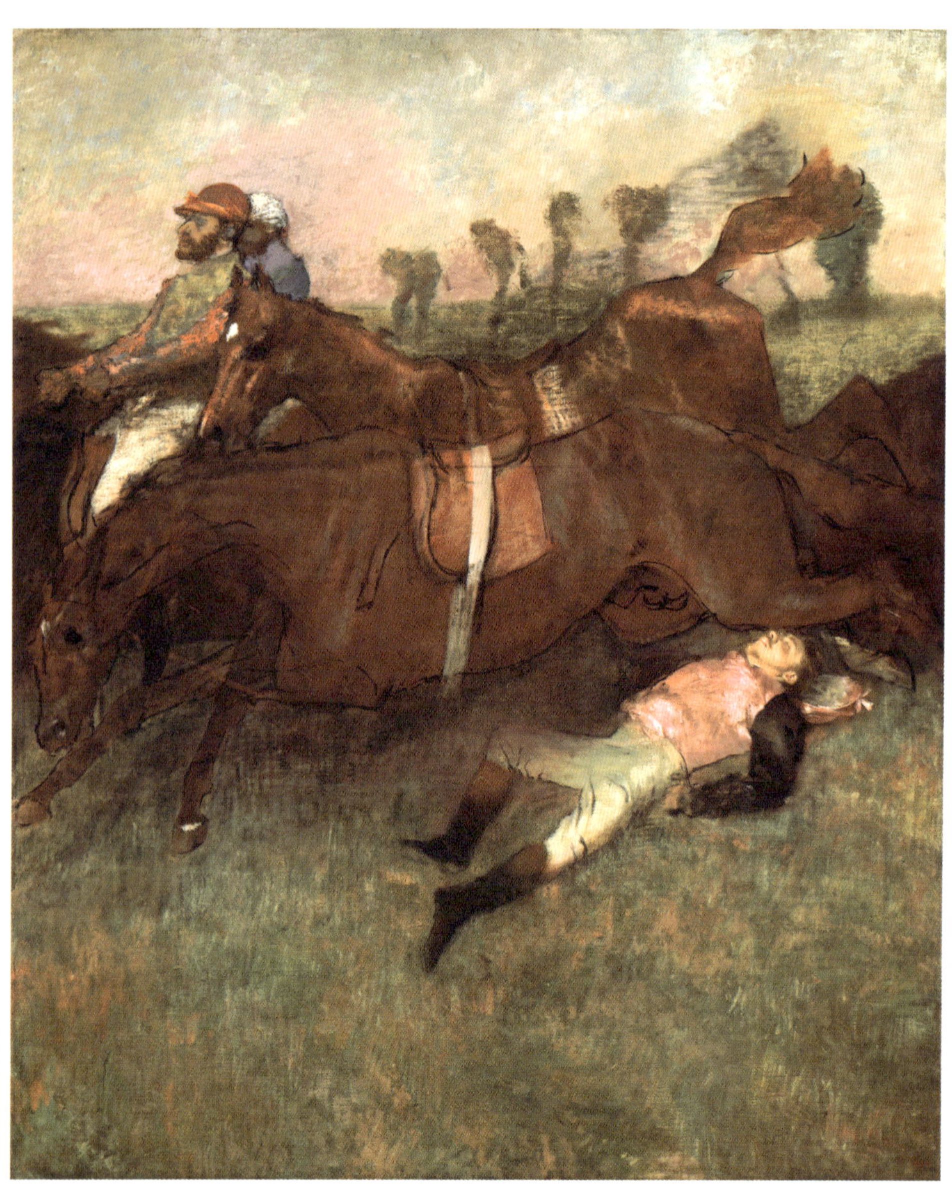

54. *Scene from the Steeplechase: The Fallen Jockey*, 1866, reworked
1880–81 and *c.* 1897. Oil on canvas, 180 × 152 cm (71 × 59½ in.).
National Gallery of Art, Washington, DC

CHAPTER FOUR

Changing Directions 1865–1870

'Oh Giotto! Let me see Paris, and you, Paris, let me see Giotto!'

(Degas, Notebook 22, p. 5, used between 1867 and 1874)

The second half of the 1860s was a period of adjustment for Degas. Although he had applied himself assiduously to the task of becoming a history painter during the first half of the decade, he soon realized that his preference was for painting modern subjects. His work was beginning to win regular acceptance at the annual Salon and the change that was now occurring in his art and life is reflected in the titles of those pictures that he sent for exhibition: *Scene from the Steeplechase: The Fallen Jockey* [54] in 1866, portraits on three occasions (1867, 1869, 1870) and in 1868 *Portrait of Mlle Eugénie Fiocre, à propos the Ballet 'La Source'* [56].

The variety of subject matter in these pictures indicates how Degas was trying to engage more directly with the present rather than the past. He was encouraged in this by others. First of all, there was his school friend Paul Valpinçon and his wife, Marguerite, who had an estate in Lower Normandy at Ménil-Hubert (Orne) near the National Stud at Haras-du-Pin. The local racecourse for this area was at Argentan. Degas visited the Valpinçons regularly for the rest of his life and it is almost certainly there during the 1860s that he discovered his interest in horseracing. Secondly, there were his friendships with artists who also began to flourish during these same years. Allegedly, Degas met Edouard Manet by chance while he was copying in the Musée du Louvre, *c.* 1862, and their friendship grew towards the end of the decade [57]. Manet challenged the authorities with such paintings as *Déjeuner sur l'herbe* and *Olympia*, both of 1863, and was immediately recognized as the leader of the avant-garde, although he never participated in any of the Impressionist exhibitions and remained steadfastly loyal to the Salon. Degas even painted a double-portrait of Manet and his wife,

Suzanne, at this time in which the artist is shown listening to his wife
playing the piano. The painting was a gift made in exchange for one of
Manet's own works. However, not long afterwards Manet mutilated
Degas's double-portrait believing, it appears, that his wife's face had not
been well painted. Such incidents illustrate the precarious nature of the
relationship between Degas and Manet, which, however, did survive until
Manet's death in 1883.

James Tissot was another friend of these years. Both had been taught
by Lamothe and both were interested in Renaissance art; both set out as
history painters and were excellent portraitists; and both sought for novel
ways to depict aspects of contemporary life. Tissot, unlike Degas, gained
success rapidly in Paris and London.

Beyond scenes of horseracing, the theatre and portraiture, Degas
introduced two new themes into his *oeuvre* during the late 1860s. Firstly,
there is the group of domestic subjects exemplified by such pictures as
La Mélancolie (*c.* 1867–70) in the Phillips Collection, Washington, DC,
Interior (The Rape) (*c.* 1868–69) in the Philadelphia Museum of Art,
and *Sulking* (*c.* 1869–71) in the Metropolitan Museum of Art, New
York. These are cleverly devised compositions portraying a range of
emotions, but they remain enigmatic. Interpretations of the subjects
and identifications of the sitters abound. The real question, however,
is to what extent Degas intended these pictures to be enigmatic or,
alternatively, do the difficulties of interpretation arise from the artist's
uncertainty in the portrayal of such psychologically orientated subjects
at this stage of his career?

By contrast, the second group of subjects new to Degas's *oeuvre*
could not be more clearly defined. During July and August of 1869
the artist visited the coast of Normandy, possibly at the behest of the
artist Berthe Morisot, whose family he knew well and who liked to
take their holidays near the sea. Degas frequented Dives-sur-Mer and
Villers-sur-Mer near Houlgate close to the popular resorts of Deauville
and Trouville. Here he undertook in the open air a series of forty
or so pastels of the sea and the shoreline, which in the course of his
development to this date are totally unexpected [78–82].

The determination with which Degas set about portraying scenes
of modern life gave added impetus to his drawings. His addiction to
the art of the past, which he never abandoned, was still an important
contributory factor to the way he interpreted the present. The *Portrait
of Mlle Eugénie Fiocre*, for example, has a composition evoking earlier
treatments of *The Finding of Moses*, and in the horseracing scenes
there are distant echoes of Gozzoli's fresco of *The Journey of the Magi*
(*c.* 1459) in the Palazzo Medici-Riccardi, Florence [see 24], and of Paolo

Uccello's *Battle of San Romano* (*c.* 1450). Such connections are not of course direct quotations and may not have been uppermost in Degas's mind at the relevant time, but they do underline how in his case the integration of the past with the present through copying could be a springboard for innovation.

Neither at this stage did Degas's meticulous preparations for a painting change. He continued to perfect his established procedure, extending from compositional drawings through individual studies to closely observed details of settings. He began to use his Notebooks with even greater relish for recording motifs and observations that might be useful for his depiction of modern life. The degree to which Degas broadens his repertoire in his Notebooks to include everyday incidents, aspects of the social scene, caricature, as well as landscape, is remarkable. Nonetheless, the radical shift that occurs in Degas's work during the late 1860s could not have happened without his regard for traditional practices and therein lies the paradox of his art. Or, as he expressed it to Daniel Halévy, 'Revolutionary! Don't say that. We are *tradition* itself. It can't be said too often. And perhaps Titian will say a few words to me as he steps from his gondola.'

Ample evidence, however, for this change in Degas's art lies in his drawing techniques. This is the moment when the influence of Ingres is again resurgent, particularly in the drawings made in connection with his portraits. The handling of the pencil or black chalk, which Degas favoured at this date for the preparation of his portraits, is wonderfully refined. Although the outlines are sometimes loose and the shading often perfunctory, the overall effect is one of great clarity. There is a crystalline quality in the treatment of the light falling across the facial features and the folds of the garments, just as there is exactitude in perfecting details of pose and setting. The full range of the pencil is used beginning with the point to produce sharp outlines before being turned on its side to make areas of shading that suggest the texture and weight of clothes [57, 58, 60]. The black chalk adds a softer, slightly blurring effect and permits a broader characterization and a more fulsome representation of garments [59]. The same media (sometimes with the addition of charcoal) also remained the principal means of preparation for the horseracing scenes, such as *Scene from the Steeplechase: The Fallen Jockey* [54, 61–63, 65]; for the pure genre subjects such as *Interior (The Rape)*; and for those paintings that hover between genre and straight portraiture: *Woman with Chrysanthemums* (1865) in the Metropolitan Museum of Art, New York, and *The Orchestra of the Opéra* (*c.* 1870) in the Musée d'Orsay, Paris. Pencil seems to have been particularly effective at suggesting the power and speed of horses or the sheen of their coats.

At the same time, however, Degas was introducing different techniques into his working methods. He began to use the brush for his drawings applying *essence* in combination with pastel, gouache, wash and oil, often on commercially coloured papers. Sometimes he prepared the paper himself by staining the surface with coatings of *essence* or oil [68–71, 74, 75]. Paper was the customary support, but different kinds of stiff card are occasionally in evidence. Some of these combinations of media are complicated and difficult to disentangle without recourse to the conservation studio.

Two fine examples of these more elaborate drawings might have formed part of the preparatory process for such compositions as *The Duet* (c. 1868–70) at Dumbarton Oaks, Washington, DC, or *Interior (The Rape)* [74, 75], but in the case of the long series of jockeys it was more a case of Degas creating his own visual dictionary for future reference [68, 69, 71]. The jockeys are studies of the greatest fluency remarkable not only for the artist's powers of observation and eye for different viewpoints, but also for the eloquent *mise-en-page*, which is only comparable with the practices of Jean-Antoine Watteau in the early eighteenth century.

Drawing with the brush, as in watercolour, promoted fluency just as it imposed a certain economy. *Woman Looking through Binoculars* (c. 1866–68) was a figure no doubt seen by Degas at a racecourse [72]. The outline of the three-quarters length figure made with *essence* is roughly brushed in with gouache highlights in the hair, on the forehead and on the hands. These focal points anchor the figure. The twist of hair descending down the right side of the face balances the raised arm on the left. There is an implicit geometry in the pose when it is looked at carefully, but Degas's reaction is instinctive and in seizing this moment he has produced one of the defining images of modern life – the viewer viewed or the gazer's gaze returned. No wonder Degas repeated the motif three times in rapid succession: he clearly liked the impact it made [73].

Essence liberated Degas and his style became more improvisatory. Drawings made with the brush in fact imply alternating methods of painting and drawing and herald a practice that became one of the main features of Degas's later work. Some of the studies of jockeys could well have been made in connection with the painting *The Parade (Racehorses before the Stands)* (c. 1866–68) [55], which is itself a work executed in *essence* on paper mounted on canvas with evidence of underdrawing in pen and ink. By such means Degas undermined the academic distinction between painting and drawing.

Another medium that the artist chose to test out at this time was pastel, which was usually the preserve of portraiture. Degas does indeed

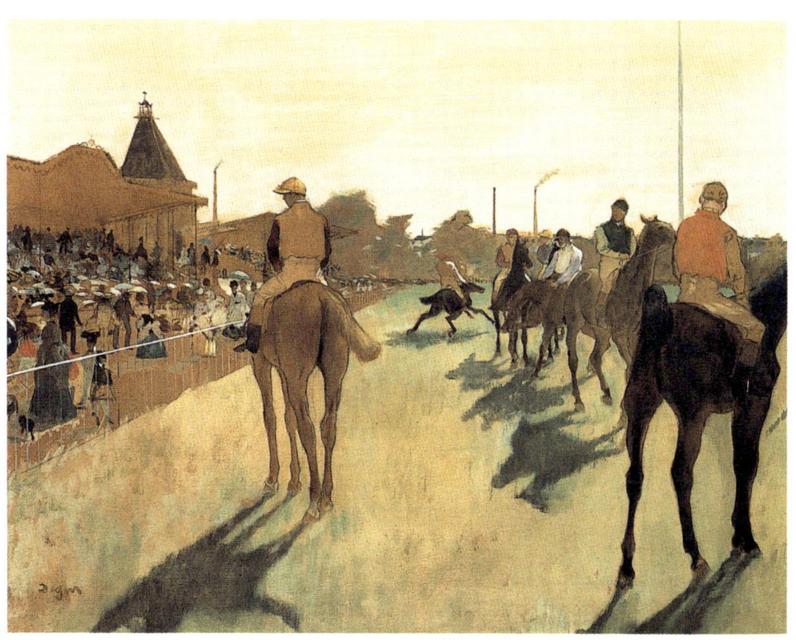

55. *The Parade (Racehorses before the Stands), c. 1866–68.*
Essence on paper mounted on canvas,
46 × 61 cm (18⅛ × 24 in.). Musée d'Orsay, Paris

honour this tradition in extremely competent images of Mme Théodore
Gobillard [76] – a member of the Morisot family – and of his own sister
Thérèse [77], both dating from 1869. But he also, more significantly,
produced a whole series of seascapes and coastal views inspired by his
visit to the English Channel in the same year [78–82]. Where Claude
Monet, following Eugène Boudin, chose to depict a popular resort
such as Trouville, Degas gives little indication of holidaymakers. Like
paintings of the sea at Trouville made by Courbet and James McNeill
Whistler in the mid-1860s, Degas concentrates on different times of
day, changing atmospheric effects and varied meterological conditions
– sunlight, dampness, light breezes and sudden gusts of wind. The
handling of the pastel is amazingly adroit – smoothly applied with
delicate nuances in some areas and roughly treated in others. Above all,
there is an eloquent sense of space and an aching feeling of emptiness.

A demonstration of the complexities in Degas's art that suddenly
appeared during the second half of the 1860s is provided by the painting
Portrait of Mlle Eugénie Fiocre: à propos the Ballet 'La Source' (1867–68)

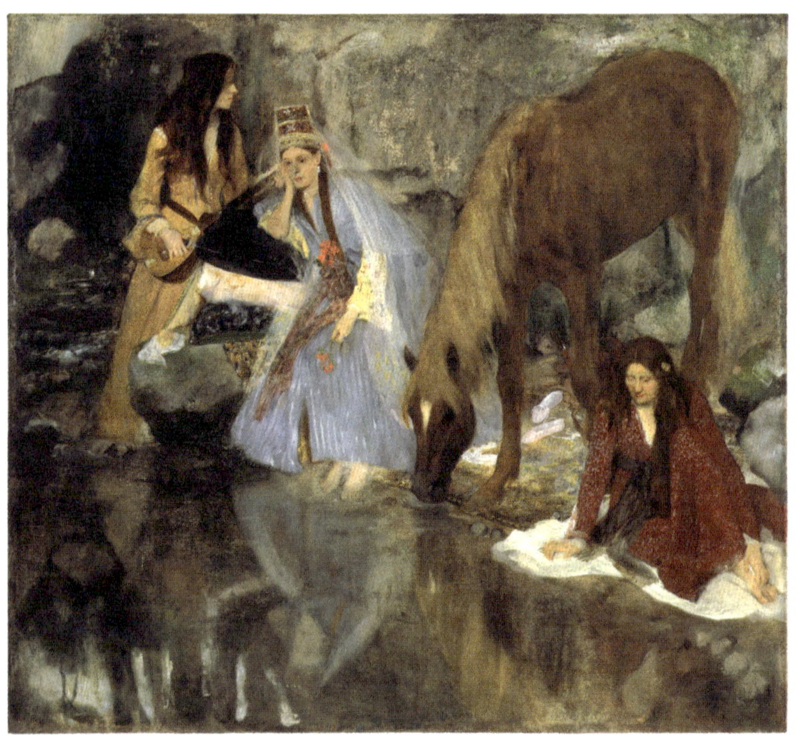

56. *Portrait of Mlle Eugénie Fiocre: à propos
the Ballet 'La Source', 1867–68.*
Oil on canvas, 130 × 144 cm (51⅛ × 56¼ in.).
Brooklyn Museum, New York

[56]. For one thing, it crosses many boundaries: part history painting,
part portrait, part ballet picture and part orientalist fantasy, without
obviously being any one of these things. But it is these very uncertainties
that Degas celebrates and exploits, not perhaps deliberately at this
early date, but in a prescient way. The ballet *La Source* was given its
first performance on 12 November 1866. The choreography was by
Arthur Saint-Léon and the music by Ludwig Minkus and Léo Delibes.
Luminaries such as Ingres and Giuseppe Verdi attended the dress
rehearsal. The renown of the ballet was such that it was performed at
the inauguration of the new Opéra building designed by Charles Garnier
in January 1875. The leading role of Nouredda, a Georgian princess,
was danced by Eugénie Fiocre whose powers as a dancer were more than
matched by her charms beyond the stage door. Degas is in fact painting

one of the most recognized dancers in Paris, but he chooses virtually to ignore her status and principal attributes. The scene is taken from the first act of the ballet where the princess rests with her retinue beside a mountain stream and is soothed by music played on a gusle (form of mandolin) to which she will eventually dance. Fiocre seems to be bathing her feet in the water – her pink ballet shoes put to one side – while the horse lowers its head to drink. By supporting her head with her hand she indicates the traditional pose for a recumbent figure, which sometimes signified melancholy, and so the ultimate paradox of the picture is that it appears to negate the physical effort that is associated with ballet or the promotional efforts equated with celebrity status. In the performance itself the princess does rest by the water before embarking upon a vigorous dance – presumably after putting her ballet shoes on again. Similarly, although an actual horse was used on stage, the viewer of this picture is not sure whether the scenery for *La Source* is realistic or simply an exercise in *trompe-l'oeil*. Furthermore, Degas tantalizes the viewer further by giving no indication as to whether this is a break in rehearsal or an actual performance.

Degas's preparations for the *Portrait of Mlle Eugénie Fiocre* were elaborate. He made portrait drawings of the dancer, compositional studies, oil sketches and individual studies of the figures and the horse [64], as well as for other details.

This single painting dating from a pivotal moment in Degas's career, therefore, is especially revealing. The subject incorporates two elements that the artist will seize upon for further examination and then develop as the principal motifs of his mature work – dancers and horses. At the same time his treatment of the subject before him is not straightforward: indeed, it is enigmatic. And the preparatory process itself may appear to be traditional whereas it is in fact by no means conformist or closely circumscribed by convention. By the end of the 1860s Degas had laid out his credentials as an artist, combining highly accomplished skills with a strongly independent approach to subject matter. How far his talent would develop was now the fundamental question.

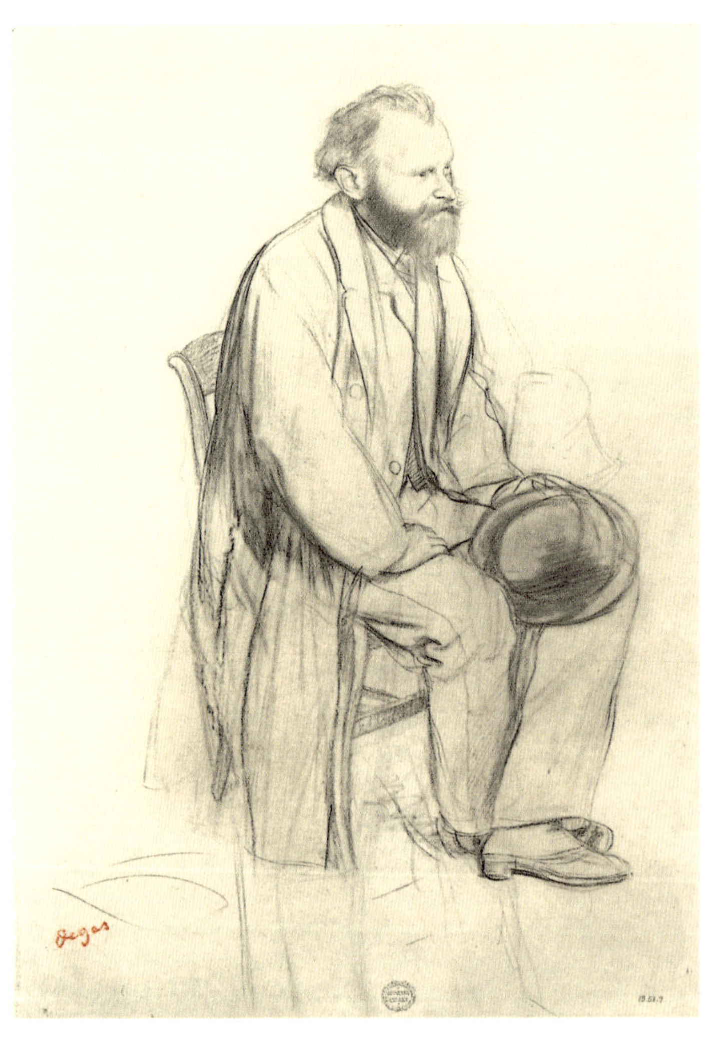

ABOVE
57. *Edouard Manet Seated*, c. 1866–68.
Pencil and black chalk, 33.1 × 23 cm (13 × 9 in.).
Metropolitan Museum of Art, New York

OPPOSITE
58. *Julie Burty*, c. 1867.
Pencil heightened with bodycolour, 36.1 × 27.2 cm (14¼ × 10¾ in.).
Fogg Museum, Cambridge, Massachusetts

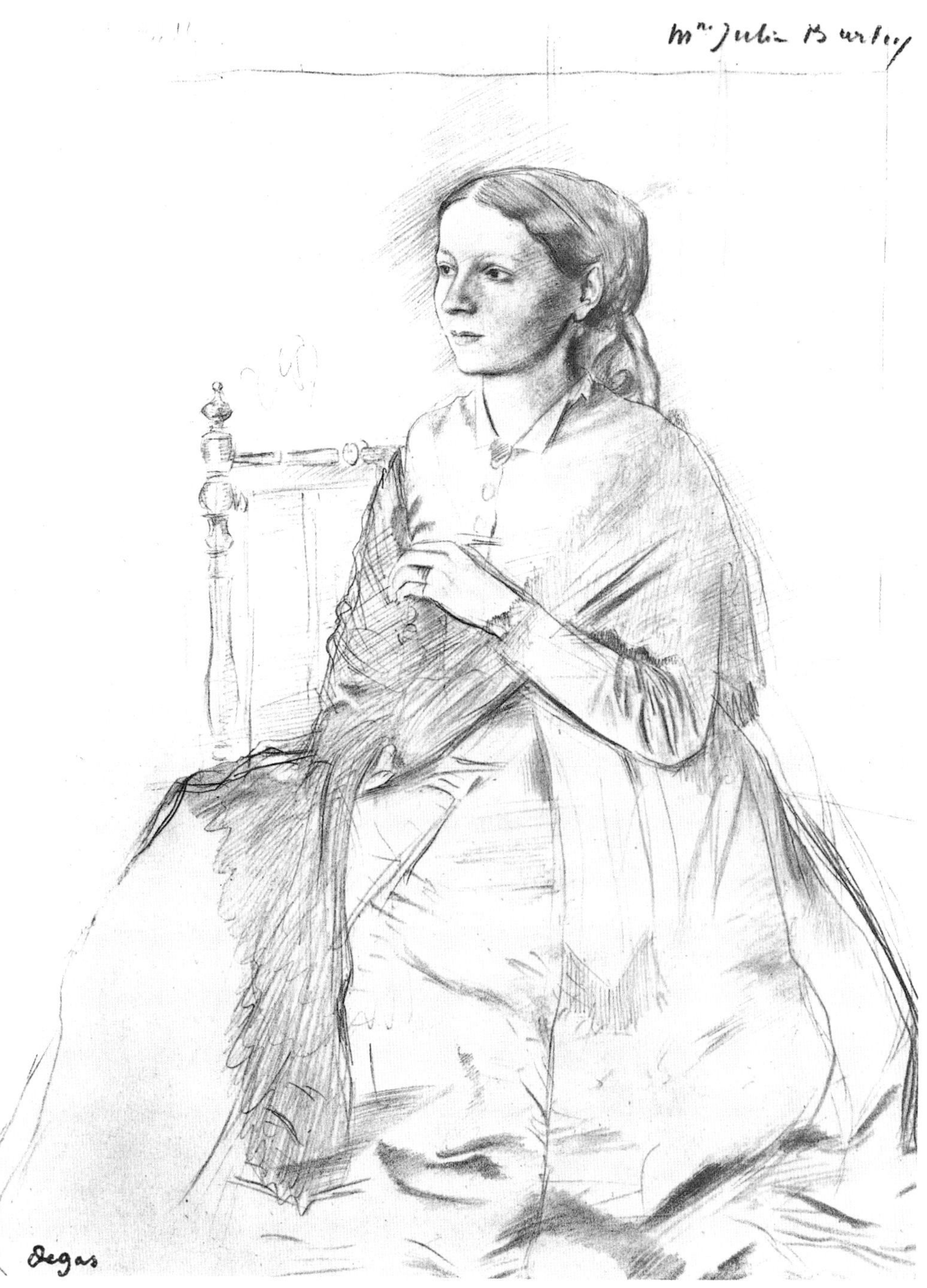

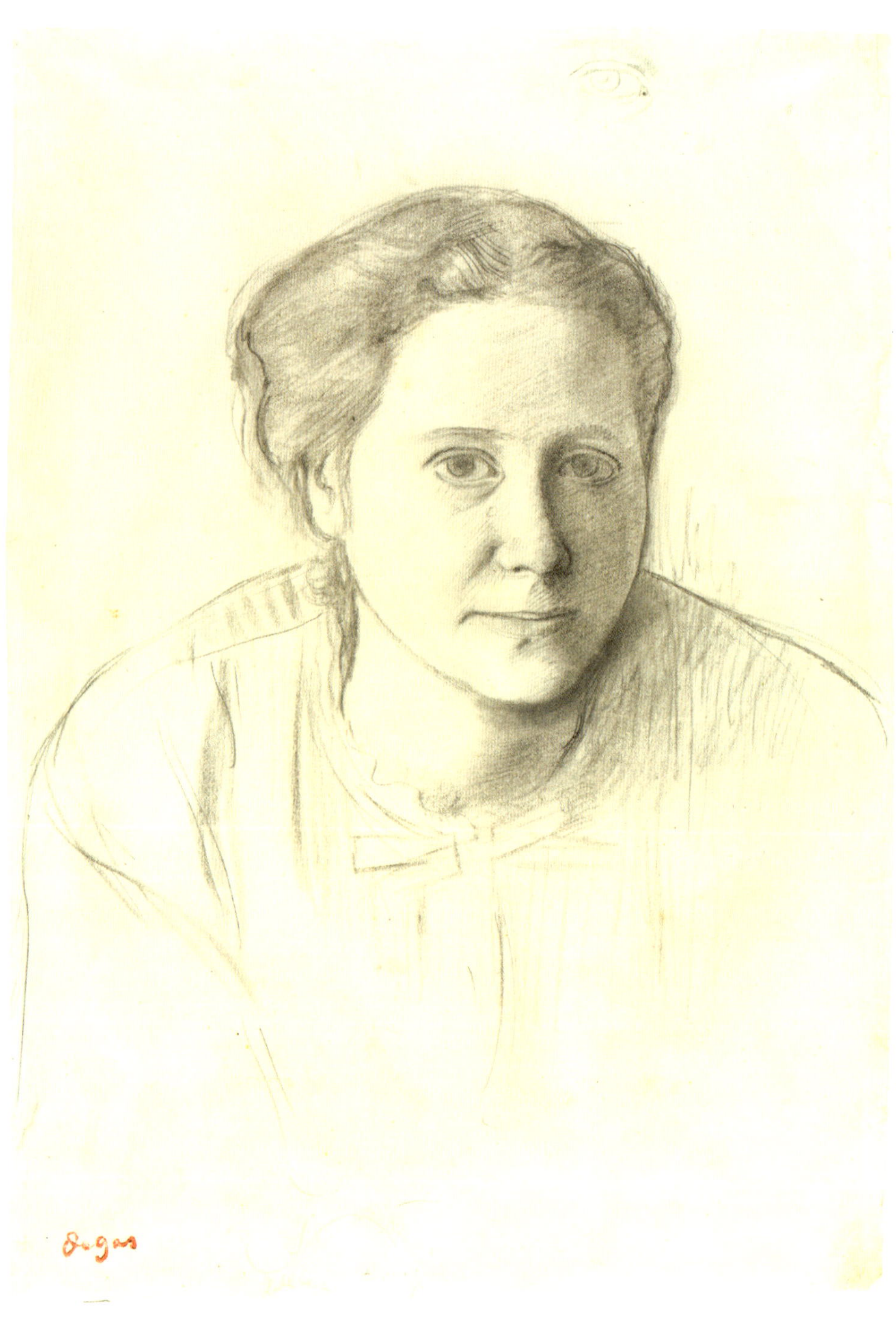

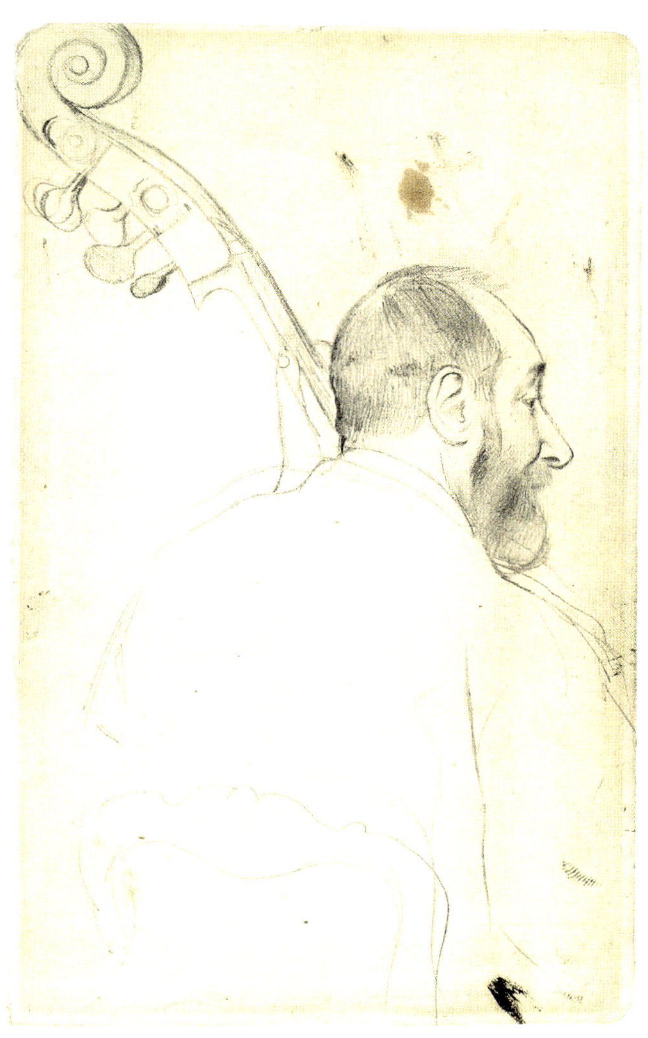

59. *Victoria Dubourg, c. 1866.*
Black chalk and pencil, 30.9 × 21.9 cm (12⅛ × 8½ in.).
Cleveland Museum of Art

ABOVE
60. *Achille Henri Victor Gouffé, c. 1868–69.*
Pencil, 32.1 × 22.7 cm (13⅛ × 9¼ in.).
Pierpont Morgan Library, New York

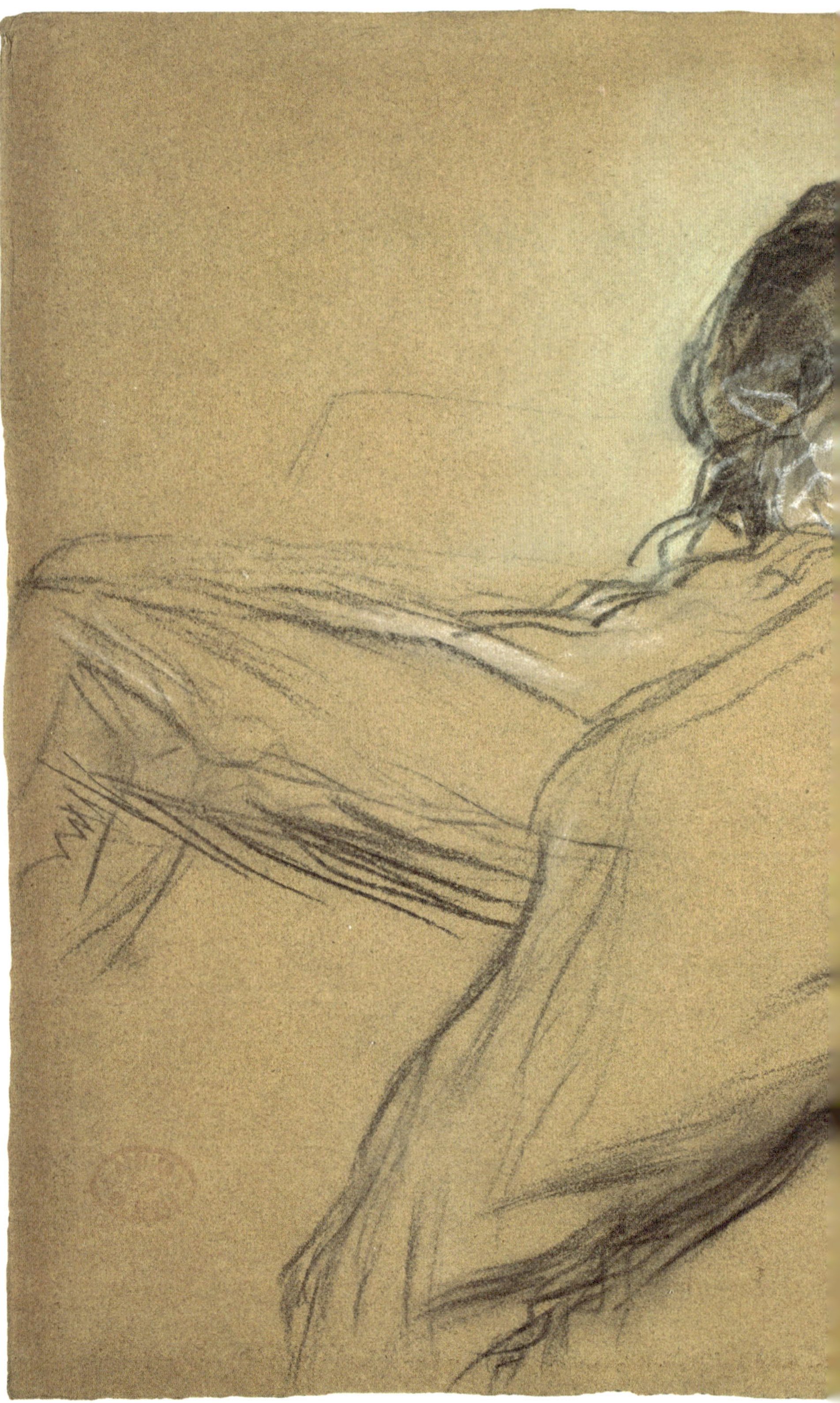

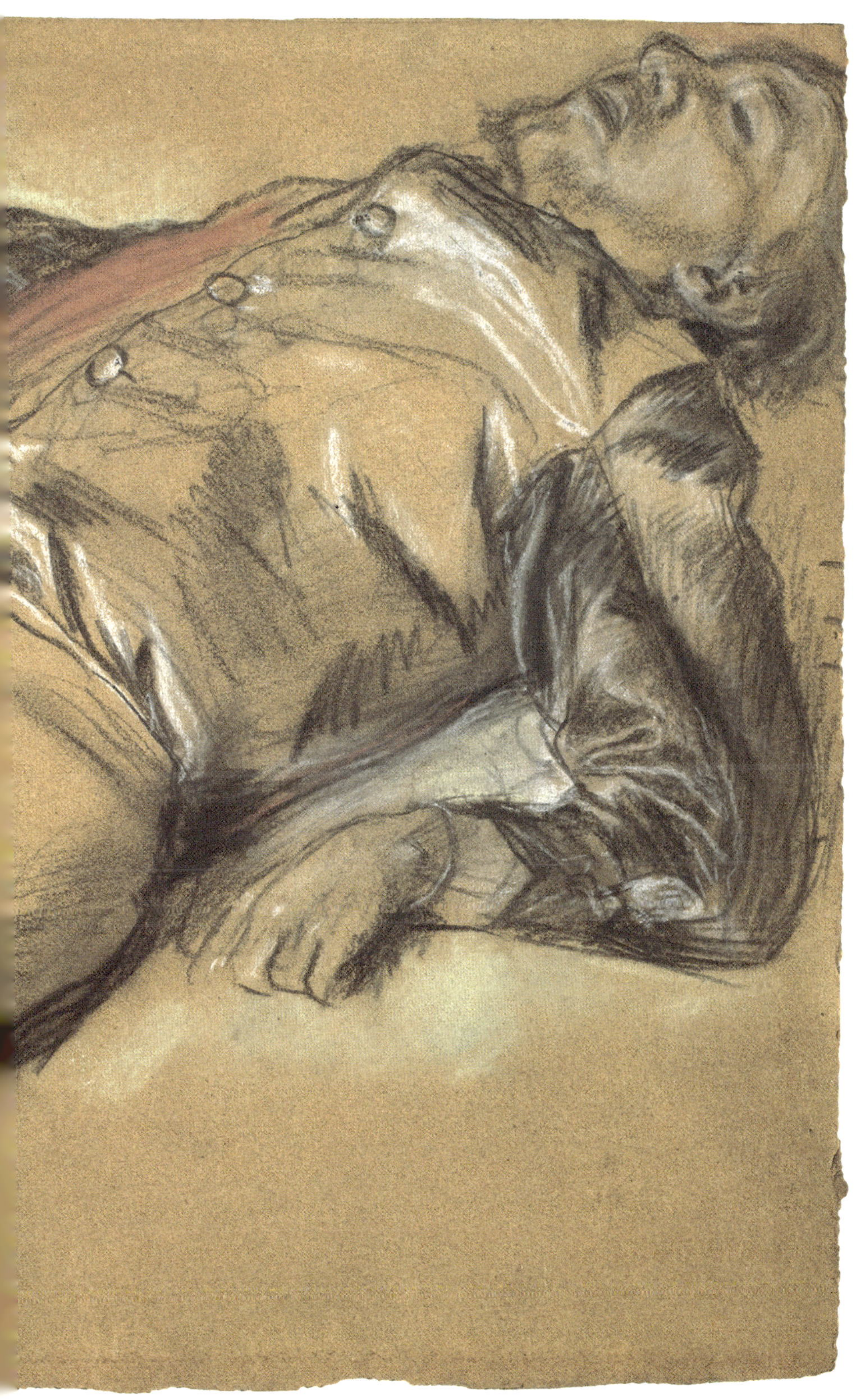

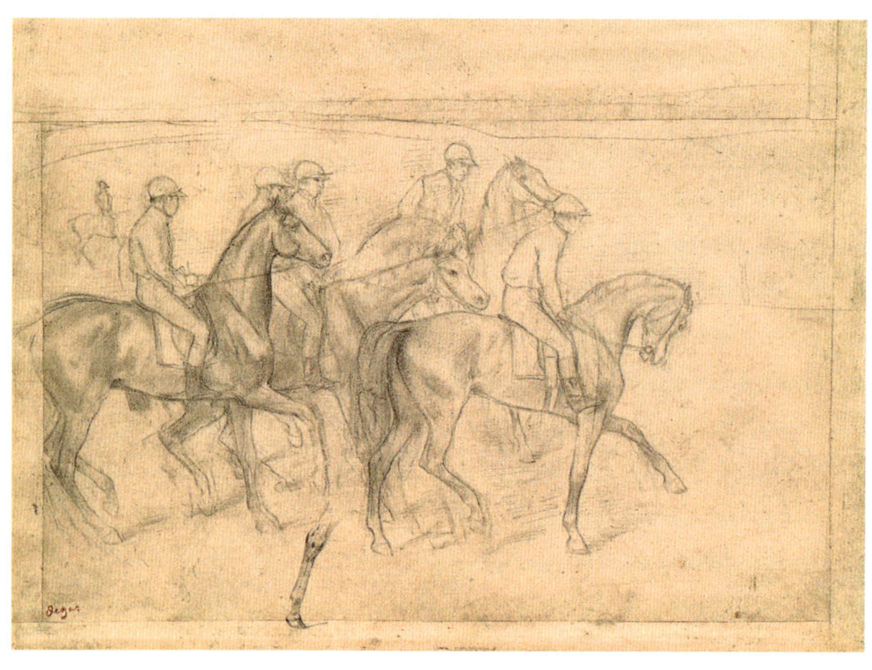

PREVIOUS PAGES
61. *Fallen Jockey, c.* 1866.
Black chalk and pastel heightened with body
colour on brown paper, 26.6 × 35.2 cm
(10½ × 13⅞ in.). National Gallery of Art,
Washington, DC

ABOVE
62. *At the Races, c.* 1860.
Pencil, 34.9 × 48.3 cm (13¾ × 19 in.).
Sterling and Francine Clark Art Institute,
Williamstown, Massachusetts

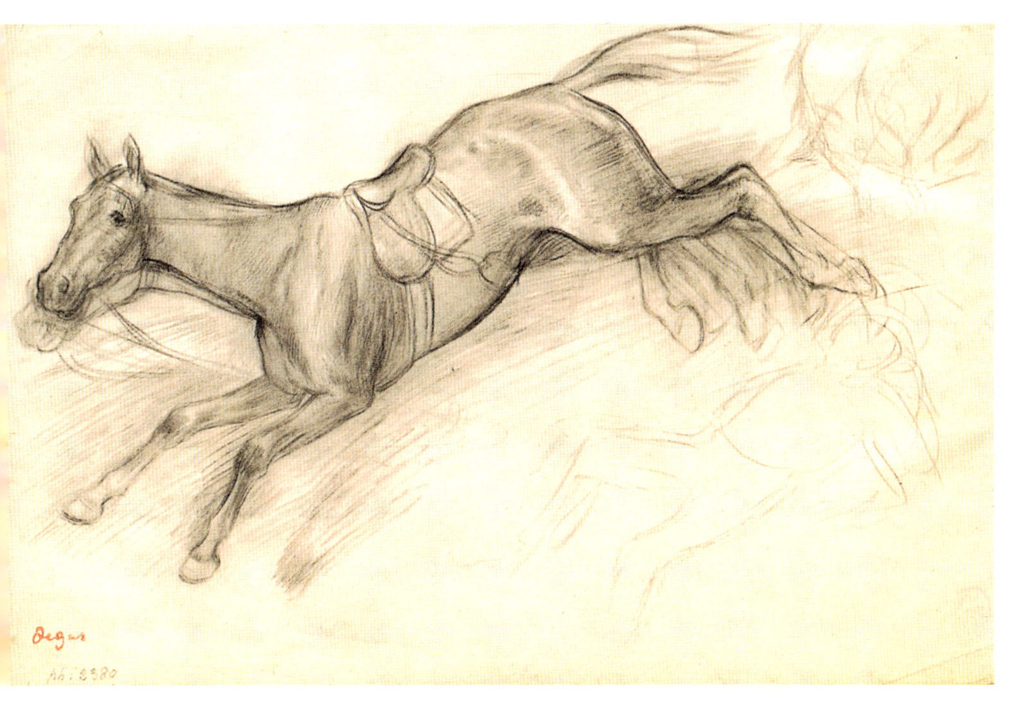

63. *The Bolting Horse, c. 1866.*
Pencil and charcoal, 23.1 × 35.5 cm (9⅛ × 14 in.).
Sterling and Francine Clark Art Institute, Williamstown,
Massachusetts

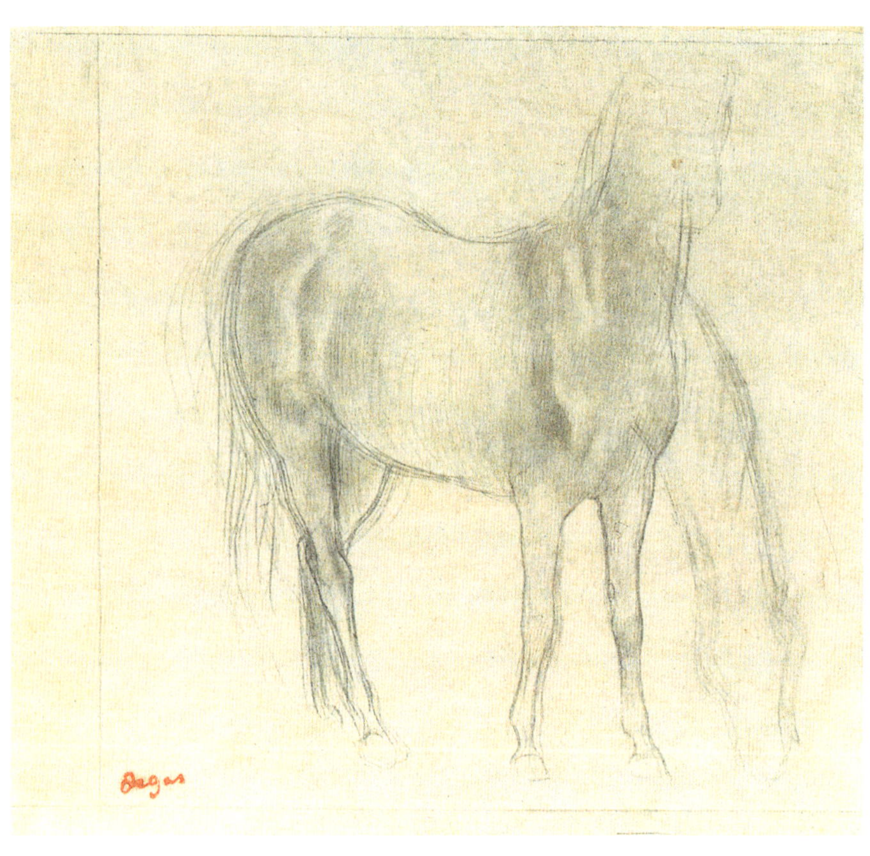

ABOVE
64. *Study of a Horse*, c. 1865–68.
Pencil, 23.7 × 26.3 cm (9¼ × 10⅛ in.).
Boymans-van Beuningen Museum,
Rotterdam

OPPOSITE
65. *Horse Walking*, 1866–68. Charcoal on brown
paper, 32.4 × 20.5 cm (12¼ × 8 in.).
Pierpont Morgan Library, New York

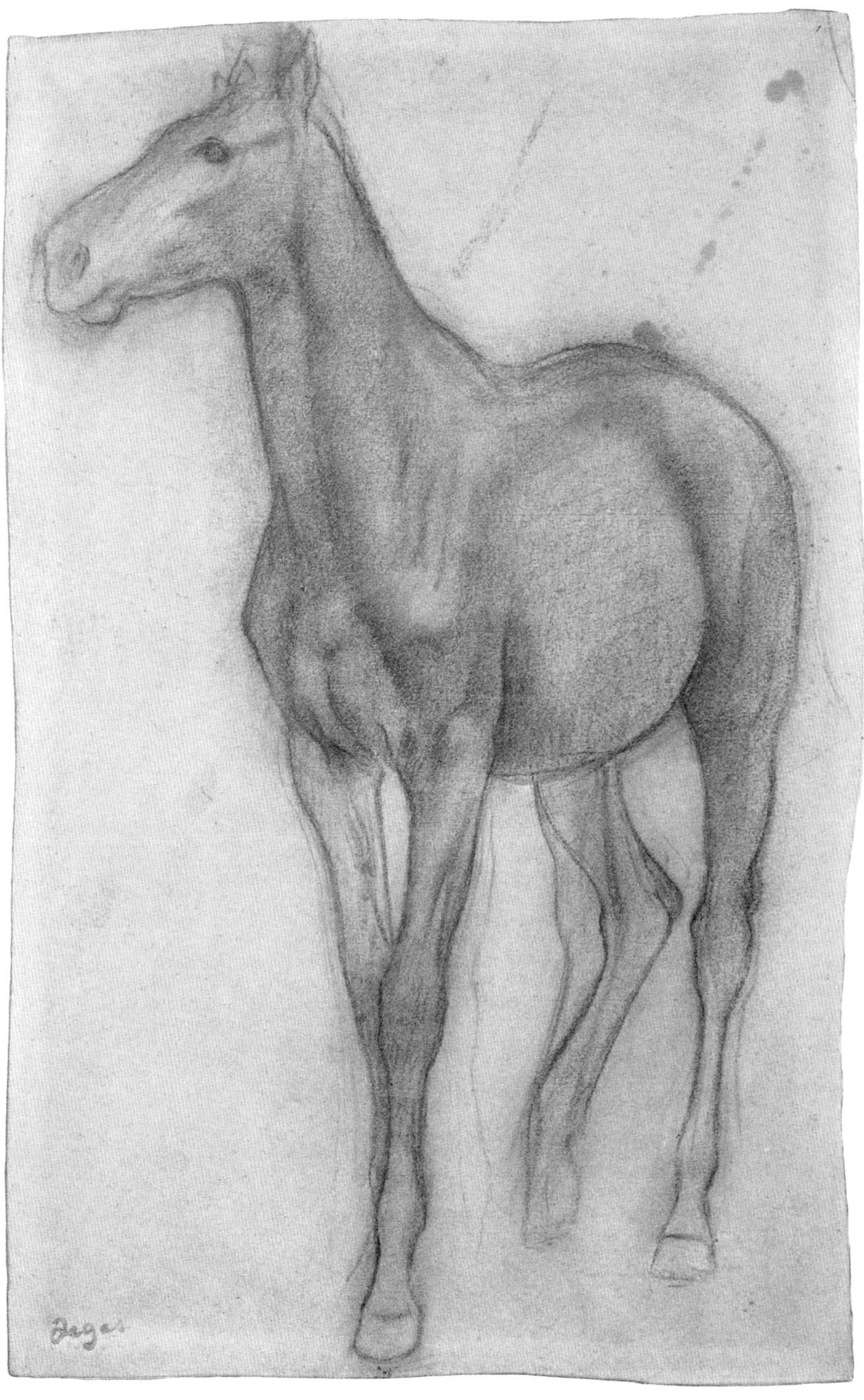

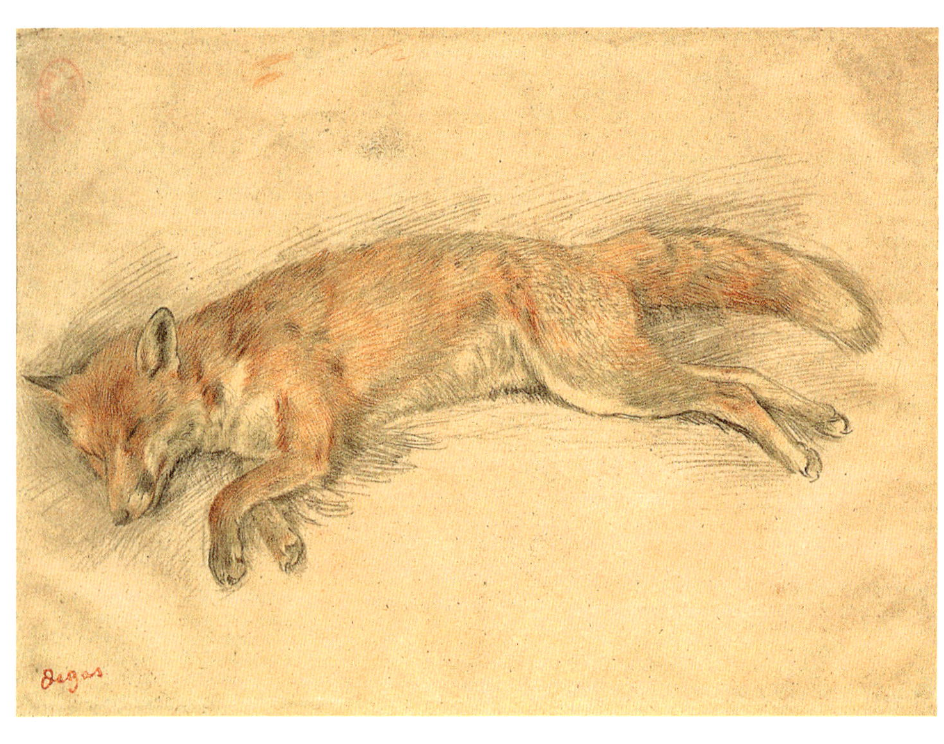

66. *Dead Fox*, *c.* 1864–68.
Black and red chalk, 20.6 × 27.9 cm (8⅛ × 11 in.).
Sterling and Francine Clark Art Institute, Williamstown,
Massachusetts

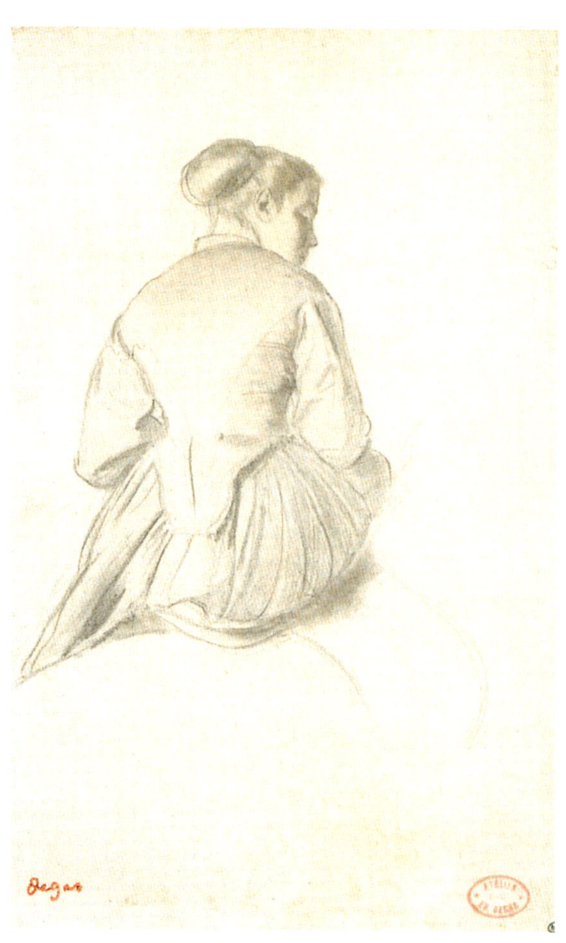

67. Woman Rider Viewed from the Back, 1867–68.
Pencil, 31.5 × 19.7 cm (12⅜ × 7¾ in.).
Musée d'Orsay, Paris

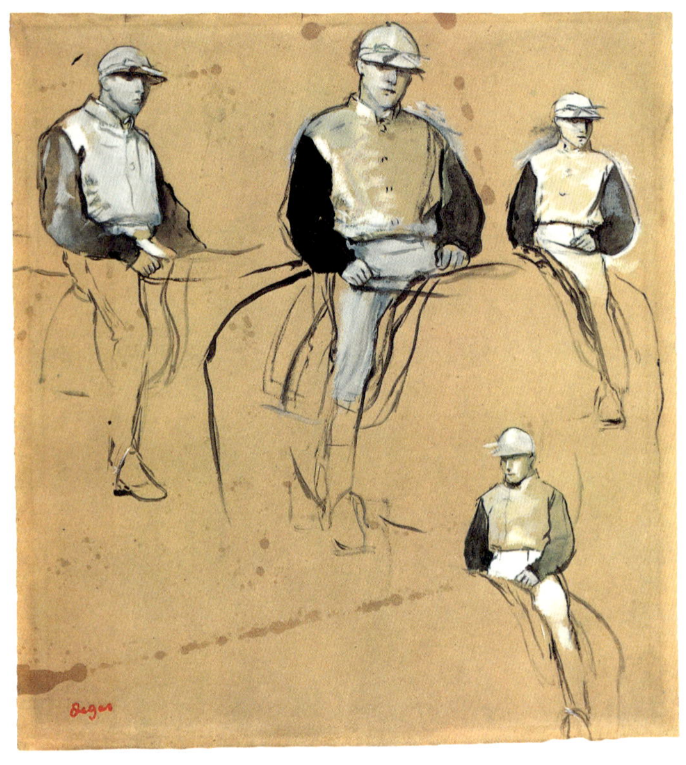

ABOVE

68. *Four Studies of a Jockey, c.* 1868–70.
Essence and black ink heightened with
bodycolour on ochre-coloured paper prepared
with oil, 31 × 18 cm (12¼ × 7⅛ in.).
Private collection

OPPOSITE

69. *Four Studies of a Jockey, c.* 1868–70.
Essence and black ink heightened with body
colour on ochre-coloured paper prepared with oil,
45 × 31.5 cm (17¾ × 12⅜ in.).
The Art Institute of Chicago

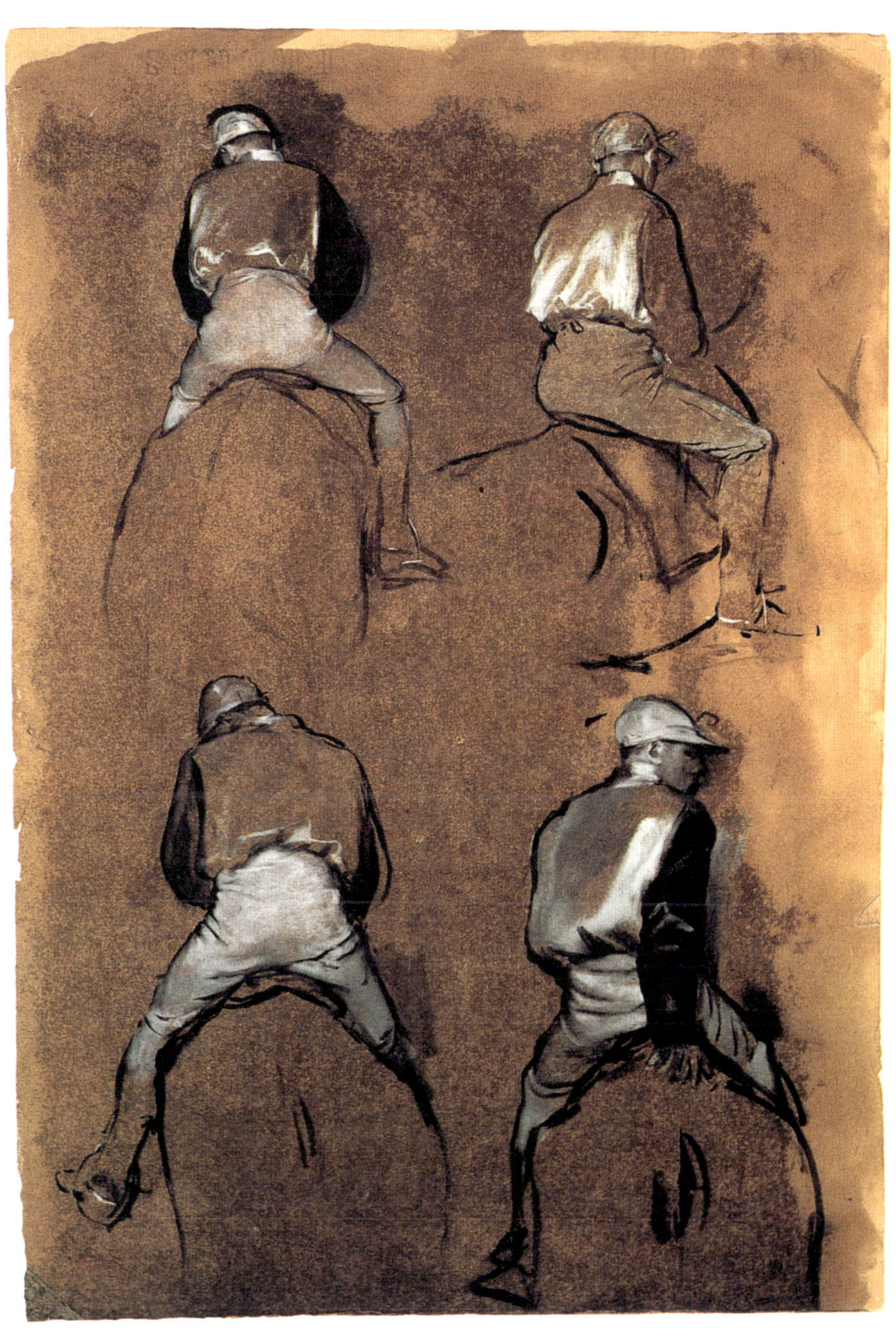

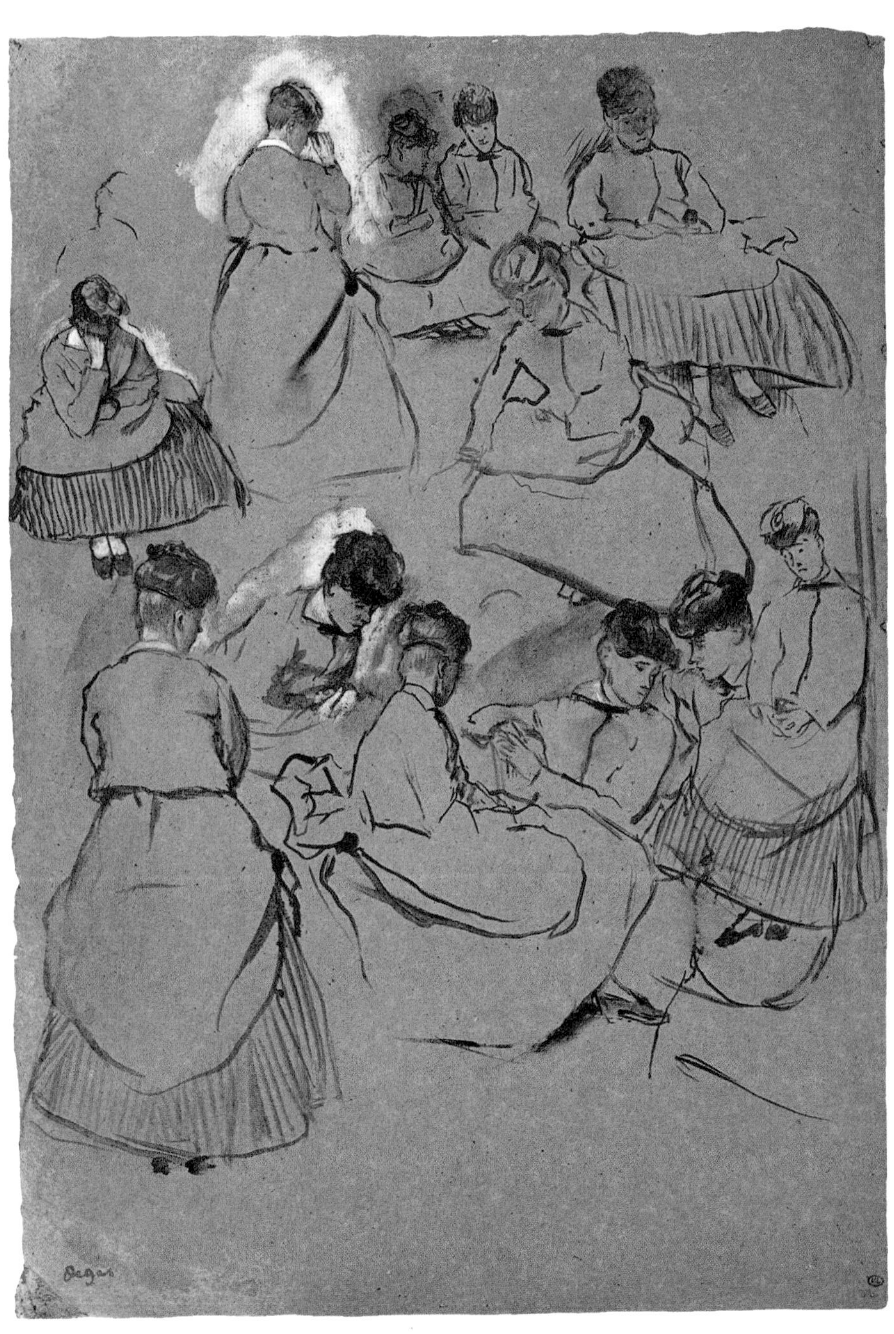

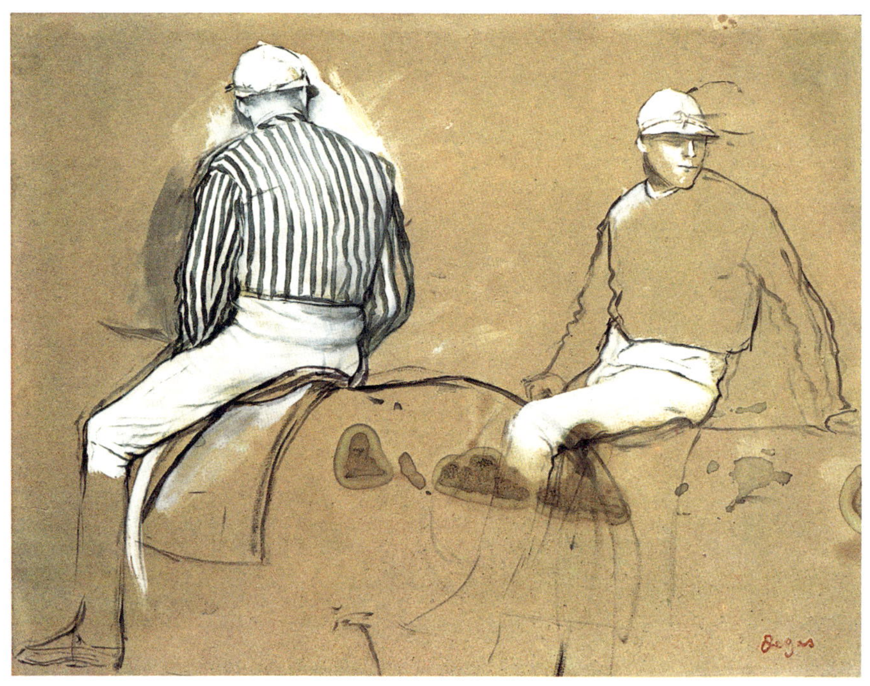

OPPOSITE
70. *At the Racecourse*, 1868–72.
Essence and black ink heightened
with bodycolour on ochre-coloured
paper prepared with oil,
45 × 31 cm (17¾ × 12¼ in.).
Musée d'Orsay, Paris

ABOVE
71. *Study of Two Jockeys*, c. 1868–70.
Essence and black ink heightened with
bodycolour on ochre-coloured paper prepared
with oil, 23 × 30 cm (9 × 11¾ in.).
Private collection

Changing Directions 1865–1870   101

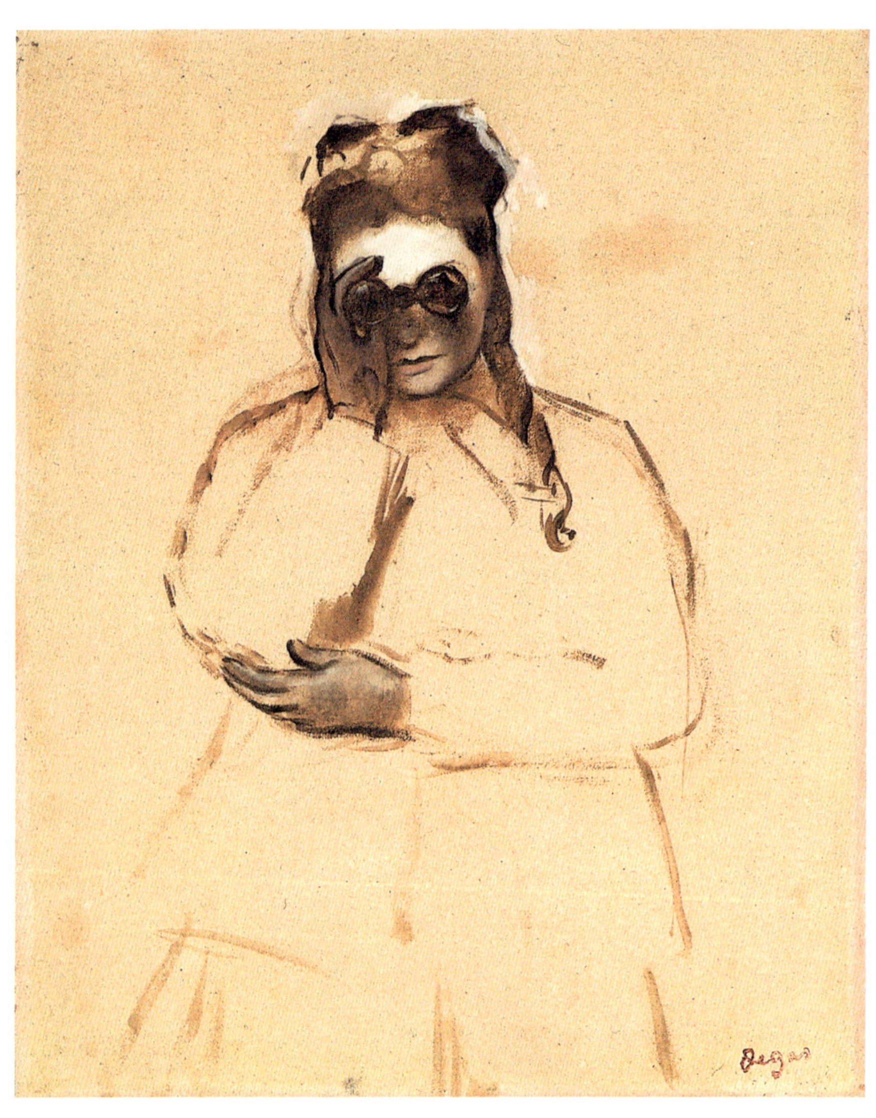

72. *Woman Looking through Binoculars*, c. 1866–68.
Essence on pink paper, 28 × 22.7 cm (11 × 9⅞ in.).
British Museum, London

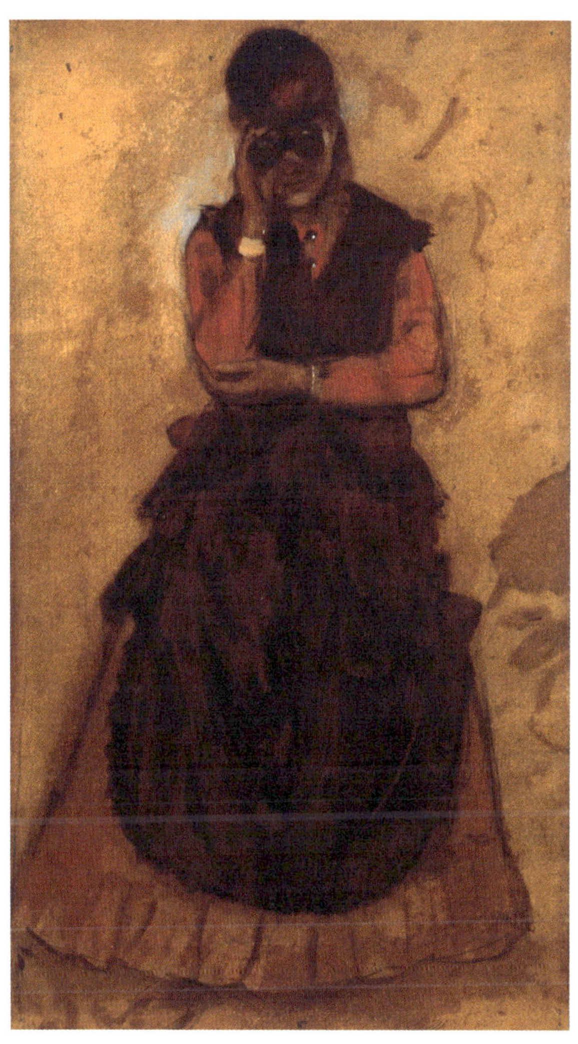

73. *Woman Looking through Binoculars*, c. 1866–68.
Essence and black chalk mounted on canvas,
31.4 × 19 cm (12⅜ × 7½ in.).
Burrell Collection, Glasgow

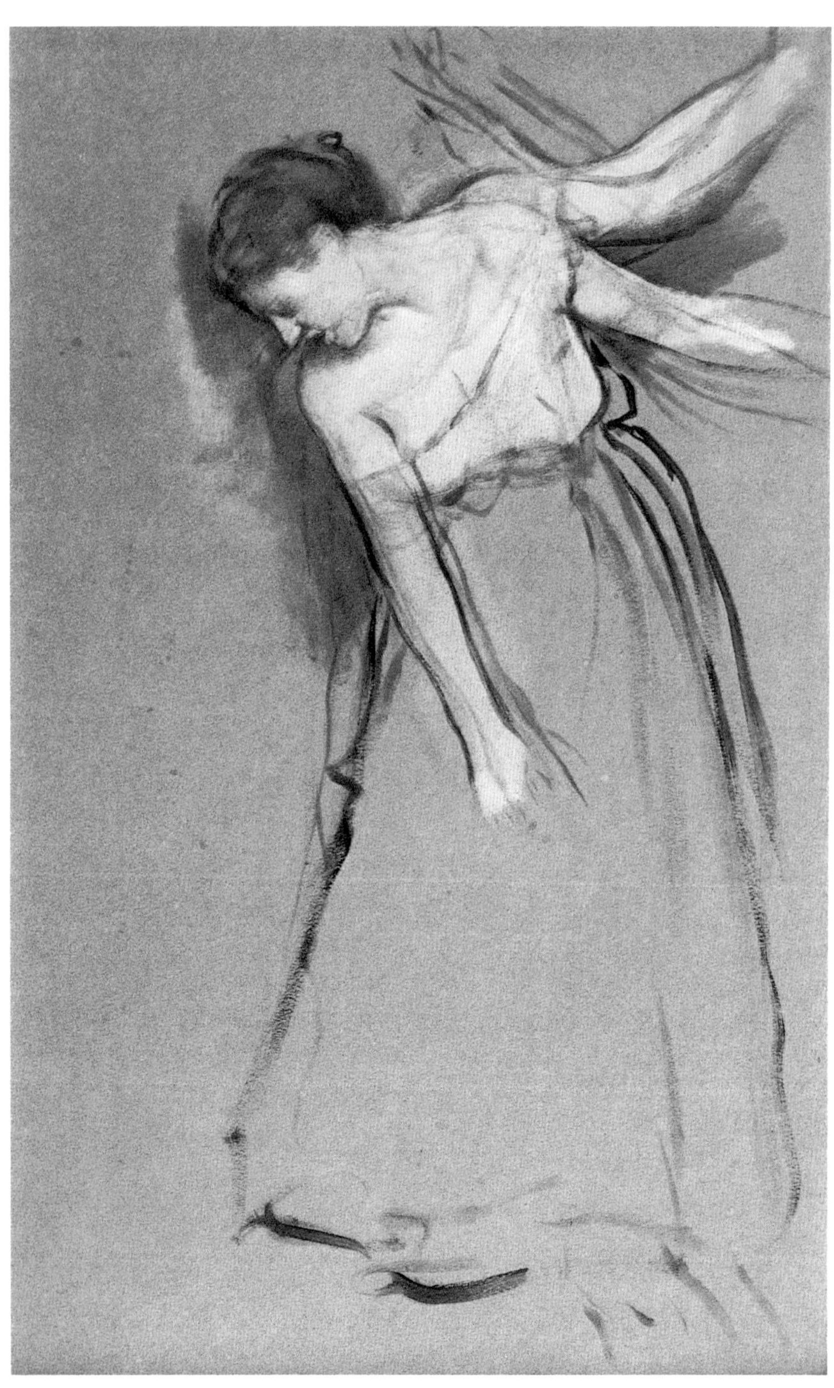

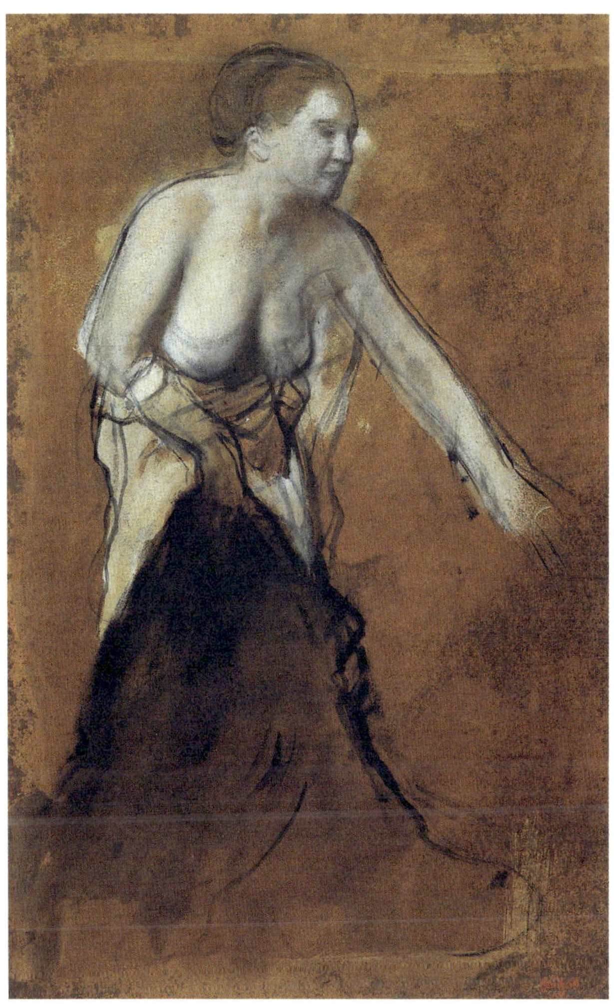

74. *Woman Standing with Arms Extended*, *c.* 1867–68.
Essence and black ink heightened with bodycolour on ochre-coloured
paper prepared with oil, 47.5 × 30.3 cm (18¾ × 11⅞ in.).
Private collection

75. *Woman Standing with Bared Torso*, *c.* 1867–68.
Essence and black ink heightened with bodycolour on ochre-
coloured paper prepared with oil, 47 × 30 cm (18½ × 11¾ in.).
Kunstmuseum, Öffentliche Kunstsammlungen, Basel

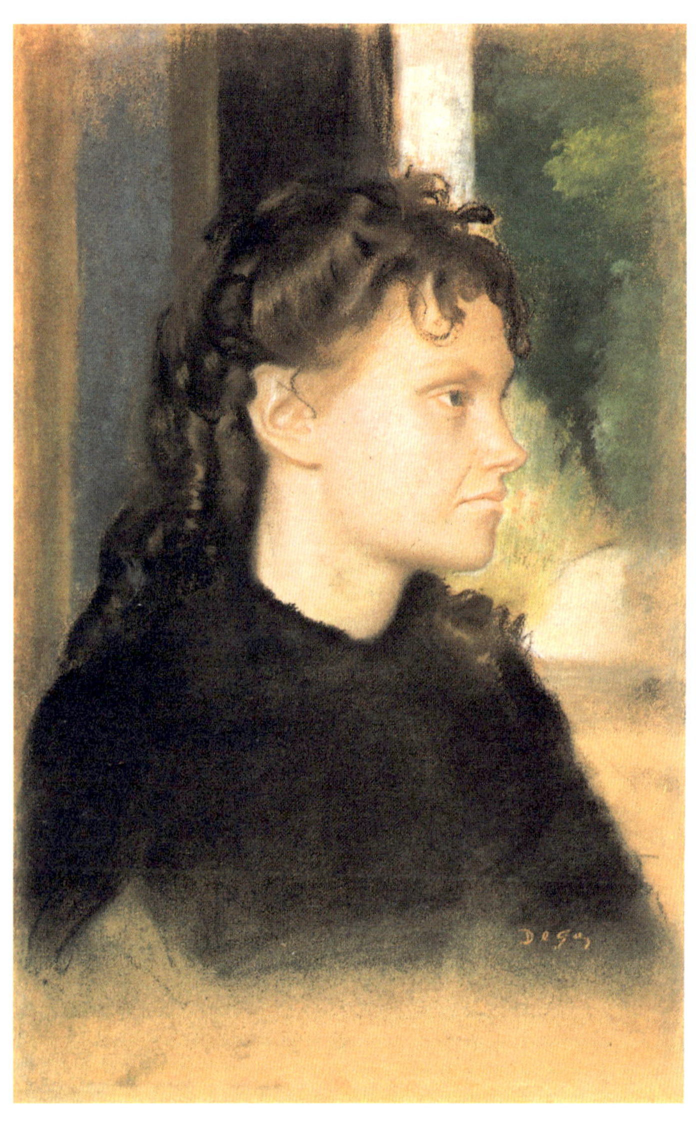

76. *Madame Théodore Gobillard (née Yves Morisot)*, 1869.
Pastel, 48 × 30 cm (18⅞ × 11¼ in.).
Metropolitan Museum of Art, New York

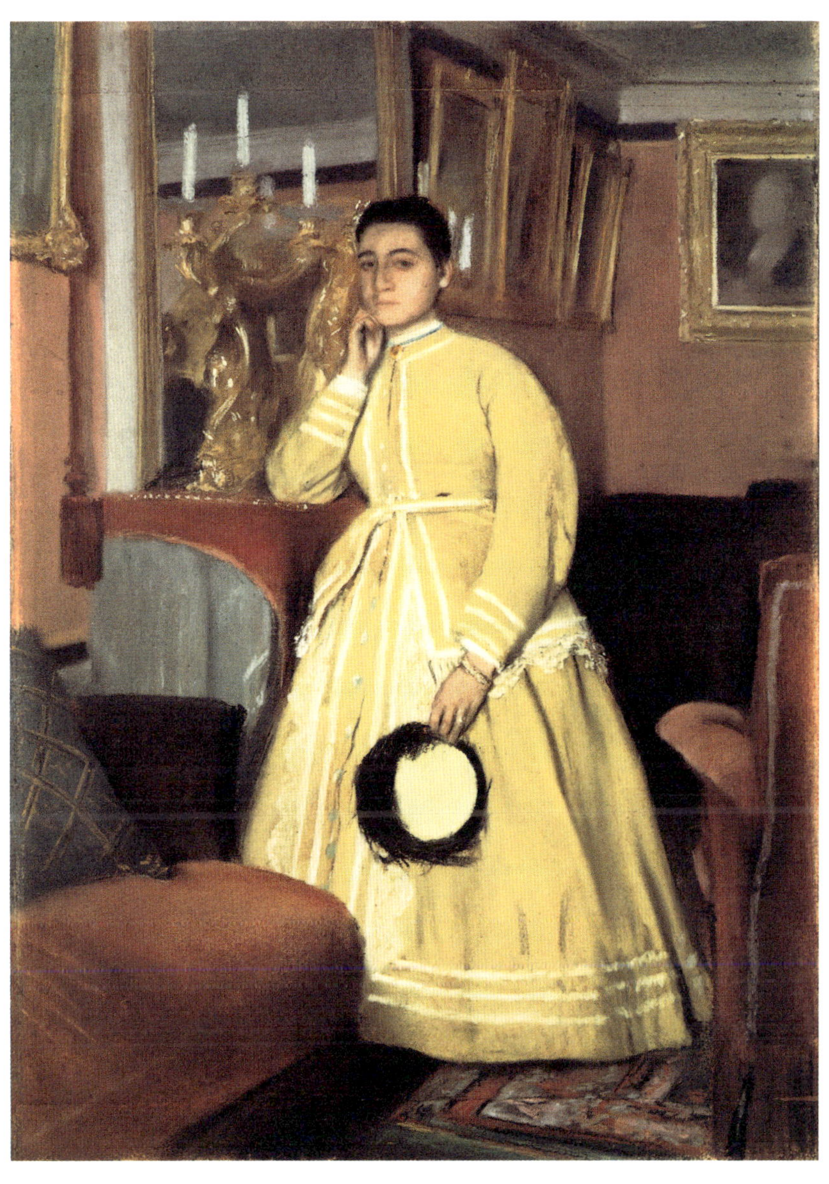

77. Madame Edmondo Morbilli (née Thérèse Degas), 1869.
Pastel, 51 × 34 cm (20 × 13⅛ in.).
Private collection

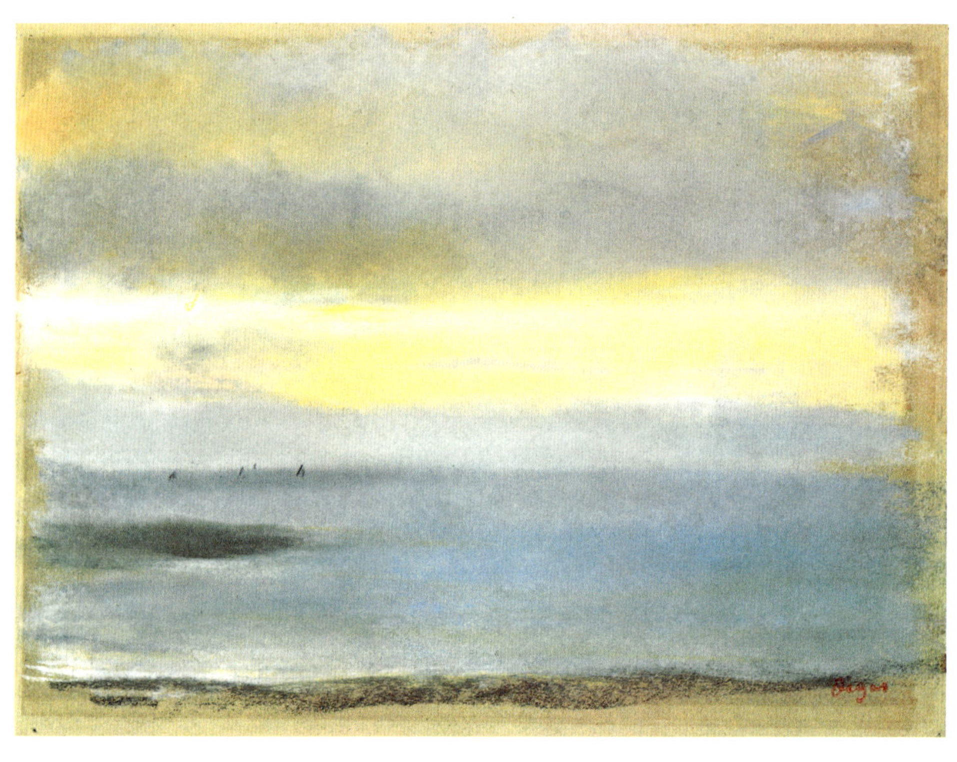

78. *Strip of Coast at Sunset*, 1869.
Pastel on brown card, 21.5 × 30 cm (8½ × 11¼ in.).
Private collection

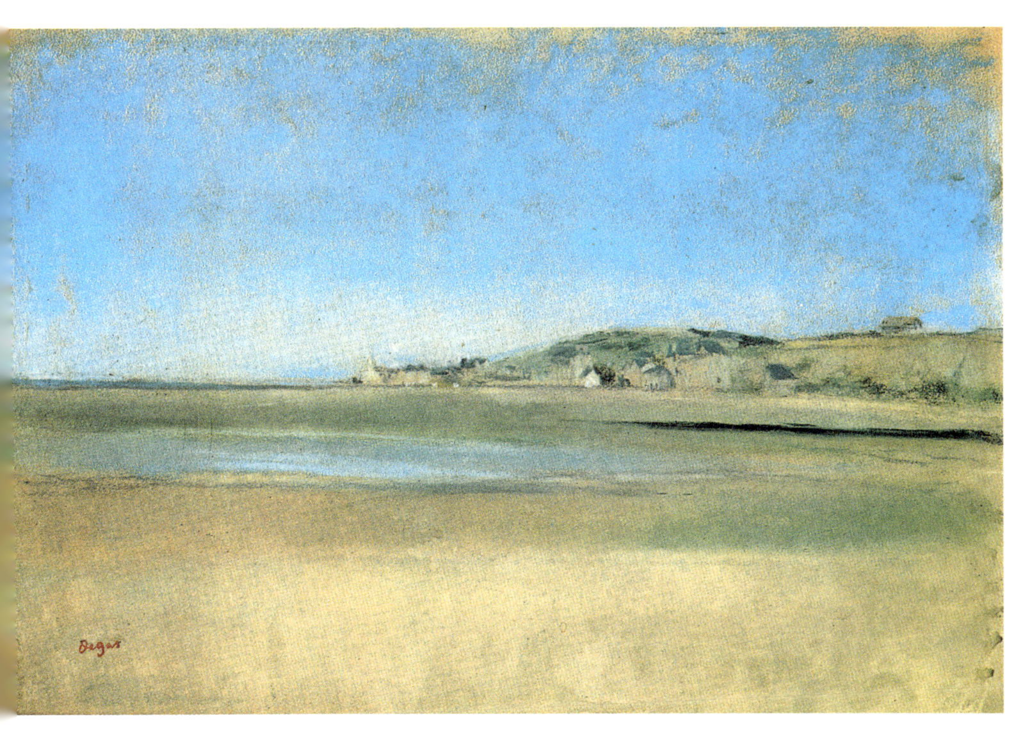

79. *Houses by the Sea*, 1869.
Pastel on buff paper, 31.4 × 46.5 cm (12⅜ × 18½ in.).
Musée d'Orsay, Paris

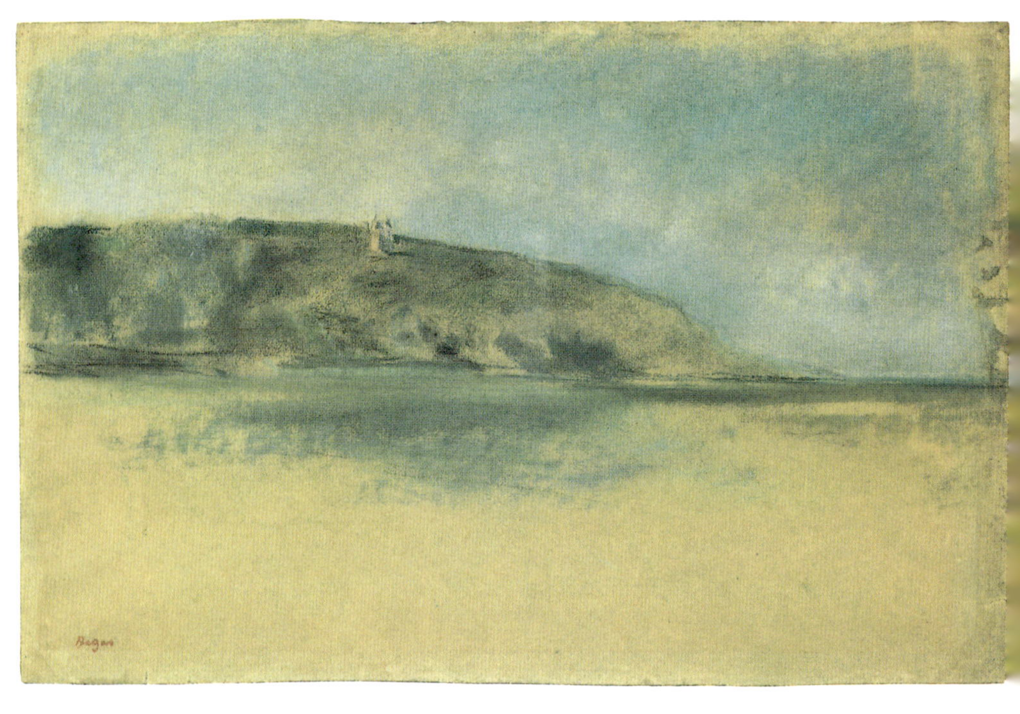

PREVIOUS PAGES
80. *Marine*, 1869.
Pastel on buff paper, 31.4 × 46.9 cm (12⅛ × 18½ in.).
Musée d'Orsay, Paris

ABOVE
81. *Estuary*, 1869.
Pastel on beige paper, 31.5 × 48.5 cm (12⅛ × 19⅛ in.).
Von der Heydt Museum, Wuppertal

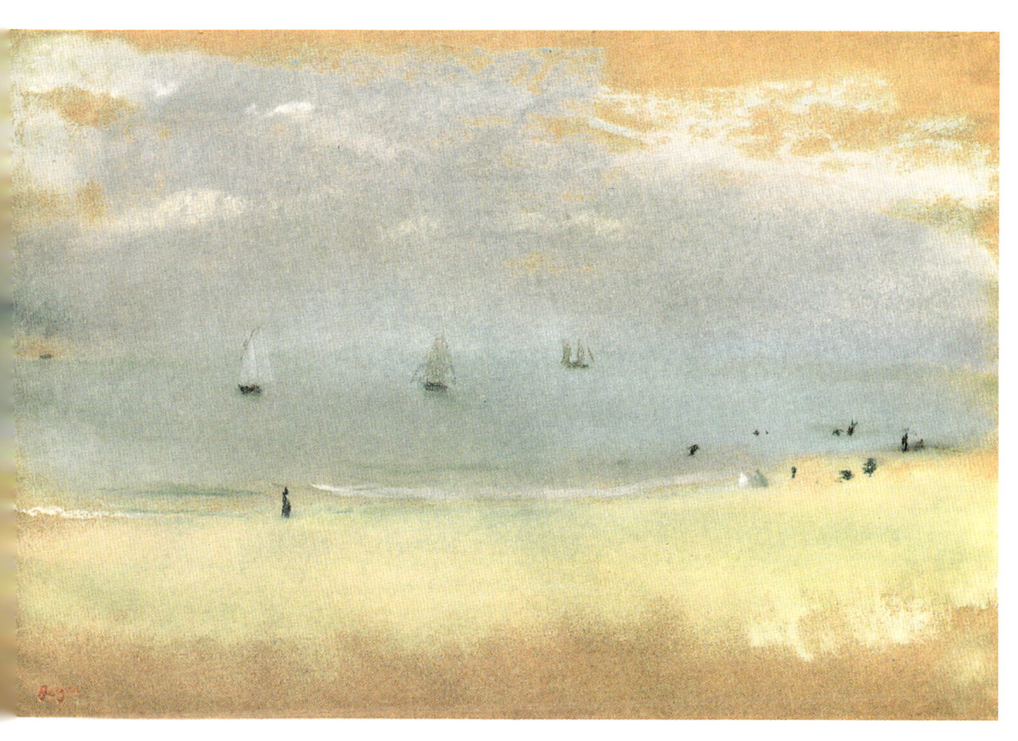

82. *Beach with Yachts at Sea*, 1869.
Pastel on buff paper, 31.4 × 46.9 cm (12⅜ × 18½ in.).
Musée d'Orsay, Paris

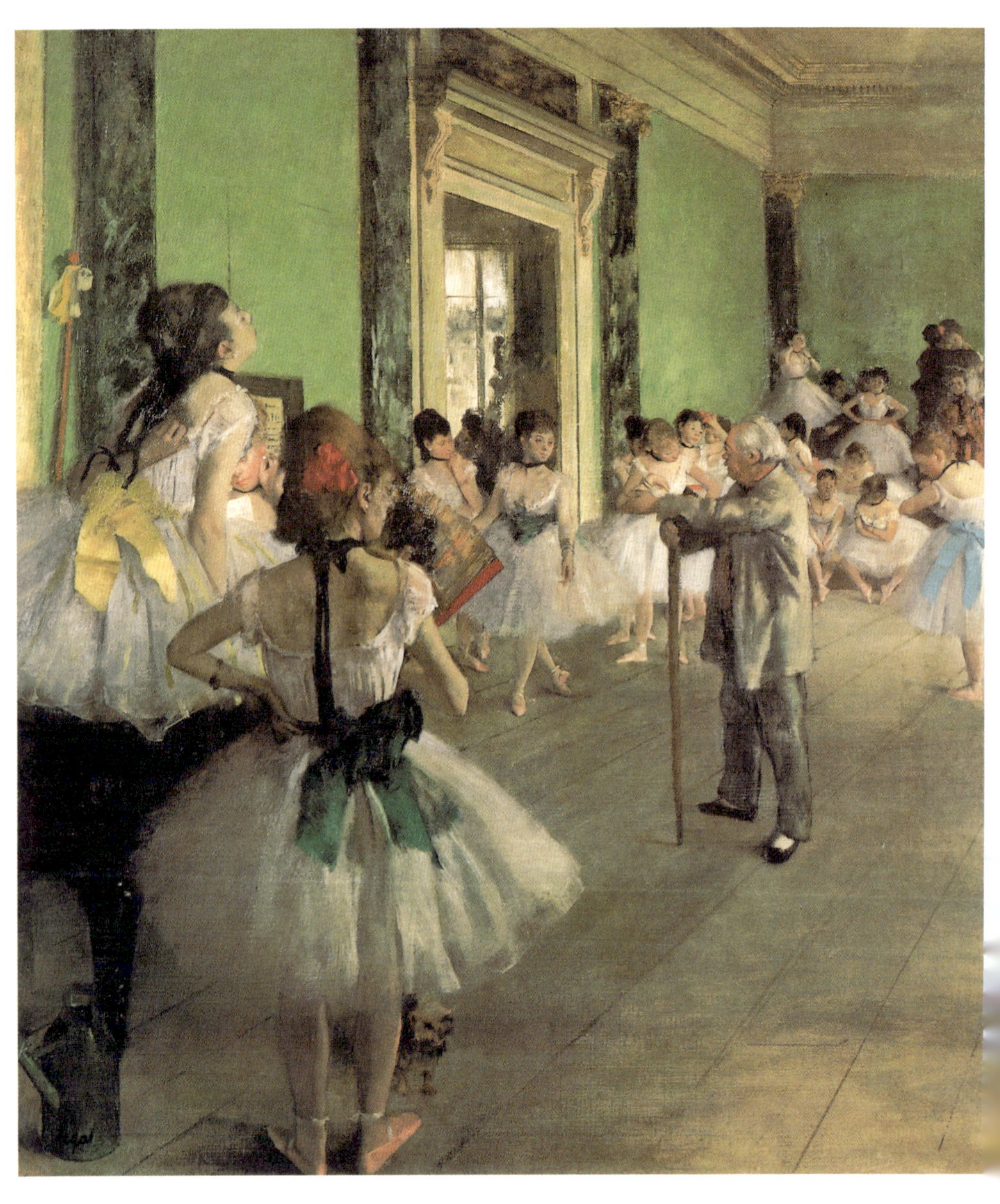

83. *The Dance Class, c.* 1873–76.
Oil on canvas, 85 × 75 cm (33½ × 29⅝ in.).
Musée d'Orsay, Paris

CHAPTER FIVE

Confronting the Modern World 1870–1879

'A painter of modern life was born, and a painter who derived from no one, who resembled no one else, who brought a totally new flavour to art, totally new procedures of execution.'

(J. K. Huysmans in *L'Art Moderne* published in 1883, but written earlier in a review of 1880 recalling Degas's work at the second Impressionist exhibition of 1876)

Degas was not alone in pursuing a new type of art at the beginning of the 1870s. Other artists, such as Monet, Renoir, Pissarro, Sisley and Cézanne, were also tackling subjects inspired by modern life while at the same time formulating a new style and experimenting with new techniques. What united them was the determination to usurp the authority of the Académie des Beaux-Arts and to broaden the scope of art in both content and style so that it could become a more accurate reflection of their own times.

Manet was the figurehead of this new movement soon to be dubbed Impressionism, but he refused to belong to any formal group of artists and always saw himself as acting independently. Impressionism as such was anticipated by two specific movements associated with mid-century painting in France: the Barbizon School, which placed great emphasis on rural naturalism, and the Realists who favoured themes of contemporary significance.

The early 1870s marks the birth of Impressionism in terms of artistic intent and practice, but as a loose confederation of like-minded artists what it lacked was a proper focus or identity as a movement. This was provided in 1874 by the formation of the Société Anonyme des Artistes, Sculpteurs, Graveurs, etc., which formally announced the arrival of Impressionism as an avant-garde movement. One of the purposes of the Société was to create an outlet for works of art made by those artists who had become members or who were invited as special guests. The annual Salon, where it was necessary for artists to exhibit work if they were to gain patronage and so become financially successful, was the main event in the Paris art world. The Salon jury, however, was increasingly reluctant to accept paintings that did not comply with the official teaching of the

Académie des Beaux-Arts and so on an almost regular basis a number
of works submitted by those artists who rejected that teaching were
overlooked. The situation became so bad that in 1863 the Emperor
Napoleon III instructed that an alternative exhibition should be
organized in addition to the main Salon. This was given the name of the
Salon des Réfusés. Both Manet and Courbet followed this lead in 1867 at
the Exposition Universelle by setting up separate pavilions to show their
own work outside the main exhibition space. Such independent acts were
seen as ways of undermining the authority of the Académie des Beaux-
Arts and were therefore healthy precedents for the Impressionists.

The exhibitions put on by this new group were a great deal
smaller, shorter in duration and less formal than the Salon. There
was no permanent exhibition venue and premises had to be found
on each occasion. Most importantly, there was no official jury and
rewards system. The exhibitions were reviewed by critics, but often
unfavourably and sometimes with considerable hostility or deliberate
misunderstanding. Those critics who were enthusiastic tended also to
be writers who in their own field shared the same aims as the artists.
The caricaturists were especially productive in lampooning the various
exhibits on show at the eight Impressionist exhibitions.

The artists included in the Impressionist exhibitions held between
1874 and 1886 were surprisingly diverse, but the presence of Caillebotte,
Cassatt, Degas, Monet, Morisot, Pissarro, Renoir and Sisley gave
the movement cohesion as well as an acknowledged independence.
Differences of opinion naturally emerged over the years and Degas in
particular was vociferous in his views about whose work should be shown
and whose work should not. Camille Pissarro, by contrast, was always
a mediator, especially in those exhibitions held during the first half of
the 1880s, and he himself was the only Impressionist who exhibited
work consistently at all eight exhibitions. Some painters appeared to
hedge their bets and continued to send work to the Salon while others
remained loyal to the new arrangements. Tensions arose between
those who were essentially landscapists and those who were figurative
painters. Symptomatic of this ongoing debate were the preparations
for the fifth Impressionist exhibition held in 1880 when Degas insisted
on the inclusion of the realist painter Jean-François Raffaëlli and then
deliberately abstained from the seventh exhibition held in 1882.

There was also the question of how the aims of style and technique
of the Impressionists should be developed, particularly when younger
artists – Gauguin, Seurat, Signac – were introduced to the group.
Similarly, it was difficult to assimilate an artist such as Odilon Redon,
who was sympathetic to the Impressionist cause but had a totally

different agenda for his own art, which became more and more steeped in symbolism. The cessation of the Impressionist exhibitions after 1886 was not in the end due to any of these personal tensions, but more to increasing difficulties of organization on practical grounds. The growth in importance of dealers (such as Paul Durand-Ruel; Boussod, Valadon & Co.; Georges Petit; and Bernheim Jeune), who were less interested in group shows and more in one-man exhibitions, was seen as an attractive alternative. Artists succumbed to the temptation of working in a more regulated way and under contract as opposed to suffering the anxieties of the open market. Degas, however, did not follow his colleagues in this respect, preferring to promote his work in Paris and the rest of Europe, as well as overseas, through favoured dealers such as Durand-Ruel and Ambroise Vollard.

The numerous works contributed by Degas to the eight Impressionist exhibitions illustrate contemporary subjects almost exclusively, with only one exception – *Young Spartans Exercising* (*c.* 1860) [see 34] in 1880, which was listed in the catalogue but apparently not actually shown. The subjects include scenes of the ballet, horseracing, café-concerts, laundresses, women washing or bathing in private and even criminals on trial. Neither did he limit himself to displaying paintings: fans, pastels, drawings and prints helped to widen the representation of his work.

Degas's total conversion to the portrayal of modern life at the beginning of the 1870s was a gradual process, but he was well prepared for such a shift in emphasis: he was an acute observer, a consummate draughtsman and possessed remarkable powers of detachment. What he was attempting to do was in many ways comparable with the description of society found in novels by Emile Zola, Jules and Edmond de Goncourt, J. K. Huysmans and Guy de Maupassant. And his work had a similar impact.

On Friday 13 February 1874 Edmond de Goncourt visited Degas and recorded in his *Journal*:

> Yesterday I spent the whole day in the studio of a strange painter called Degas. After a great many essays and experiments and trial shots in all directions, he has fallen in love with modern life, and out of all the subjects in modern life has chosen washerwomen and ballet-dancers. When you come to think of it, it is not a bad choice.
>
> It is a world of pink and white, of female flesh in lawn and gauze, the most delightful of pretexts for using pale, soft tints.
>
> He showed me, in their various poses and their graceful foreshortening, washerwomen and still more washerwomen…

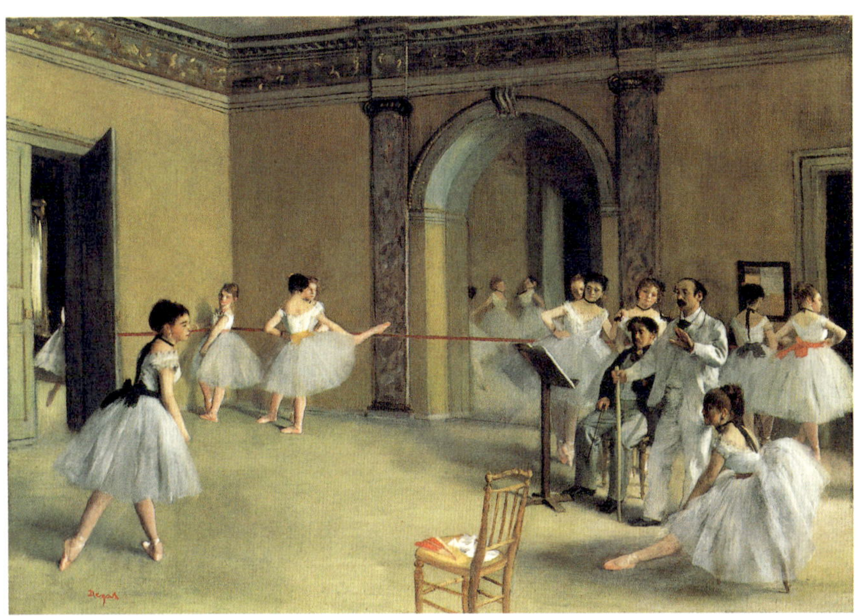

84. *Dance Class at the Opéra*, 1871.
Oil on canvas, 32 × 46 cm (12⅝ × 18⅛ in.).
Musée d'Orsay, Paris

speaking their language and explaining the technicalities of the
different movements in pressing and ironing.

Then it was the turn of the dancers. There was their green-room
with, outlined against the light of a window, the curious silhouette
of dancers' legs coming down a little staircase, with the bright red
of a tartan in the midst of all those puffed-out white clouds, and a
ridiculous ballet-master serving as a vulgar foil. And there before
one, drawn from nature, was the graceful twisting and turning of
the gestures of those little monkey-girls.

An original fellow, this Degas, sickly, neurotic, and so ophthalmic
that he is afraid of losing his sight; but for this very reason an
eminently receptive creature and sensitive to the character of
things. Among all the artists I have met so far, he is the one who
has best been able, in representing modern life, to catch the spirit
of that life.

This is an early and shrewd assessment of Degas's particular traits, together with his strengths and weaknesses, but it is clear that Degas is already an artist to note. No doubt aware of the interest that his work was generating, Degas increased his output dramatically during the 1870s.

The subject that captivated the artist most once his examination of modern life was underway was the ballet. Starting late in his career in 1871 when he was already aged thirty-seven, Degas remained in thrall to dancers for the rest of his life. In all, the paintings, gouaches, pastels and drawings of dancers that he produced number over half of his total *oeuvre*. These works were immediately popular and have been so ever since. Degas had a musical background and so his interest in ballet was not a new development in his personal life, but his depiction of dancers was a landmark in the history of art. Ballet in Paris was performed at the Opéra, located at the start of Degas's lifetime in the Rue Le Peletier close to Montmartre and near his family home. It was this grand, much-loved building that is the setting for his earlier compositions even after it burnt down in October 1875. Already though, before the fire, the old Opéra on Rue Le Peletier was condemned and a new building commissioned from Charles Garnier. Work had started on this in 1861 and Garnier's building (the Palais Garnier still in use today) at the top of the Avenue de l'Opéra opened in January 1875. This then became the focus of Degas's attention.

At first Degas kept his distance, viewing performances from the auditorium across the orchestra pit with glimpses of dancers on the stage beyond (*Musicians of the Orchestra*, c. 1870–71, Städelsches Kunstinstitut, Frankfurt-am-Main, *The Ballet from 'Robert le Diable'*, 1872, Metropolitan Museum of Art, New York, or the picture of the same title of 1876 now in the Victoria and Albert Museum, London). Even so, this viewpoint allows for some dramatic effects – cropping, foreshortening and stark contrasts of light and dark – that are innovatory in this context. The superb pictures of rehearsals and classes set in cavernous rooms away from the auditorium in the Opéra show a similar restraint [83–86]. The distribution of figures and treatment of space are more old-fashioned, referring back in some ways to the *fêtes galantes* of Watteau in the eighteenth century.

Only with time did Degas finally gain admittance to backstage areas of the Rue Le Peletier Opéra where he could observe the dancers at close-quarters and more informally. These areas comprised the rooms where classes were conducted, the more glamorous *foyer de la danse* where dancers could meet and mingle with their admirers either before or after performances, the dressing rooms, and the wings where performers gathered while a performance was in progress. Degas probably gained

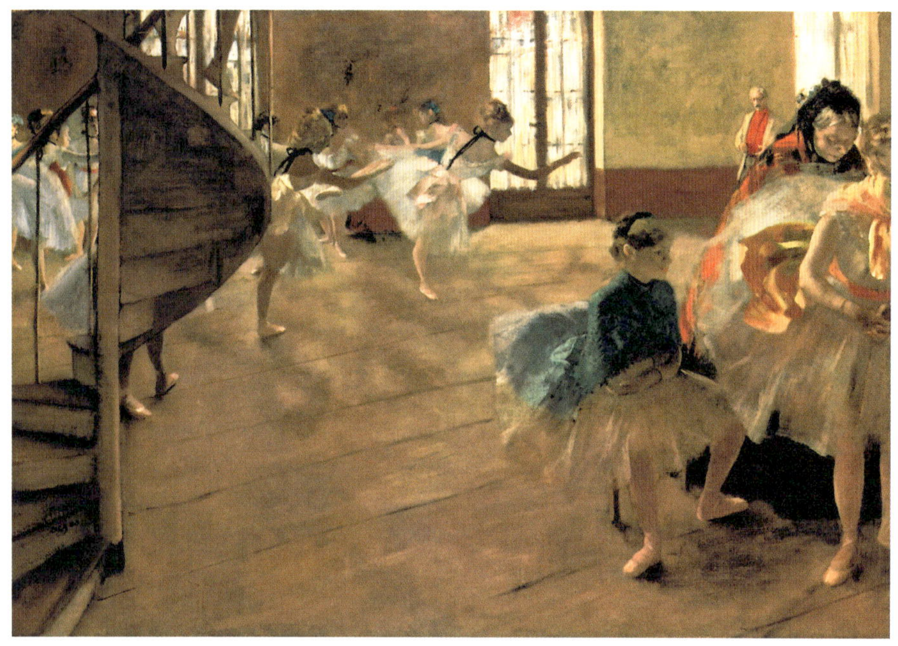

85. *The Rehearsal, c.* 1874.
Oil on canvas, 58.4 × 83.8 cm (23 × 33 in.).
Burrell Collection, Glasgow

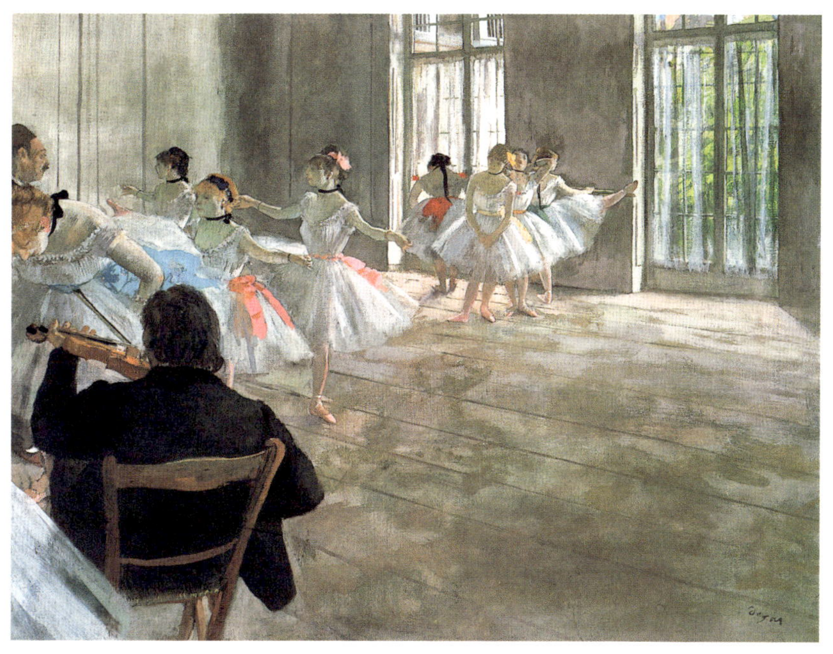

86. *The Dance Class*, *c.* 1874–78.
Oil and tempera on canvas, 47 × 61.3 cm (18½ × 24⅛ in.).
Shelburne Museum, Vermont

access to these areas through the influence of friends such as Count
Ludovic Lépic and Ludovic Halévy, both balletomanes who were annual
subscribers (*abonnés*) with special privileges [92]. It is likely that Degas
himself was a subscriber, although not on a regular basis owing to his
fluctuating financial situation. Certainly he knew many of the dancers
by name and made formal portraits of some of them out of the theatre
[93]. Backstage the artist learnt about the art of classical dance. First of
all, there were technical aspects of positions, balance, routine exercises
and movements, including turns, leaps and extensions. Secondly, there
was the human aspect, observing the life of ballerinas from the earliest
stages of their development as children (known as *les rats*) chaperoned
by solicitous mothers before advancing through the *corps de ballet* to
the highest level of prima ballerina. Above all, there was the physical
commitment of dancers working to the point of exhaustion, injury or
collapse. In these respects it might be said that ballet was a metaphor for
Degas's own practices as an artist and this association became stronger
the longer he engaged with the ballet.

The drawings of dancers made by Degas during the 1870s fall into
several categories. During the first half of the decade, while devising
elaborate compositions for his paintings, he would observe poses from
the life noting them down with the brush in *essence*, which facilitated
speed of execution [94–97, 105]. Then he would ask the dancer to
model the final pose for him in the studio. These drawings are usually
in pencil on tinted papers and squared for enlargement [98, 99, 101].
They combine a winning dexterity with telling precision, as well as
very skilful differentiations of texture between skin, hair, gauze and
satin. Technically these are among the greatest drawings of dancers
that Degas ever made. At the same time, he began to draw hundreds
of rapid studies in black chalk or charcoal backstage, which were often
annotated with details of dress, position, colour, light and occasionally a
name [102, 103]. Some were made in his Notebooks [104]. This was the
way that Degas learnt about the ballet and became acquainted with the
vocabulary of dance. He accumulated these studies for future reference.
Unlike other artists, or indeed photographers, who tackled this subject
there is no attempt to prettify or glamorize the ballet: dancers of all
ages perspire, grimace, ache, groan, stretch and strain, collapse with
exhaustion or wait patiently until needed [106–108].

According to Vollard, Degas once remarked, 'People call me the
painter of dancing girls. It has never occurred to them that my chief
interest in dancers lies in rendering movement and painting pretty
clothes.' A marked feature of the drawings of dancers dating from
the second half of the 1870s is the increasing use of pastel in finished

compositions made as works of art in their own right [109–114]. These were probably made as a result of Degas becoming more aware of the intensity of light in theatres, which enhanced colours. Nobody in France at that date could make pastels of this supreme quality and his use of the medium was by no means restricted to dance.

The males in Degas's ballet scenes have no great prominence and neither are they numerous, but they do have important responsibilities. Jules Perrot, for example, was a leading dancer and choreographer at the Paris Opéra in the early 1830s when Romantic ballet was at its height. When his contract was not renewed he became a peripatetic performer and producer in London and Milan before moving on to St Petersburg where he became ballet master at the Imperial Theatres from 1849 until 1860. On returning to Paris he had hoped for a similar post at the Opéra, but was disappointed, although as Degas shows in several works, he taught there unofficially [115, 116]. The artist was also mindful of the male violinists who worked as répétiteurs in dance classes and had a fairly low status as musicians. These figures occur in some paintings and pastels during this decade and are often overwhelmed by the number of dancers surrounding them. Degas tends to introduce an element of caricature into these depictions, emphasizing age, unkempt appearance and unsophisticated playing styles [117–119].

The paintings, pastels and drawings of the ballet made by Degas during the 1870s are not just testimony to his growing maturity as an artist. They also show him with great specificity coming to terms with a contemporary subject that absorbed all his attention. What he does in these particular works is to map out the world of ballet as he saw it. In doing this he has left a highly personal record of the ballet in Paris at that time. Such was Degas's enthusiasm he was no doubt already devising ways in which he could continue his exploration of the ballet in future decades.

The other subject that dominated Degas's output, but not quite to the same extent as the ballet, was horseracing. He had begun his investigation of horses, steeplechasing and racing in the mid-1860s, building up his knowledge of the animals, jockeys and spectators. Degas seems to have found it difficult to achieve paintings that satisfied his own high standards and frequently reworked those he had in his studio, or had left unfinished, before returning to them at various intervals. In fact, he exhibited only two such paintings in the Impressionist exhibitions: *The Carriage Leaving the Races in the Countryside* (Museum of Fine Arts, Boston) in 1874 and *Jockeys before the Start* (Barber Institute of Fine Arts, Birmingham) in 1879. Degas did not stop adding to his material for his racecourse pictures, but he did not devise any new compositions until the 1880s and 1890s. However, just as in the 1860s he had concentrated on the jockeys, during the 1870s he examines the gentlemen riders, grooms or trainers – all expert horsemen in their own right [120]. Their particular skills and quiet professionalism were clearly much respected by Degas who takes a great deal of trouble with such details as dress, balance, stirrups and reins. Where the jockeys are full of tension, these riders calmly and diligently work the horses.

Degas's exploration of modern life during the 1870s extended well beyond the Opéra and the racecourse. He was fascinated by all manner of pursuits, among which laundresses were at the forefront. He depicts laundresses, washerwomen and ironers fetching and carrying or at work with hot irons. The hours were long (5 am to 11 pm), the wages were low and the conditions horrific, particularly the heat and the claustrophobic spaces. The ironers did not wear much clothing and drank in order to offset their misery. Degas was sympathetic to the plight of the laundresses and for him they epitomized Paris. As he wrote in a letter to Tissot in 1872 from New Orleans: 'Everything is beautiful in this world of the people. But one Paris laundry girl, with bare arms, is worth it all for such a pronounced Parisian as I am.'

Degas also attended café-concerts where, as in the music-hall tradition, popular entertainment was staged with singers and comic acts as the warm-up routine. The success of the café-concerts began in the 1830s and continued to thrive at the end of the century, by which time they had been commandeered in part by the avant-garde. The atmosphere at café-concerts was rumbustious, rowdy and sexually charged. Drinks were served throughout. Entry prices were low, which enabled a wide cross-section of society to attend. In summer café-concerts, as at the Alcazar-d'Eté and the Ambassadeurs in the Champs-Elysées, were held in the open air. Living on the edge of Montmartre, Degas would have witnessed numerous performances at café-concerts. On such occasions he would begin with quick sketches of the singer, observing deportment and characteristic gestures, thus preserving for posterity the idiosyncratic singing styles of performers such as Emma Valadon, called Thérèsa, and Emilie Bécat. As in the early ballet pictures, Degas views the stage at first from in front, thereby including some members of the audience and the musicians [123, 124]. He also paid close attention to details such as the awnings, stage props and the light given out by the globe lamps. When Degas moves nearer to the stage, or even on to it, he produced dramatic close-up views of singers in mid-performance [125]. Some of these anticipate cinematic techniques.

Another startling viewpoint was offered by a circus performer known as Miss La La, who Degas saw on four occasions at the Cirque

Fernando on the Boulevard Rochechouart in January 1879. Miss La La was renowned for the strength of her mouth and jaw. Being hoisted to the roof of the circus on a pulley holding on by her teeth was one of her acts. Degas was obviously intrigued by the image of the figure dangling overhead in the cavernous space of the Circus. The act perhaps reminded him of the angels or other figures he had seen in frescoes in Italian churches. He made preparatory drawings for the painting *Miss La La at the Cirque Fernando* (1879) in the National Gallery, London [87], in pastel and black chalk until he had settled upon the best viewpoint for the figure [88], but the perspective of the roof caused him some difficulty and he had to take advice.

By concerning himself with the public spectacle of modern Paris Degas was widening the sociological basis of his work, which now extended from the glamour of the Opéra to the lowest trades. It is typical of Degas that he enjoyed exploring the overlaps between these two worlds [126]. It is in fact in these interstices from which much of the tension in his work is derived. More and more during the 1870s Degas frequented those places where both ends of the spectrum comingled or simply passed one another by – backstage at the Opéra, the café-concert, the brothel.

Degas's initial interest in the female nude began in the 1860s when he was preparing such pictures as *Scene of War in the Middle Ages* [see 39], but it took him several years before returning to the subject. Renewal of interest came with a group of some fifty monotype prints on the subject of the brothel or scenes of prostitution done *c.* 1876–77. Pierre-Auguste Renoir remarked that the compositions had the 'grandeur of an Egyptian relief', and later Picasso, who owned examples, was also impressed by them. These magnificent monotypes (some overdrawn with pastel) were far removed from the studies made from nude models posed in the studio for the history paintings; they show life in the raw [127]. From these Degas gained sufficient confidence to develop the motif of modern women seen in the domestic environment, which he moved towards during the late 1870s until making it one of his main subjects from the 1880s onwards [128, 129].

Degas's depiction of women, however, was not restricted to interiors such as brothels. One of Degas's most accomplished works is *Women on the Terrace of a Café, Evening*, which was shown at the Impressionist exhibition of 1877 [130]. The horizontal composition is divided vertically by pillars articulating the space in which four women are seated in pairs, They are in conversation, but are positioned asymmetrically. The street is behind them. The different angles of their bodies and the random distribution of the chair backs suggest the disarray of a busy café, but the centre is firmly anchored by the woman who is seen almost full face

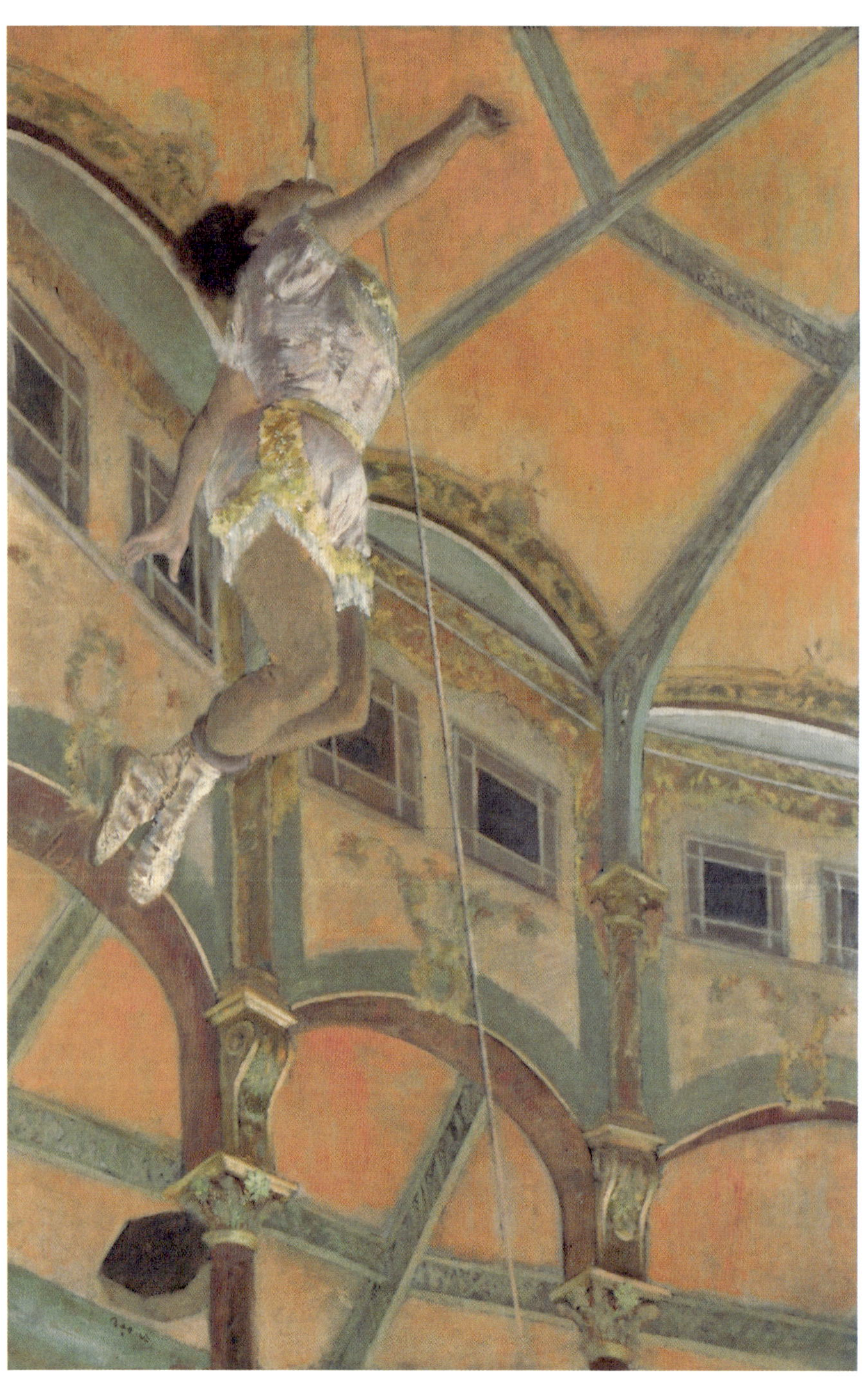

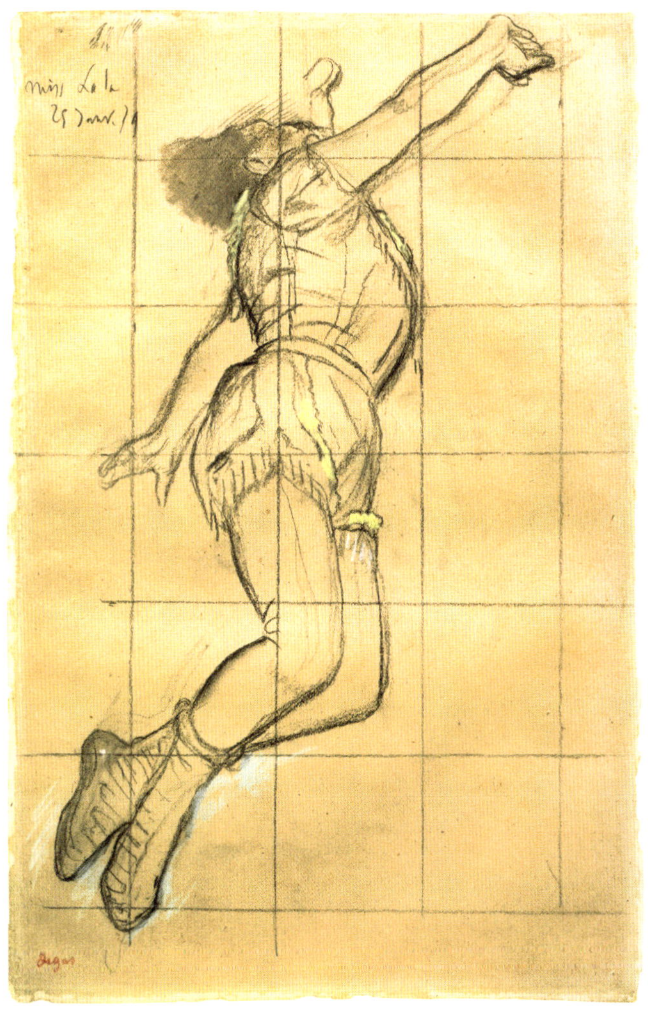

OPPOSITE

87. *Miss La La at the Cirque Fernando*, 1879.
Oil on canvas, 117.2 × 77.5 cm (46 × 30½ in.).
National Gallery, London

ABOVE

88. *Miss La La at the Cirque Fernando*, 1879.
Black chalk with pastel, 47 × 32 cm (18½ × 12⅝ in.), squared.
Barber Institute of Fine Arts, Birmingham

and makes a vulgar sexual gesture with her thumb held against her teeth. Degas uses a vivid blue pastel to give her prominence. Indeed, this blue is perfectly pitched as it is intensified by the internal lighting of the café while being seen against the penumbra of night falling outside.

There also exists a superb group of pastel studies of women in day dress on a special outing. The grandest of these, showing three women, is inscribed, 'Portraits en frise pour décoration dans un apartement' [132]. This was shown at the sixth Impressionist exhibition of 1881, but the project for which it was drawn, together with others, is unknown and perhaps was never even undertaken. Presumably it was some kind of mural decoration unless it was for a screen. The figures in all the related studies have dignity and monumentality: they are in the act of looking as though visiting a gallery or a museum. Two of the models can be identified: the American artist Mary Cassatt in the centre and the actress Ellen André on the right. A memorable feature of these studies is the *mise-en-page*, especially in the study of Ellen André alone where the right half of the sheet is left totally blank [133]. The fact that these studies were made for a decorative scheme may again have put Degas in mind of the fresco cycles he saw in Italy. And it is perhaps no accident that the studies made for this scheme may have been transmuted into the compositions of visits to the Musée du Louvre featuring Mary Cassatt. Dating from *c.* 1879–80, these were made in oil, pastel and as prints [89]. The development and replication in different media is symptomatic of Degas's energized approach to these new subjects. The prints of Mary Cassatt in the Louvre (specifically the Etruscan Gallery and the Picture Gallery) were among those intended for the publication *Le Jour et la Nuit*, which was to have been issued monthly with original prints by Degas, Pissarro, Cassatt and Bracquemond in addition to text. The publication never appeared probably because there were no backers, but the ideas for it that were jotted down by Degas in Notebook 30 (pp. 208–202 [sic]) in May 1879 amount to an index of life in Paris. The fact also that the sixteen or so prints undertaken by Degas for this project combine different techniques, unorthodox methods and innumerable states indicate the artist's creative restlessness.

The choice of modern urban subject matter, therefore, was undoubtedly a stimulant to Degas's imagination, but equally it gave him an incentive to experiment. Towards the end of the 1870s the need to convey the endless ebb and flow of the contemporary world encouraged Degas to test out new formats and new techniques as a way of seeking new solutions. Preeminent among these initiatives was the daring sculpture *Little Dancer Aged Fourteen* shown at the sixth Impressionist exhibition of 1881, where it caused a furore [90]. This was the only

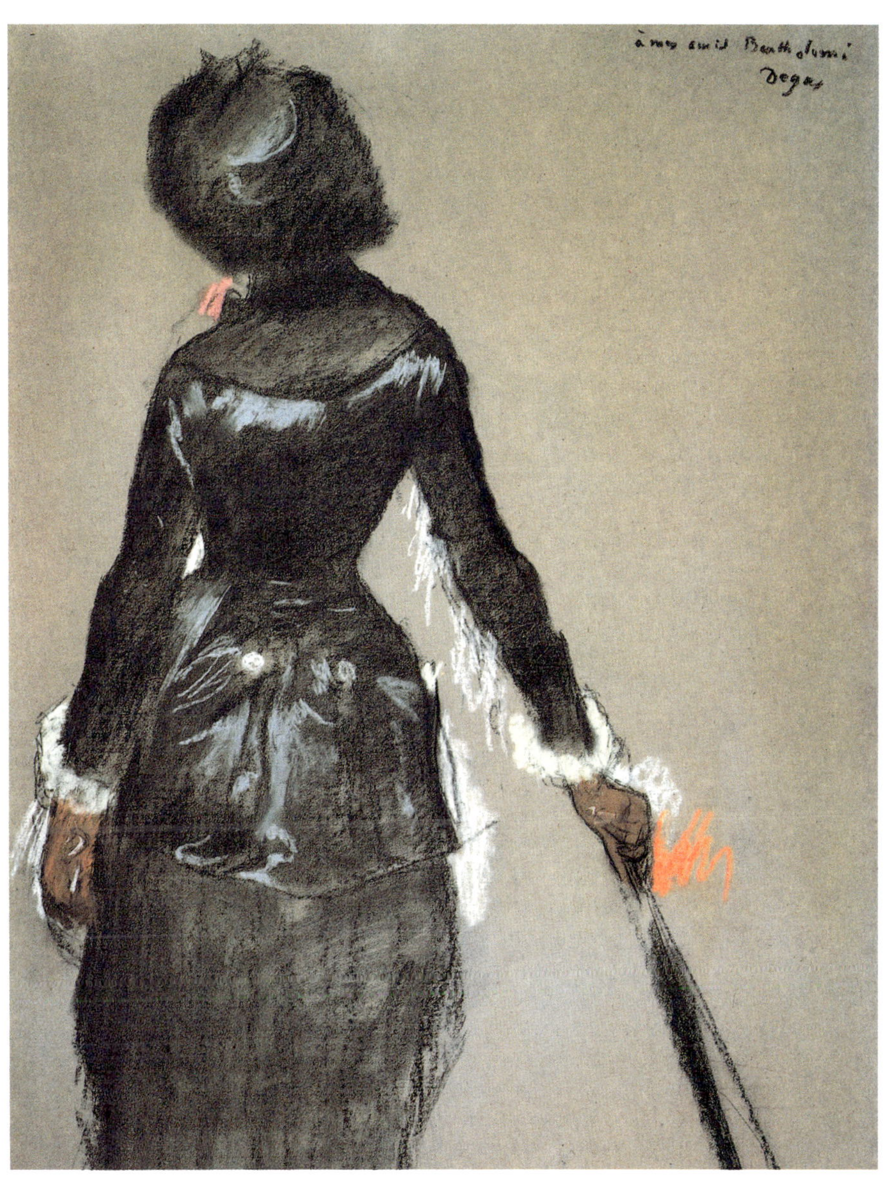

89. *Mary Cassatt at the Louvre*, 1880.
Pastel on grey paper, 63.5 × 48.9 cm (25 × 19¼ in.).
Philadelphia Museum of Art

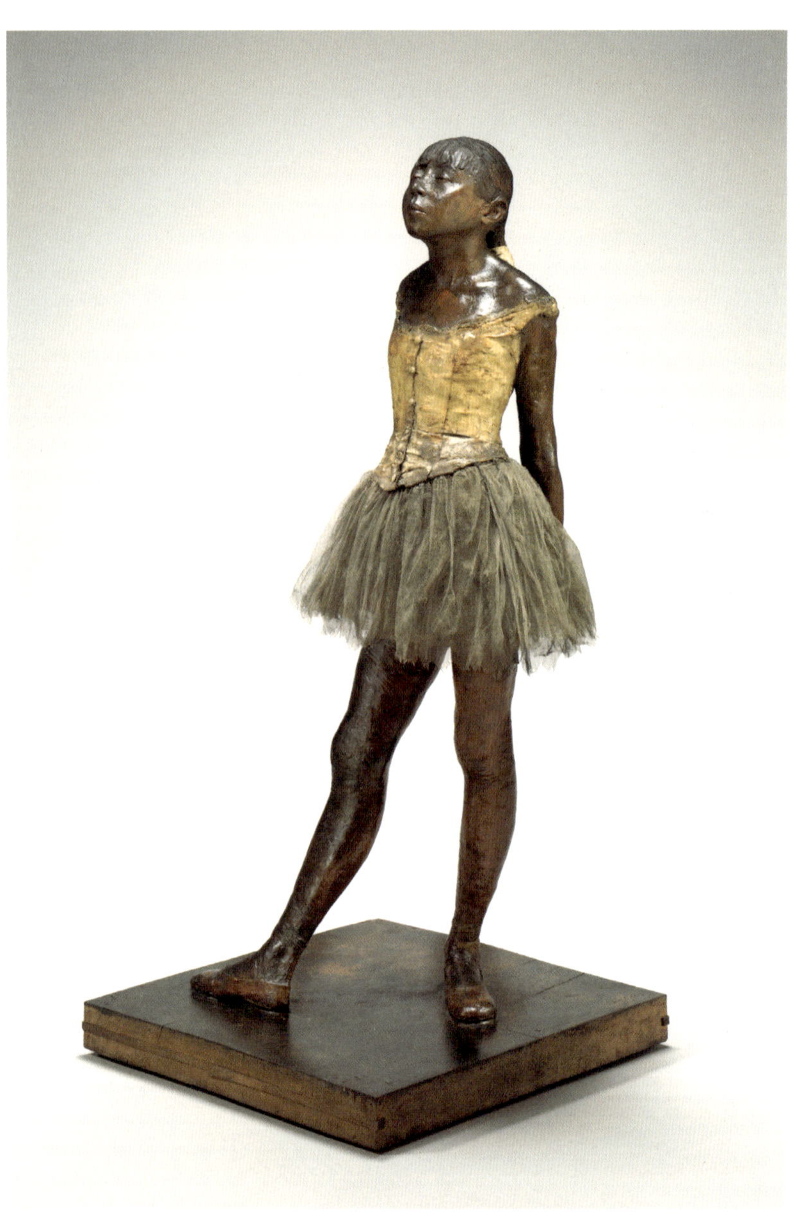

90. *Little Dancer Aged Fourteen*, 1878–81.
Wax and fabric, h. 99 cm (39 in.).
National Gallery of Art, Washington, DC

sculpture exhibited by Degas in his lifetime. The figure was modelled in wax supported on a metal armature. The wax is now in the National Gallery of Art in Washington; it was cast in bronze only after the artist's death. What was exceptional was that the wax figure was dressed in real fabrics: muslin skirt, lace-trimmed bodice, ballet shoes, and a wig made of genuine hair tied at the back with a satin ribbon. These features reinforced the sense of realism. Added to this was the fact that choosing a very young girl who was in training to be a dancer instead of someone better known in the dance world was courting controversy.

The model was Marie van Goetham, who was a dance student at the Paris Opéra. Her family was originally from Belgium – her mother a laundress and her father a tailor – who happened to live near Degas. In preparation for the sculpture the artist made nine sheets of drawings totalling some twenty-six studies of the dancer from a similar number of viewpoints [134–136]. Effectively, Degas circulated round the figure emphasizing her physiognomy, the curvature of her spine, the position of her feet and the angle of her head. The drawings, some showing the model naked, have strong contours that are often redrawn and have rapidly applied heightening in pastel and white chalk. The sense of verisimilitude exuded by this sculpture is only matched by the thoroughness of Degas's preparations, perhaps necessitated by his comparative lack of experience in making sculpture.

Another departure was the artist's sudden interest in fans framed as pictures [137]. He made about twenty-five in total, nearly all of which date from 1879 when Degas, together with Pissarro, included five examples in the Impressionist exhibition of that year. The scenes he selected are from the ballet and only one shows a café-concert. The principal association of the fan is with the eighteenth century as an aristocratic accessory, but the Impressionists (including Gauguin, in addition to Degas and Pissarro) saw the painted fan in a more democratic light and as a way of promoting wider sales at cheaper prices than those charged for their oil paintings. For an artist like Degas, however, the appeal of the fan may have been more for the creation of new compositions or adapting existing ones specially to fit this difficult format.

Equally inventive was Degas's attitude to printmaking in the mid-1870s when he began to put particular emphasis on monotypes. The monotype, which is created in two ways, was for him a form of drawing. The 'light-field' manner was produced by making a free-hand design in printer's ink directly onto a blank plate. The 'dark-field' type was produced by inking the whole plate first and then wiping parts of it clean or partially clean in accordance with the selected design. The point about monotypes, however, is that the number of impressions was severely limited and in most cases to a single impression, but occasionally two, with the second impression being much fainter. Degas decided to heighten the impressions with pastel or gouache after he pulled them so that the monotype itself served as a dark background or priming for the final image. Many of the subjects of modern urban life explored by Degas during the 1870s were by the close of the decade treated as monotypes and then developed further by the addition of pastel or gouache [115, 123–125, 127–130]. By doing this Degas was extending the practical application of drawing, which he continued in the 1880s and 1890s.

The originality that Degas brought to his art in the 1870s is best summarized by his *Portrait of Edmond Duranty*, which was shown at the fourth Impressionist exhibition of 1879 and had the rare (indeed unique) distinction of being seen again at the fifth in 1880 following the sitter's recent death [91]. The portrait, executed in tempera and pastel on linen, was eloquently described at the time by Huysmans, who praised Degas for the analytical powers of his drawing and the accuracy of his colours:

> M. Duranty is shown amidst his prints and books, seated at his
> writing table, his slender, nervous fingers, his keen and mocking
> eye, his searching, piercing look, his expression as of an English
> comedian, and his dry little laugh into the stem of his pipe pass
> before me again as I look on this canvas where the character of this
> curious analyst is so well rendered.

Duranty was a novelist, erudite journalist and art critic associated in the first instance with the defence of Realism and then of Naturalism. The friend of Manet and of Zola, he was also close to Degas, who became his executor. For the Impressionist exhibition of 1876 Duranty had written a pamphlet entitled *La Nouvelle Peinture*, which is in effect a manifesto for avant-garde painting.

> Farewell to the human body treated like a vase, with an eye for
> the decorative curve. Farewell to the uniform monotony of bone
> structure, to the anatomical model beneath the nude. What we
> need are the special characteristics of the modern individual – in
> his clothing, in his social situations, at home, or on the street.

For Duranty, as for Huysmans, Degas was the greatest exponent of this new ambition in art which was best served through drawing. For Duranty 'drawing is such an individual and indispensable means of expression that one cannot demand from it methods, techniques or points of view. It fuses with its goal, and remains the inseparable companion of the idea.' Degas's *Portrait of Edmond Duranty* does indeed represent a fusion of painting and drawing both in the way it has been achieved and in the way in which it appears to the onlooker.

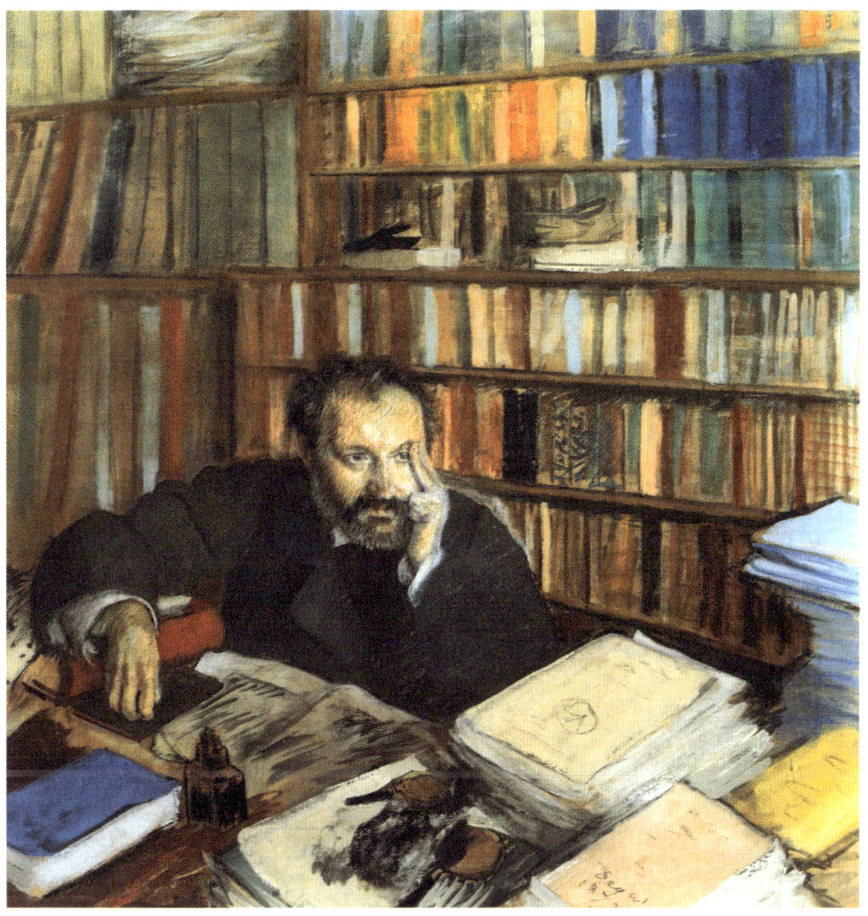

91. *Portrait of Edmond Duranty*, 1879.
Tempera and pastel on linen, 100.6 × 100.6 cm
(19⅛ × 19⅛ in.). Burrell Collection, Glasgow

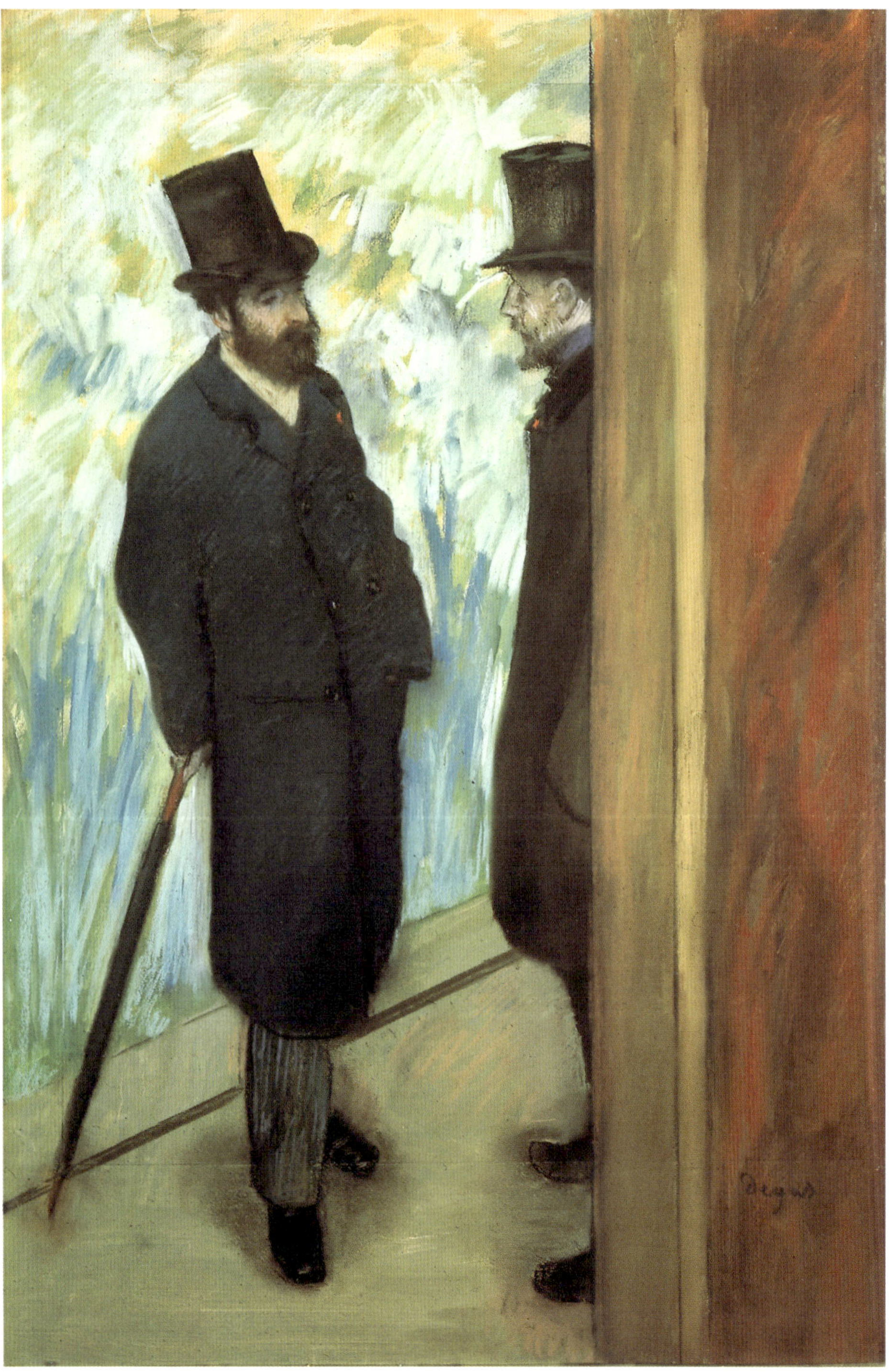
Degas

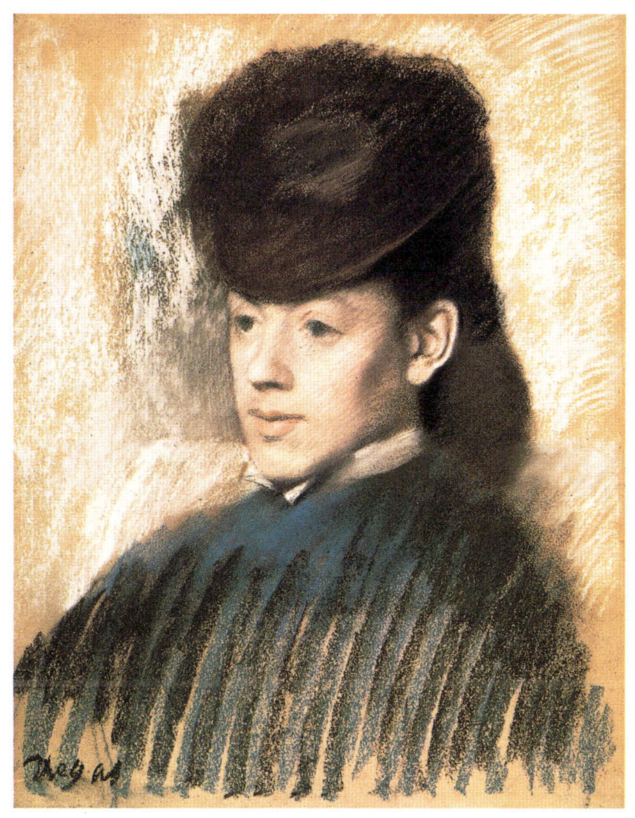

OPPOSITE
92. *Portraits of Two Friends (Ludovic Halévy and Albert Boulanger-Cavé) Backstage at the Opéra*, 1879.
Pastel on beige paper, 79 × 55 cm (31⅛ × 21⅝ in.).
Musée d'Orsay, Paris

ABOVE
93. *Mlle Malo*, c. 1875.
Pastel on beige paper, 52 × 41 cm (20⅞ × 16⅛ in.).
Barber Institute of Fine Arts, Birmingham

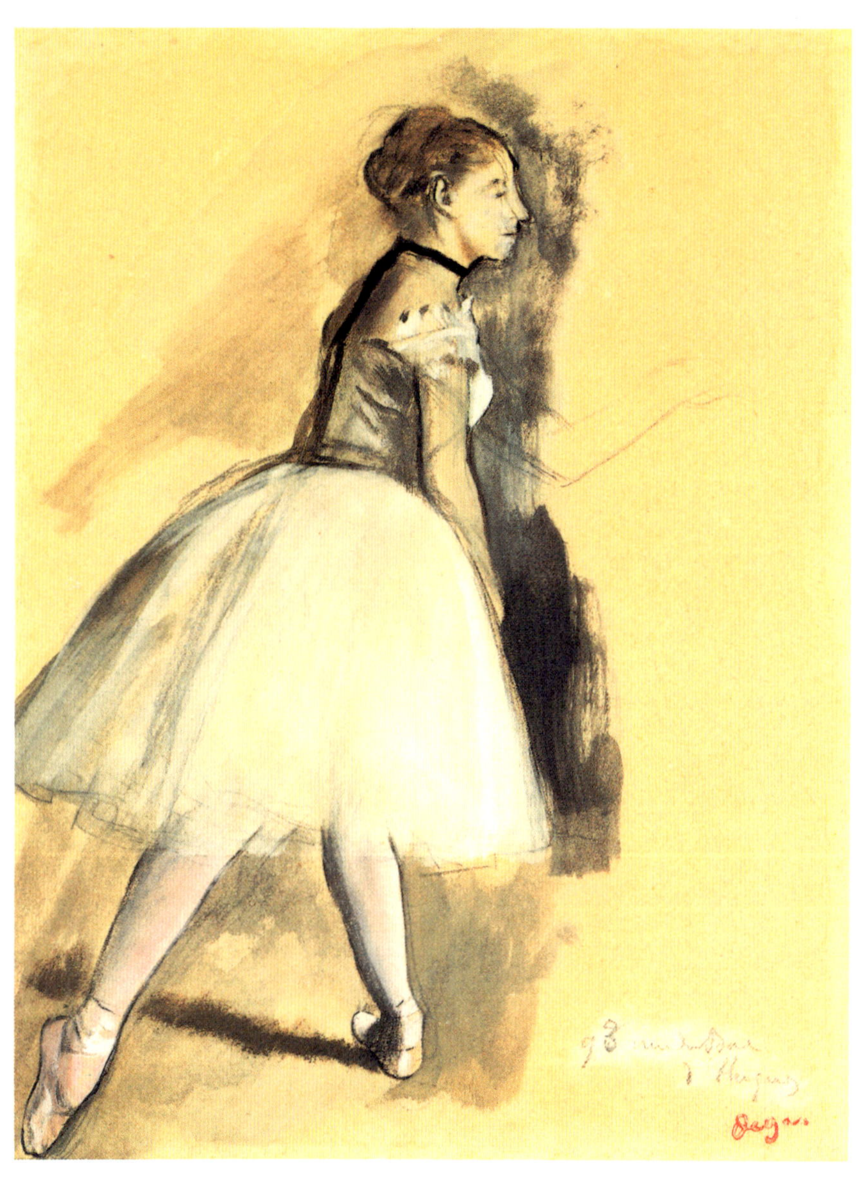

94. *Study for 'Foyer de la Danse à l'Opéra'*, 1872.
Essence over pencil heightened with bodycolour
on beige paper, 27.1 × 21 cm (10⅝ × 8¼ in.).
Private collection

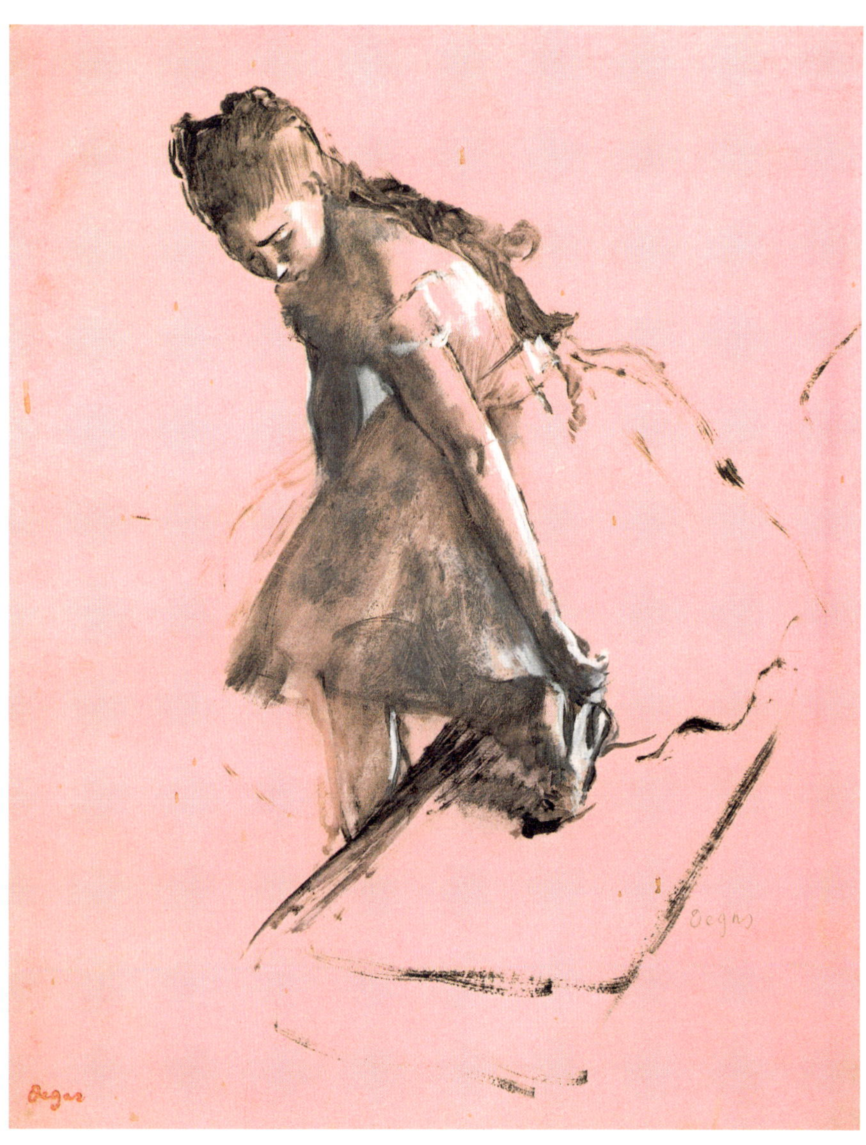

95. *Dancer Adjusting her Shoe, c.* 1874.
Essence with brown ink and oil heightened
with bodycolour on pink paper, 40 × 32 cm
(15¼ × 12⅝ in.). Private collection

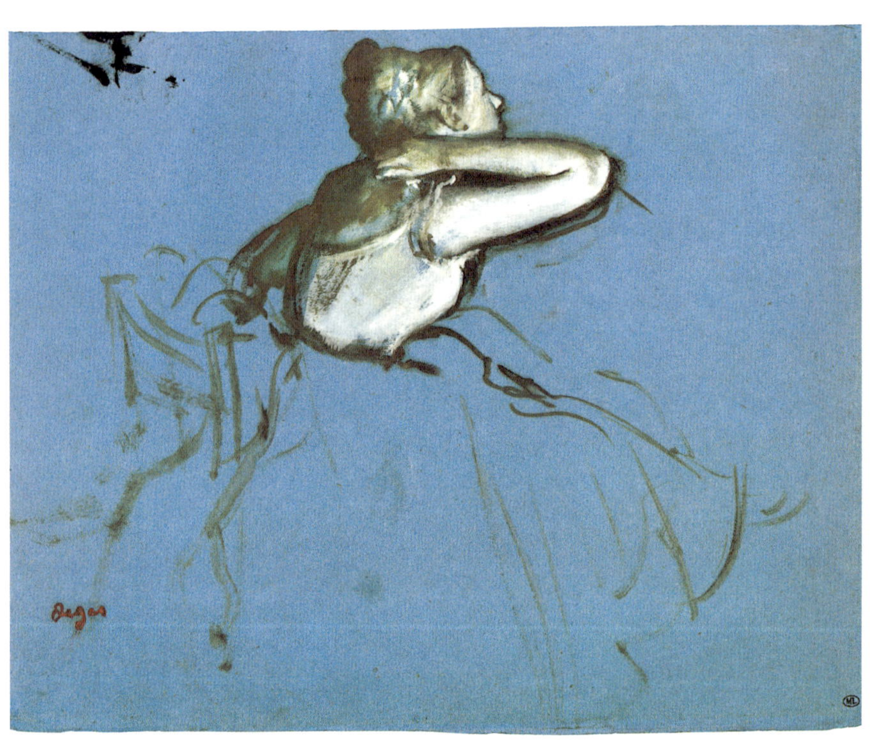

96. *Seated Dancer Seen in Profile Facing*
Right Scratching her Neck, 1873.
Essence with brown ink on blue paper,
23 × 29.2 cm (9 × 11½ in.).
Musée d'Orsay, Paris

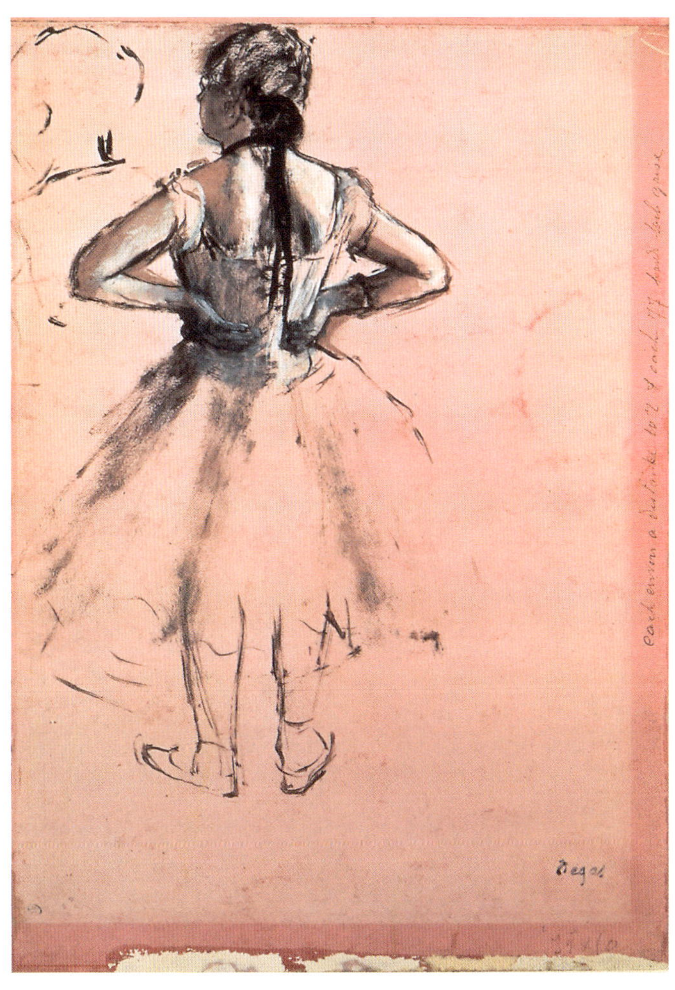

97. *Standing Dancer Seen from the Back, c. 1873.*
Essence with brown ink on pink paper, 39.4 × 27.8 cm
(15½ × 11 in.). Musée d'Orsay, Paris

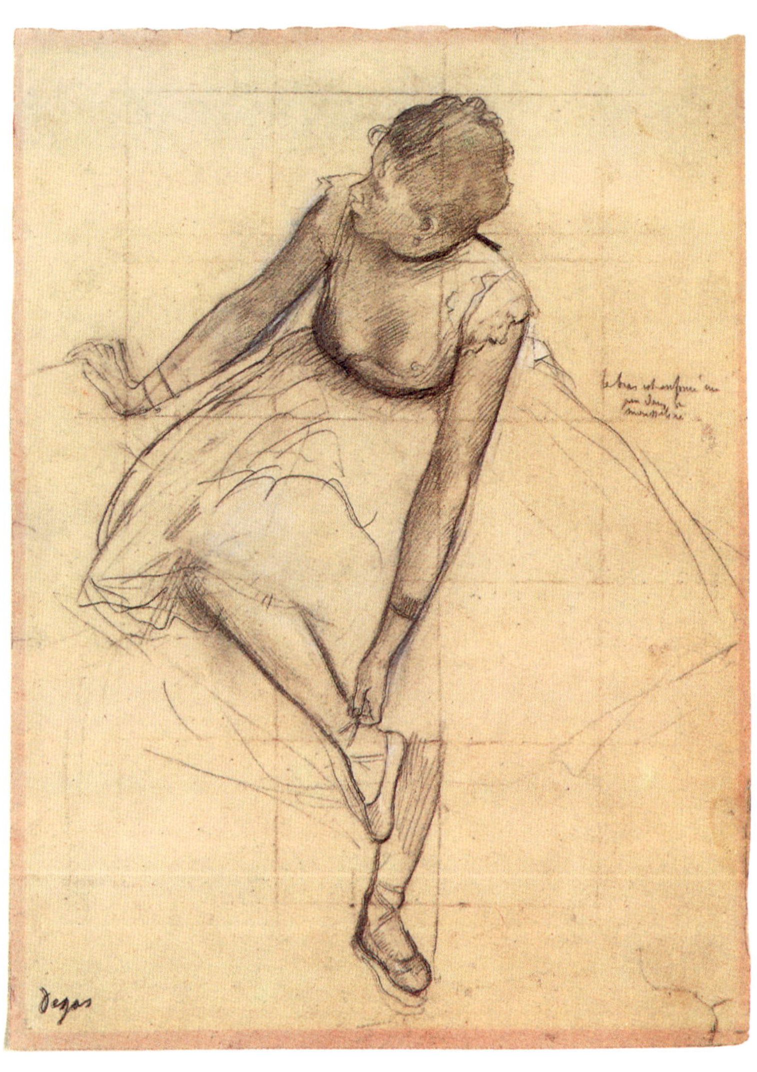

98. *Dancer Adjusting her Shoe*, c. 1872–73.
Pencil heightened with white chalk on discoloured pink paper,
32.7 × 24.4 cm (12⅞ × 9⅝ in.), squared.
Metropolitan Museum of Art, New York

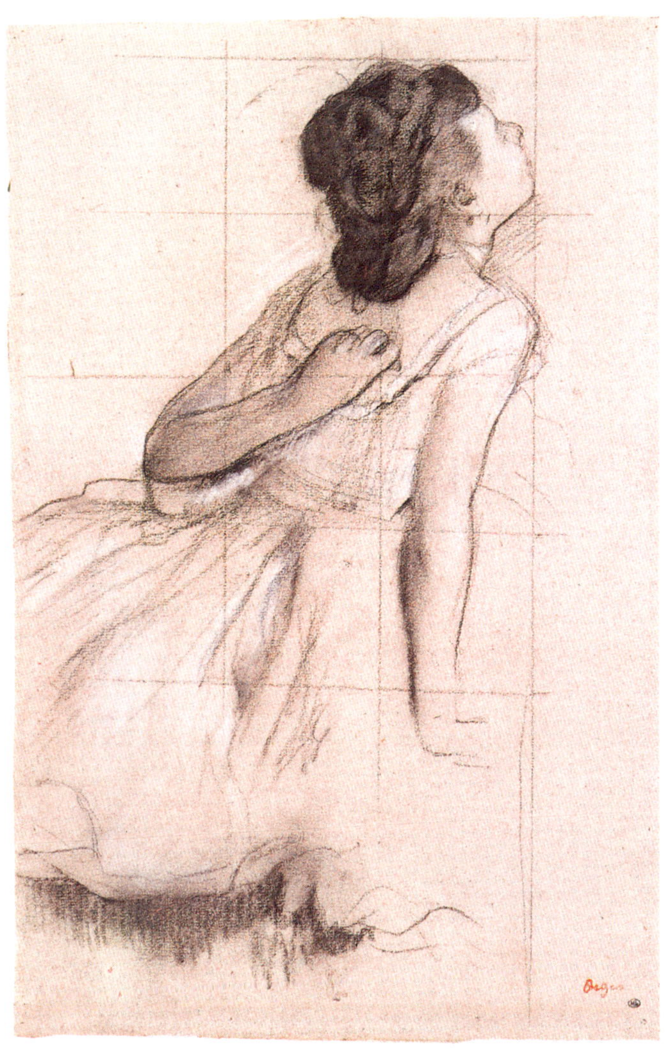

99. *Seated Dancer Scratching her Back*, c. 1873–74.
Black chalk heightened with white chalk on pink paper,
46.5 × 30.8 cm (18⅜ × 12⅛ in.), squared.
Musée d'Orsay, Paris

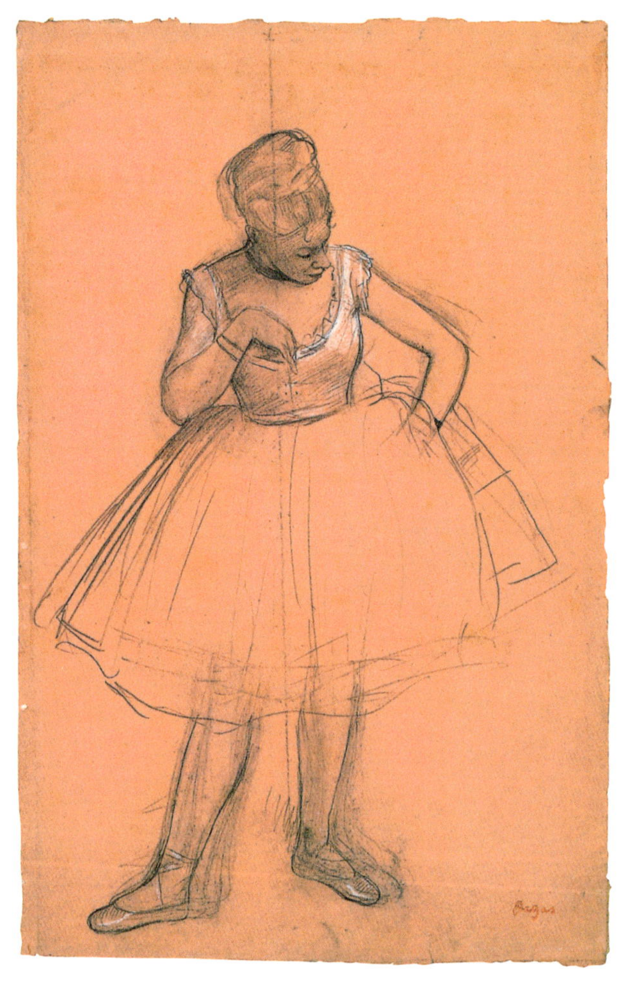

ABOVE
100. *Dancer Adjusting her Costume*, c. 1872–73.
Pencil heightened with white chalk on pink paper,
42.2 × 27.2 cm (16½ × 10⅝ in.).
Detroit Institute of Arts

OPPOSITE
101. *Dancer Shown in Position Facing Three-Quarters Front*, c. 1872.
Pencil and black chalk heightened with white chalk on pink paper,
41 × 27.6 cm (16⅛ × 10⅞ in.), squared.
Fogg Museum, Cambridge, Massachusetts

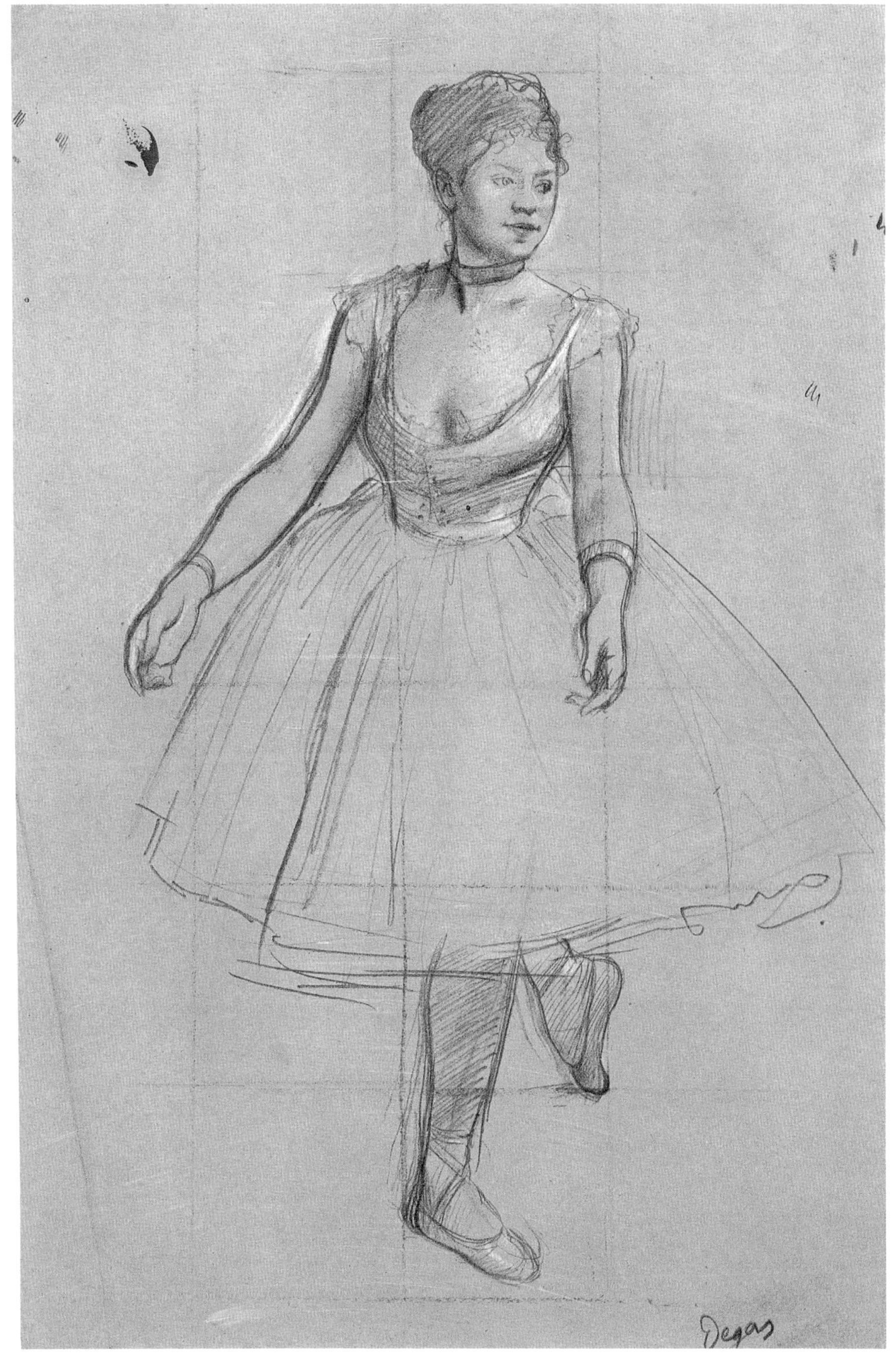
Degas

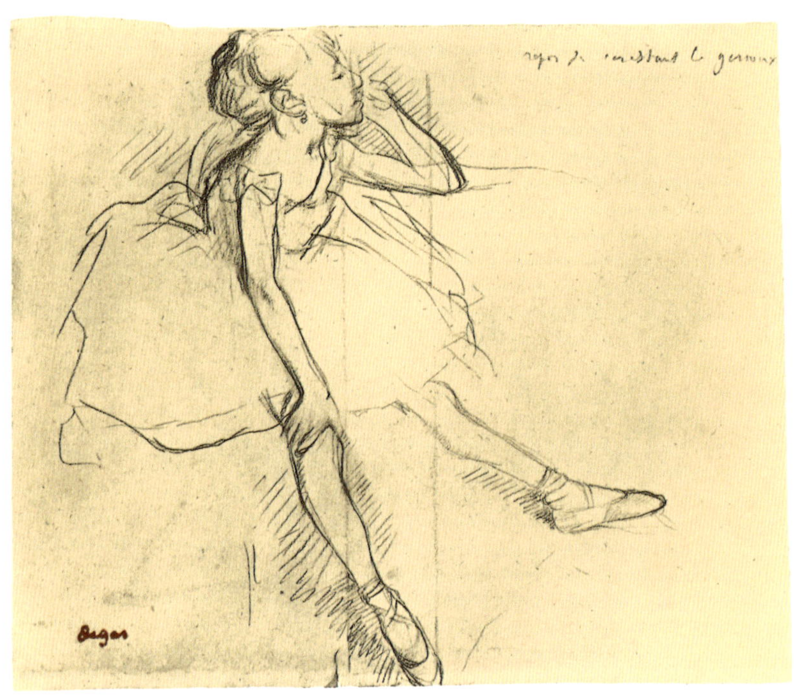

102. *Young Girl in Repose, c. 1878–80.*
Charcoal, 24.8 × 29.5 cm (9¼ × 11⅛ in.).
Minneapolis Institute of Arts

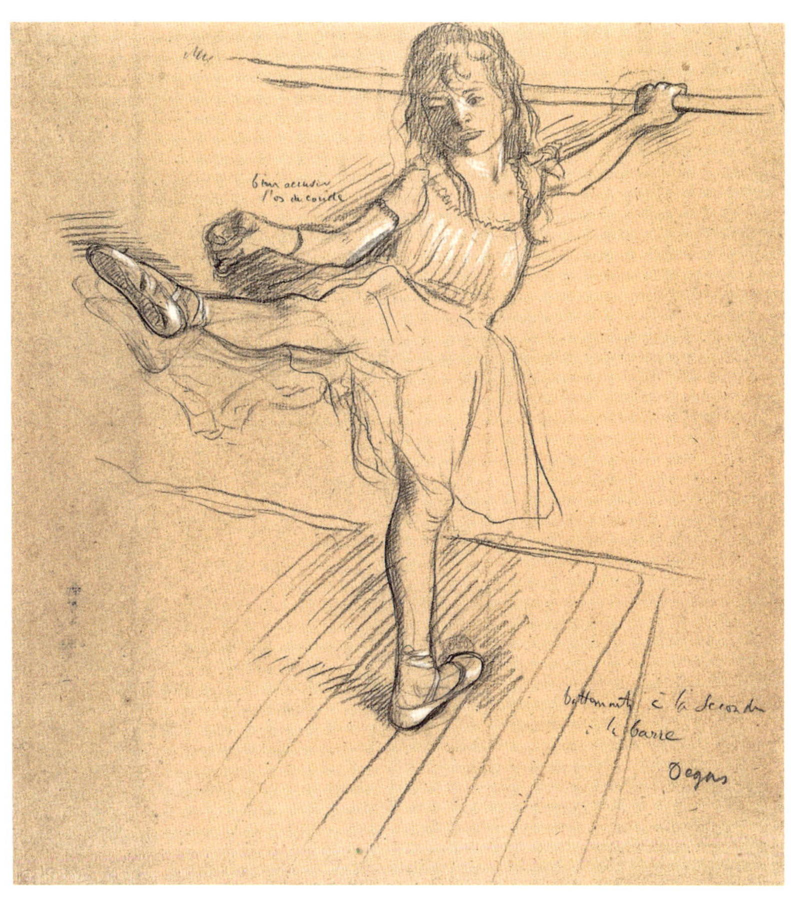

103. *Young Girl Practicing at the Bar*, c. 1878–80.
Charcoal heightened with white chalk, 31.1 × 29.2 cm (12⅛ × 11½ in.).
Metropolitan Museum of Art, New York

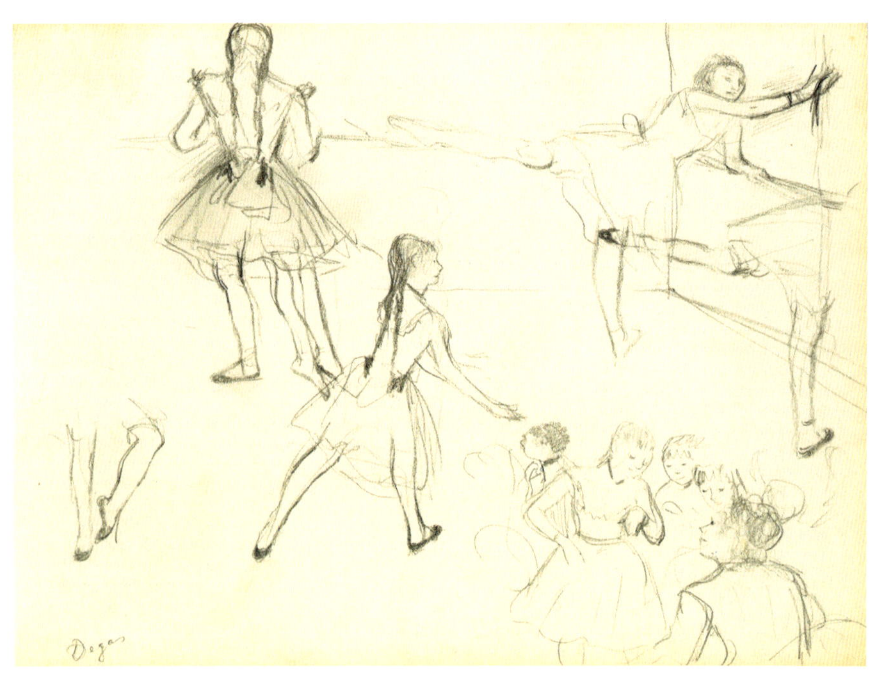

104. *Ballet Dancers Rehearsing*, Notebook 28, p. 25, *c.* 1877.
Pencil, 25 × 34 cm (9⅞ × 13⅜ in.).
J. Paul Getty Museum, Los Angeles

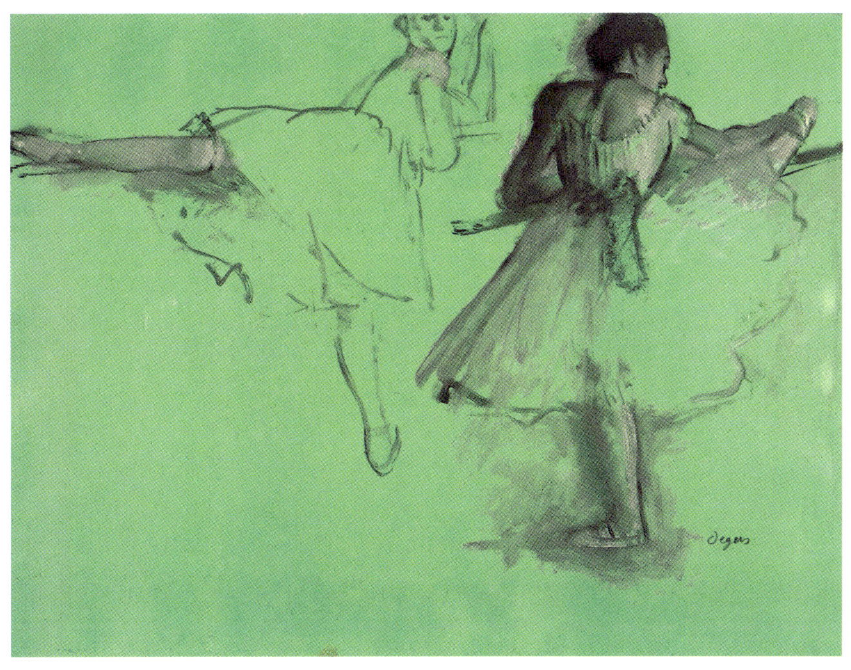

105. *Study for 'Two Dancers at the Bar'*, c. 1876–77.
Essence with sepia ink heightened with bodycolour on green paper,
47.4 × 62.7 cm (18⅞ × 24⅝ in.).
British Museum, London

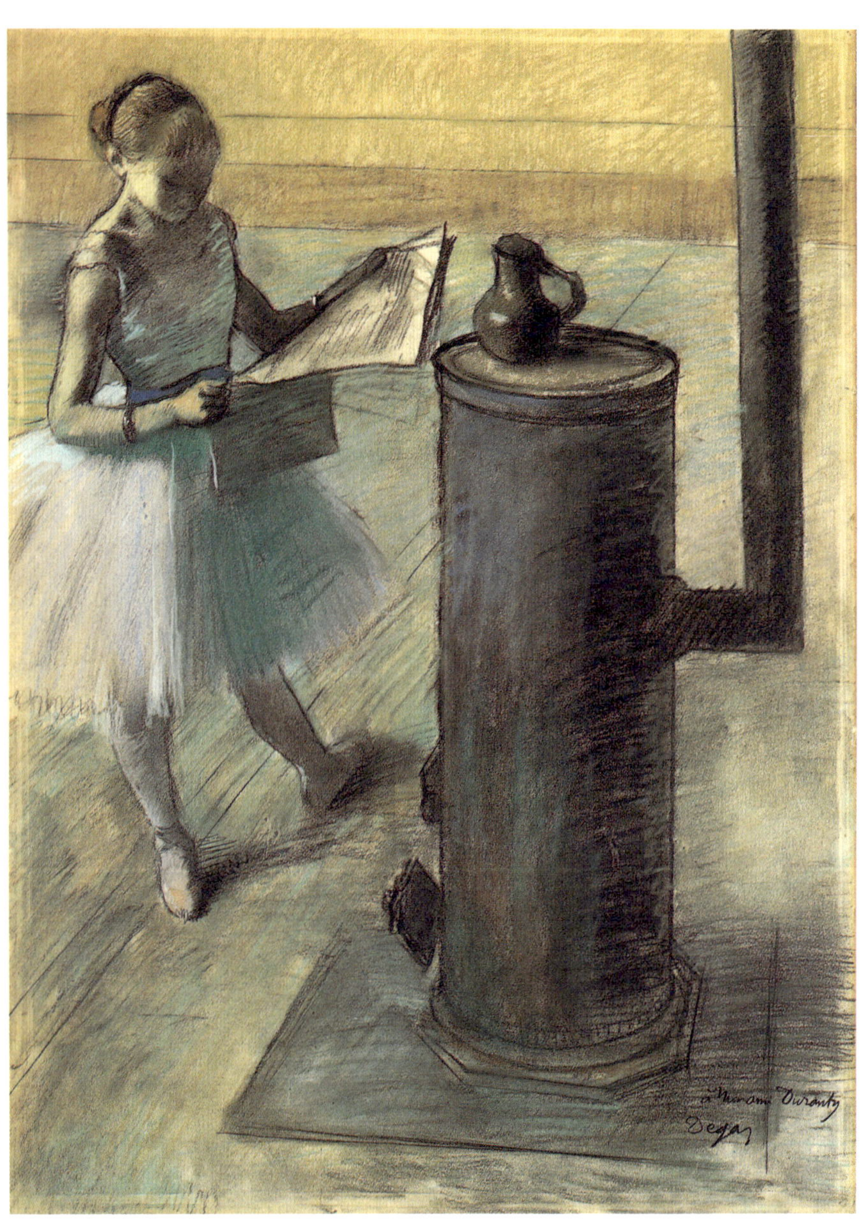

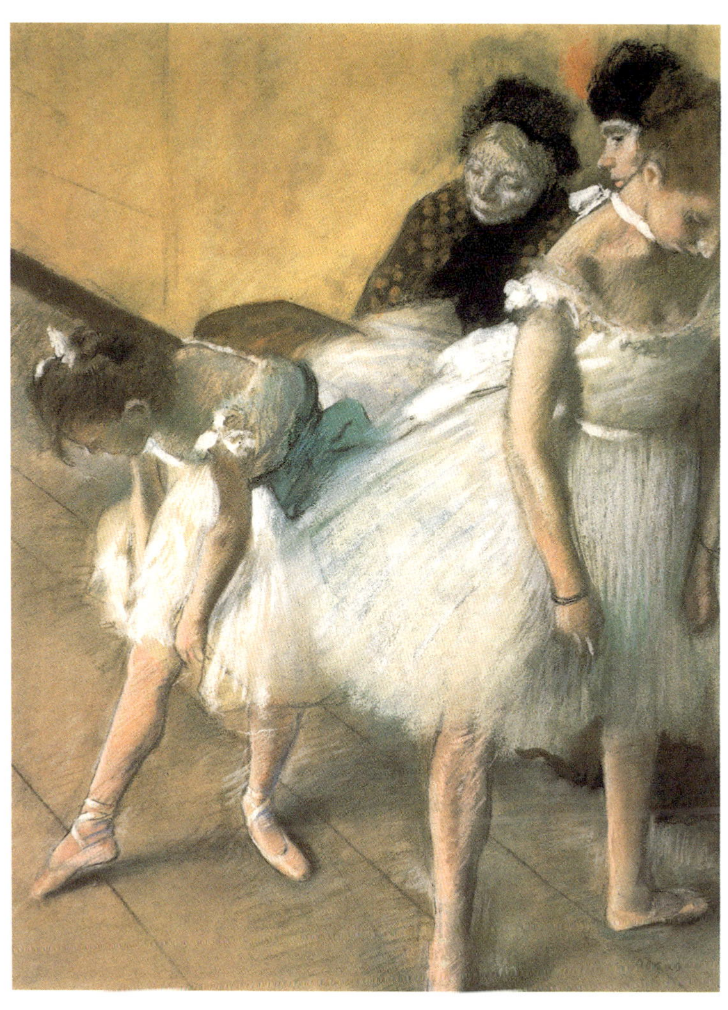

OPPOSITE
106. *Dancer Taking a Rest*, c. 1879.
Pastel and black chalk mounted on board,
76.5 × 55.5 cm (30¼ × 21⅞ in.).
Private collection

ABOVE
107. *The Dance Examination*, c. 1879.
Pastel and charcoal, 63.4 × 48.2 cm (25 × 19 in.).
Denver Art Museum

108. *Dancer Seen against the Light*, c. 1878–80.
Charcoal heightened with white chalk and bodycolour on
grey paper, 48.8 × 30.6 cm (19¼ × 12 in.).
Staatliche Kunsthalle, Karlsruhe

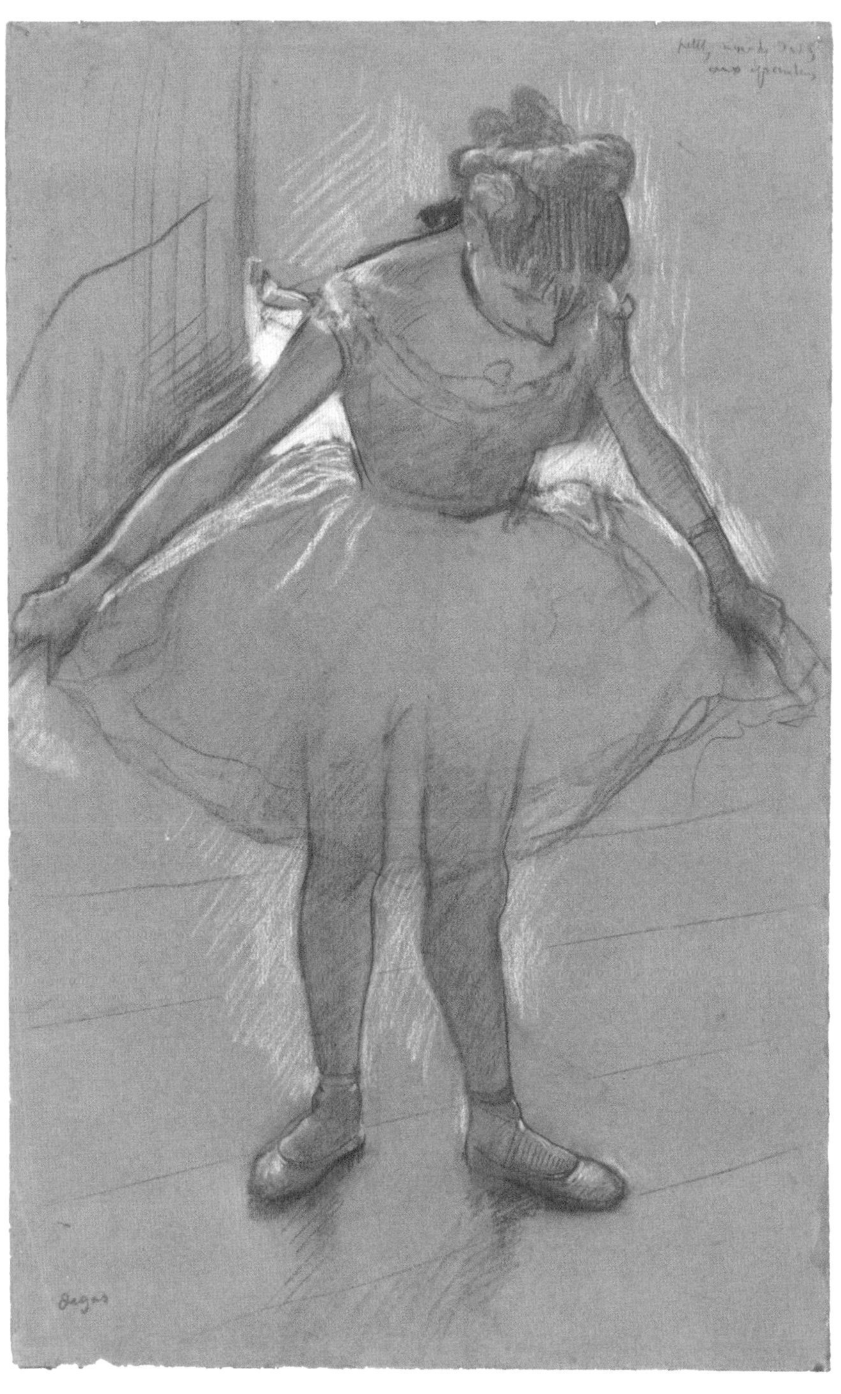

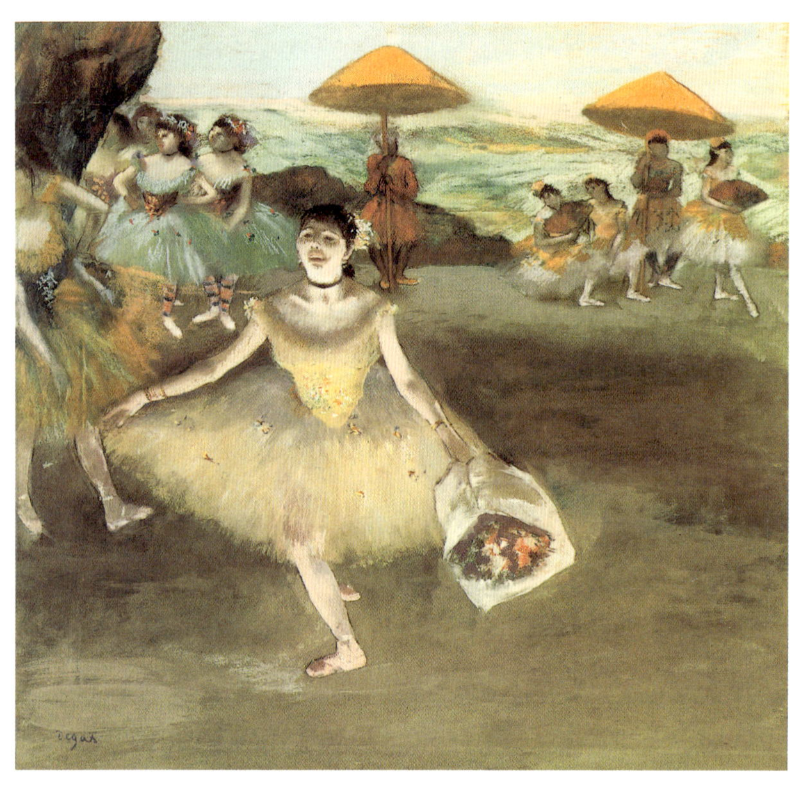

109. *Dancer with a Bouquet, Bowing*, 1877.
Pastel, 72 × 77.5 cm (28⅛ × 30½ in.).
Musée d'Orsay, Paris

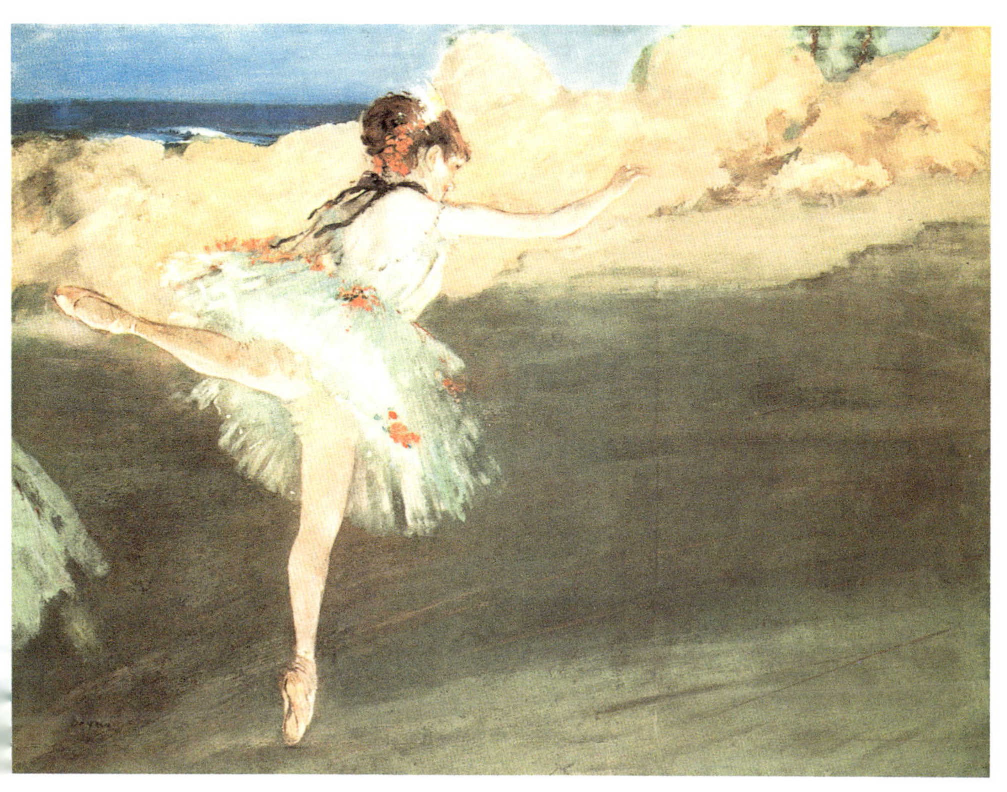

110. *The Star, Dancer on Pointe, c. 1878–80.*
Pastel and gouache, 56.5 × 75.6 cm (22¼ × 29¾ in.).
Norton Simon Art Foundation, Pasadena

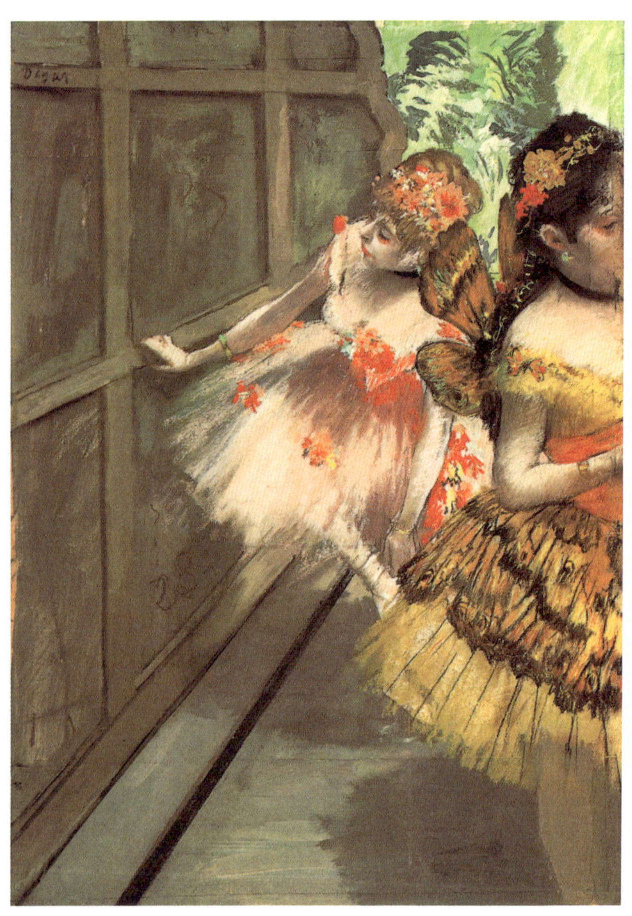

ABOVE

111. *Dancers in the Wings*, *c.* 1876–78.
Pastel gouache, tempera and essence on paper mounted on board,
69.2 × 50.2 cm (27¼ × 19¾ in.).
Norton Simon Art Foundation, Pasadena

OPPOSITE

112. *Dancers in Green*, *c.* 1880.
Pastel and gouache, 64 × 36 cm (25¼ × 14⅛ in.).
Thyssen-Bornemisza Museum, Madrid

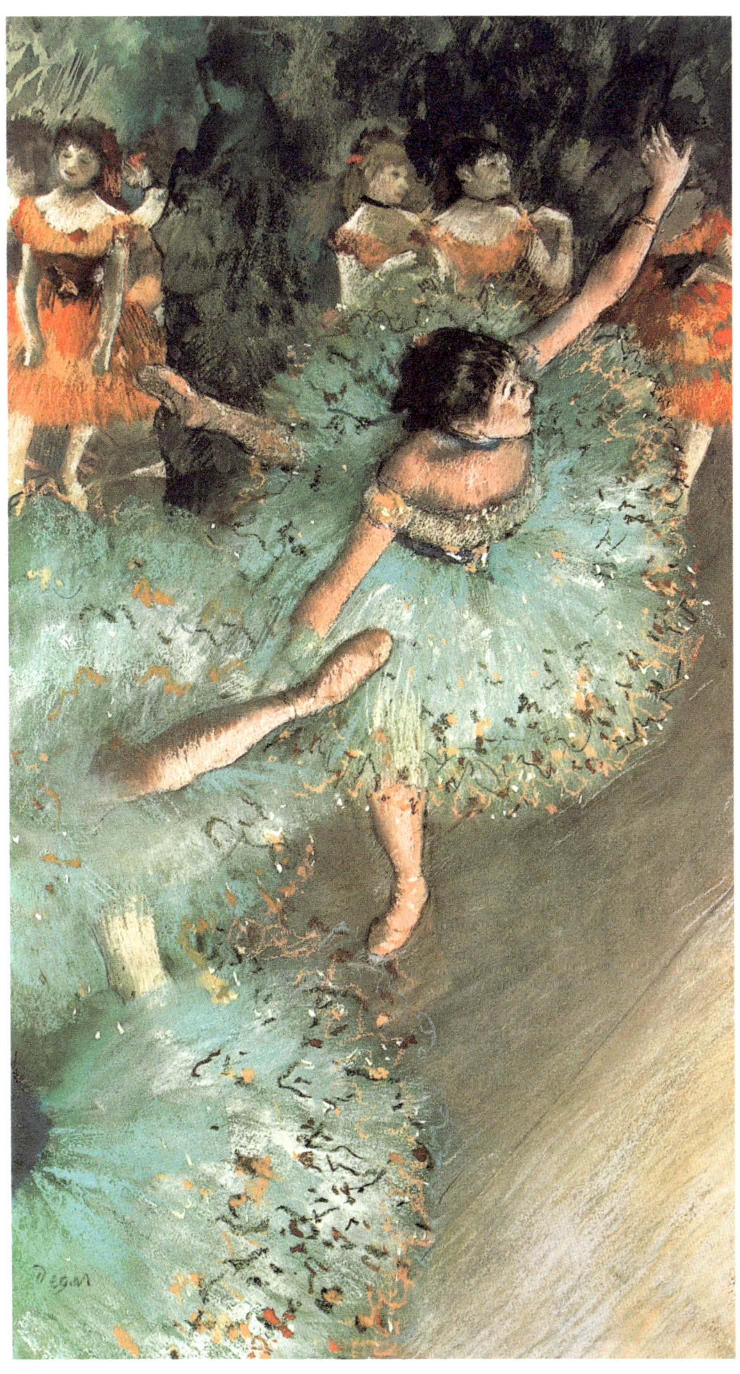

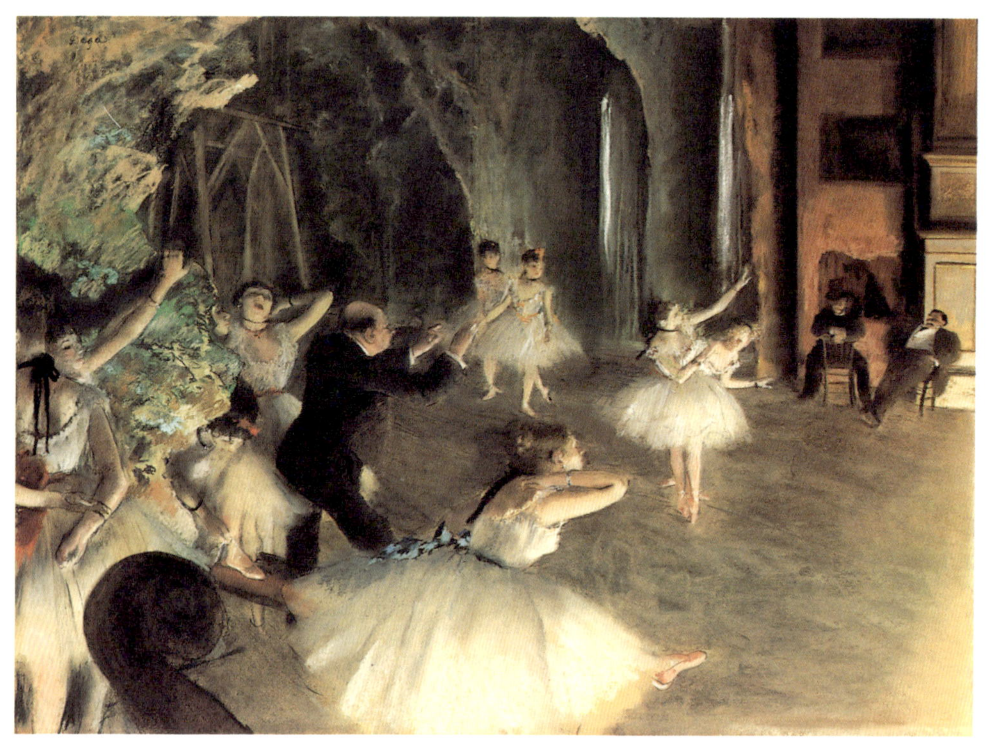

ABOVE
113. *Rehearsal on Stage*, *c.* 1874.
Pastel over brush and ink on paper laid down on board
and mounted on canvas, 53.3 × 72.3 cm (21 × 28½ in.).
Metropolitan Museum of Art, New York

OPPOSITE
114. *Dancer in her Dressing Room*, 1879.
Pastel on canvas, 87.9 × 37.7 cm (34⅝ × 14⅞ in.).
Cincinnati Art Museum

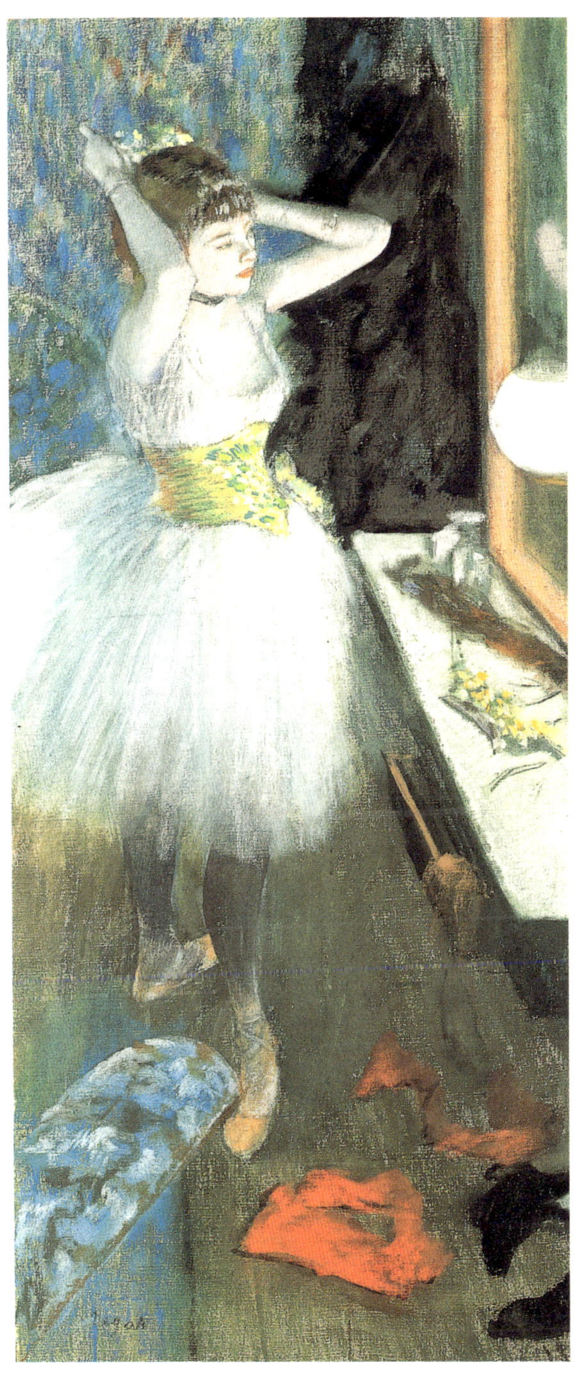

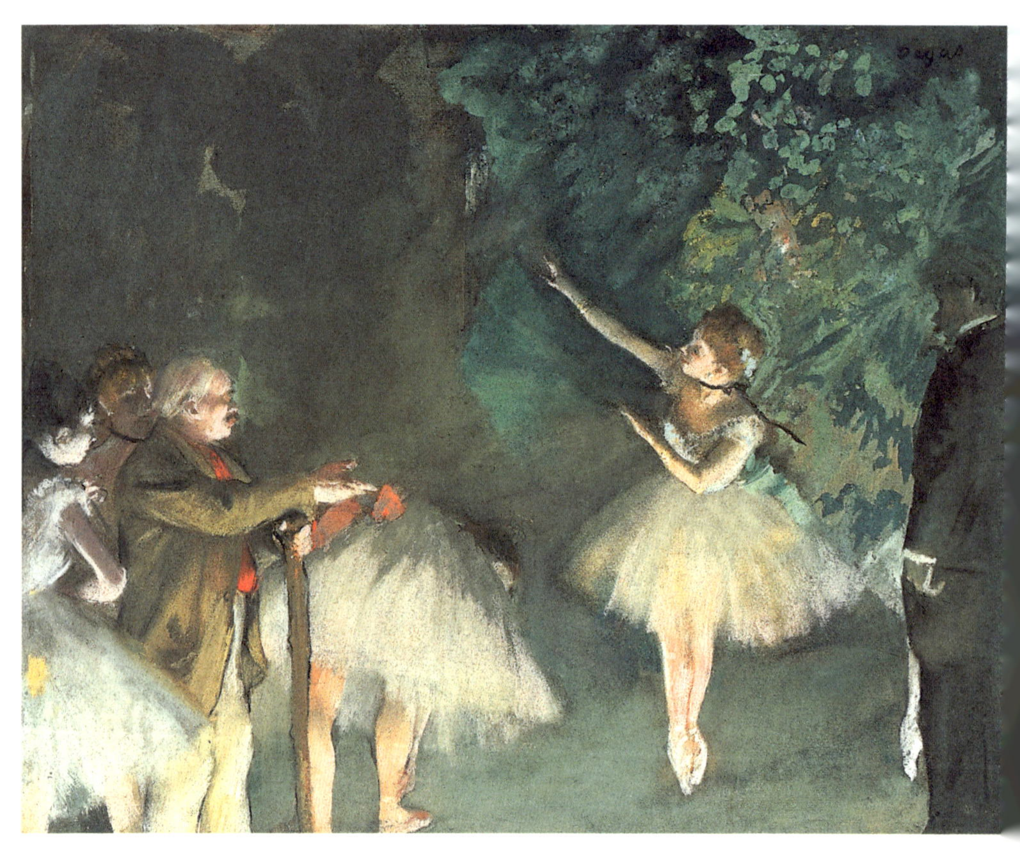

115. *Rehearsal of the Ballet, c.* 1876.
Pastel and gouache over monotype,
55 × 67.9 cm (21⅛ × 26¾ in.).
Nelson-Atkins Museum of Art, Kansas City

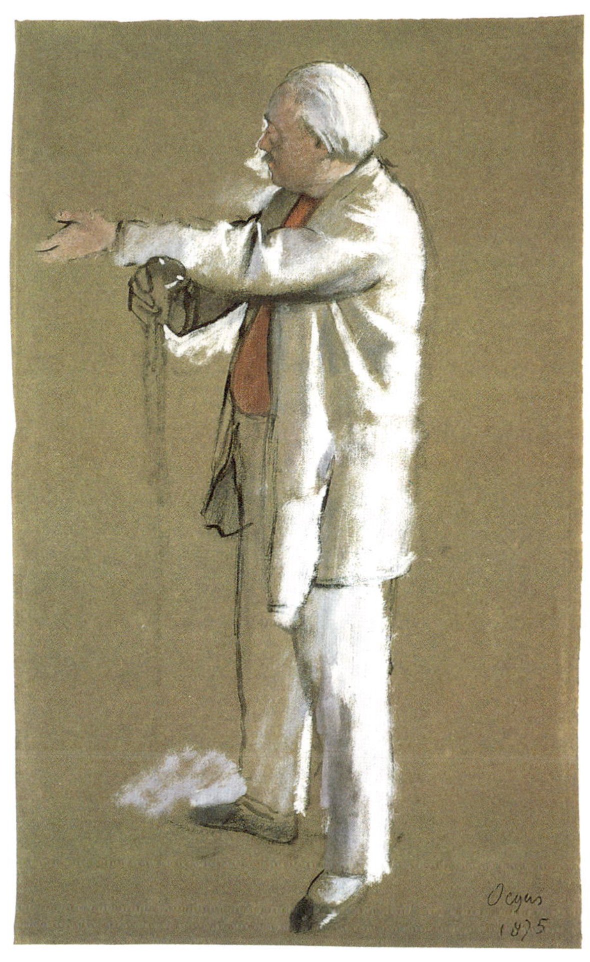

116. *Jules Perrot*, 1875.
Essence on brown paper, 48 × 30 cm (18⅞ × 11¼ in.).
Philadelphia Museum of Art

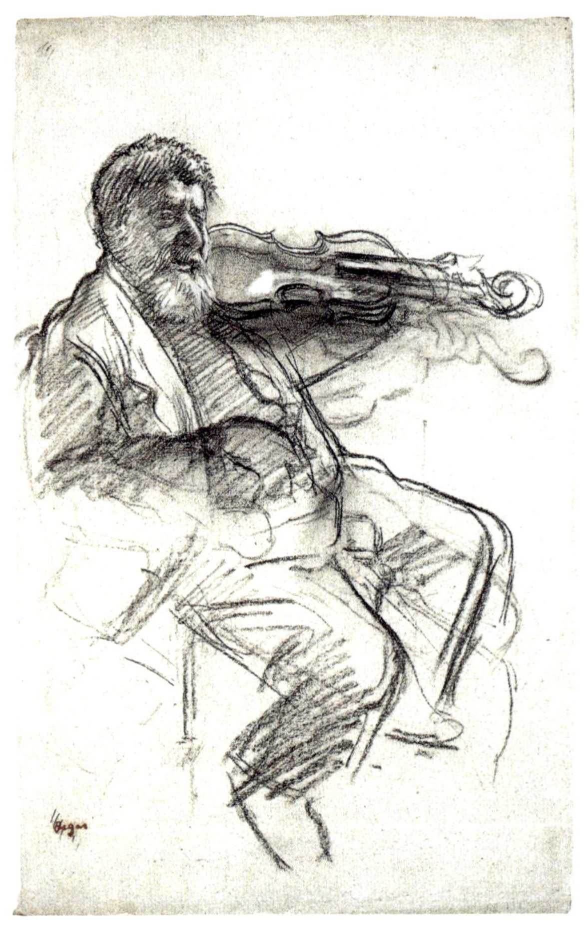

ABOVE
117. *Seated Violinist*, c. 1879.
Charcoal heightened with white chalk on grey-blue
paper, 47.9 × 30.5 cm (18⅞ × 12 in.).
Museum of Fine Arts, Boston

OPPOSITE
118. *Seated Violinist*, c. 1879.
Pastel and charcoal on green paper,
39.2 × 29.8 cm (15½ × 11¼ in.), squared.
Metropolitan Museum of Art, New York

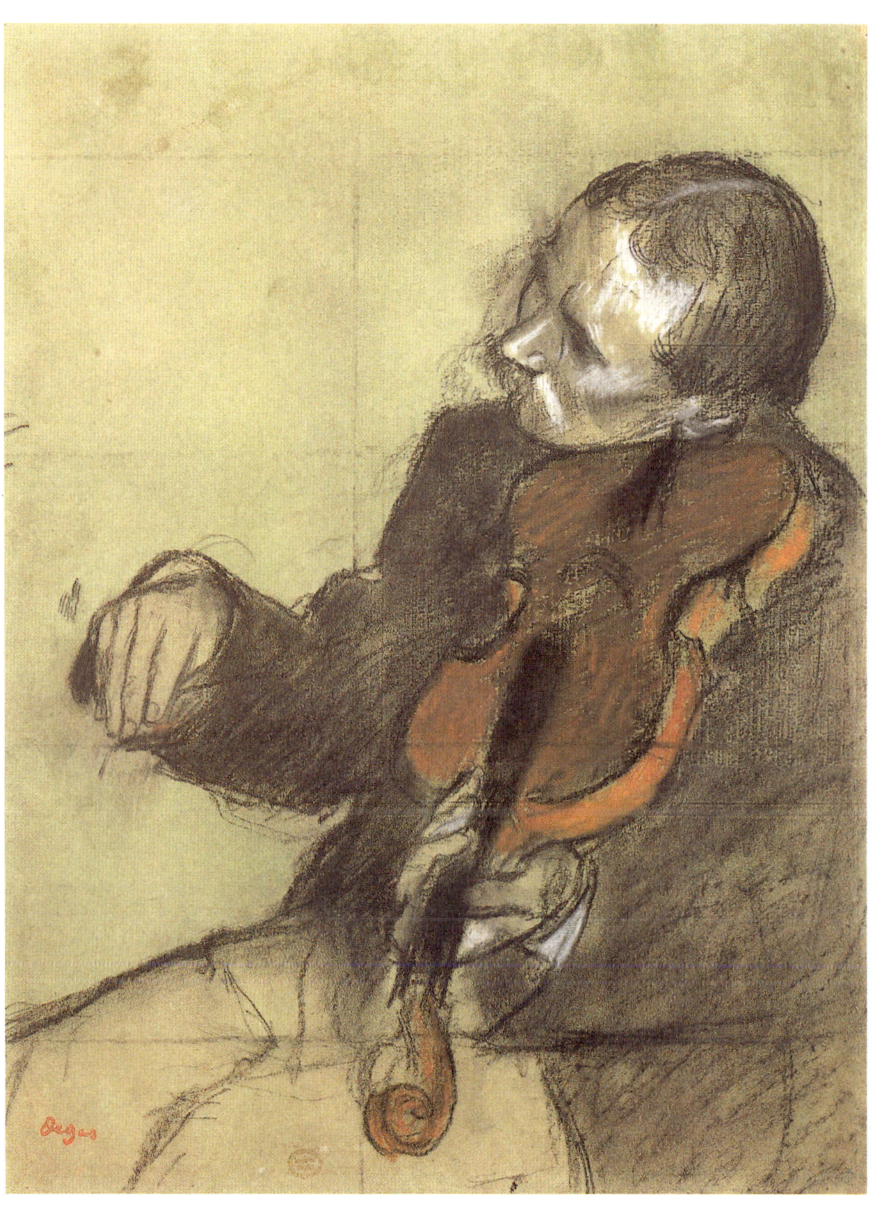

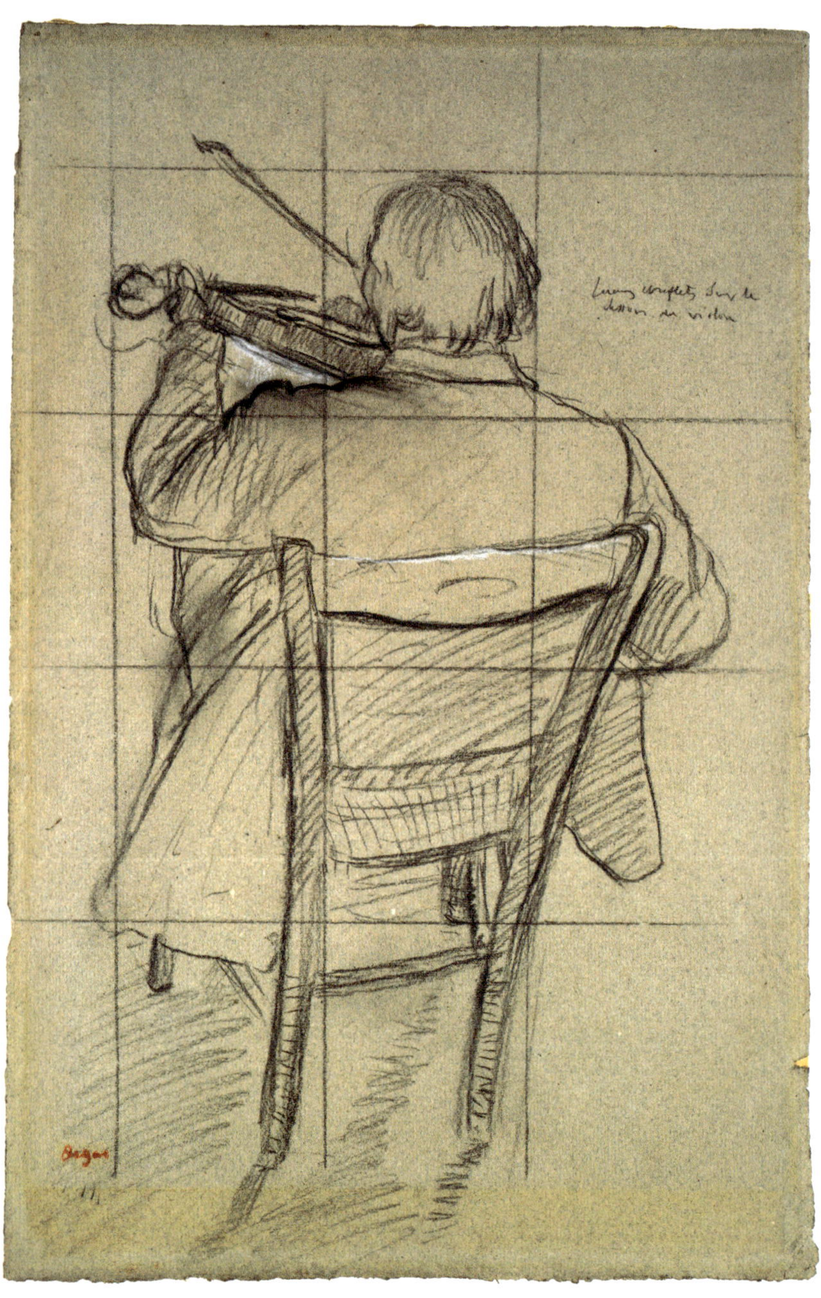

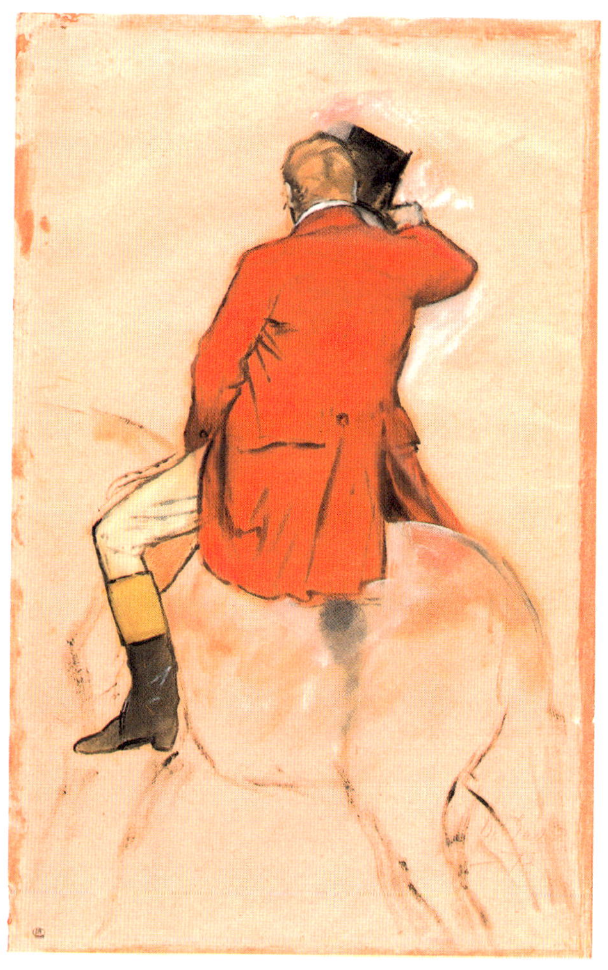

OPPOSITE
119. *Seated Violinist Seen from the Back*, c. 1879.
Charcoal heightened with white chalk,
48 × 31.5 cm (18⅞ × 12⅜ in.), squared.
Ashmolean Museum, Oxford

ABOVE
120. *Rider in Red Coat Seen from the Back*, 1873.
Essence and gouache on pink paper, 43.6 × 27.6 cm
(17⅛ × 10⅞ in.). Musée d'Orsay, Paris

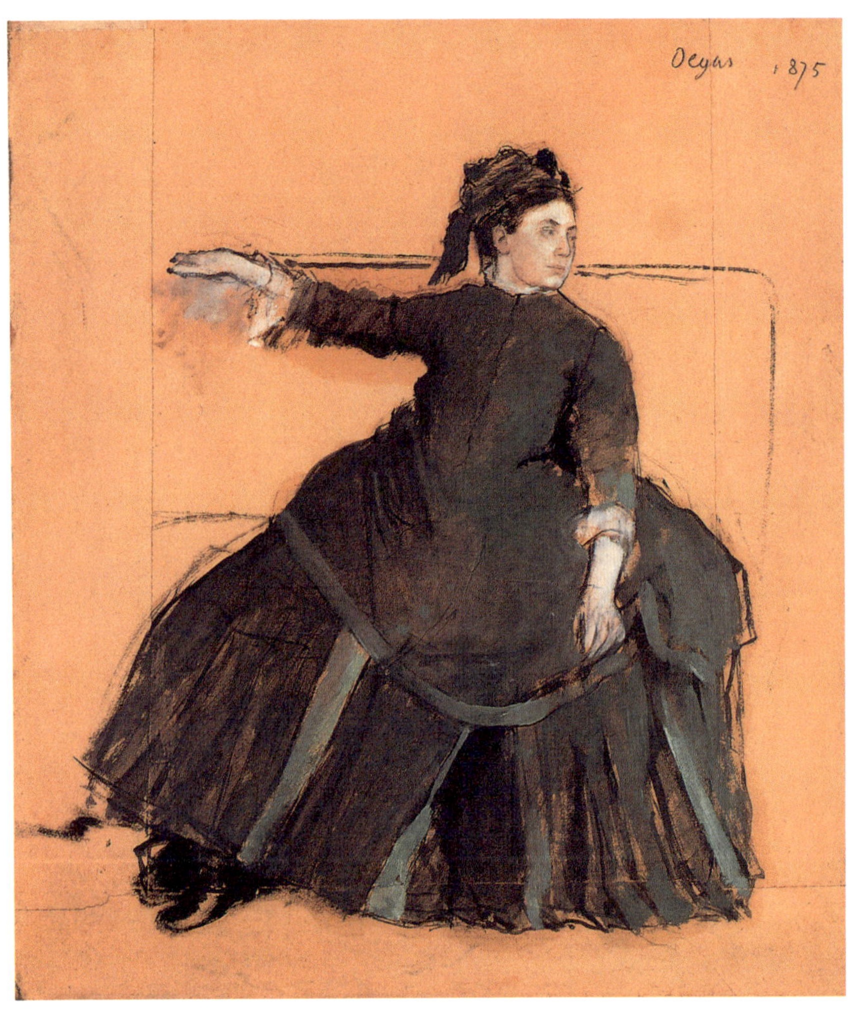

ABOVE
121. *Woman Seated on a Divan*, 1875.
Essence with sepia ink, oil and pastel over pencil
on pink paper, 48 × 42 cm (18⅞ × 16½ in.).
Metropolitan Museum of Art, New York

OPPOSITE
122. *Carlo Pellegrini*, c. 1876–77.
Oil on paper, 62.6 × 34.2 cm (24⅝ × 13½ in.).
National Gallery, London

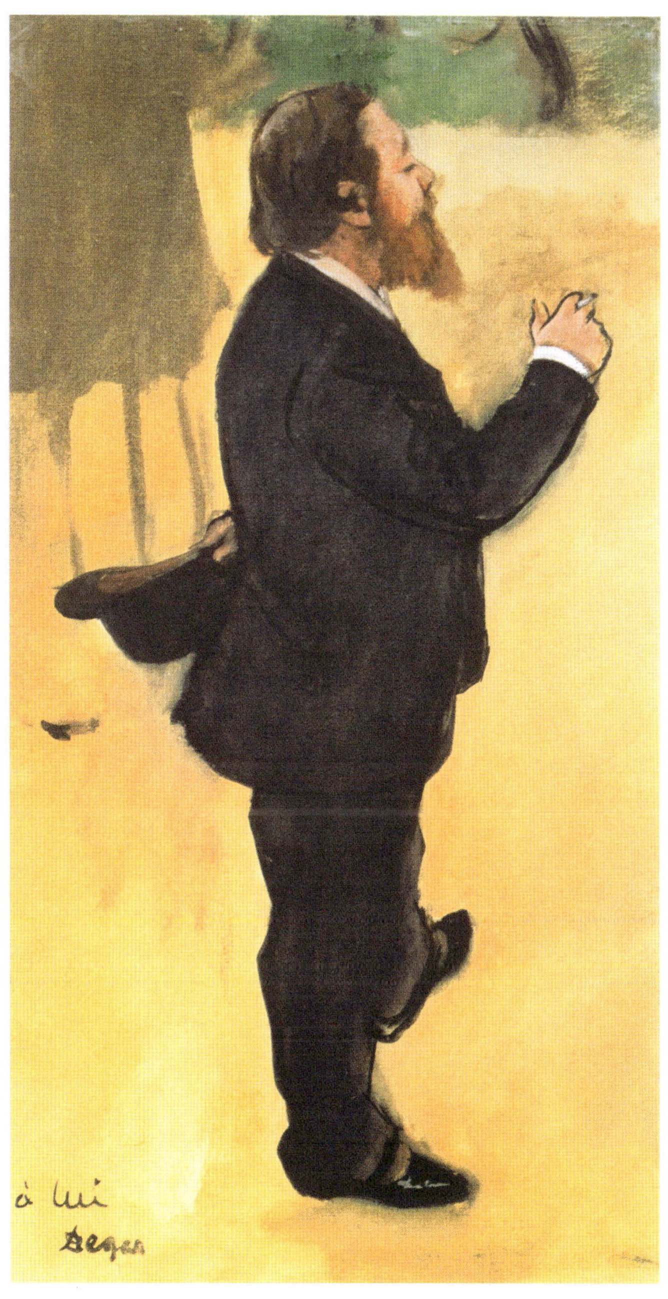

123. *Café-Concert des Ambassadeurs, c.* 1875–77.
Pastel over monotype, 37 × 27 cm (14½ × 10⅝ in.).
Musée des Beaux-Arts, Lyon

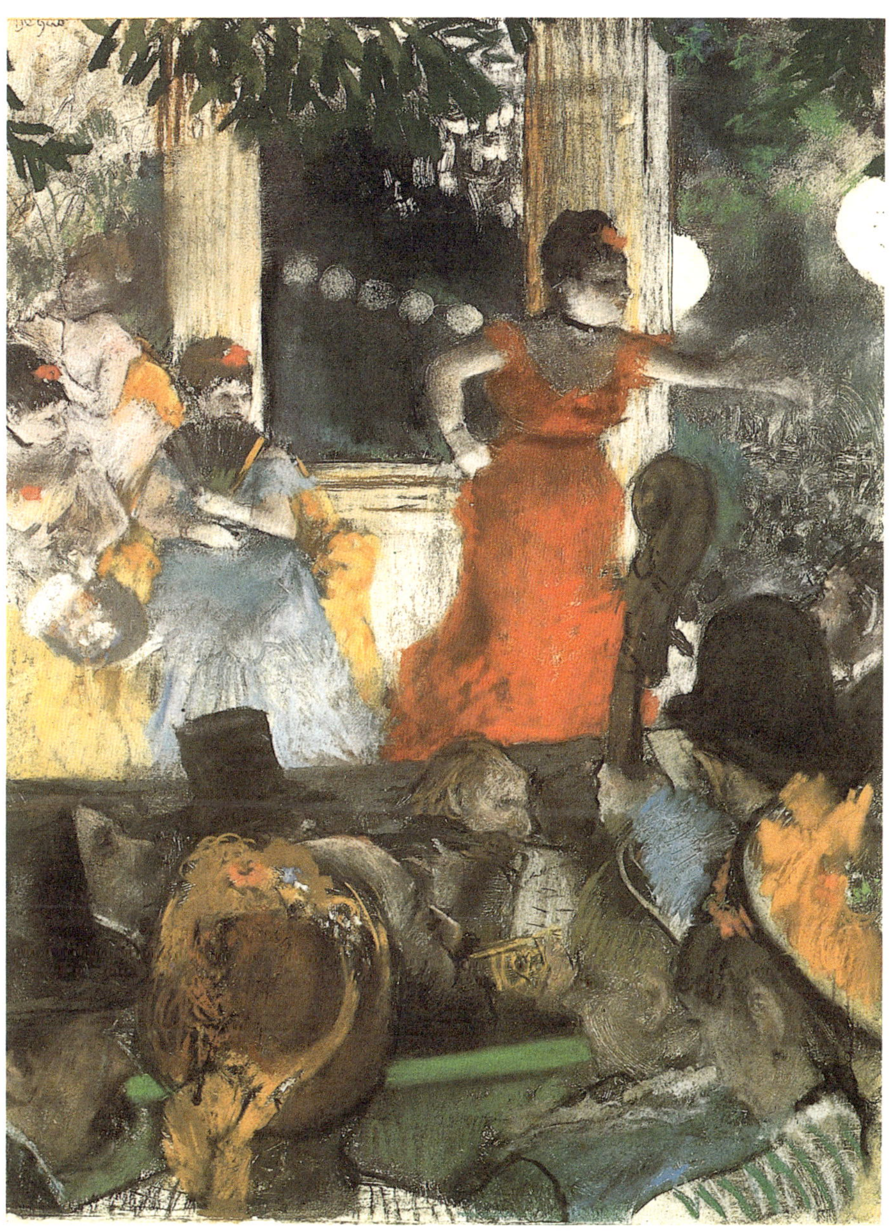

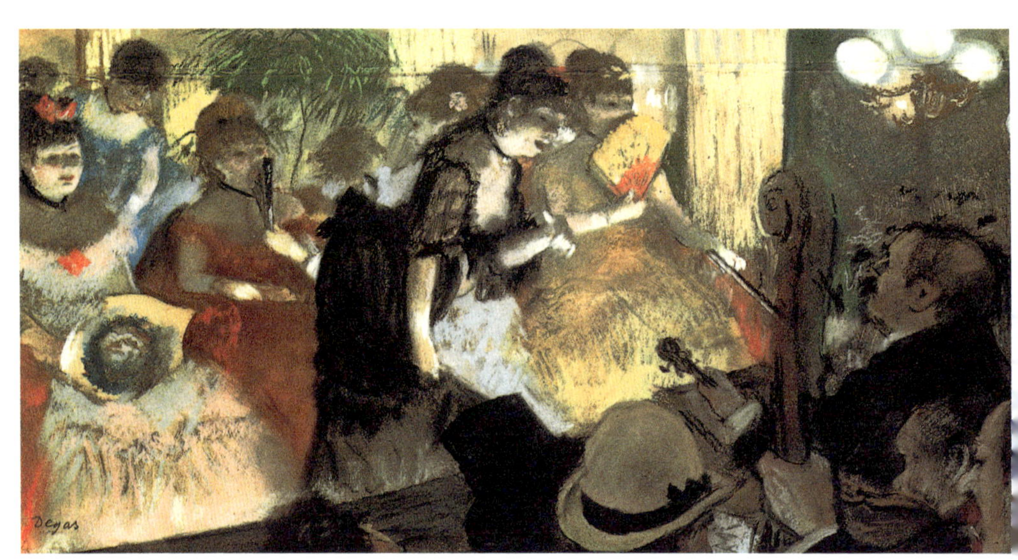

124. *Cabaret*, 1876.
Pastel over monotype, 24.2 × 44.5 cm (9½ × 17½ in.).
Corcoran Gallery of Art, Washington, DC

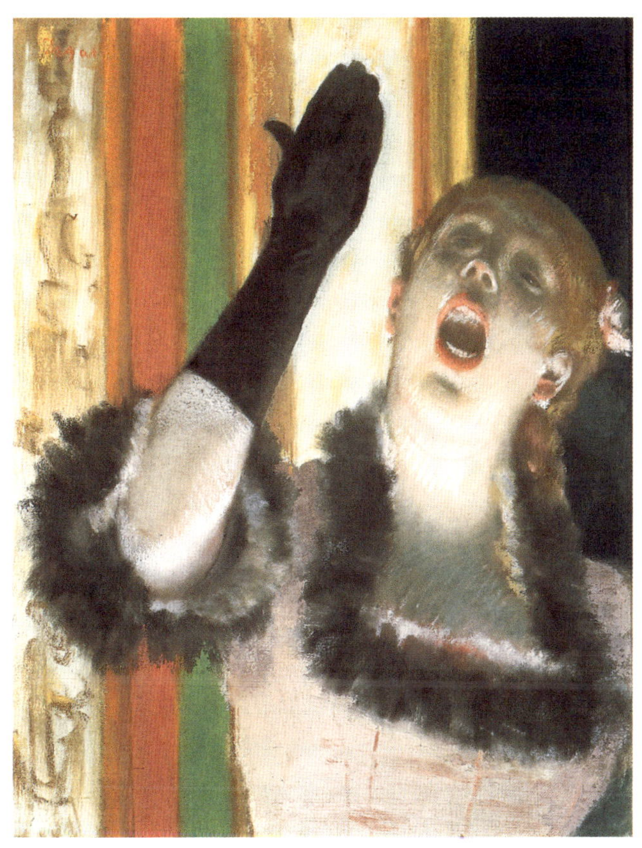

125. *Singer with a Glove*, 1878.
Pastel over monotype, 53.2 × 41 cm (20⅞ × 16⅛ in.).
Fogg Museum, Cambridge, Massachusetts

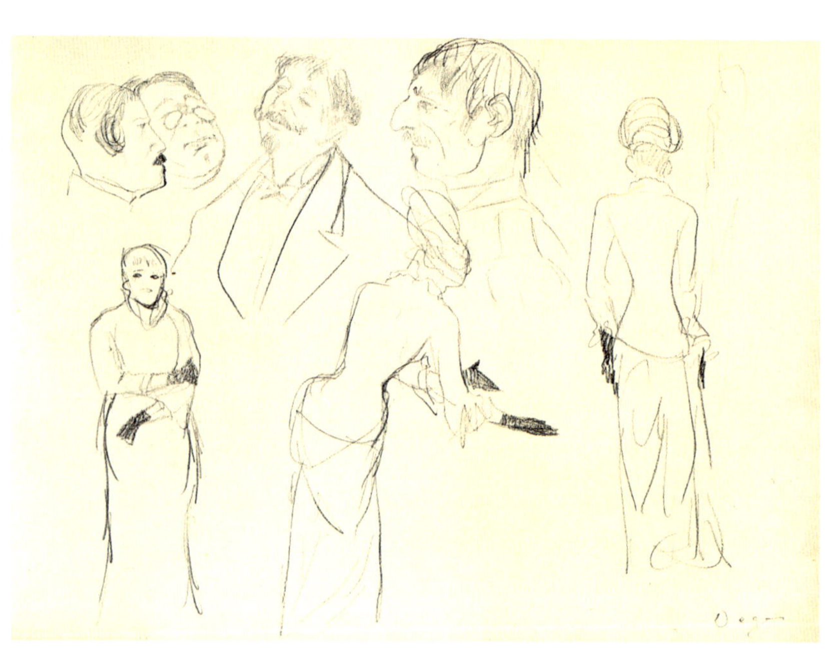

ABOVE
126. *Seven Rapid Sketches*,
Notebook 29, p. 5, *c.* 1878.
Pencil, 25.1 × 43.5 cm (9⅞ × 17⅛ in.).
Pierpont Morgan Library, New York

OPPOSITE
127. *After the Bath*, *c.* 1876–77.
Pastel over monotype, 21 × 16 cm (8¼ × 6¼ in.).
Pierpont Morgan Library, New York

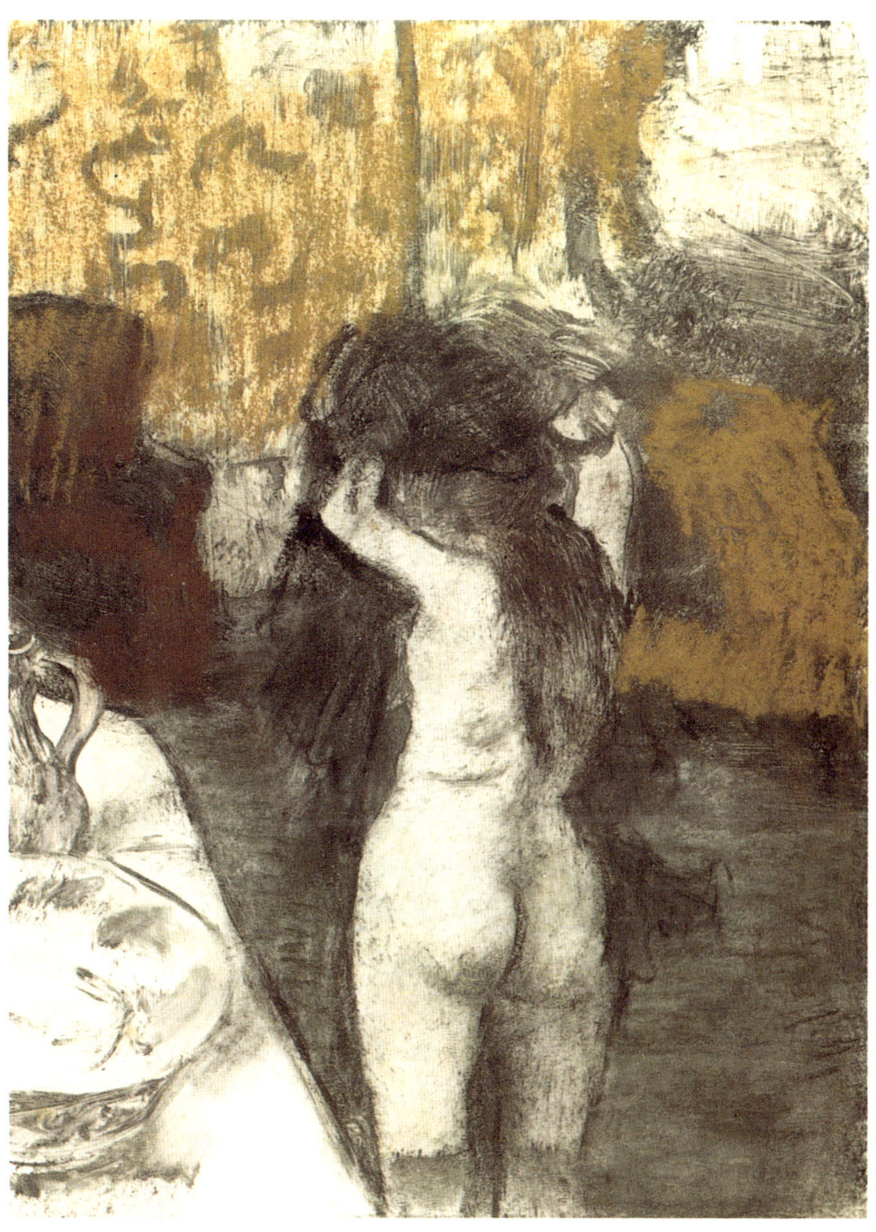

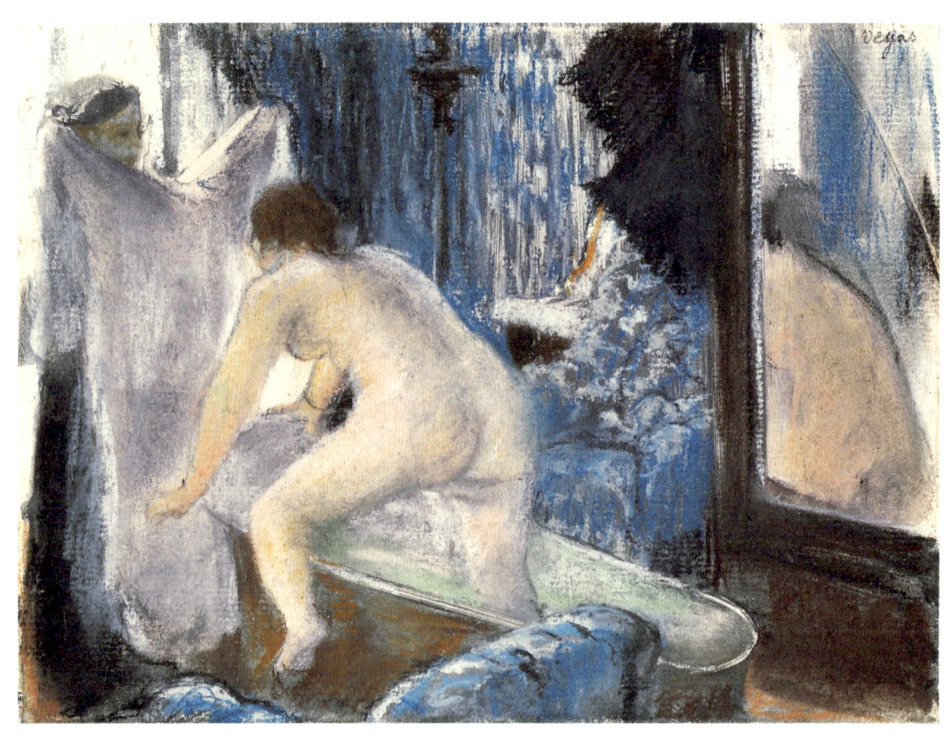

128. *Woman Getting out of her Bath*, *c.* 1876–77.
Pastel over monotype, 15.9 × 21.6 cm (6¼ × 8½ in.).
Norton Simon Art Foundation, Pasadena

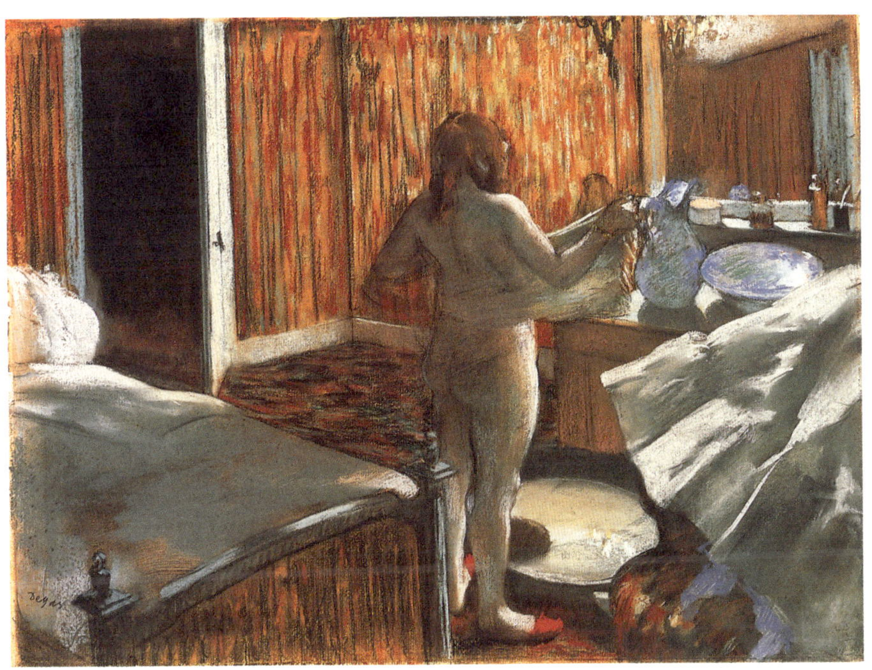

129. *Woman Drying Herself after the Bath*, 1876–77.
Pastel over monotype, 45.7 × 60.3 cm (18 × 23¾ in.).
Norton Simon Art Foundation, Pasadena

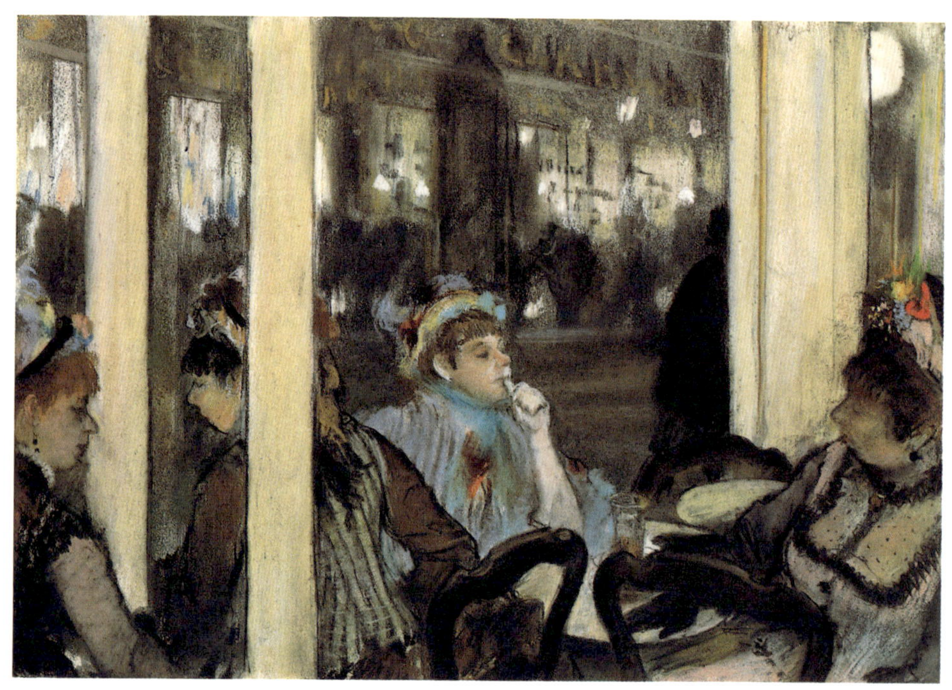

130. *Women on the Terrace of a Café, Evening,* 1877.
Pastel over monotype, 41 × 60 cm (16⅛ × 23⅝ in.).
Musée d'Orsay, Paris

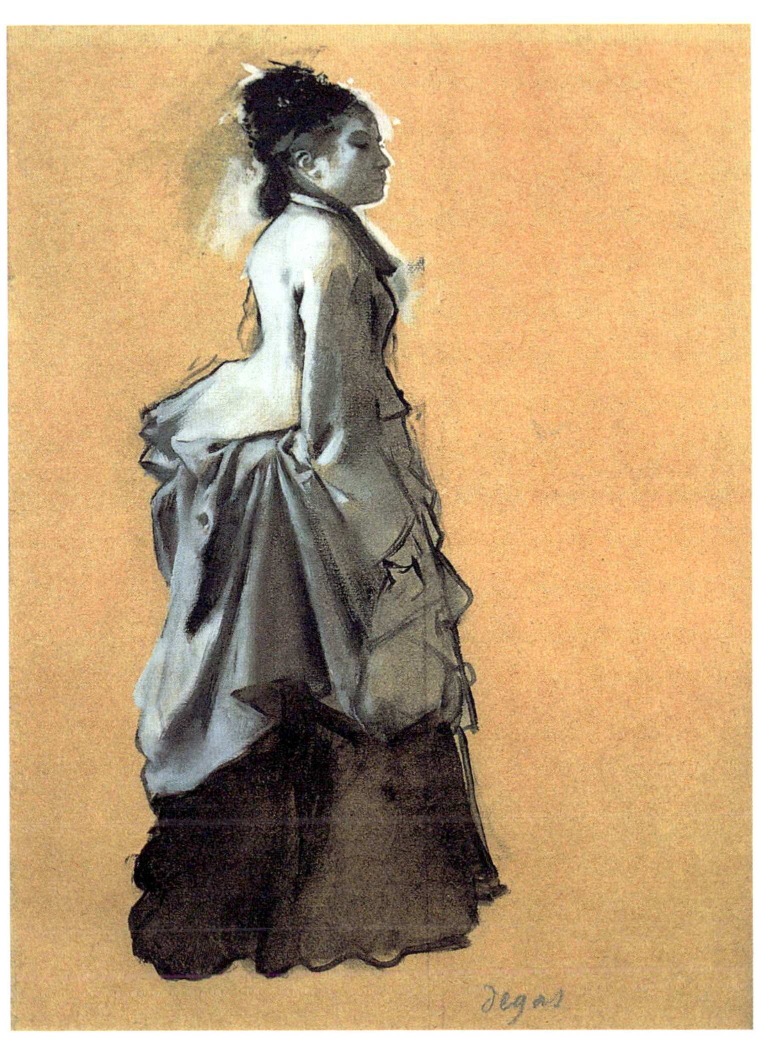

131. *Young Woman in a Day Dress*, c. 1879.
Essence with sepia ink and gouache on red-brown
paper, 32.5 × 25 cm (12¼ × 9⅞ in.).
Fogg Museum, Cambridge, Massachusetts

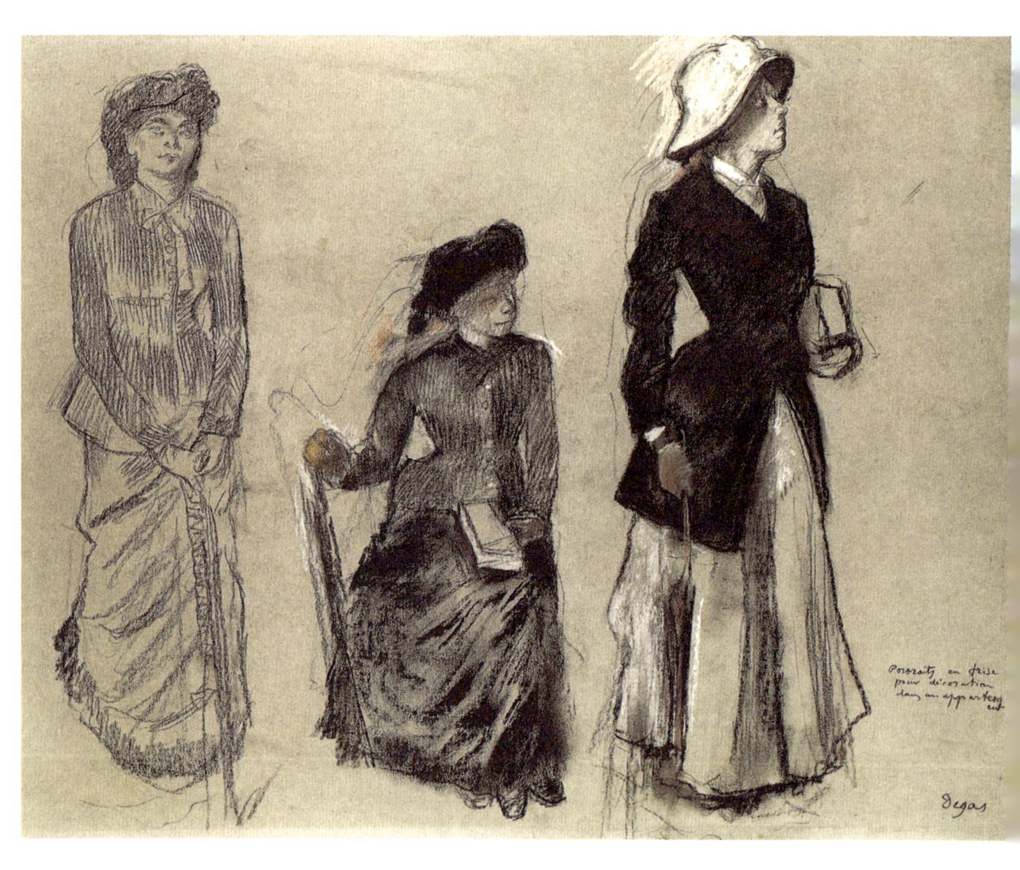

132. *Portraits in a Frieze*, *c.* 1879–80.
Pastel, charcoal and black chalk on grey
paper, 50 × 65 cm (19⅛ × 25⅝ in.).
Private collection

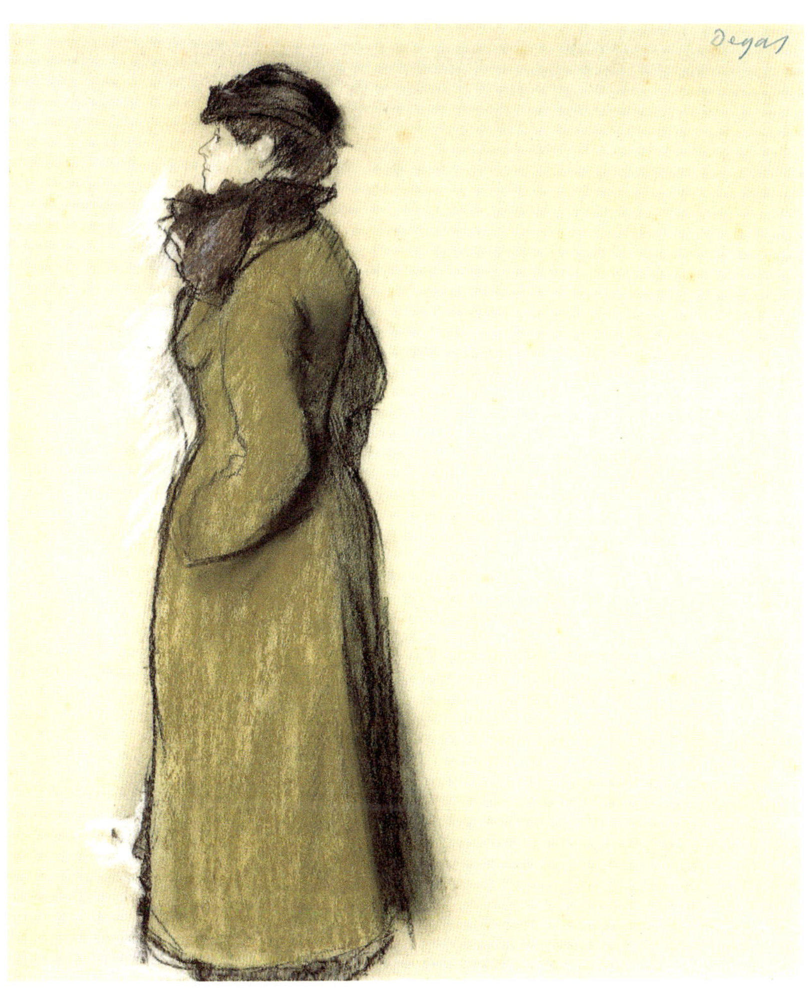

133. *Ellen André, c.* 1879.
Pastel on grey paper, 48 × 42 cm (18⅞ × 16½ in.).
Private collection

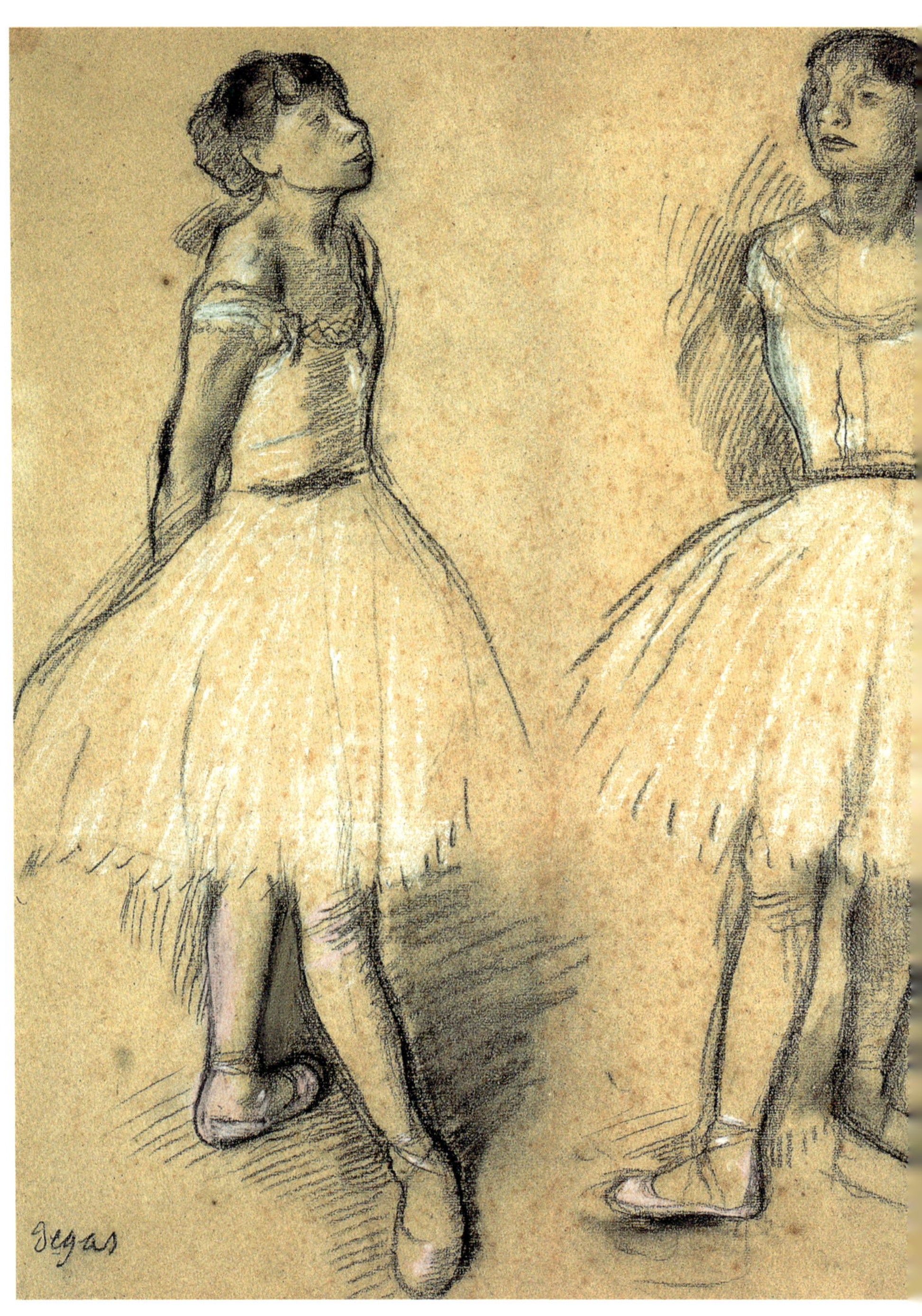

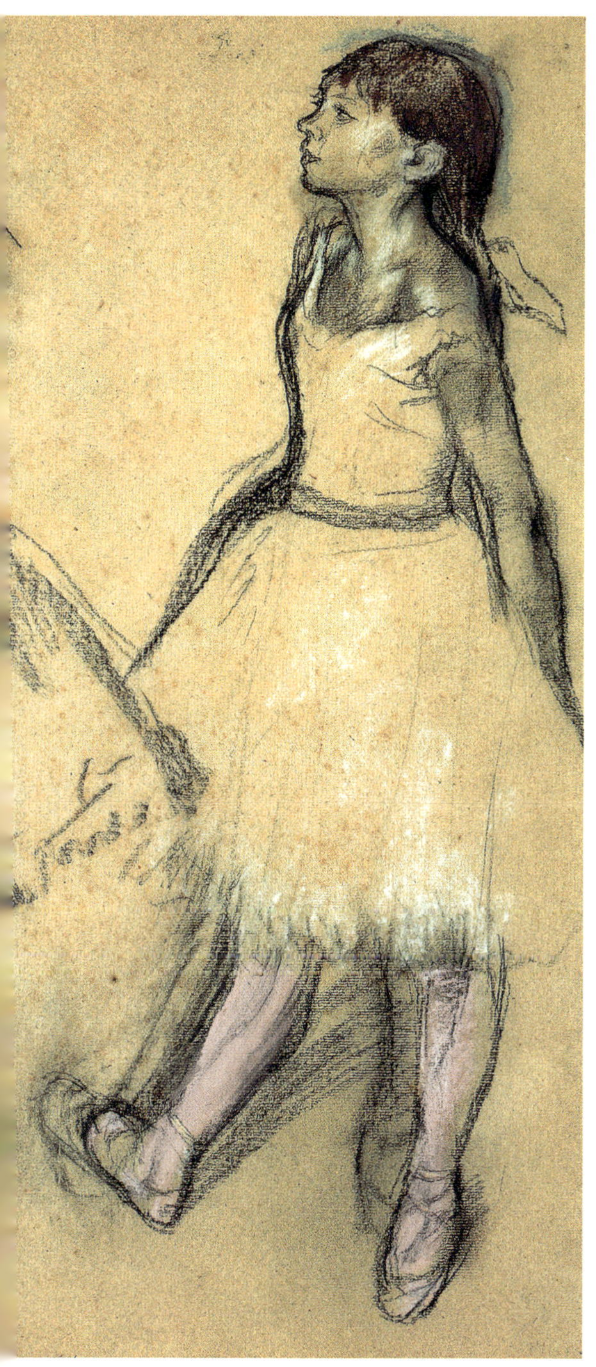

134. *Three Studies of a Dancer in Fourth Position, c.* 1878–81. Charcoal and pastel with stump and wash, 48 × 61.5 cm (18⅞ × 24¼ in.). The Art Institute of Chicago

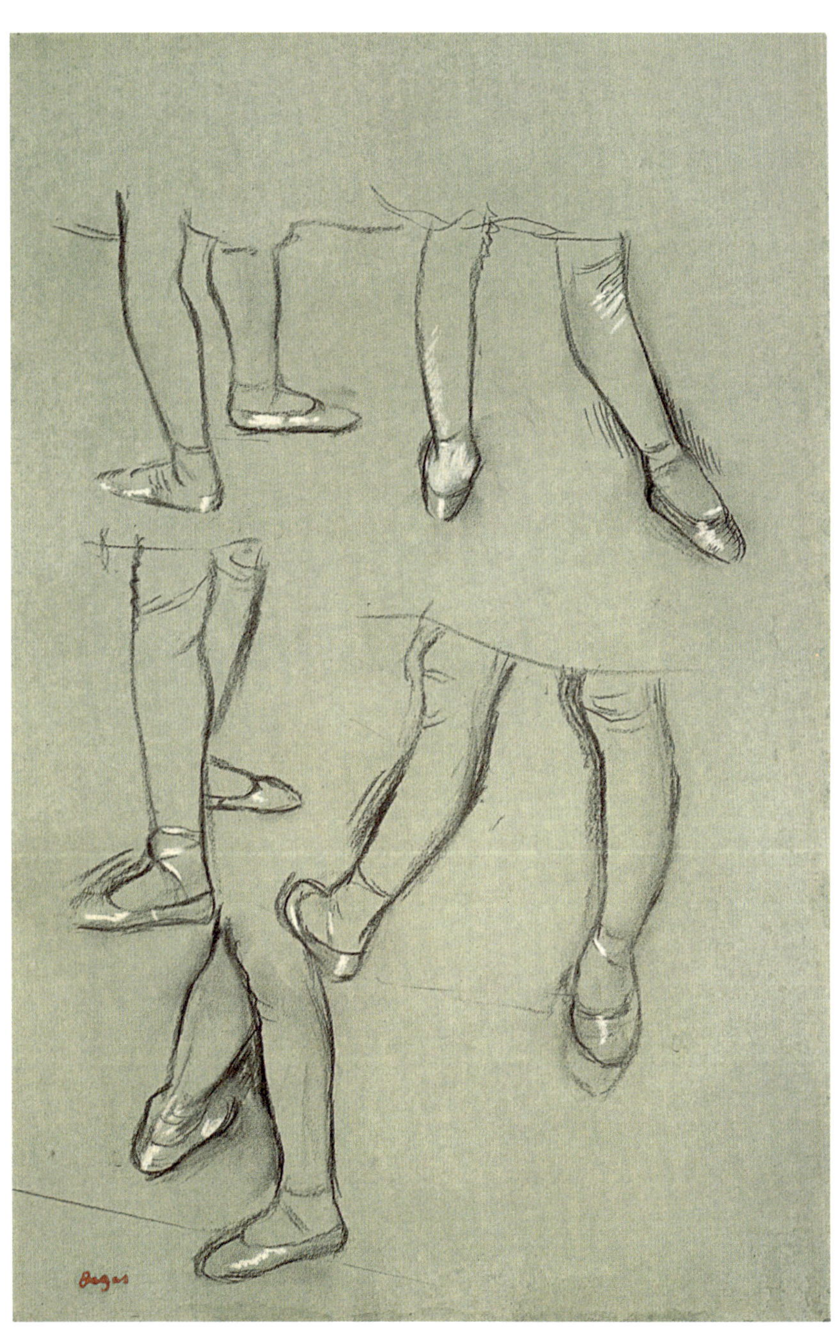

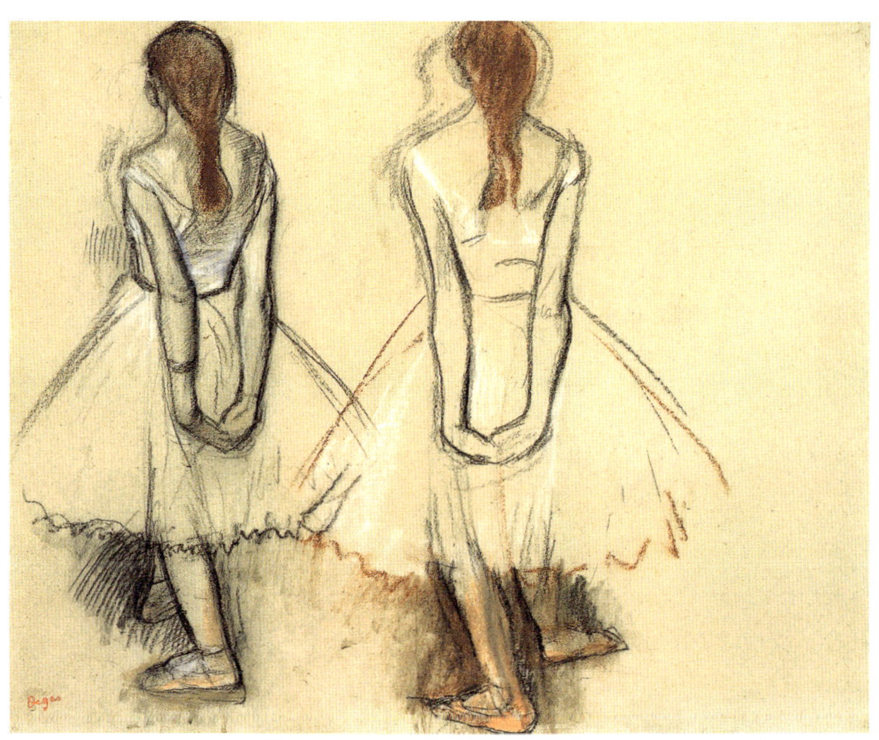

OPPOSITE
135. *Study of a Dancer's Feet*, c. 1878–81.
Pencil, charcoal and pastel on green paper, 48.2 × 30.5 cm
(19 × 12 in.). Private collection

ABOVE
136. *Two Studies of a Dancer*, c. 1878–81.
Charcoal, pastel and wash, 47.2 × 58.8 cm (18⅝ × 23⅛ in.).
Private collection

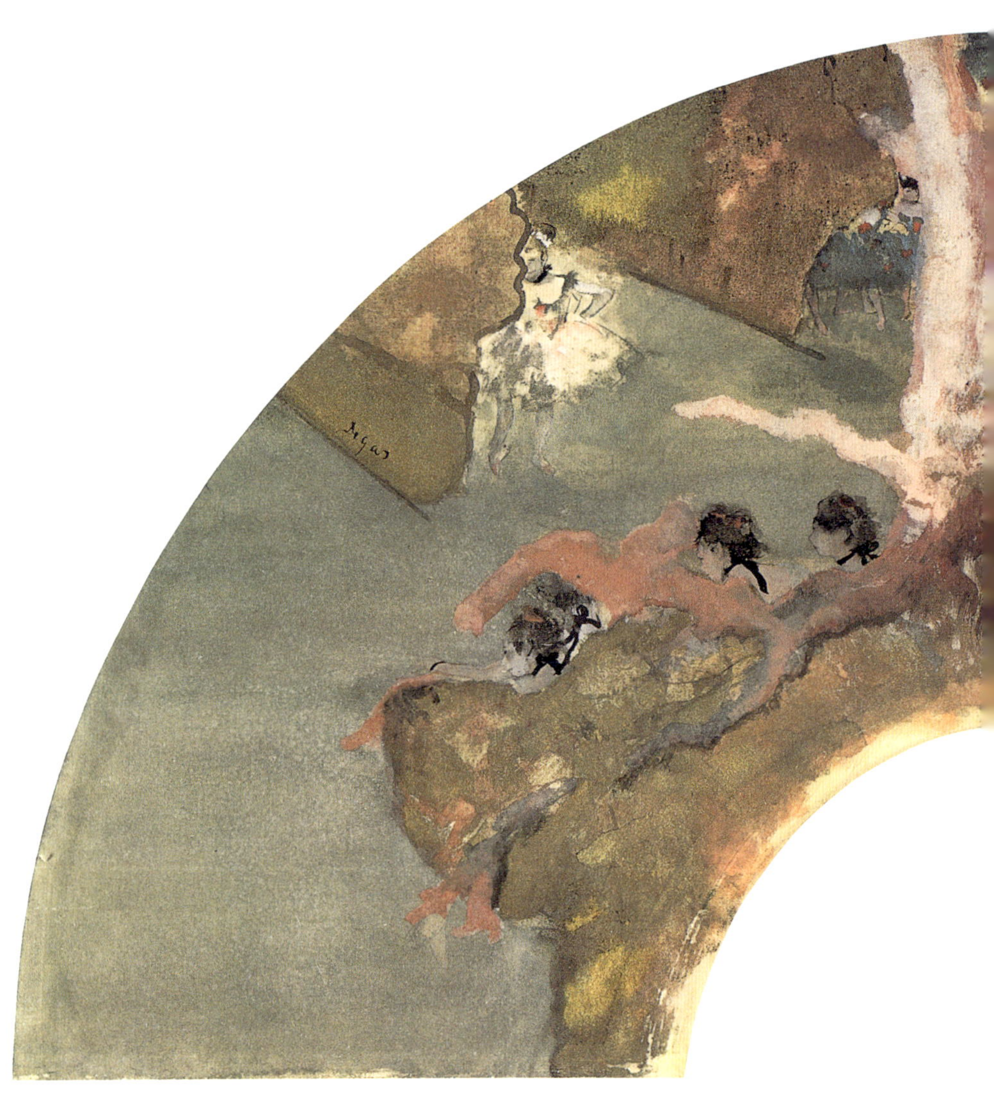

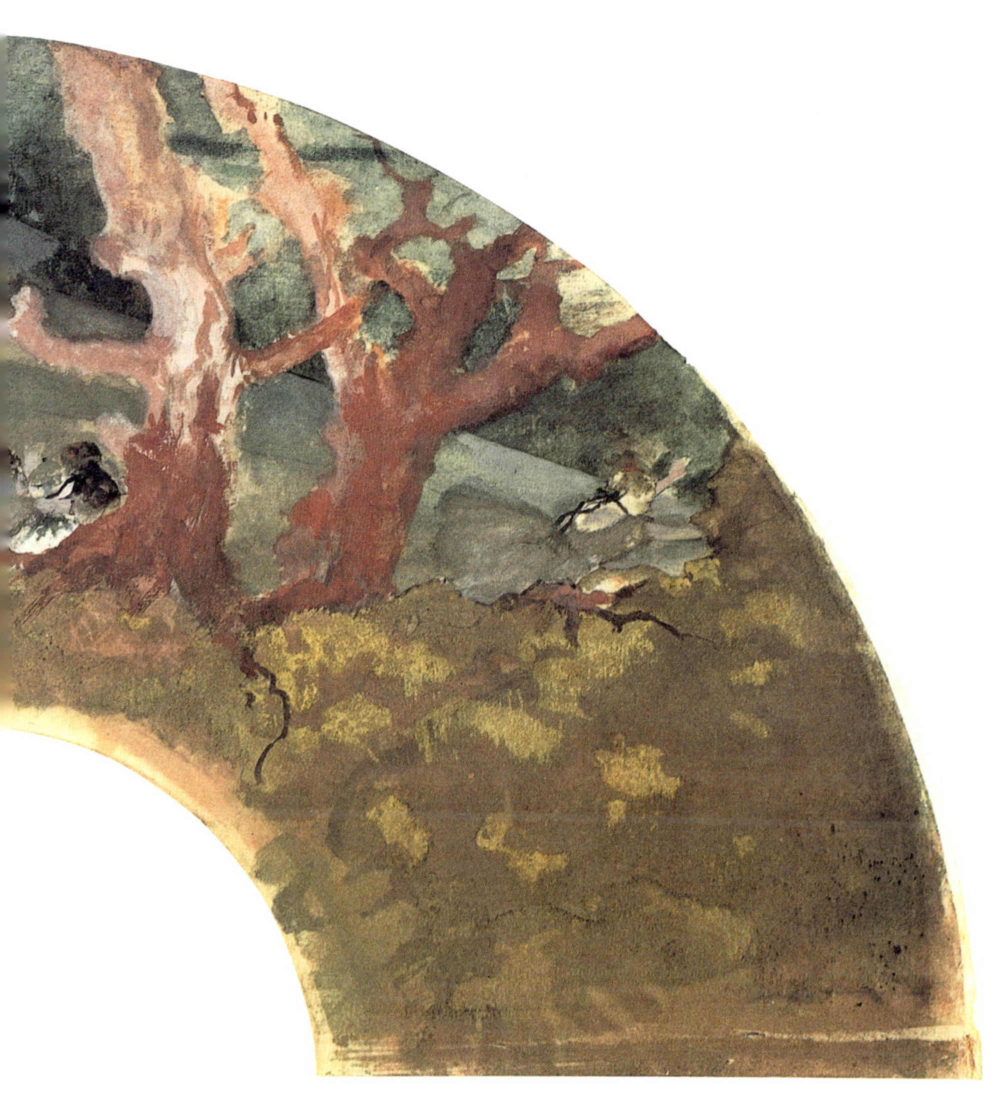

137. *Fan: Dancers and Stage Scenery, c.* 1878–79.
Gouache with gold highlights, 31 × 61 cm (12¼ × 24 in.).
Private collection

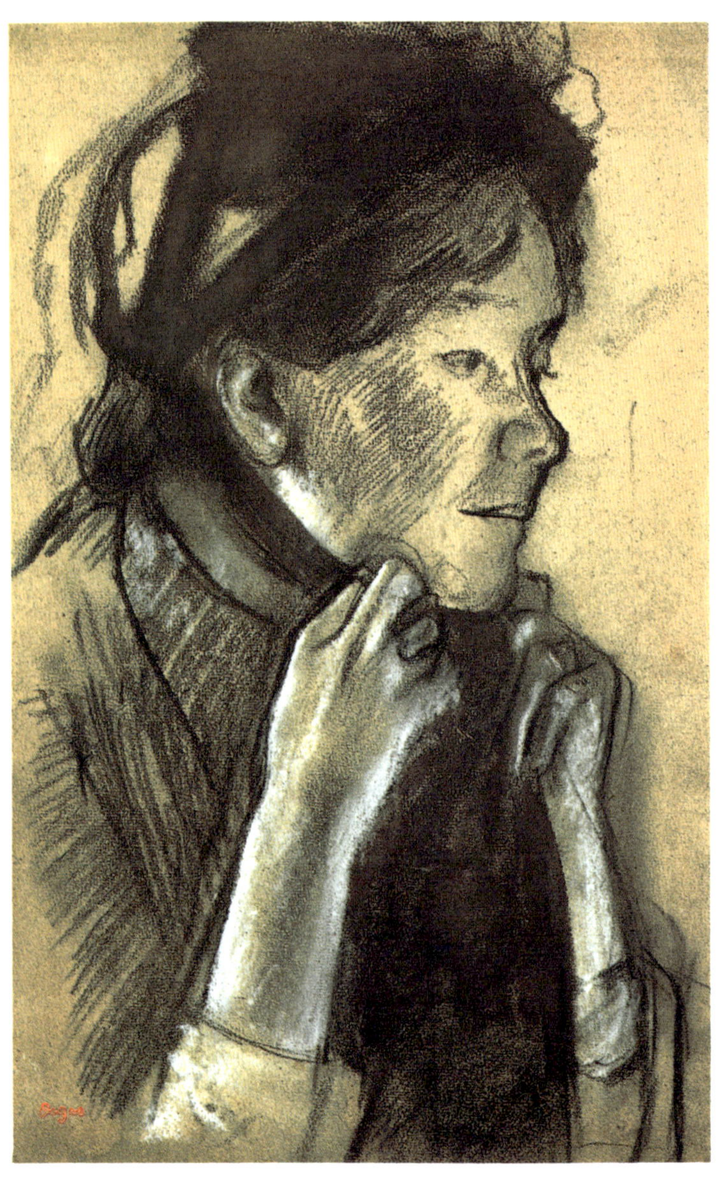

138. *Woman Tying the Ribbons on her Hat, c.* 1882.
Charcoal and pastel on grey-beige paper, 48 × 31 cm (18⅞ × 12¼ in.).
Musée d'Orsay, Paris

CHAPTER SIX

Retreat into the Studio 1880–1890

'Degas is a primitive lost in our civilization of black tail coats.'

(Octave Mirbeau in *La France*, 15 November 1884)

The decade of the 1880s was a time of transition for the Impressionists. The momentum generated by the exhibitions held in the 1870s was faltering owing to tensions between the artists and the realization that the aesthetic principles of Impressionism had for the most part been established, even if they had not yet been fully appreciated by the wider public. The question now was how to develop the Impressionist style beyond the basic premise of merely reproducing the world as it appeared to the eye. Each artist responded to this conundrum in different ways. Monet and Alfred Sisley investigated nature with greater intensity; Pissarro experimented for a time with new techniques and then found new subjects that he could paint in series; Renoir turned to the past and rediscovered Raphael and Ingres before moving to the South of France; and Cézanne went south to Provence where he became increasingly more reclusive. Degas remained in Paris and developed a tendency to retreat into his studio to work in isolation, although well into the 1890s he was to maintain an active interest in the urban motifs that he had explored in the 1870s.

The younger generation was now also beginning to make an impact on the avant-garde scene. Several of those artists known as Post-Impressionists – Gauguin, Van Gogh, Toulouse-Lautrec – had begun their careers under the mantle of the Impressionists. However, the reactions of the Post-Impressionists to the modern world differed from those of their immediate predecessors. The Impressionists at first aimed to paint directly what they saw in front of them, whereas the Post-Impressionists were more concerned with expressing their personal feelings about the world in the light of experience. Gauguin, for example, chose to turn his back on modernity and created his own private mythology; Vincent van Gogh yearned to discover the very essence of nature; and Henri de Toulouse-Lautrec took refuge in the night life of Montmartre. All three artists were indebted to Degas in their different ways. If the Impressionists, therefore, concerned themselves most with looking and analysing, the Post-Impressionists preferred imagining and conceptualizing.

The stylistic strategies that the Post-Impressionists employed to achieve their ends did create a certain unity. Essentially, for them the process of painting was reductive and intellectual. Simplified compositions, clear but supple outlines, flattened forms and broad areas of strong colour resulted in a pictorial synthesis that was in many ways diametrically opposed to the immediacy of Impressionism. Ultimately, the treatment of subject matter in Post-Impressionism leans towards Symbolism, just as in its stylistic inclinations it heralds Abstraction. Thus, the aesthetic shift that occurs during the 1880s is one that is away from direct representation and more towards invented or imaginary compositions based on an observed reality refined or distilled in the studio. Drawing remained an instinctive and spontaneous response to an artist's surroundings, but when carried out in the privacy of the studio it became a vehicle for recreating spontaneity and therefore the principal means of achieving a pictorial unity whereby reality was transformed into illusion. The fragmentary and the transitory were now being rejected in preference for the synthetic and the universal. During the 1880s and 1890s Degas's example was an important element in these developments and the emphasis he placed on his drawings, especially his pastels, was crucial.

By the time that Edmond Duranty had published his call to arms in *La Nouvelle Peinture* in 1876 Degas had to a certain extent already fulfilled expectations by creating an art that was 'infused with the sap of life'. And Degas had also proved himself to be more than capable of executing the writer's prescriptions in his choice of subject matter:

> A back should reveal the temperament, age, and social position, a pair of hands should reveal the magistrate or the merchant, and a gesture should reveal an entire range of feelings. Physiognomy will tell us with certainty that one man is dry, orderly, and meticulous, while another is the epitome of carelessness and disorder. Attitude will reveal to us whether a person is going to a business meeting, or is returning from a tryst…Hands kept in pockets can be eloquent.

Degas had so far applied this principle for such subjects as the ballet, the racecourse and the café-concert and clearly heeded it in his depiction of laundresses and prostitutes. To these he now added the milliners whose work he began to observe at the beginning of the 1880s [138,

146–150]. This subject inspired four oil paintings and some seventeen magnificent pastels made between 1879 and 1886. The compositions of these works signal the change that came about in Degas's style during the first half of the 1880s. The spatial organization is complicated in the way it is divided up by pieces of furniture – display tables, work surfaces, mirrors and seats – and the viewpoints are oblique and high. Diagonals are emphasized so as to join disparate parts of the composition together. Degas now moves much closer to the figures and makes them more monumental in scale. A remarkable aspect of Degas's visual record of milliners is the manner in which the hats form the principal feature regardless of the presence of figures. The milliners are often half-hidden by the displays while the heads and faces of the clients are often obscured by the special choreography employed in trying on a hat. Typically, Degas is conflating two types of painting that in the past would have been kept separate: genre and still life. In short, hats for Degas are the urban equivalent of Monet's water-lilies at Giverny.

As so often with Degas though, there are further ambiguities in his compositions of milliners. These stem from the social conditions. At the start of the nineteenth century milliners made their hats and offered them for sale in boutiques that they might own or rent, but the opening of department stores (Le Bon Marché in 1852, Les Grands Magasins du Louvre in 1863, Au Printemps in 1865, A la Ville de Saint Denis in 1868) and the growth of mechanization meant that the profession was being modernized. Hats were now also sold in department stores in designated areas on specific floors involving special displays to attract customers. Similarly, hats could be a feature of window displays. Degas gives no clue in his compositions as to the status of the milliners he is depicting and neither is it absolutely clear whether the viewer is in the shop itself or looking through a window. Furthermore, to us now it is not always apparent which figure is the milliner and which the client. Although in reality such social distinctions were clear cut, Degas chooses to blur them.

Like laundresses, milliners were often seen in the streets of Paris delivering their wares to clients in hat boxes. They too worked long hours and were often put on night shifts. Normal working hours could also be extended in accordance with the seasons so that periods of intense activity were punctuated by layoffs, which meant that other forms of employment might be necessary for survival. Milliners, therefore, like dancers and laundresses, were socially vulnerable and could be taken advantage of. A great deal of contemporary literature highlights their predicament. Degas, however, does not depict laundresses or milliners in a demeaning or suggestive way. Rather, he stresses their technical skills or their professional competence. Indeed, his milliners have an air of

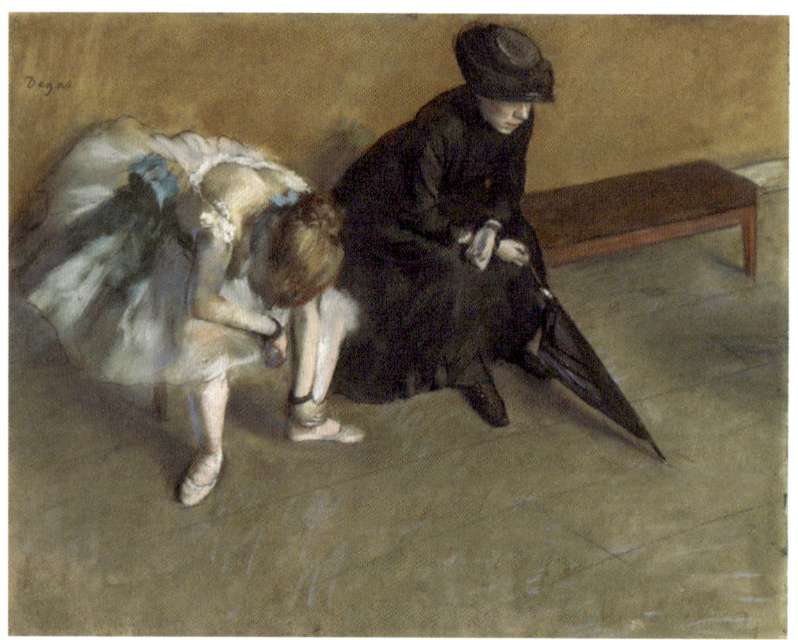

139. *Waiting, c.* 1880–82.
Pastel, 48.3 × 61 cm (19 × 24 in.).
J. Paul Getty Museum, Los Angeles, and Norton Simon
Art Foundation, Pasadena

refinement in so far as their code of practice – gesture, conversation, appraisal, advice, judgment – is based on that of the people to whom they are selling. Again, Degas blurs the social distinctions as much as he defines them and it is the social tensions that derive from this situation that make his work so compelling.

Similarly, as with the dancers, part of Degas's fascination with milliners stemmed from the parallels that he could see with his own role as an artist. Just as the search for technical perfection through endless toil and physical exertion that characterized a dancer's life was a metaphor for Degas the artist, so too was the life of the milliner. He took great pleasure in accompanying female friends (for example, Mary Cassatt or Mme Emile Straus) to dressmakers and milliners to inspect the fabrics and the colours, in the same way as he enjoyed seeing 'the red hands of the young women who hold the pins'. Again, it is the technical skills found in hat-making – cutting, blocking, finishing, trimming – combined with the intensive labour involved in the process that Degas finds sympathetic and suggestive of his own situation.

It is no coincidence that at the time Degas was giving careful consideration to his choice of subject matter he was also revising his compositional procedures. This revision is most evident in his treatment of the ballet and the racecourse, which during the 1870s he had rendered with what the British artist Sir William Rothenstein termed 'the colour and movement of romantic art' while providing 'the clear form dear to the classical spirit'. Yet by the end of the 1870s and at the start of the 1880s in certain pastels – *Au Théâtre* (c. 1880–81) [151], *Dancers on the Stage* (c. 1883) [152] and *The Entrance of the Masked Dancers* (c. 1884) [153] – Degas was exploiting such excessively steep viewpoints in such severely compressed spaces involving foreshortening and overlapping that he was in danger of becoming mannered. Indeed, the writer and critic Félix Fénéon described *Dancers on the Stage* with his usual pungency as 'an entanglement of extended arms and legs like an image of an epileptic Hindu god'. And so, in order to counteract any further developments in this direction Degas started to devise simpler compositions built around one or two carefully selected motifs.

A consummate example of this reductive process is the pastel *Waiting* (c. 1880–82), which shows two figures seated on a bench in a room or passageway of the Opéra [139]. A dancer in a tutu clasps her left ankle, perhaps in pain, while another young woman sombrely dressed in out-door clothes and with an umbrella looks downwards at the ground. Degas's own title for this superb work is not known and the subject is open to interpretation: is this a break in a rehearsal or a pause before the announcement of the result of a dance examination? The space is as anonymous as are the two figures. They form such a contrast in their dress and demeanour – one in white and the other in black, one 'active' and the other 'passive' – and nothing is indicated of the relationship between them. The sense of isolation is as palpable as in paintings by Edward Hopper, just as the boldness of the composition, the positioning of the figures, the rich tonal qualities of the setting and the delicate accents of the blue and purple highlights attest Degas's technical skills at their finest. No wonder the artist's Italian friend, Federico Zandomeneghi, felt disposed to make a copy of *Waiting* at a later date (c. 1895).

The motif of the dancer clasping her ankle, or the nearly related one of the dancer adjusting her shoe, were ones that Degas resorted to frequently during the early 1880s. He no doubt observed such scenes from life backstage at the Opéra and then if necessary recreated them in his studio with the aid of models – possibly the dancers themselves. A whole cluster of pastels and drawings in charcoal or black chalk testify to his fascination with these and similar motifs [154–158]. The figures are all seen in close up from above with dramatic foreshortening, but also with an undeniable emphasis on the texture of materials – bows, ribbons [159], gauze. It is from these groups of powerful drawings, all rapidly made and committed to paper with great panache, that Degas selected one or more specifically for use in finished pastels made for sale, such as *Waiting* [139] and *Dancers Resting* [160].

Similar groups of drawings were made in connection with painted compositions of ballet dancers, in which Degas pursued his idea of devising long horizontal compositions resembling friezes with figures strung out across the surface. The width of these canvases is more than twice their height. Here the artist is probably recalling the fresco cycles or sculptured reliefs of the Italian Renaissance, as well as demonstrating his knowledge of Japanese prints and his interest in contemporary photography. The challenge for him was to retain the monumentality of the figures within a strictly prescribed format. Shallow diagonals, repoussoir effects, oblique wide-angle viewpoints with a gradual recession into depth often emphasized by contre-jour lighting effects are the means by which he achieved these uncluttered scenes. The figures are either isolated, in pairs, or arranged in groups. Degas articulates the space by simple devices such as benches (*The Dancing Lesson*, c. 1880 [140]), musical instruments (*Dancers in the Rehearsal Room with a Double Bass*, c. 1885, in the Metropolitan Museum of Art, New York) and architectural features, particularly floorboards and windows (*Ballet Rehearsal*, c. 1885, in Yale University Art Gallery, New Haven). The numerous drawings required for this type of composition extended Degas's repertoire of dancers [161]. He accumulated literally hundreds of drawings in his studio where he could either make direct use of them or else, like a musician, employ them on other occasions as a basis for improvisation. The ballet paintings of the 1880s therefore tend to be an aggregate made up of stock drawings adjusted to need.

The new compositional procedures that governed the ballet pictures also applied to Degas's depictions of jockeys. This was a subject that had fallen into abeyance during the 1870s, but captivated the artist again during the 1880s and 1890s [164–166]. Previously, the location and social ambiance of the racecourse had absorbed Degas's attention, but on reinvestigating the subject he concentrates more on the riders themselves, placing them prominently in the foreground. They jostle nervously moments before the start of a race with the figures overlapping one another, recalling carvings on ancient sarcophagi. The landscape settings are abbreviated, or only vaguely sketched in, so as not to distract from the silhouetted forms of the horses and their riders dressed in their colourful silks. These compositions are full of tension with the powerful horses prancing and shying as the jockeys struggle to control their mounts. Rather than creating a special format, as in the narrow horizontal compositions adopted for the ballet, Degas retains rectangular or square formats for his racing scenes.

The studies of jockeys and horses for the paintings and pastels of the 1880s are comparable with those for the dancers in so far as they provided Degas with a portfolio of images that could be referred to or reworked over an extensive period of time. The rhythmic actions associated with riding are captured by flurries of lines and frequently redrawn outlines [167]. Occasionally, as with the dancers, Degas returns to basics and outlines the form of a jockey in the nude as if reverting to his practices for the history paintings of the 1860s [168]. Degas also takes an interest in the physique and physiognomy of the jockeys – chinless, inexperienced youngsters contrasted with burly, thickset amateurs. There is an immense energy about these drawings even though they are studies made in connection with the preparations for a race rather than during the race itself with the riders fully committed. As ever, Degas's forensic approach favours those moments when humanity reveals its frailties.

The drawings of the horses are even more revealing of Degas's powers of investigation [141]. As the nineteenth century progressed, both scientists and artists began in earnest to study animals in motion. The horse was of particular interest and Degas would have been aware

140. *The Dancing Lesson, c.* 1880.
Oil on canvas, 39.4 × 88.4 cm (15½ × 35¼ in.).
Sterling and Francine Clark Art Institute,
Williamstown, Massachusetts

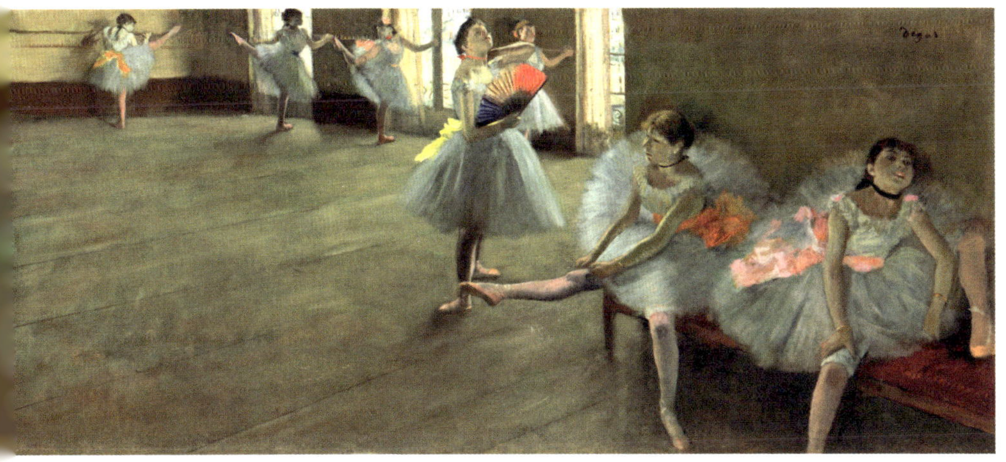

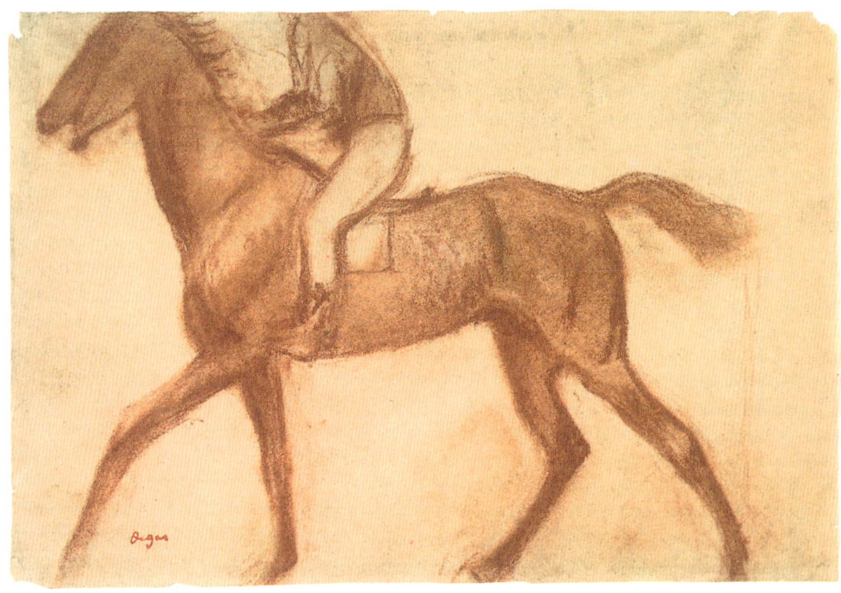

141. *Mounted Jockey Seen in Profile (after Eadweard Muybridge)*, 1889.
Red chalk, 28.3 × 41.8 cm (11⅛ × 16½ in.).
Boymans-van Beuningen Museum, Rotterdam

of the researches of Dr Etienne Jules Marey published in the journal *La Nature* in 1878 and the lectures and photographic experiments conducted in Paris by Eadweard Muybridge, culminating in his study in eleven volumes, *Animal Locomotion* (1887). The findings of these two men, which extended to the human body as well, coincided with Degas's first sculptures of horses in motion and must also have informed his further analysis of dancers.

Degas's attendance at the Opéra and the racecourse fell off during the 1880s when he was reassessing his compositional procedure, but never ceased totally. The drawings he horded in his studio were an invaluable record of previous work and at the same time a stimulus to further activity. Memory also played a vital role in the art of drawing and the more Degas became restricted to working in his studio so it too became one of the principal components of his graphic practices. The chief exponent of training the visual memory for drawing was Horace Lecoq de Boisbaudron, whose treatise *L'Education de la Mémoire Pittoresque* was first published in 1848 and reissued in 1862. Lecoq de Boisbaudron was a Salon painter, but ended up as an influential teacher of drawing. His principal theory was that in order to become artists students needed to learn to analyse forms with the greatest care. This could be done if they concentrated on the essentials and committed them to memory before redrawing them away from the model or motif. A surprising number of artists – among them Manet, Pissarro, Gauguin, Van Gogh, Rodin, Matisse – were advocates of this method. And Degas was particularly enamoured of it, judging by his statement made to Jeanniot:

> If I were to open an Academy, I would have a house with five floors. The model would be on the ground floor with the first year students. The best pupils would go to the fifth.

The method encouraged close examination, but, in the case of a lapse of memory, instinct would take over. By such means drawing ceased to be a way of passively recording what was in front of the artist and instead became a method of recollection. Ultimately, this practice, which positively encouraged imaginative recreation, could lead to a freer form of personal expression.

Evidence of Degas applying powers of observation to his art by the use of memory lies in his love of mimicry. Valéry describes the artist in old age taking pleasure in travelling on an open-air bus to watch the other passengers. Degas imitates for Valéry a woman he saw settling into her seat arranging her clothes and belongings with the utmost fastidiousness and then beginning the whole process again. The artist said it was a 'whole routine, intensely personal, followed by another apparently stable condition of equilibrium which lasted only for a moment'. This kind of observation made from life could be most effectively drawn on paper with the aid of memory. As Degas told Jeanniot:

> It is very good to copy what one sees; it is much better to draw what you can't see any more but in your memory. It is a transformation in which imagination and memory work together. You only reproduce what struck you, that is to say, the necessary. That way, your memories and your fantasy are freed from the tyranny of nature. This is why pictures made in such a way, by a man who has a cultured memory and knows the old masters and his craft, are almost always remarkable works – look at Delacroix.

And to Delacroix's name, that of Degas's should be added.

No finer demonstration of Degas's authority as a draughtsman exists than the series of female nudes in pastel that he sent to the eighth and last Impressionist exhibition held in 1886. Many aspects of Degas's art are on display in the 'Suite de nuds de femmes se baignant, se lavant, se séchant, s'essuyant, se peignant ou se faisant peigner' ('Suite of female nudes bathing, washing, drying themselves, wiping themselves, combing themselves or being combed') [169, 173, 178–180, 182]. Degas seems to have intended to show ten pastels covering these activities of personal toilette, but on the basis of contemporary reviews by such writers as Gustave Geoffroy, Fénéon and Octave Mirbeau only six, or possibly seven, were actually exhibited and even some of these are not absolutely clearly identifiable today. What is apparent, however, is that Degas's suite of female nudes is the most sustained and audacious exploration in nineteenth-century France of this much vaunted and highly traditional subject in art. Degas combines his profound knowledge of the treatment of the female nude from Antiquity through the Renaissance to the eighteenth century with his singularly powerful resolve to present the subject as one of the greatest significance for his own time. In this respect, these works alone are enough to place Degas as the heir of Titian, Rembrandt, Goya or Delacroix, and to be the forerunner of Picasso and Matisse.

Degas's preoccupation with the female nude extends throughout his career from the time of the early history paintings to the final decade. The monotypes of brothel scenes made during the mid-1870s, but not seen publicly during the artist's lifetime, are a sudden immersion in a topic that has to be seen in the context of the social mores of late nineteenth-century France. It is not known to what extent they are imaginary or based on personal experience in the use of brothels, but it must at least be the case that Degas visited them and knew prostitutes. The fifty or so images are technically astounding in the use of a difficult medium, but even more amazing is how overtly sexual they are and how comprehensive [142]. Yet in the final analysis there is a surprising degree of objectivity and even sympathy for the plight of these women who lived and worked in the twilight world of the 'maisons closes'.

During the early and mid-1880s Degas continued to explore the theme of individual women performing their toilette alone in the privacy of their rooms in both monotypes and pastels [170–172]. These, too, are intimate and direct images in which personal maids sometimes participate, suggesting therefore that Degas is sometimes depicting bourgeois households as opposed to prostitutes.

The pastels shown in the eighth Impressionist exhibition are only one sample of Degas's depictions of the female nude in pastel made during the 1880s. Another exhibition held at the dealers Boussod, Valadon & Co. two years later in 1888 and organized by Theo van Gogh, the brother of Vincent, included nine more examples dating from this same decade. Gauguin saw this exhibition and made copies of some of the items in it [143].

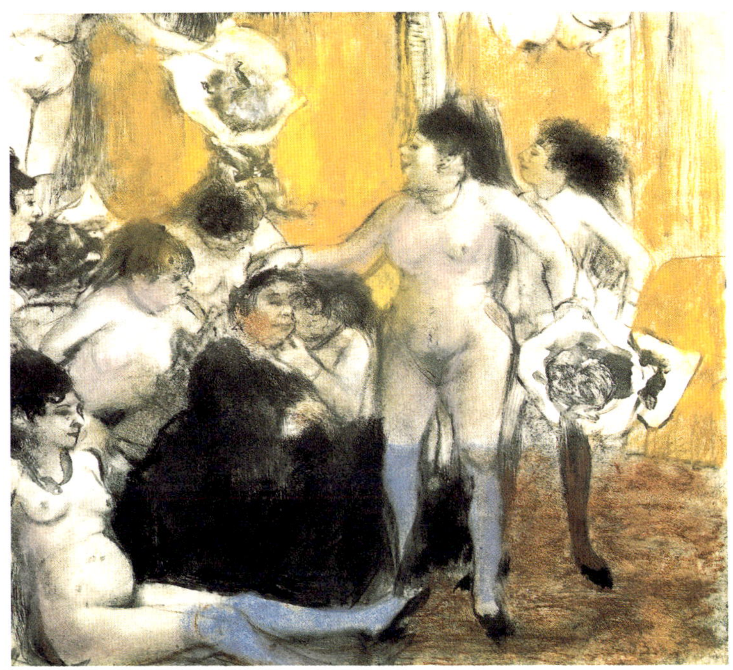

142. *The Madam's Birthday*, 1876–77.
Pastel over monotype, 26.6 × 29.6 cm (10½ × 11⅝ in.).
Musée Picasso, Paris

On both occasions, in 1886 and 1888, the critics were respectful in acknowledging Degas's virtuosic display, but there was puzzlement over the artist's intentions. Conservative viewers, who were used to seeing their women blandly represented in the guise of Venus or the Three Graces, were shocked by the social improprieties, while supporters of the avant-garde were intrigued by the brazen approach to this most traditional theme and at the same time bemused by the radical style adopted for the purpose.

The pastels themselves are notable first of all for the variety of the poses that Degas gives his women, as the generic title ('Suite of female nudes') indeed implies. They variously stand, squat, sit, stoop, kneel, or balance on one leg; they undress, dress, wash, get in or out of the bath, dry themselves, attend to their hair or have it combed for them by a maid. Nearly all the pastels are set in interiors variously equipped with tubs, baths, water jugs, towels, brushes, scissors, carpets, curtains, bed linen, comfortable arm chairs or chaises longues. The emphasis throughout is on the toilette itself with the figure, often seen in close-up,

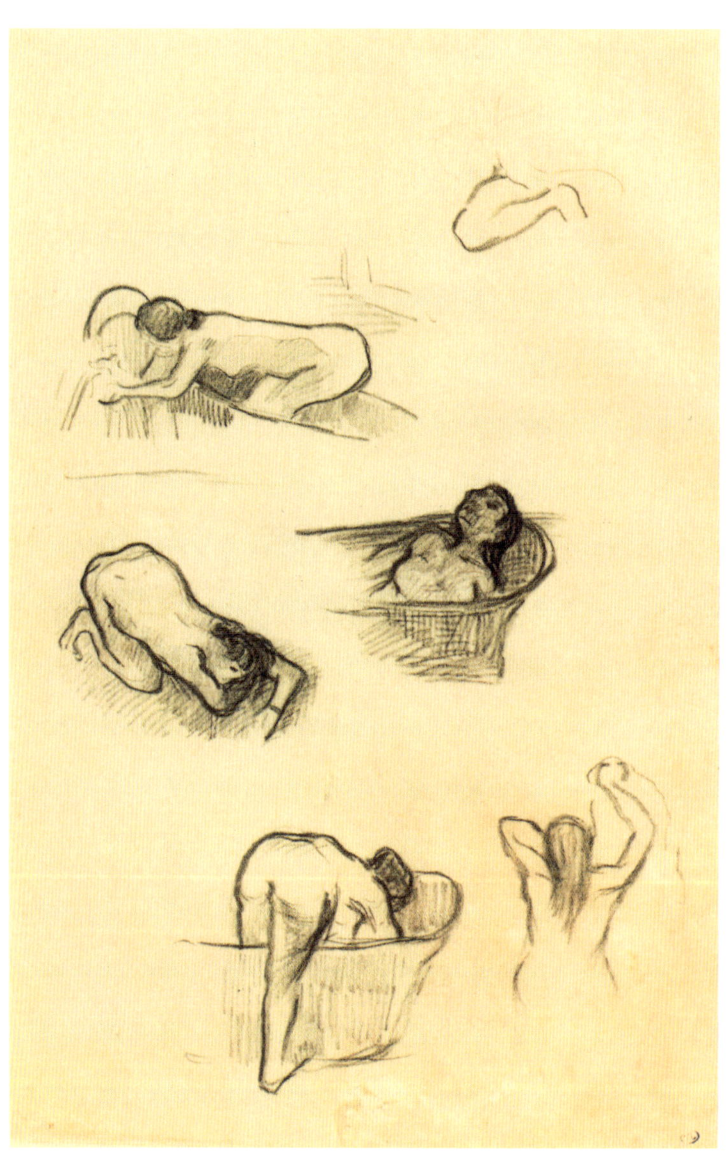

143. Paul Gauguin, *Studies of Women at their Toilette (after Degas)*,
1888. Black chalk, 34.2 × 22.8 cm (13½ × 9 in.).
Musée du Louvre, Paris

dominating the space. Any architectural features are kept to a minimum and in most cases are not attempted at all. Only one pastel (*Woman Dressing*) is set outside [178]. A few of the poses suggest specific artistic prototypes from Antiquity, but the majority are due to Degas's own powers of observation, which gives the whole group a strong sense of cohesion and stylistic unity. The squatting, stooping and lying down figures are seen from above; the seated and kneeling figures from less elevated positions; and those standing are seen from more or less the same level as the viewer. Throughout, Degas contrasts rounded forms (heads, breasts, buttocks, thighs, shoulders, hips, bellies) with the more jagged extremities derived from jutting elbows, protruding feet, bent legs, busy hands and awkward gestures. Most importantly and regardless of the variety in the poses, the self-absorption of each figure is mirrored by the physical self-containment of its form and it is this factor that provides an overarching unity to the nudes of the 1880s.

The fact that Degas chose to exhibit so many of his female nudes together implies that he might have brought all of them to the same degree of finish. But there are in fact marked differences between the pastels as regards their surfaces. *The Tub* [169] and *Woman in a Tub* [173], as well as *Woman Having her Hair Combed* [170], *The Tub* [175], *Woman Drying her Left Foot* [176], *Woman Combing her Hair* [177] and *Bather Stretched out on the Floor* [181], are all precisely drawn, firmly modelled and executed with several layers of pastel, including delicate layers of highlights. On the other hand, the two full-lengths, *Woman Dressing* [178] and *Woman Getting Up* [179], together with *Woman Bathing in a Shallow Tub* [180] and *The Tub* [182], are more dependent on charcoal and sporadic outbursts of pastel with quite extensive areas of the paper support allowed to show through.

It is unlikely that these visual disparities caused as much bemusement among the critics and viewers as the subject matter. Who are these women and where do they belong in the social hierarchy? Are they bourgeoise or are they prostitutes? Why are they depicted in this way in the privacy of their rooms performing their ablutions with no clue as to their stations in life? These are some of the questions posed by the critics and which still promote discussion today. There is no doubt that for Degas an artist drawing the female nude was to work in an honourable and venerable tradition. Equally, with this series there can be no doubt that Degas was keen to continue this tradition while at the same time updating it, or, as it were, seeing it through the prism of modernity. What struck viewers, however, was the degree of unabashed intimacy on display, which the artist himself acknowledged to Jeanniot:

> Oh! Women can never forgive me; they hate me, they feel that I am
> disarming them. I show them without their coquetry, in the state of
> animals cleaning themselves!

Similarly, to George Moore, Degas explained:

> Hitherto the nude has always been represented in poses which
> presuppose an audience, but these women of mine are honest,
> simple folk, unconcerned by any other interests than those involved
> in their physical condition. Here is another; she is washing her feet.
> It is as if I looked through the keyhole.

It is on account of such statements that Degas has in recent times been termed a misogynist and a voyeur, which are judgments that fail to take into account the social mores of late nineteenth-century France and so diminish Degas as an artist. Admittedly, advanced critics of his own day – Mirbeau, Geoffroy, Huysmans – expressed shock at the directness of the poses and sought to find a suitable vocabulary with which to describe their impact while also trying to explain Degas's purpose. The women were likened to 'amphibians' or 'frogs', described as 'riff-raff' and classified as bourgeoise, lower class, or as prostitutes. Huysmans described the figure in *Woman Getting Up* as 'a butcher's wife' [179]. Such comparisons and terminology reveal the puzzlement caused by Degas's modern approach to such a traditional subject and he himself – as so often – added to the confusion by exploiting conflicting imagery in the pastels. For instance, baths and tubs were associated at that time with prostitution, whereas the water jug was a time-honoured trope for the female form applied throughout literature and art.

A comparison between the brothel monotypes where Degas's meaning is explicit and the pastels exhibited in 1886 and 1888 surely reveals that his purpose in the pastels was to give the subject of the female nude contemporary relevance. That he succeeded in doing this is reflected not only in the immediate reaction to the pastels, but also in the discussion that is still generated by them today. Or, as Degas remarked to the painter Henri Gervex whom he had advised over his famous painting *Rolla* (1878), which had caused a similar furore, 'You see…nude models are all right at the Salon, but a woman undressing – never!' Degas's own position is reflected in his remark, 'See how different the times are for us; two centuries ago, I would have been painting "Susannah Bathing", now I just paint "Woman in a Tub".'

Valéry, who was a great admirer of Rembrandt's nudes [144], with which Degas's pastels are of sufficient merit to be illuminatingly compared, wrote:

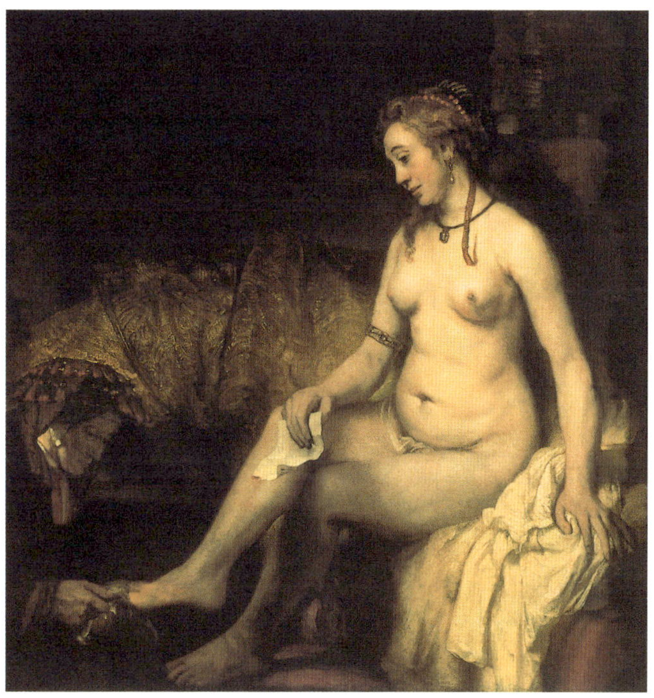

144. Rembrandt van Rijn, *Bathsheba*, 1654.
Oil on canvas, 142 × 142 cm (55⅞ × 55⅞ in.).
Musée du Louvre, Paris

Degas's lifelong quest was to discover in the nude, studied from
every angle, in an incredible variety of poses, and even in rapid
movement, the one and only linear pattern, which, while defining
a momentary pose of the body with the greatest precision, gives it
the greatest possible generalization. Grace, obvious poetry are not
his aim.

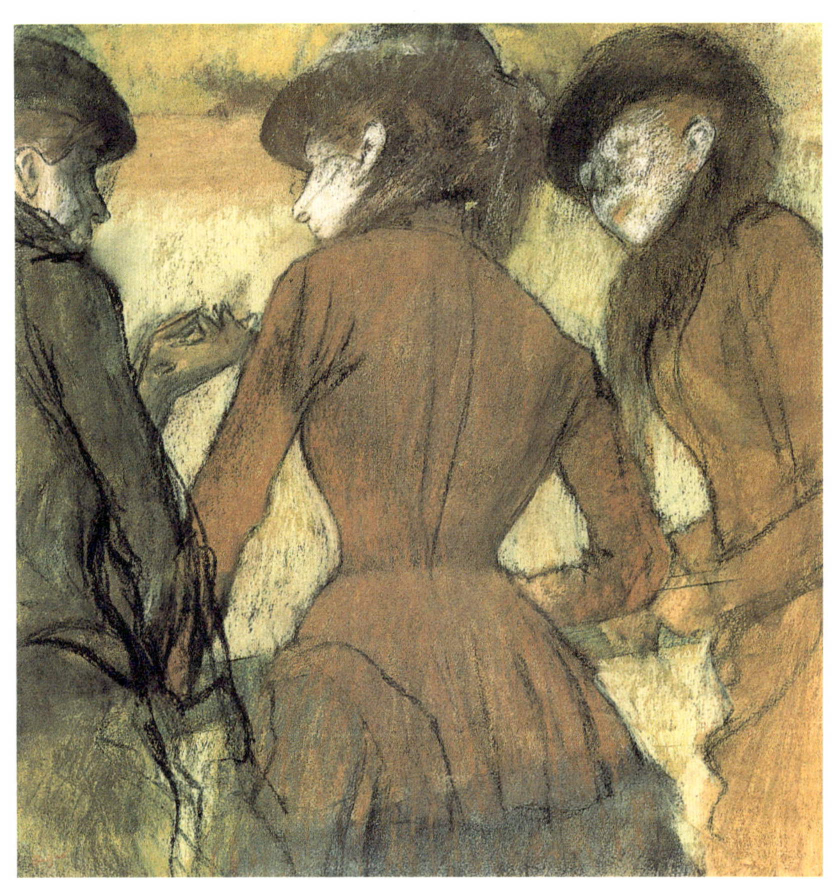

145. *Three Women at the Races, c.* 1885.
Pastel, 27 × 27 cm (10⅝ × 10⅝ in.).
Denver Art Museum

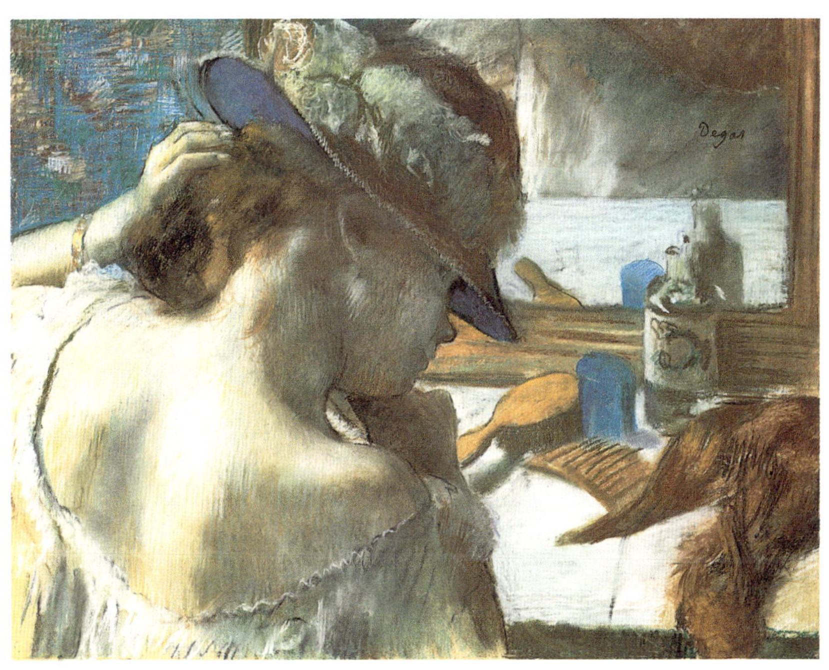

146. *At the Mirror, c.* 1889.
Pastel, 49 × 64 cm (19¼ × 25¼ in.).
Kunsthalle Hamburg

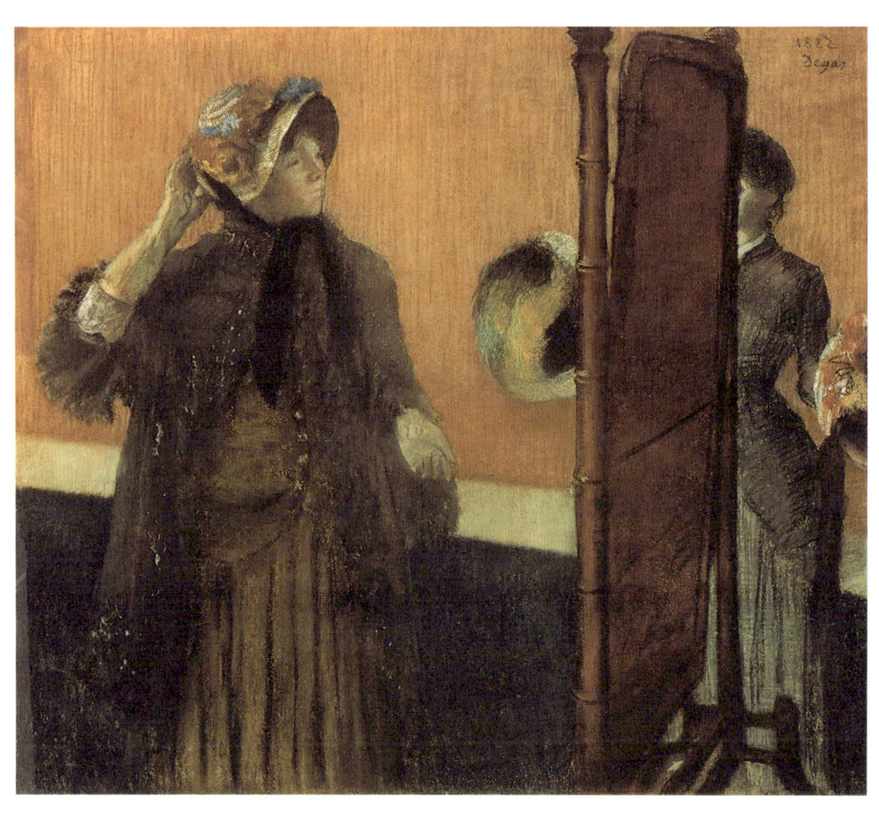

147. *At the Milliners*, 1882.
Pastel on pale grey industrial wrapping paper laid on silk,
76.2 × 86.4 cm (30 × 34 in.).
Metropolitan Museum of Art, New York

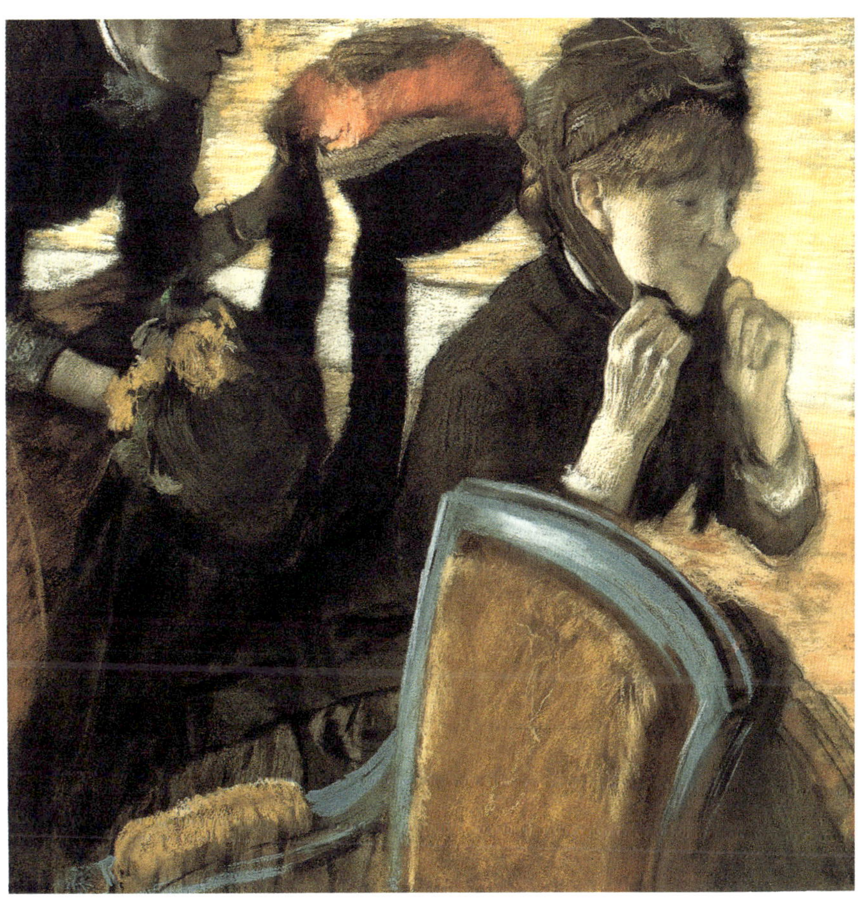

148. *At the Milliners, c.* 1882.
Pastel, 70.2 × 70.5 cm (27⅝ × 27¼ in.).
Museum of Modern Art, New York

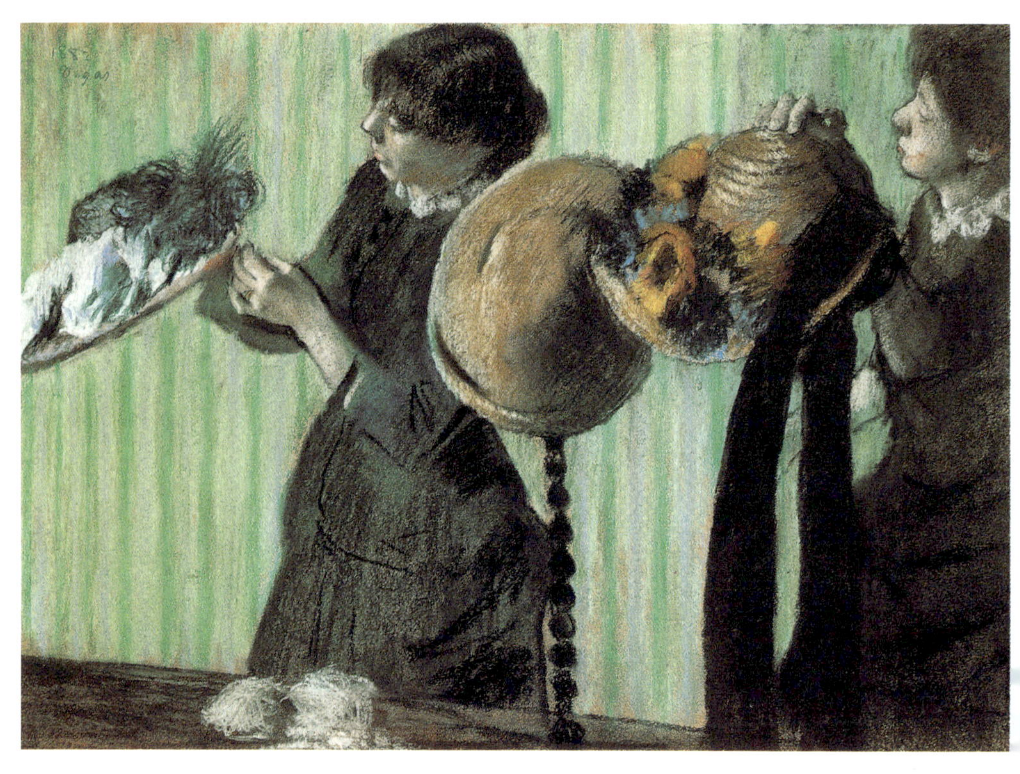

149. *The Milliner's Shop*, 1882.
Pastel, 48.9 × 71.8 cm (19¼ × 28¼ in.).
Nelson-Atkins Museum of Art, Kansas City

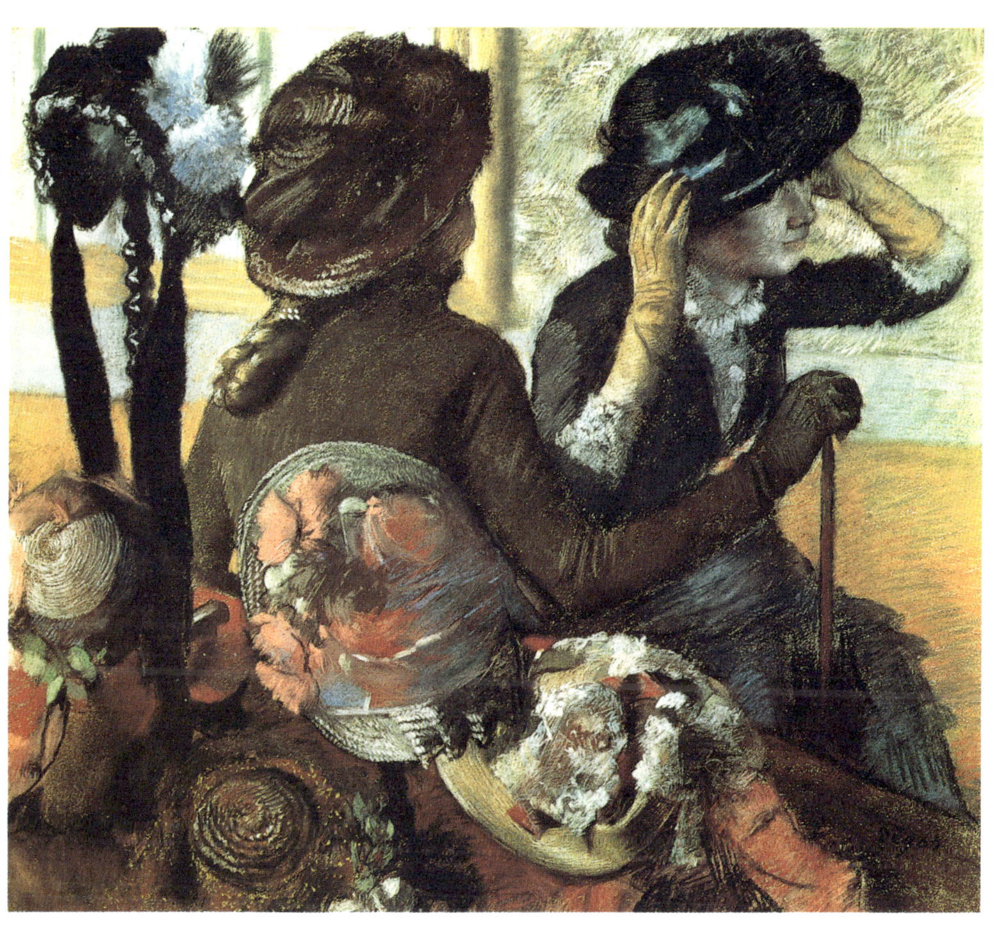

150. *At the Milliners*, 1882.
Pastel, 75.5 × 85.5 cm (29¼ × 33⅝ in.).
Thyssen-Bornemisza Museum, Madrid

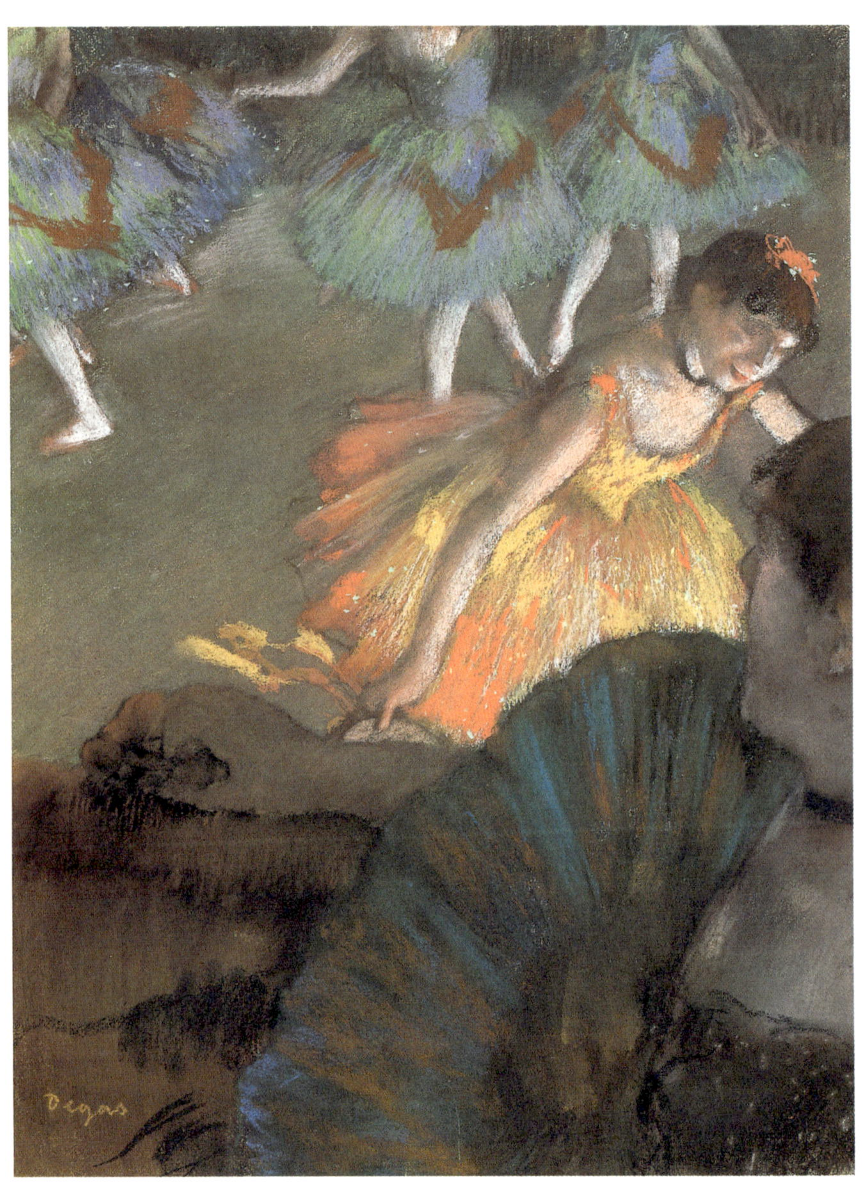

 Retreat into the Studio 1880–1890

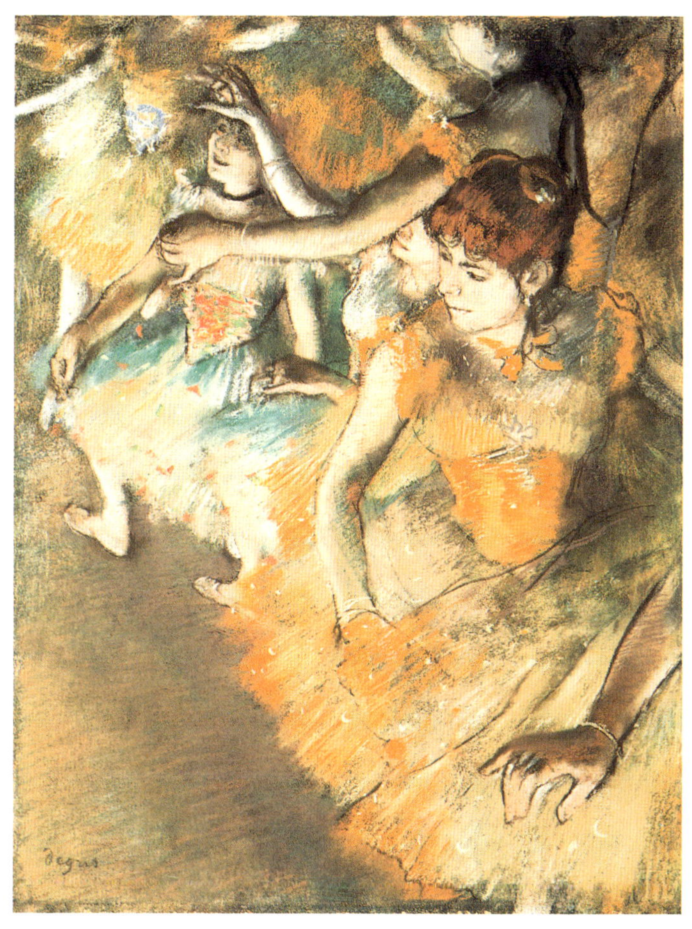

Degas

OPPOSITE
151. *Au Théâtre (Ballet from an Opera Box)*, *c.* 1880–81.
Pastel, 66 × 50.8 cm (26 × 20 in.).
Philadelphia Museum of Art

ABOVE
152. *Dancers on the Stage*, *c.* 1883.
Pastel, 64.8 × 50.8 cm (25½ × 20 in.).
Dallas Museum of Art

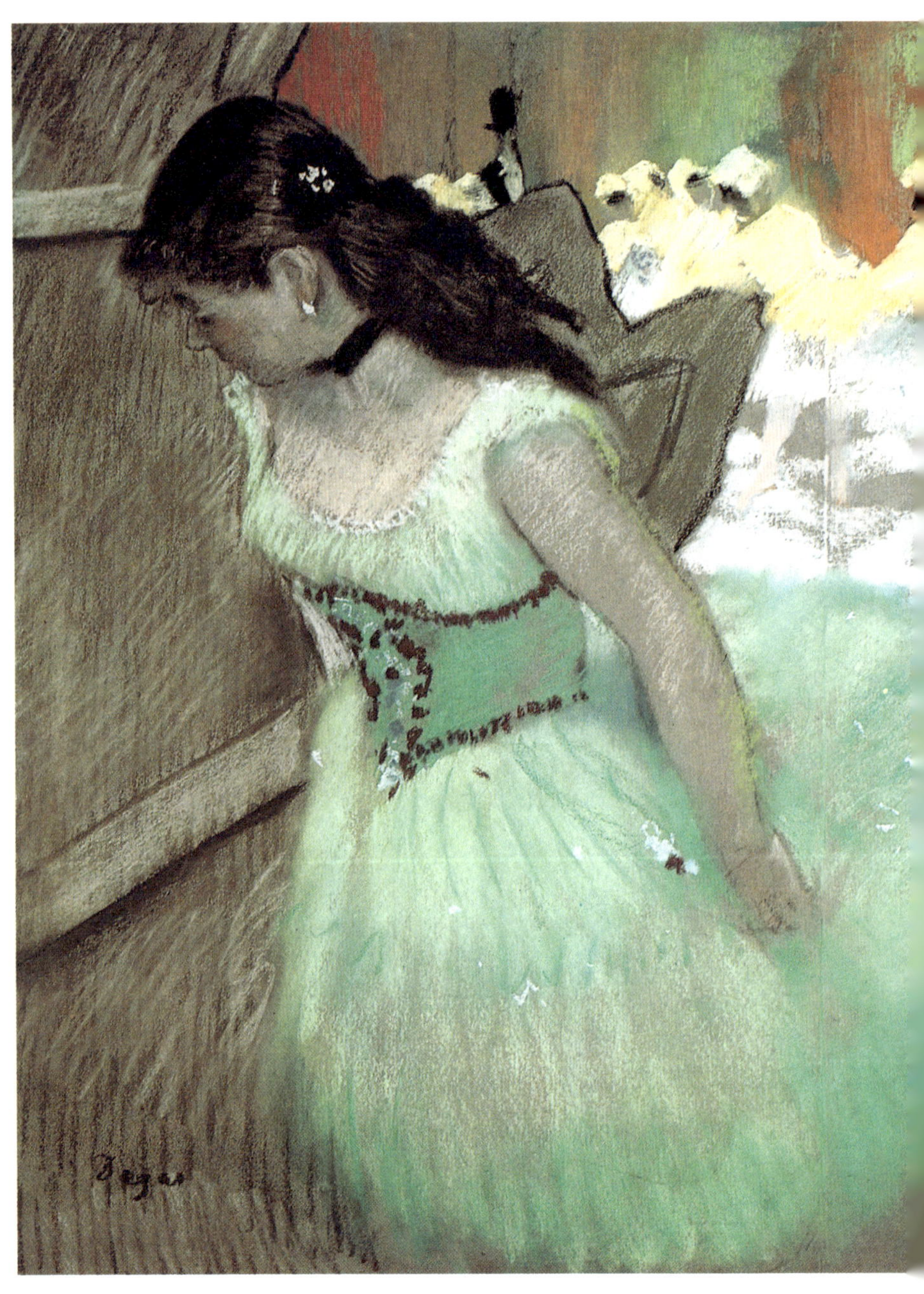

208   *Retreat into the Studio 1880–1890*

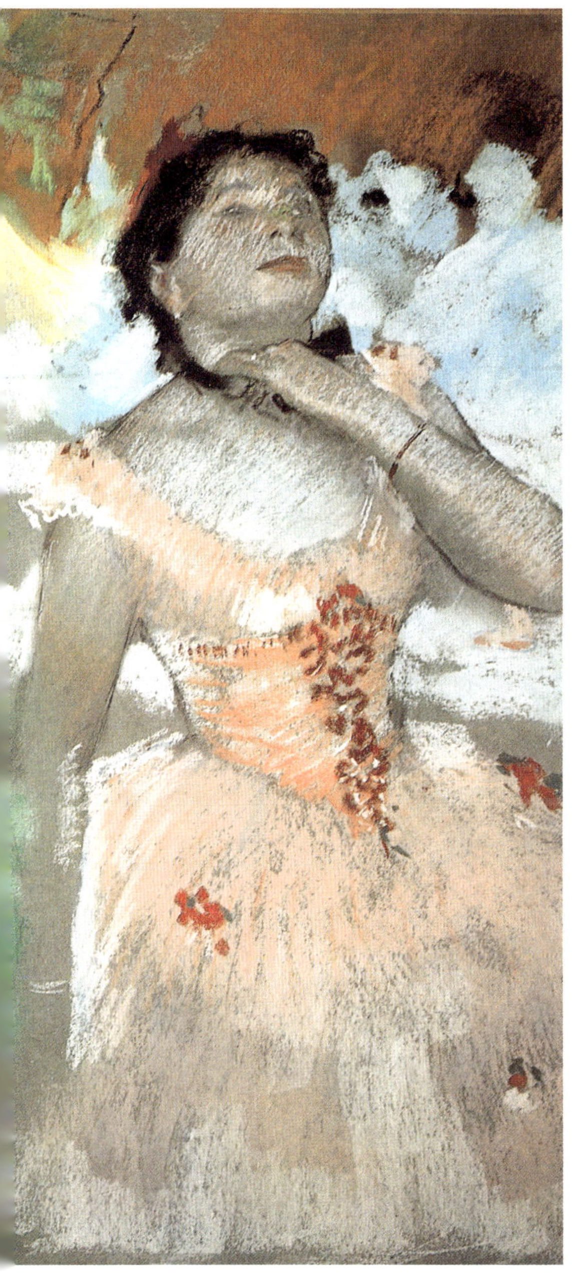

153. *The Entrance of the Masked Dancers*, c. 1884. Pastel, 49 × 64.7 cm (19⅜ × 25½ in.). Sterling and Francine Clark Art Institute, Williamstown, Massachusetts

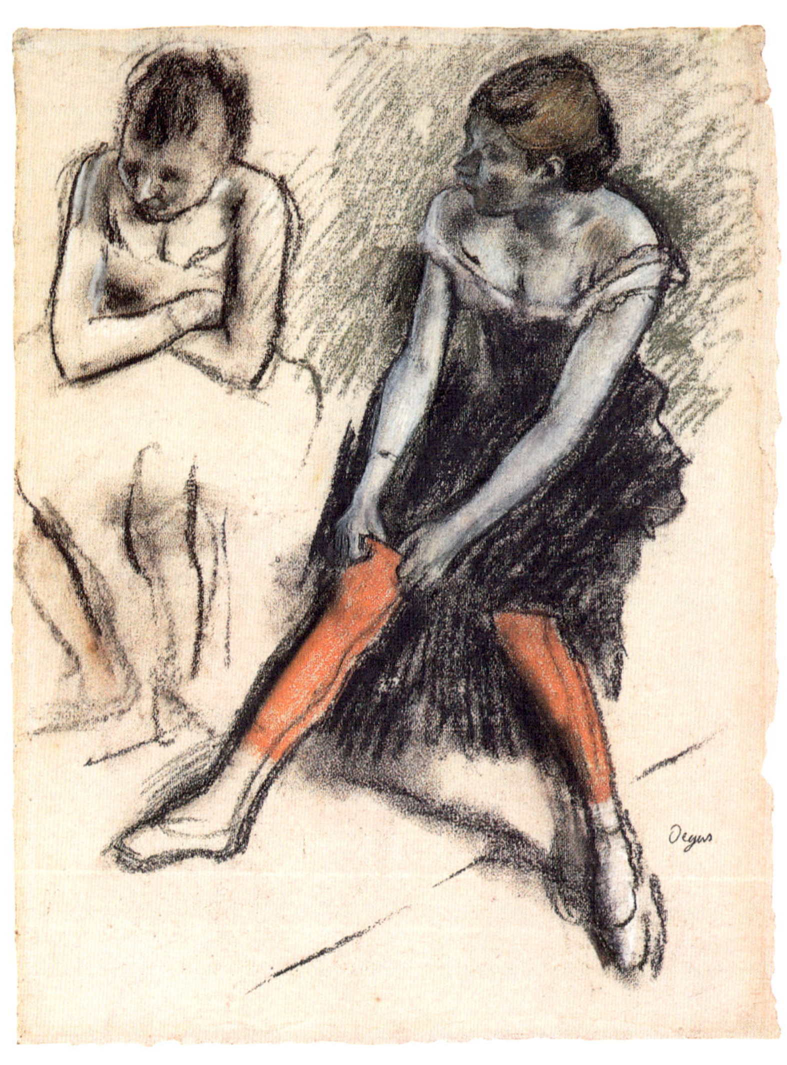

154. *Dancer with Red Stockings, c. 1884.*
Pastel on pink paper, 75.9 × 58.7 cm (29⅞ × 23⅛ in.).
The Hyde Collection, Glen Falls, New York

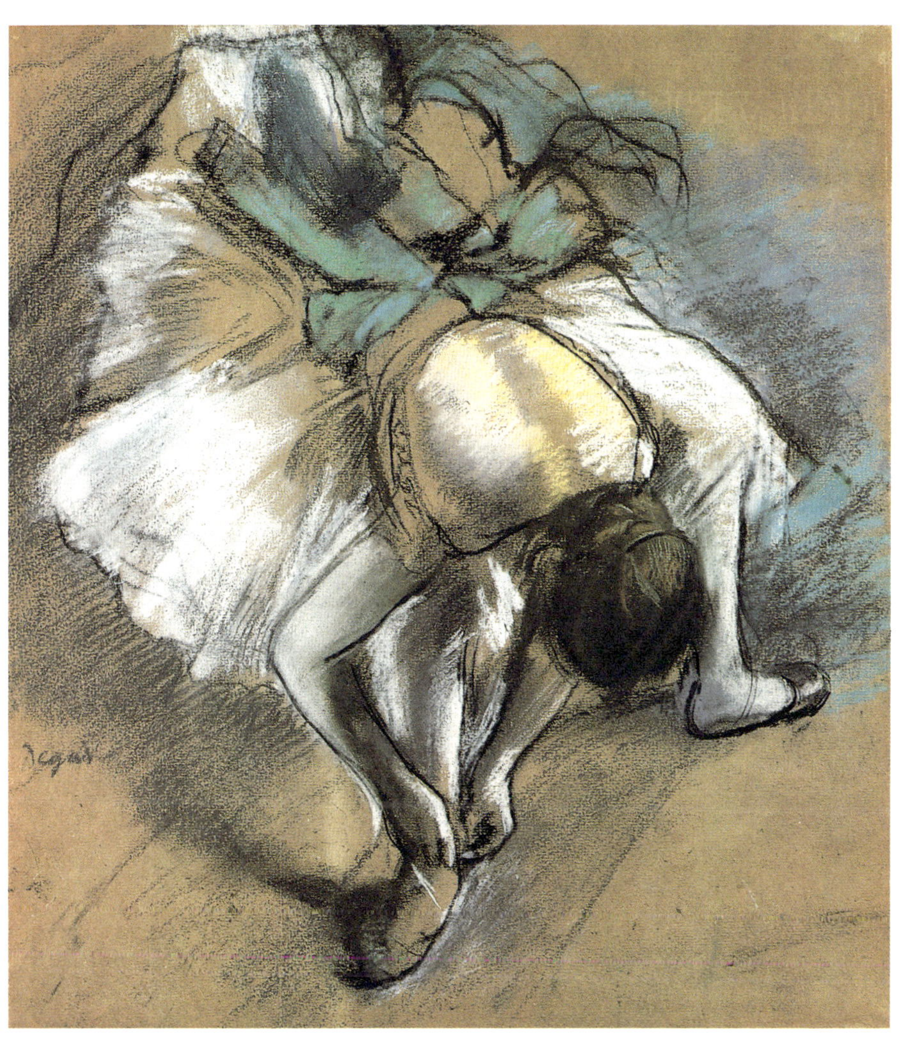

155. *Dancer Adjusting her Shoe, c.* 1880–82.
Pastel and black chalk on buff paper, 42.6 × 34.3 cm (16¾ × 13½ in.).
Private collection

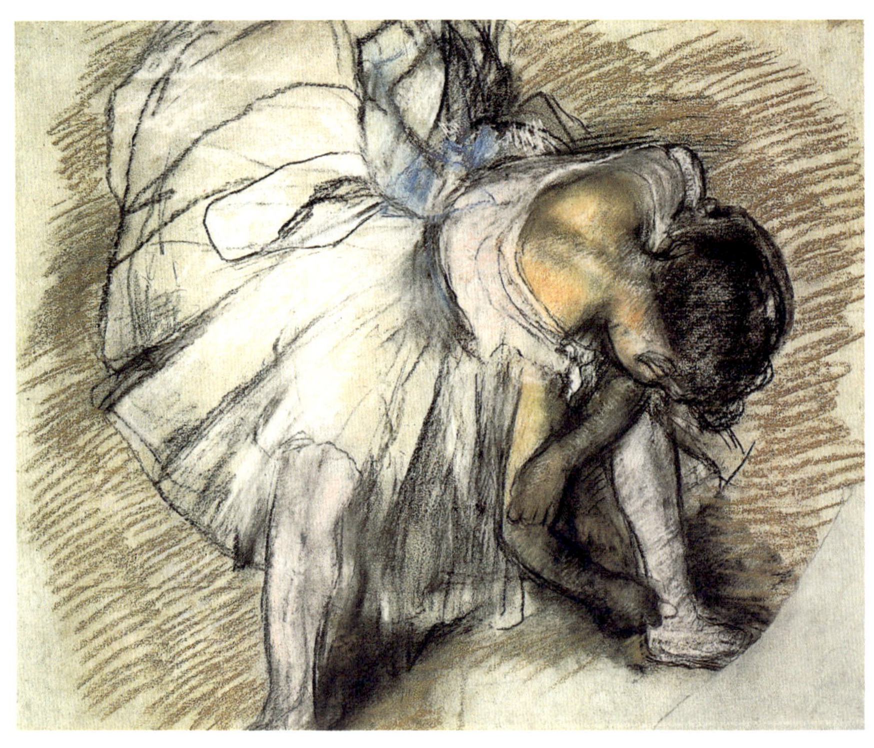

156. *Dancer Adjusting her Shoe*, c. 1880–82.
Pastel on grey paper, 48.2 × 61 cm (19 × 24 in.).
Dixon Gallery and Gardens, Memphis

OPPOSITE

157. *Dancer in Green Tutu*, c. 1880–85.
Pastel on paper, 46.9 × 33 cm (18½ × 13 in.).
Private collection

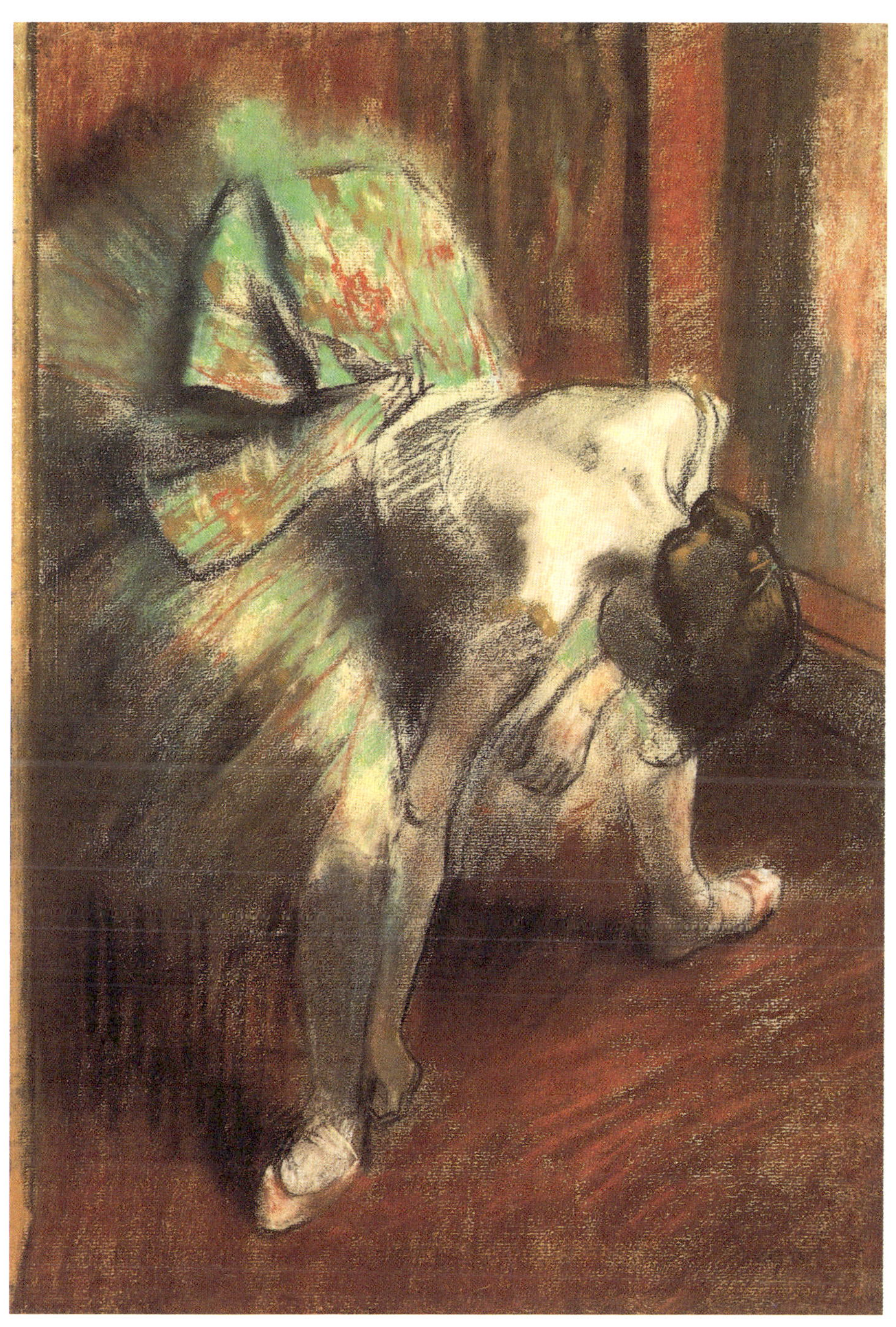

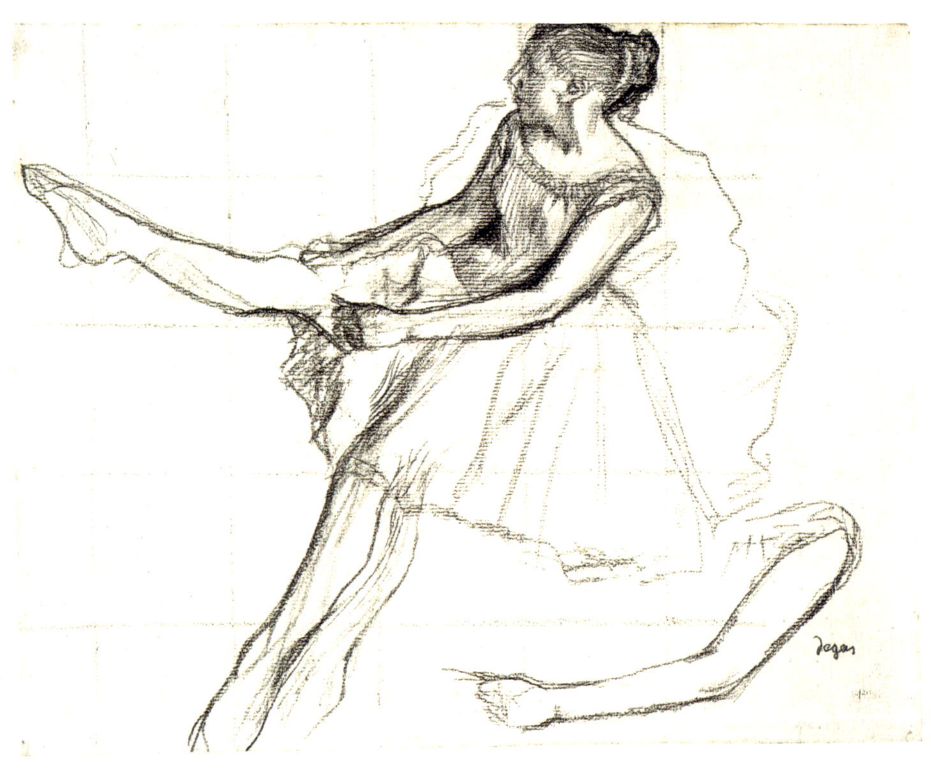

158. *Dancer Adjusting her Stocking, c.* 1880.
Black chalk, 24.2 × 31.3 cm (9½ × 12⅛ in.).
Fitzwilliam Museum, Cambridge

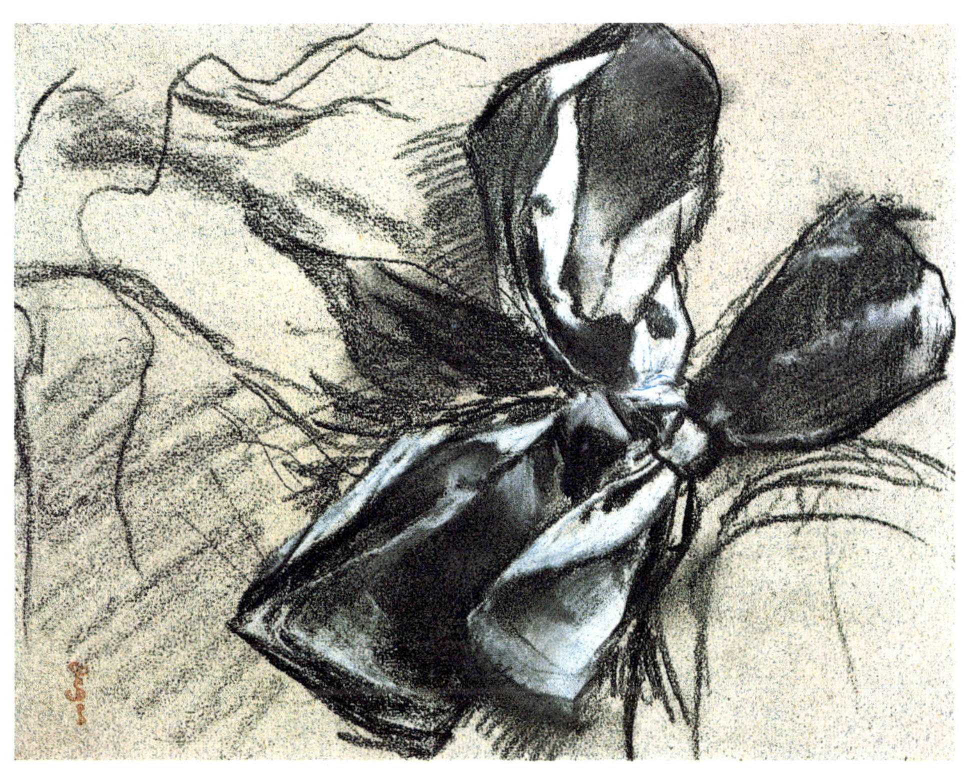

159. *Study of a Ribbon*, c. 1882–85.
Charcoal on grey-blue paper [with atelier stamp
incorrectly placed at lower left],
23.5 × 30 cm (9¼ × 11¾ in.).
Musée d'Orsay, Paris

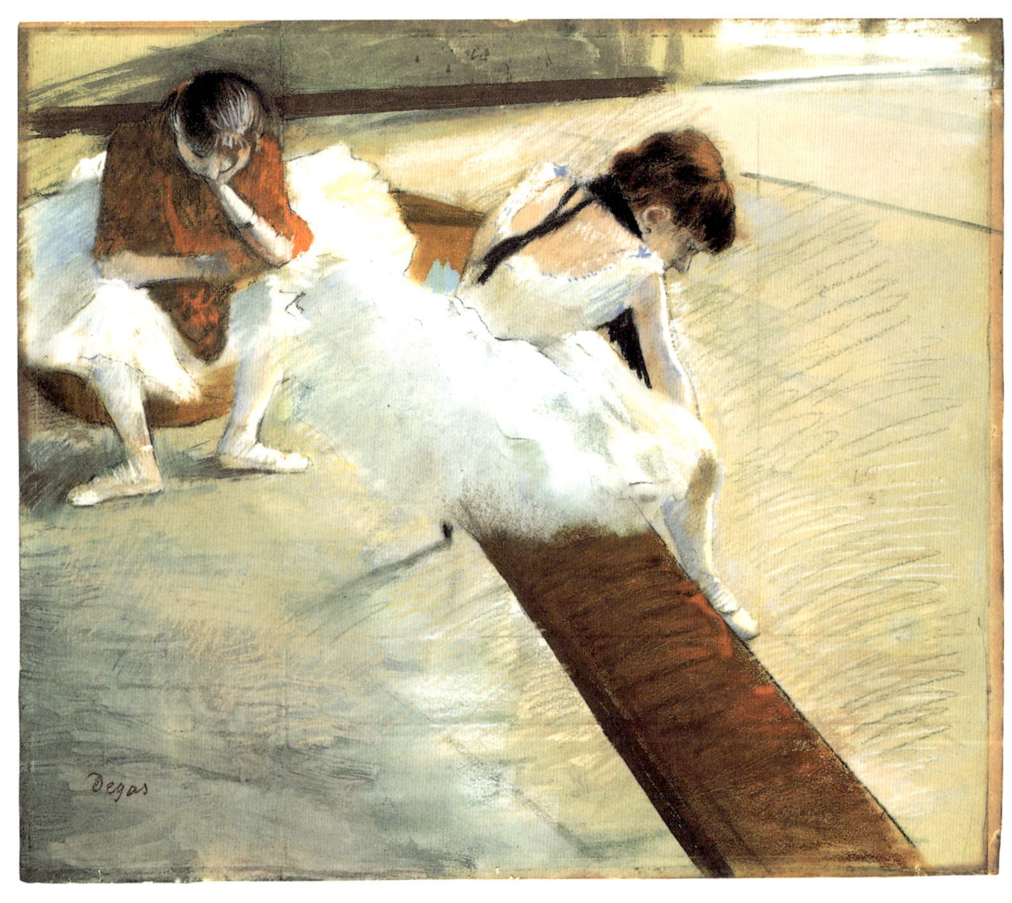

ABOVE

160. *Dancers Resting*, c. 1881–85.
Pastel on paper mounted on cardboard,
49.8 × 58.4 cm (19⅛ × 23 in.).
Museum of Fine Arts, Boston

OPPOSITE

161. *Dancer Stretching*, c. 1882–85.
Pastel, 46.7 × 29.7 cm (18⅛ × 11¾ in.).
Kimbell Art Museum, Fort Worth

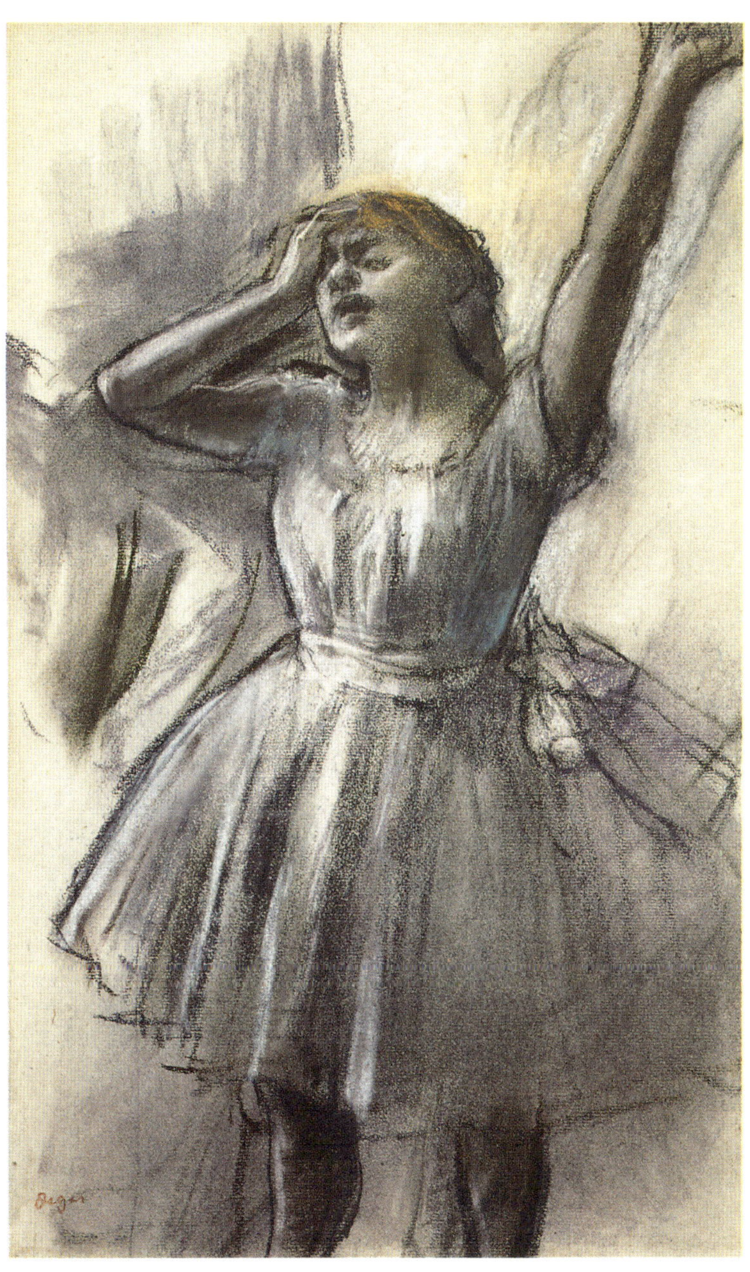

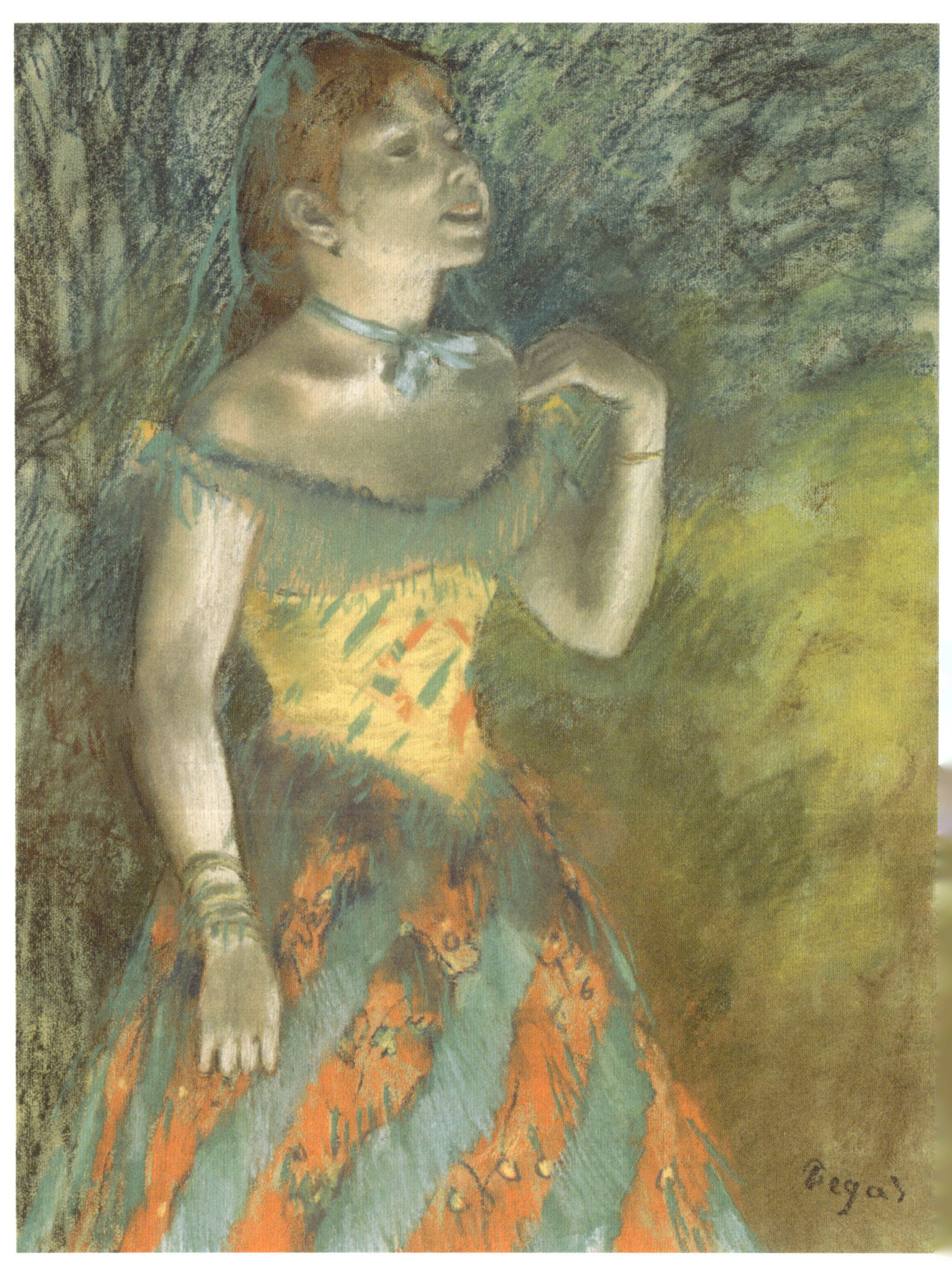

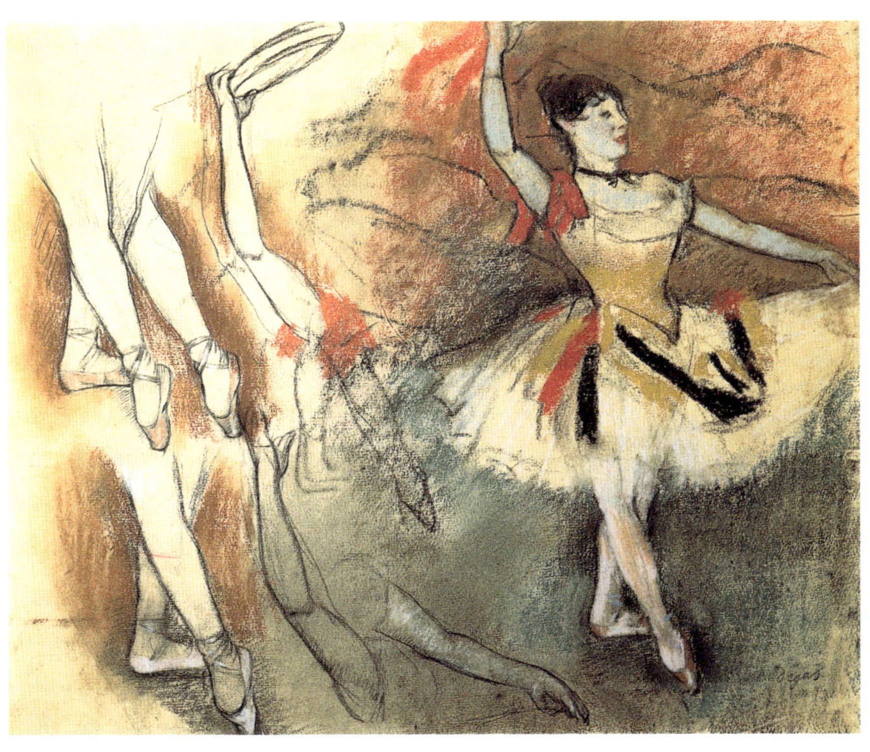

OPPOSITE
162. *The Singer in Green*, c. 1884.
Pastel on light blue paper, 60.3 × 46.3 cm (23¾ × 18¼ in.).
Metropolitan Museum of Art, New York

ABOVE
163. *Sheet of Studies: Dancer with a Tambourine*, c. 1882.
Pastel and pencil, 46 × 58 cm (18⅛ × 22⅞ in.).
Musée d'Orsay, Paris

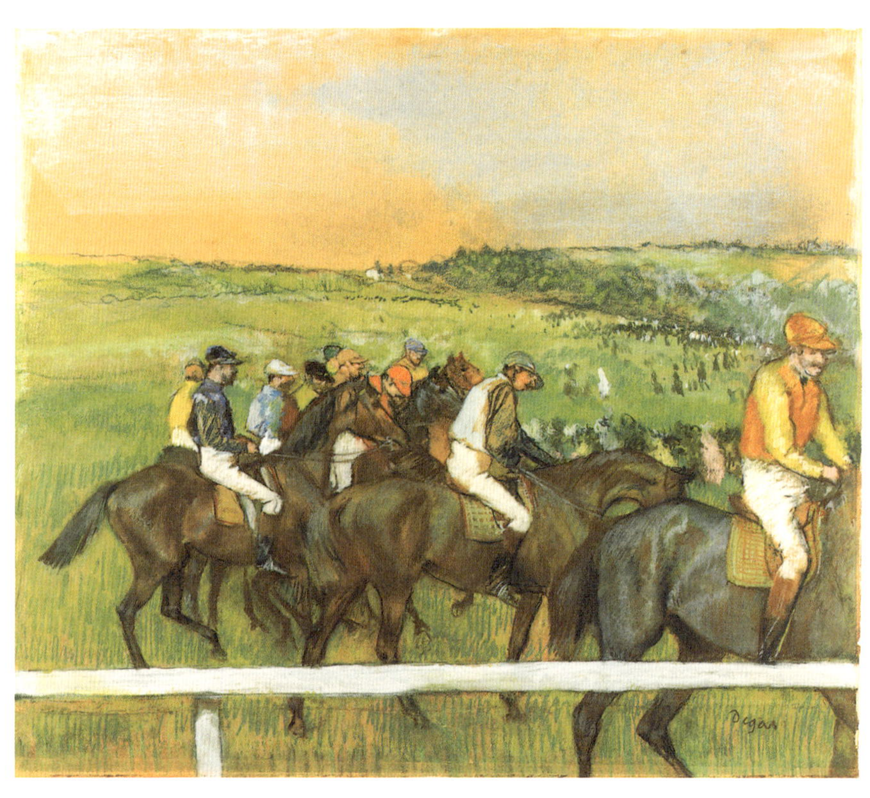

164. *Before the Race*, 1880–84.
Pastel, gouache and pencil over charcoal on tracing paper,
56.5 × 65.4 cm (22¼ × 25¾ in.).
Rhode Island School of Design, Providence

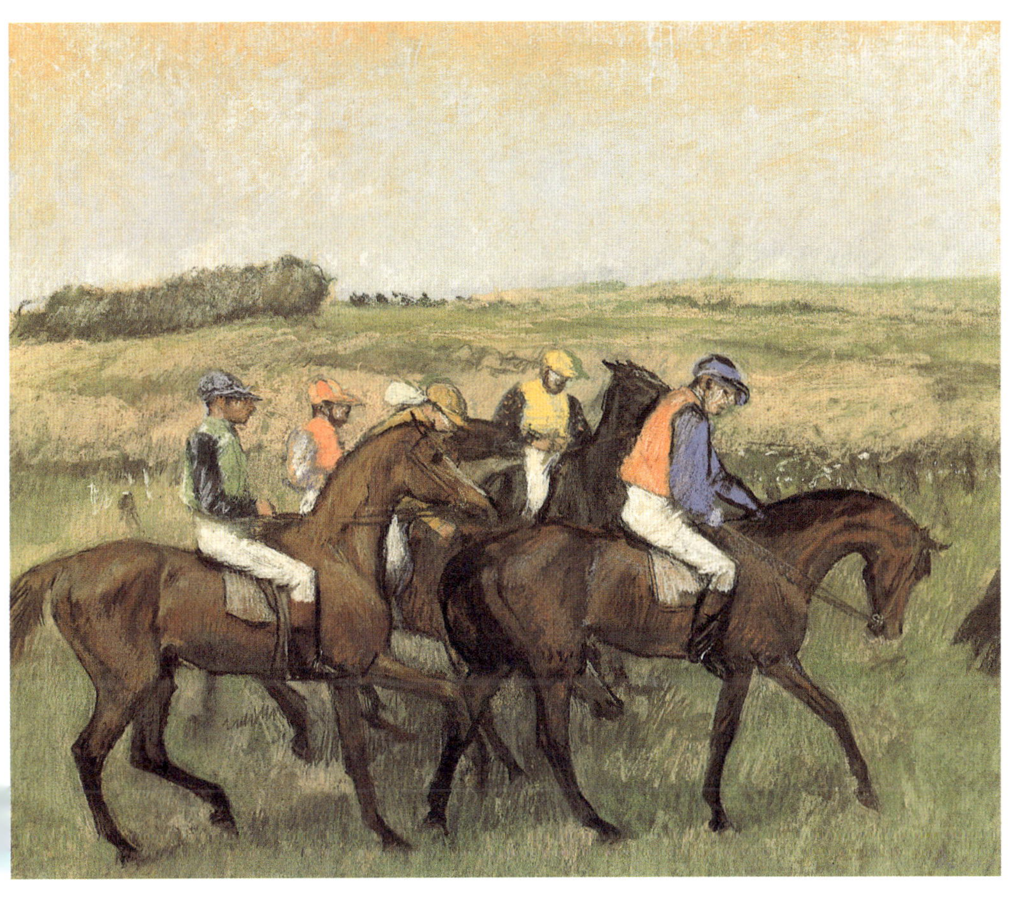

ABOVE
165. *The Racecourse, c.* 1885–87.
Pastel on cardboard, 42.5 × 49.5 cm (16¼ × 19½ in.).
Kunsthaus, Zurich

OVERLEAF
166. *Jockeys in the Rain, c.* 1883–86.
Pastel, 46.9 × 63.5 cm (18½ × 25 in.).
Burrell Collection, Glasgow

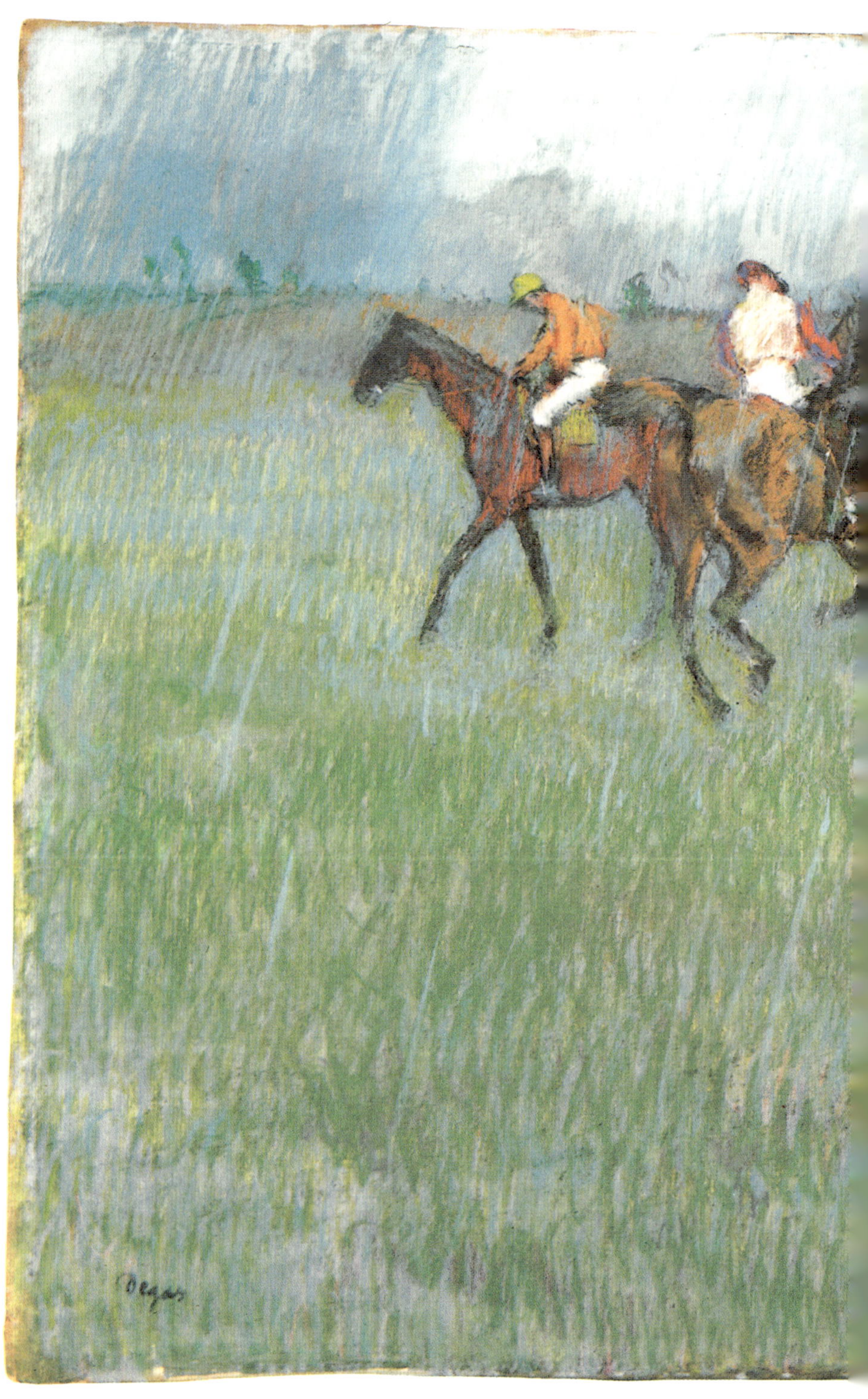

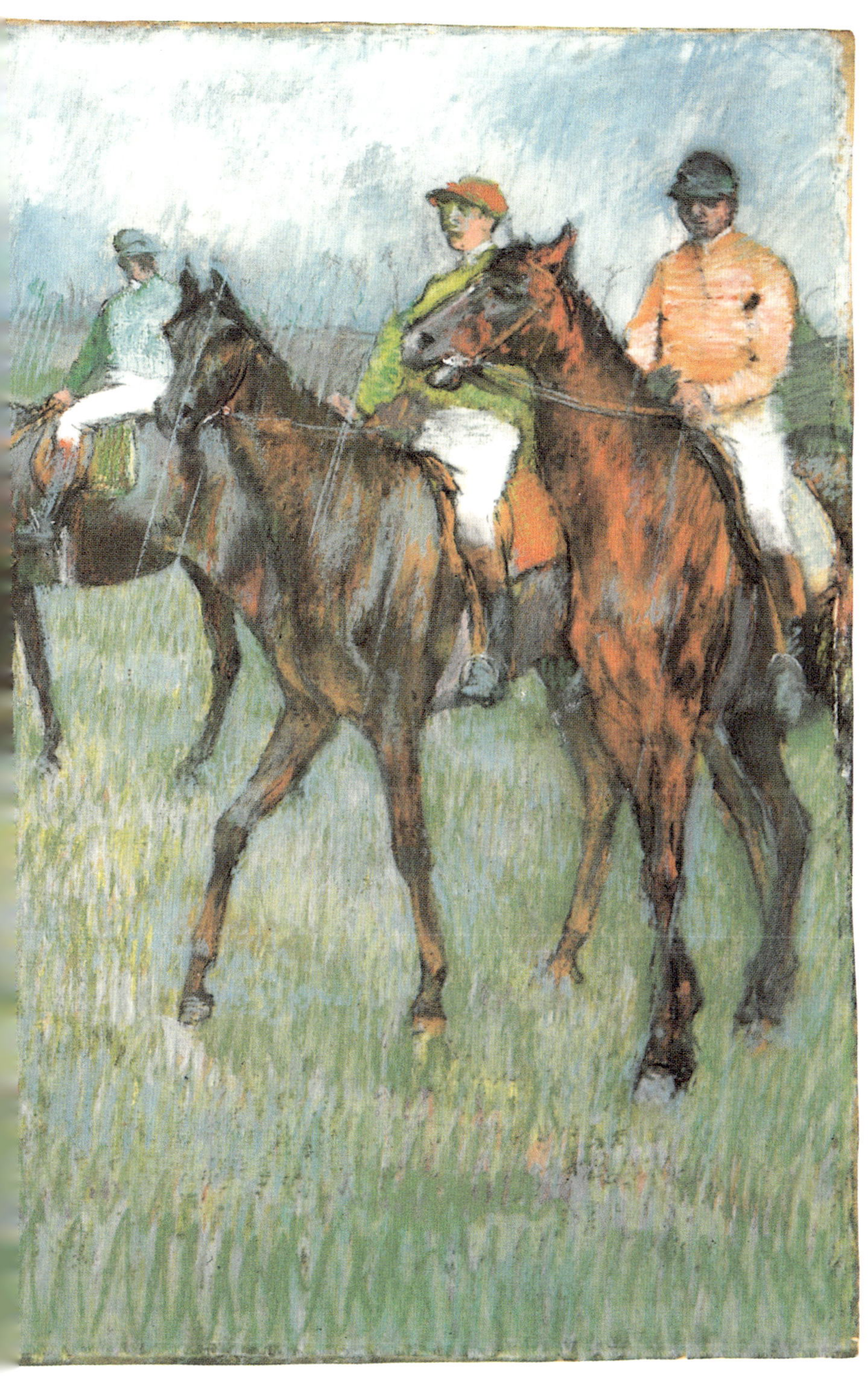

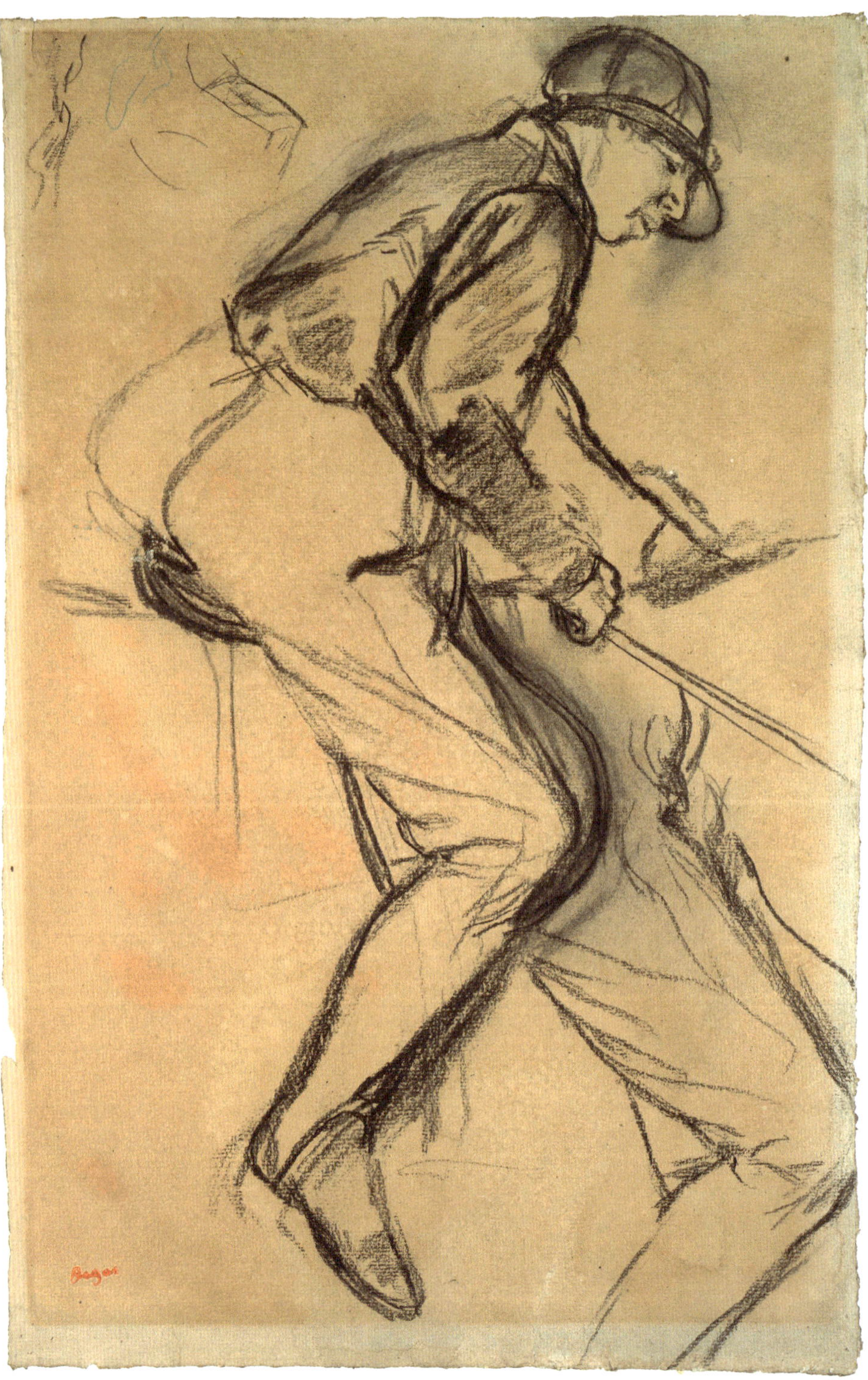

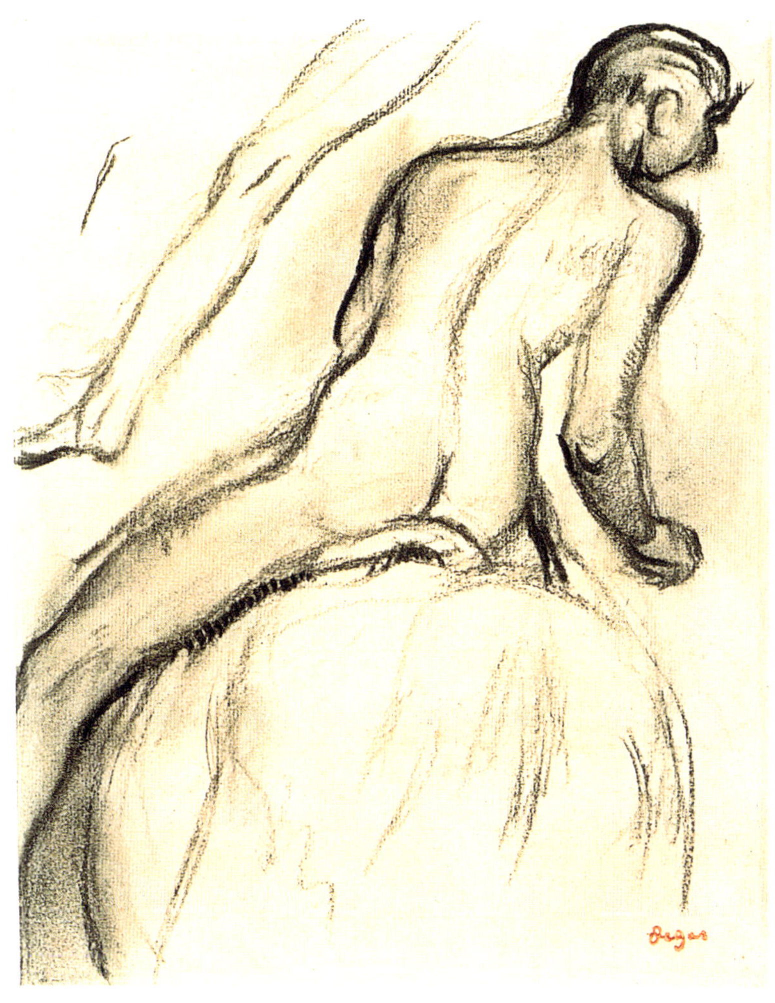

OPPOSITE
167. *Jockey in Profile, c.* 1884.
Charcoal, 48 × 31 cm (18⅞ × 12¼ in.).
Ashmolean Museum, Oxford

ABOVE
168. *Nude Study of a Jockey,* 1885–90.
Charcoal, 31 × 24.9 cm (12¼ × 9¾ in.).
Boymans-van Beuningen Museum, Rotterdam

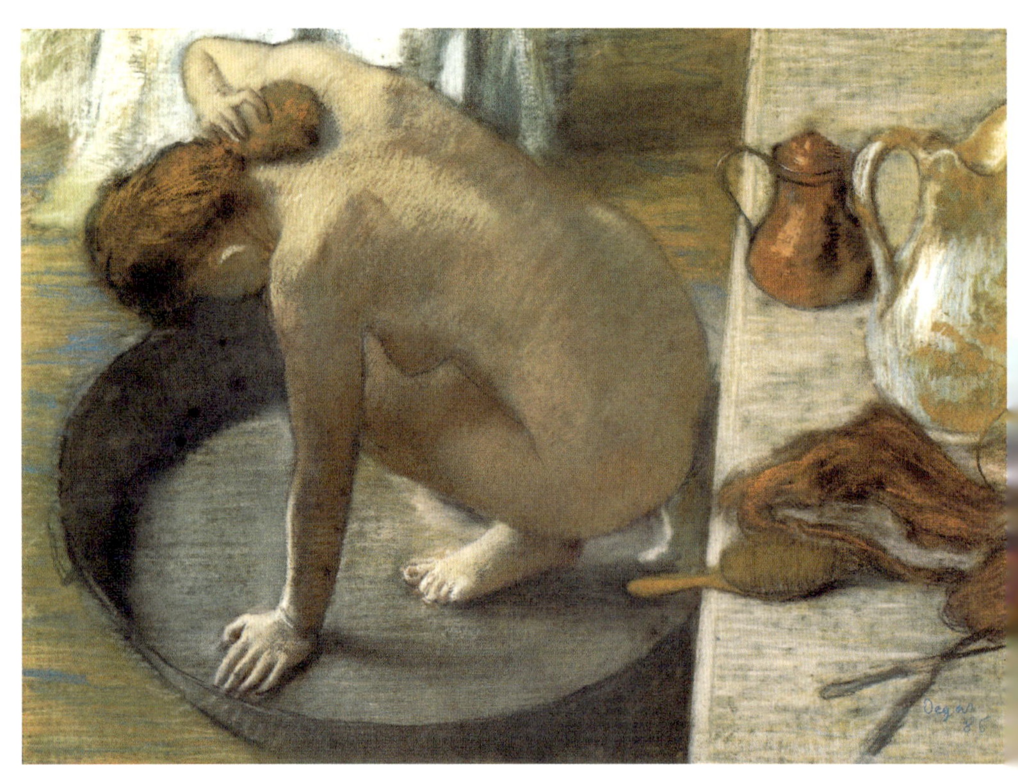

169. *The Tub*, 1886.
Pastel, 60 × 83 cm (23⅝ × 32⅝ in.).
Musée d'Orsay, Paris

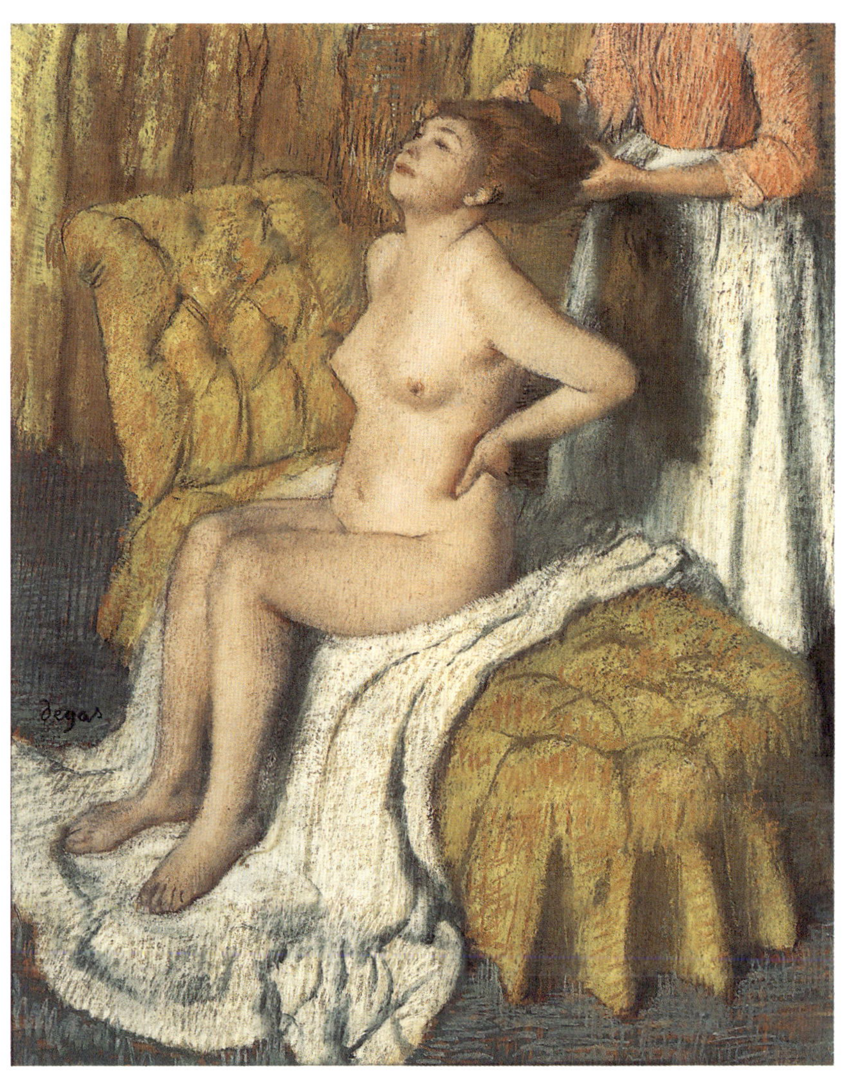

170. *Woman Having her Hair Combed*, 1886–88.
Pastel on light green paper, 74 × 60 cm (29⅛ × 23⅝ in.).
Metropolitan Museum of Art, New York

171. *Retiring*, c. 1883.
Pastel, 36.4 × 43 cm
(14⅜ × 16⅞ in.).
The Art Institute of Chicago

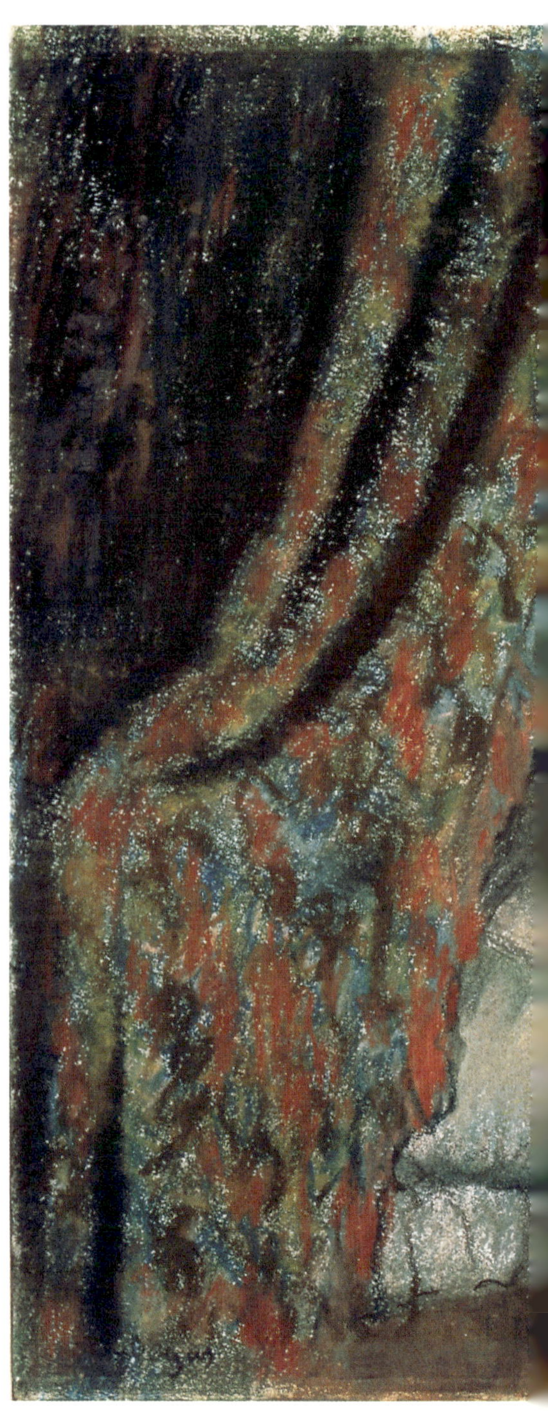

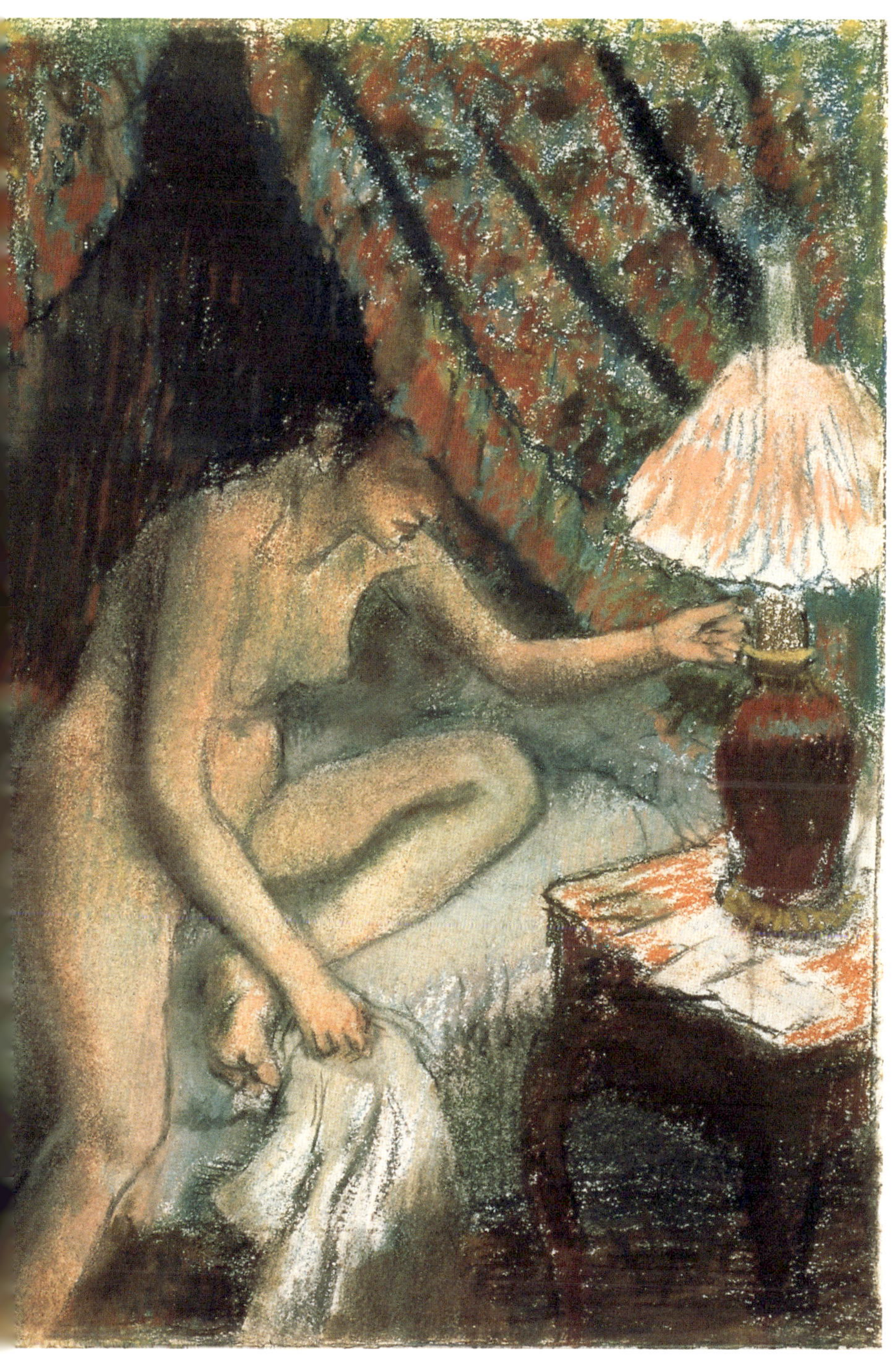

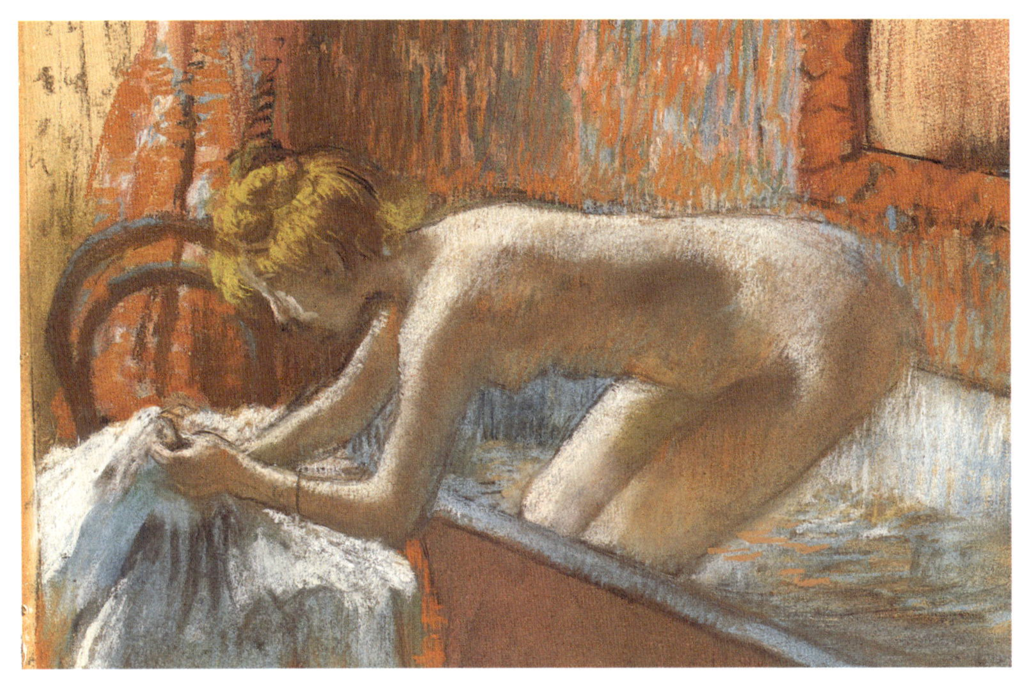

ABOVE
172. *Woman Getting out of the Bath*, *c.* 1886.
Pastel over monotype, 27.5 × 38 cm (10⅞ × 14⅞ in.).
Private collection

OPPOSITE
173. *Woman in a Tub*, *c.* 1883.
Pastel, 70 × 70 cm (27½ × 27½ in.).
Tate, London

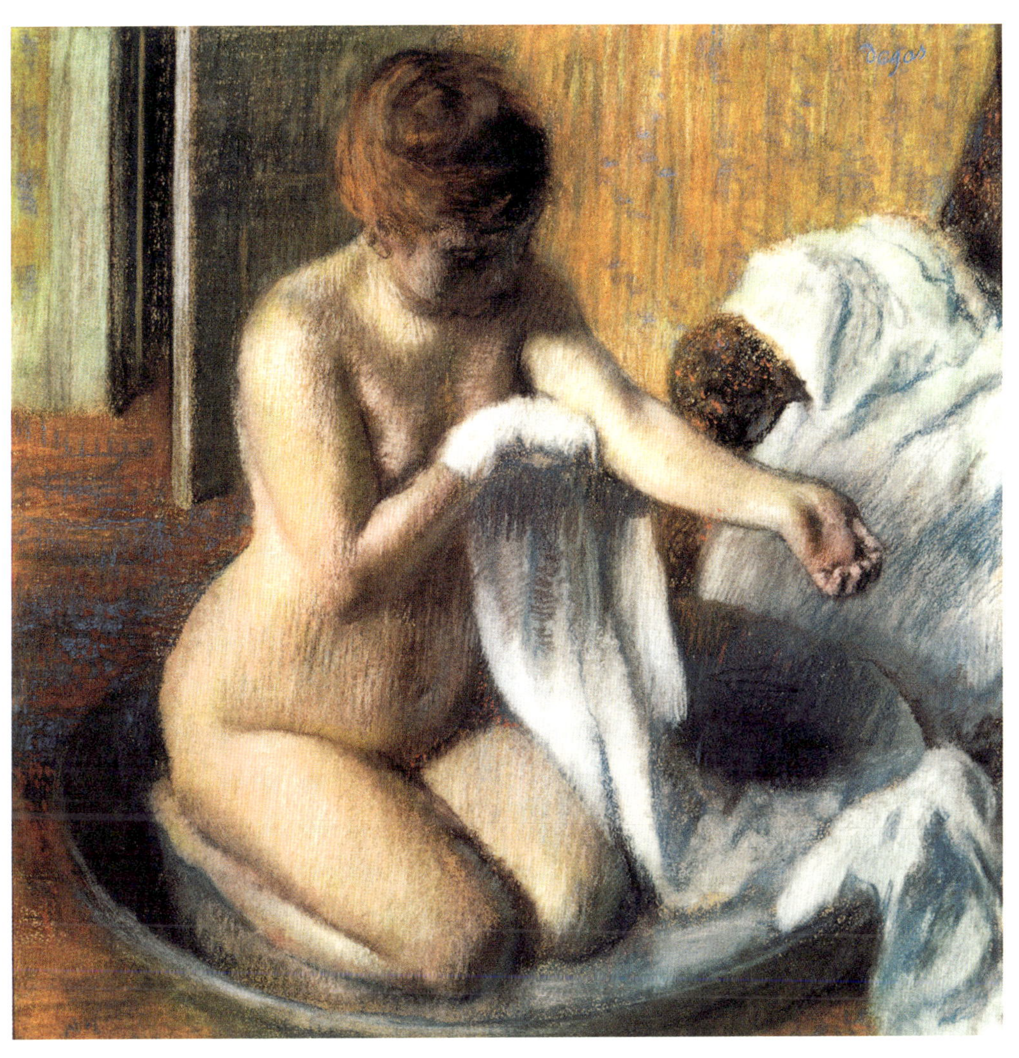

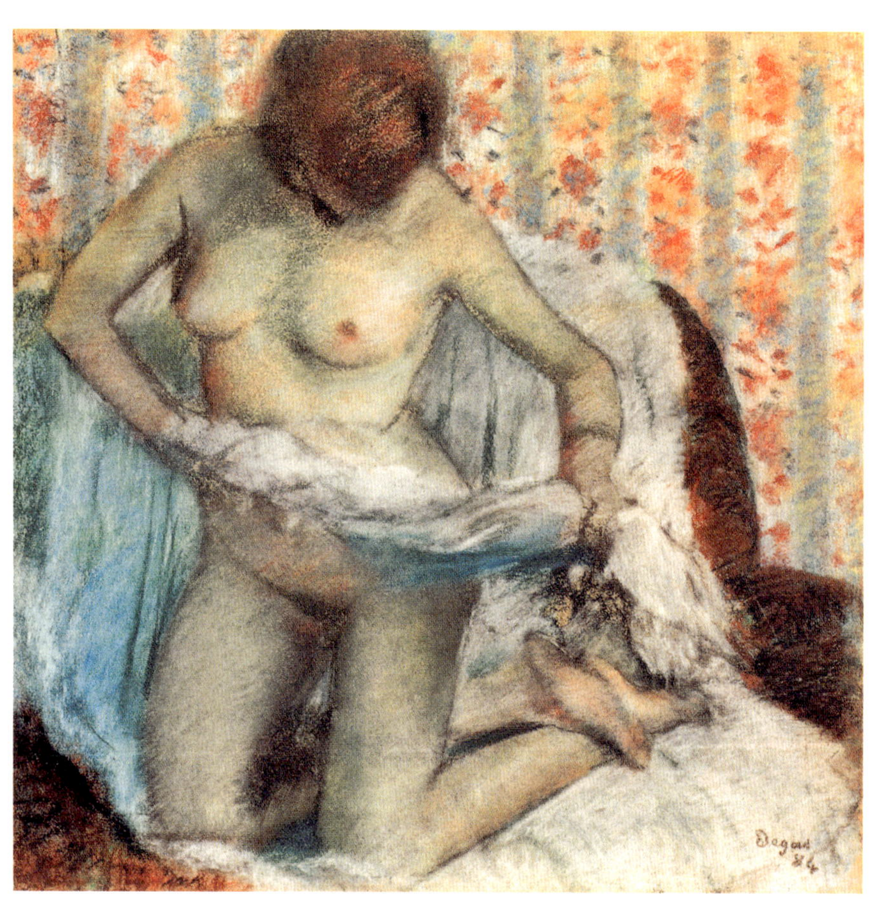

174. *Nude Woman Drying Herself*, 1884.
Pastel, 50 × 50 cm (19⅛ × 19⅛ in.).
State Hermitage Museum, St Petersburg

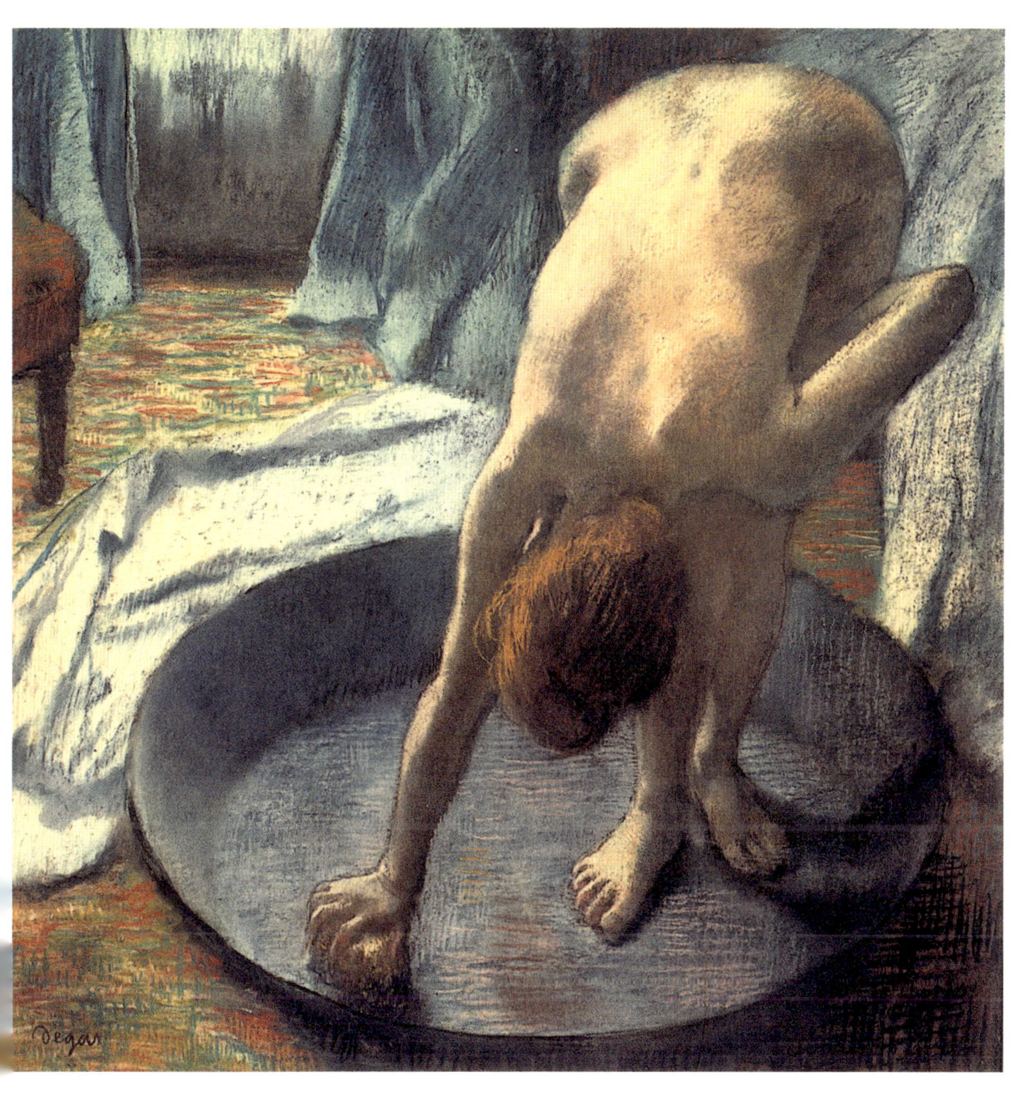

175. *The Tub*, 1886.
Pastel, 70 × 70 cm (27½ × 27½ in.).
Hill-Stead Museum, Farmington, Connecticut

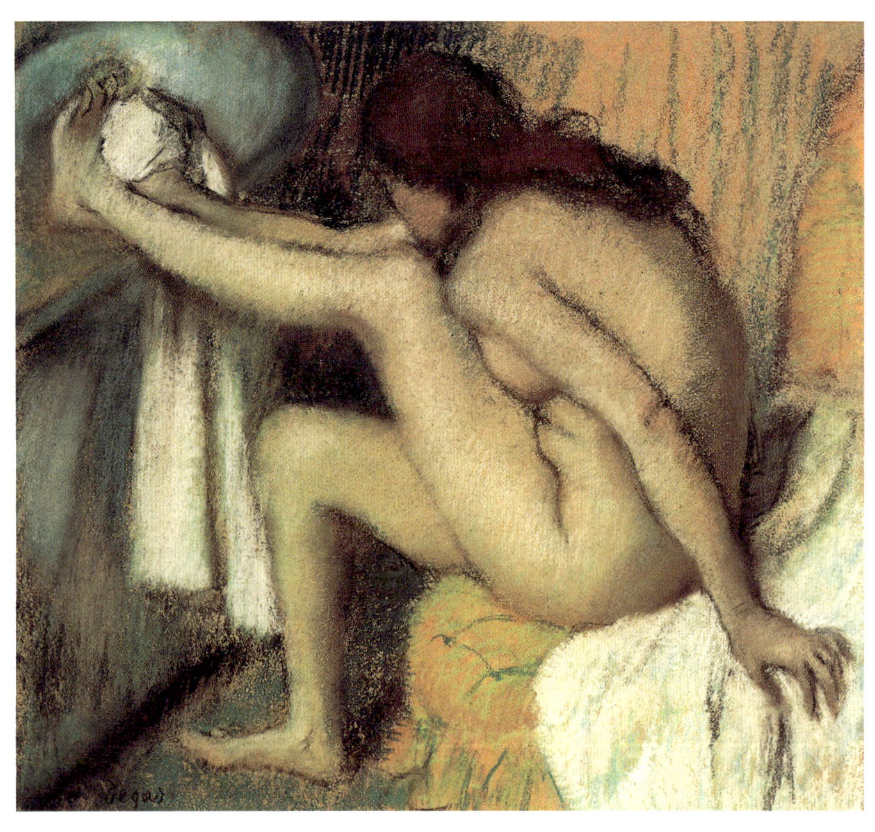

ABOVE

176. *Woman Drying her Left Foot*, 1885–86.
Pastel, 54 × 52 cm (21¼ × 20½ in.).
Musée d'Orsay, Paris

OPPOSITE

177. *Woman Combing her Hair*, 1888–90.
Pastel on light green paper mounted on board,
61.3 × 46 cm (24⅛ × 18⅛ in.).
Metropolitan Museum of Art, New York

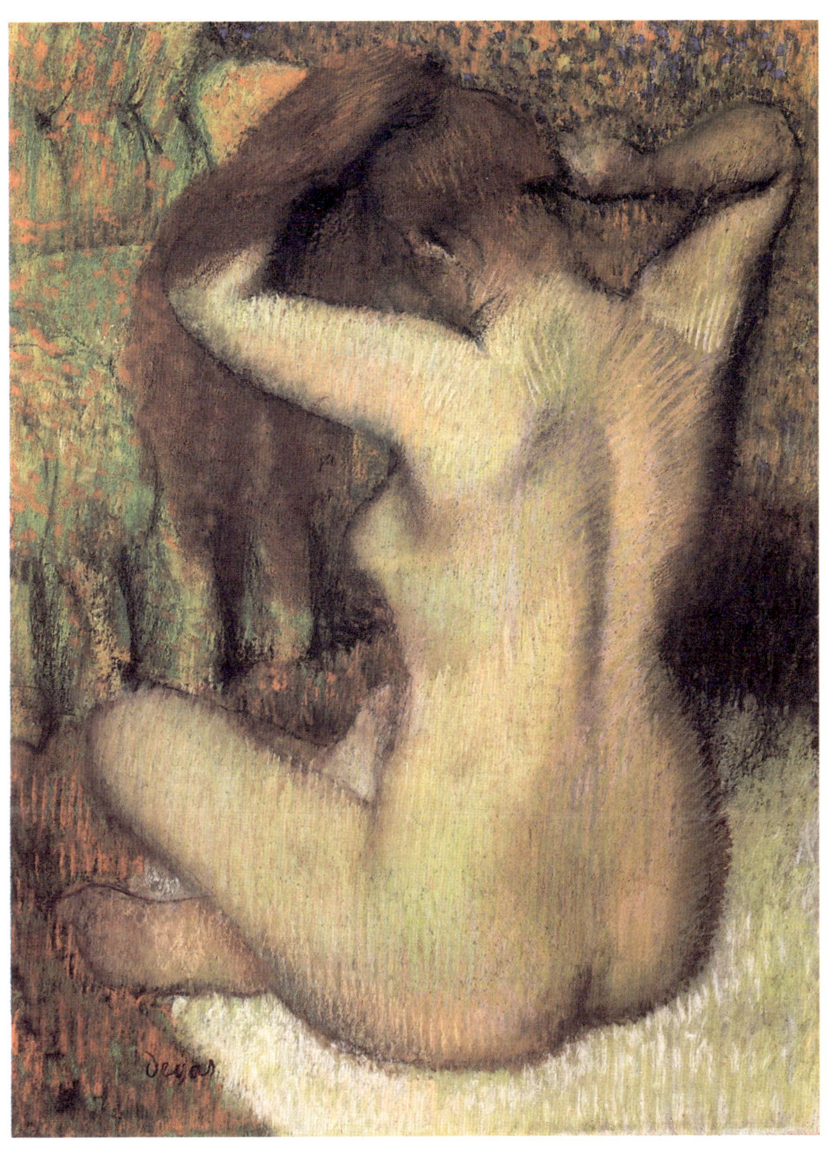

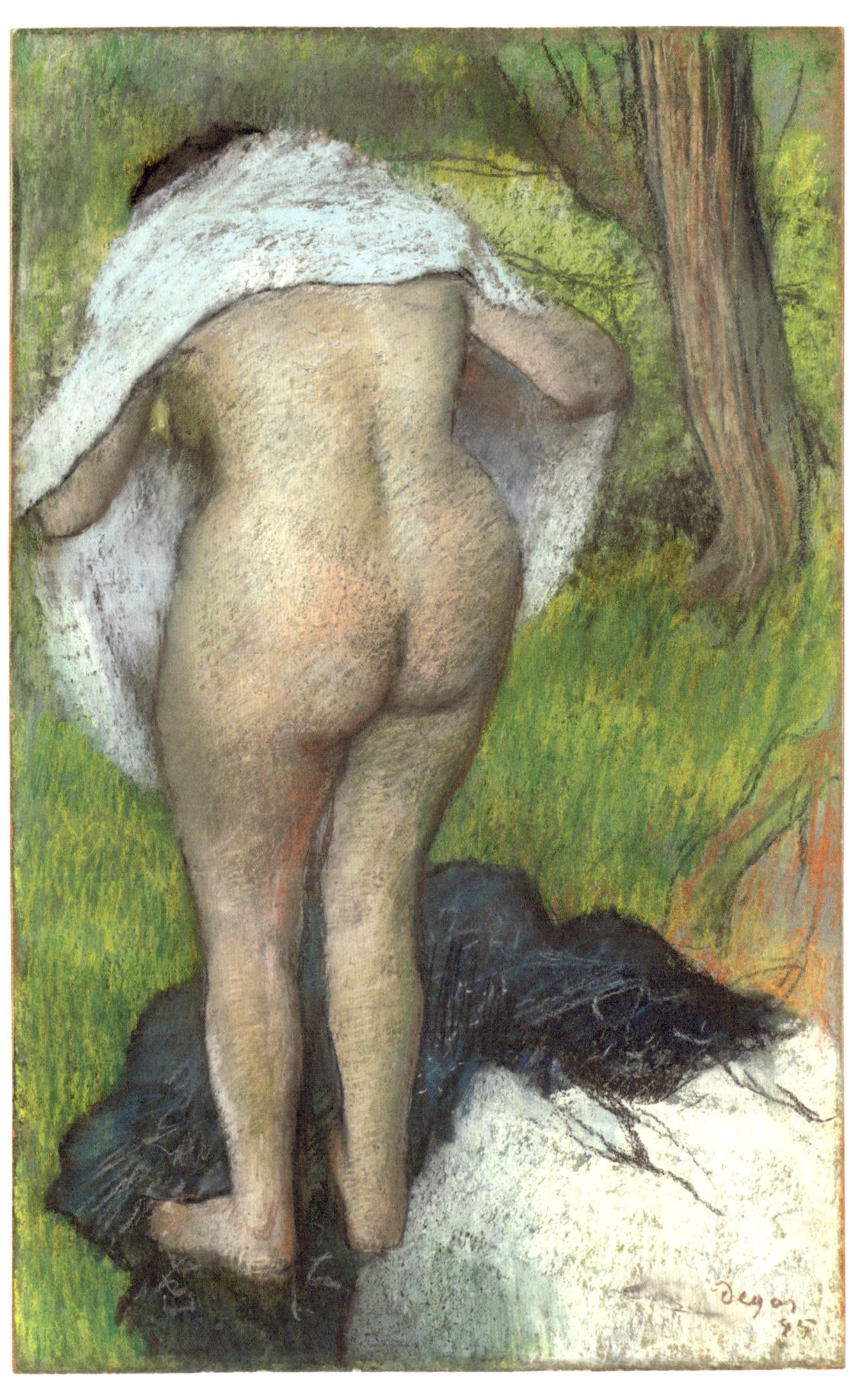

  Retreat into the Studio 1880–1890

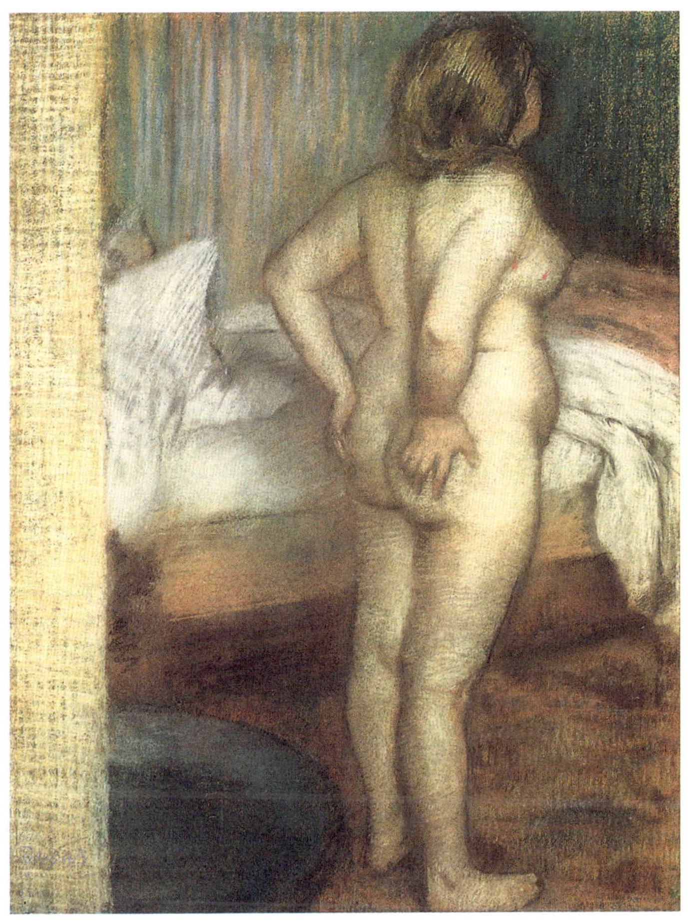

OPPOSITE
178. *Woman Dressing*, 1885.
Pastel, 80.1 × 51.2 cm (31½ × 20⅛ in.).
National Gallery of Art, Washington, DC

ABOVE
179. *Woman Getting Up*, 1885–86.
Pastel, 67 × 52.1 cm (26⅜ × 20½ in.).
The Henry and Rose Pearlman Foundation
on loan to Princeton University Art
Museum, New Jersey

180. *Woman Bathing in a Shallow Tub*, 1885.
Charcoal and pastel on light green paper, 81.3 × 56.2 cm (32 × 22⅛ in.).
Metropolitan Museum of Art, New York

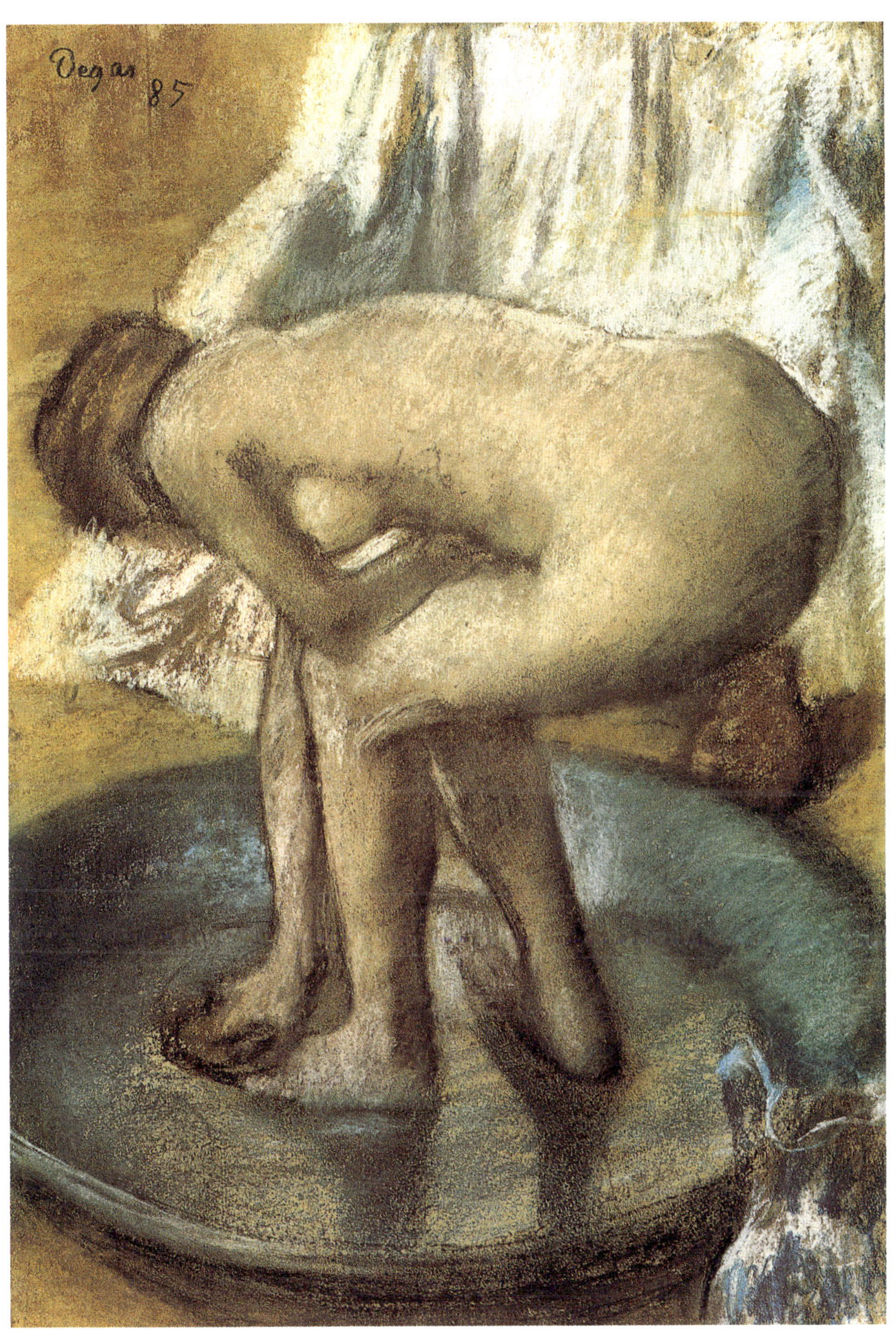

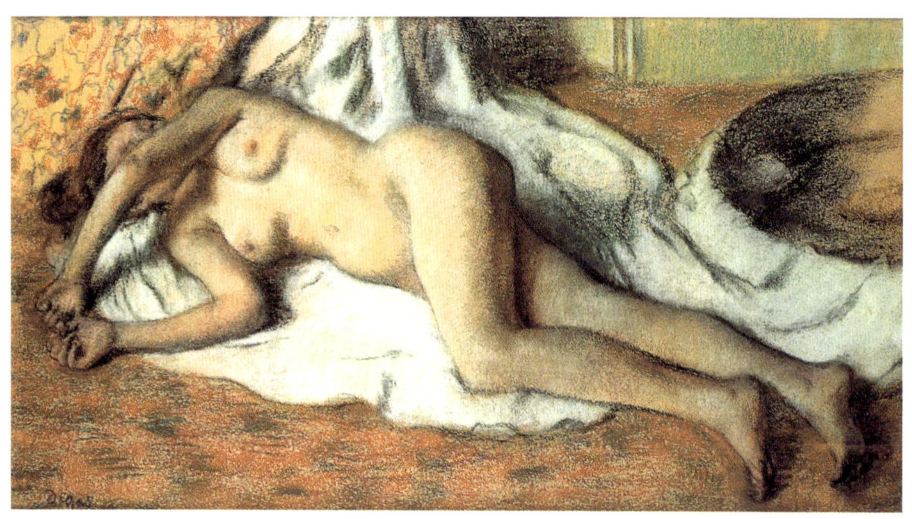

181. *Bather Stretched out on the Floor, c.* 1886.
Pastel, 48 × 87 cm (18⅞ × 34¼ in.).
Musée d'Orsay, Paris

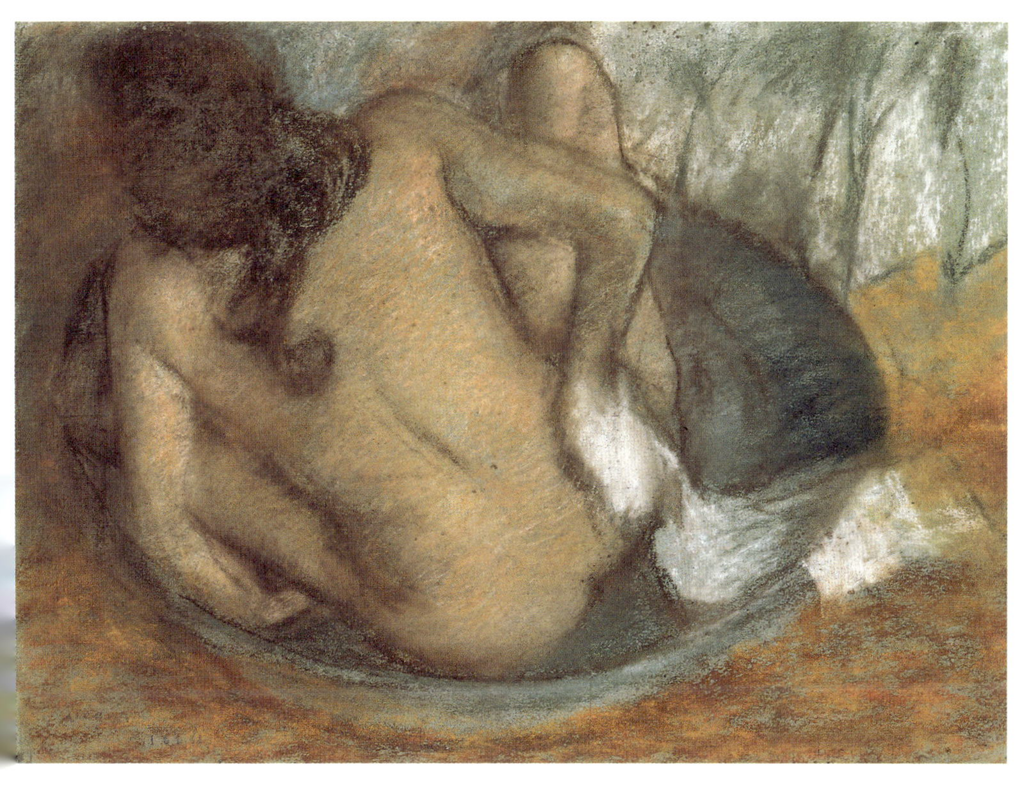

182. *The Tub*, 1884.
Pastel, 21 × 25 cm (8¼ × 9⅞ in.).
Burrell Collection, Glasgow

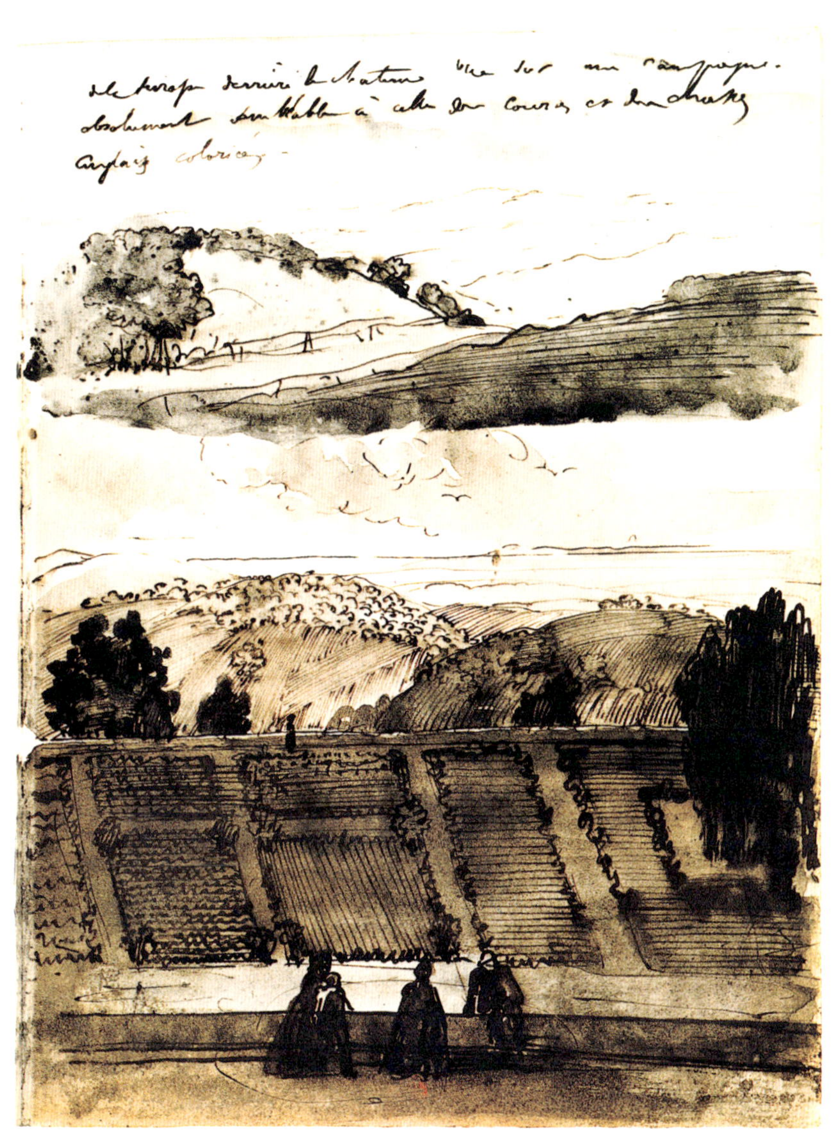

183. *Two Landscape Sketches*, Notebook 18, p. 163, 1861.
Brown ink with brown and grey wash,
25.4 × 19.2 cm (10 × 7½ in.).
Bibliothèque Nationale, Paris

CHAPTER SEVEN

Landscape Drawings

'Boredom soon overcomes me when I am contemplating nature.'

(Degas, Notebook 11, p. 66, used in Italy between 1857 and 1858)

Degas regularly claimed that his principal interest as an artist was the human figure. He believed this implicitly and he was determined that others should know it as well, to the point that it could almost be said that he conducted a propaganda campaign against landscape painting. Half in jest, he said to the dealer Ambroise Vollard:

> You know what I think of people who work out in the open. If I were the government I would have a special brigade of gendarmes to keep an eye on artists who paint landscapes from nature. Oh, I don't mean to kill anyone; just a little dose of bird-shot now and then as a warning.

And he liked to tease his close friend, the amateur artist Henri Rouart, by informing him that 'Painting is not a sport!' in the knowledge that Rouart was a gifted painter and watercolourist (he exhibited in seven of the Impressionist exhibitions) who often worked in the open air. Then there was Degas the joker, who on visiting an exhibition of Monet's landscapes was seen to turn up his collar against the draught because there was too much fresh air in the pictures. In the end, it is probably the case that Degas came to believe his own propaganda.

Looked at objectively, however, although Degas quite clearly distanced himself from such painters as Monet, Renoir, Pissarro and Sisley who were wholly or partially landscapists, there is considerable evidence to suggest that he was not quite as averse to natural beauty as he gave everybody to understand. The spontaneously written passages in his Notebooks indicate that not even Degas was totally immune to the charms of Italy – a country to which so many artists through the centuries were attached, including his famous forerunners, Claude

Lorrain and Nicolas Poussin. The years in Italy (1856–59), which involved a fair amount of travelling, saw an immediate and sympathetic response by Degas to his natural surroundings. This was evident not least in Naples where his family lived and which so many people undertaking the Grand Tour in the eighteenth century visited in order to admire the beauty of the Bay and to marvel at the powerful threat of Mount Vesuvius.

Degas was also alert to the natural scenery of France. A visit to his childhood friend Paul Valpinçon at Ménil-Hubert in Lower Normandy in 1861 induces an outbreak of almost stream-of-consciousness prose in reaction to the countryside:

> …left the road to Argentan and headed with Paul straight for Exmes. Exactly like England. Small and large meadows, all closed in by fences. Damp paths, ponds. Green and umber….Exmes, old church – how can anybody live here? Along steep and woody paths – after half an hour suddenly emerge into an avenue in a park, with gates. Beginning of the autumn, dead leaves cry out underfoot. We wait for the appearance of the horses.

The same passage reveals that Degas saw this particular countryside through the eyes of English painters – not J. M. W. Turner or John Constable, but lesser artists such as William Collins and William Mulready whose work had been shown at the Exposition Universelle of 1855. And at the same time he was reading Henry Fielding's novel *Tom Jones* (1749), which glories in traditional rural pursuits [183, 187].

Degas's resolve to resist the temptations of landscape weakened on other occasions in his career. A visit to the English Channel coast in 1869, when he worked at less popular resorts such as Villers-sur-Mer and Dives-sur-Mer, not the more fashionable Deauville and Trouville, resulted in a sudden output of over forty pastels [see 78–82]. These, as has been mentioned earlier, are almost nebulous when compared with the more socially conscious renderings of the coastal resorts undertaken by Boudin and Monet. Degas's approach is partially explained by a passage written in Notebook 23, which refers in a technical way to colour, tone and atmosphere:

> Villers-sur-Mer, sun-set, cold and dull orange-pink, whitish green neutral, sea like a sardine's back and clearer than the sky. Line of the seashore brown, the first pools of water reflecting the orange, the second reflecting the upper sky; in front coffee-coloured sand, rather sombre.

Degas was in higher spirits when he travelled with the sculptor Paul-Albert Bartholomé in 1890 to visit their friend the artist Georges

Jeanniot in Burgundy. The journey was undertaken in a tilbury (a two-wheeled horse-drawn carriage) and involved journeying south-eastwards from Paris following the river Seine to the village of Diénay, twenty miles north of Dijon. Letters written by Degas to friends show that he treated the trip as a 'progress' through the French countryside with the gastronomic delights at first perhaps of a greater significance than the visual experiences. The result was not only an unexpected breakthrough in Degas's printmaking techniques but also a whole new development in his art. Over thirty colour monotypes, some heightened with pastel, record the artist's impressions of this journey into the hinterland of France [188, 189, 202].

A similar damascene experience befell Degas in 1898 when he revisited one of the places closely associated with his childhood. This was the estuary town of Saint Valéry-sur-Somme on the coast of the English Channel near Abbeville in Picardy. It was here during the 1890s that Degas's brother René went on holiday and was often joined by the artist. When Degas suddenly decided to confront the motifs offered by this coastal resort he was ageing rapidly and the fifteen paintings and pastels he produced in 1898 are in his late style. The compositions are more linear as though enveloped in scaffolding, but the paint is dabbed on to the canvas creating a muffled effect like the use of the soft pedal on a piano. These works have a strong structural sense and are comparable with Cézanne's landscapes of Provence done during this same decade. As with the pastels of 1869, there is a melancholy air about these views of Saint Valéry-sur-Somme, which mark the start of a long process of closure to Degas's working life [201]. The opera singer Jeanne Raunay states in her reminiscences of the artist:

> Degas loved to return to this little town where his parents had taken him as a child. He found everything he had once enjoyed: the sea with all its surprises, roads bordered by old houses, the walls of a ruined tower, a monumental gate under which Joan of Arc had passed; but above all he would rediscover the first memories of his childhood, and he could recall those he had loved.

Whatever his attitude to landscape, therefore, there is a sense in which Degas could not escape it. He was, for instance, an inveterate traveller – in fact, with Monet, he was the most extensively travelled of all the Impressionists. Outside of Europe he went to America in 1872 and North Africa in 1889 and within Europe he moved easily and frequently between Italy, Spain, Switzerland, Belgium and Britain. Degas also travelled throughout France from the English Channel in the north to the Pyrenees in the south, as well as to Burgundy, Vaucluse and

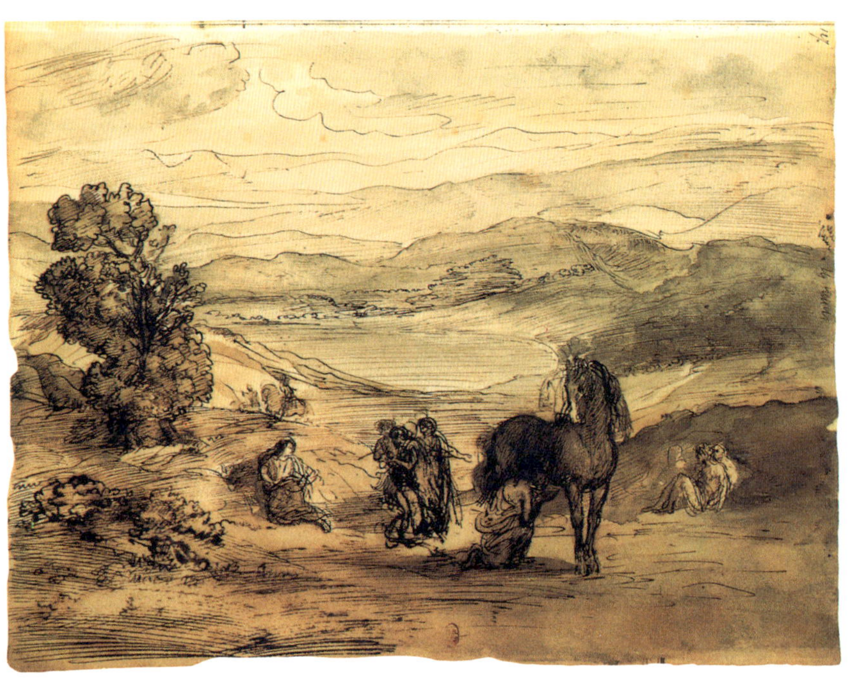

184. *Copy after Delacroix's 'Ovid among the Scythians'*, Notebook 18, p. 127, 1859.
Brown ink with brown and grey wash, 19.2 × 25.4 cm (7½ × 10 in.).
Bibliothèque Nationale, Paris

Tarn-et-Garonne, where at Montauban he paid homage to the memory
of Ingres. The frequency of the journeys increased through the 1880s
into the 1890s. The reason for this amount of travel was to see members
of his family, to spend time in the country with close friends such as the
Valpinçons, the Rouarts and the Halévys, to keep up old friendships
and, as he grew older, for health reasons, particularly to rest his eyes
from the incessant self-imposed toil of working in a darkened studio in
Paris. Degas certainly did not travel solely in order to view the landscape,
just as he eschewed fashionable resorts and obvious tourist landmarks.
Significantly, the carefully planned and closely documented journey to
Diénay and back through the Côte d'Or was not a popular route and
was not one promoted in contemporary guidebooks. Degas was not
interested in the picturesque and when he did turn his attention to the
landscape what he experienced was something much more elemental.

Landscape was also an important aspect in Degas's development as
an artist. At the start during the 1860s, when he was uncertain as to what
kind of painting he might pursue, his history pictures, notably *Young*

Spartans Exercising, The Daughter of Jephthah and *Scene of War in the Middle Ages*, necessitated landscape settings [see 34, 36, 39]. Degas's admiration for Delacroix increased when he acknowledged the latter's skill in distributing figures in a landscape without upsetting the balance between those two constituent parts of his composition – thus his early skilful copy of Delacroix's painting, *Ovid among the Scythians* [184]. Even though Degas did not pursue history painting and chose instead to depict scenes from modern life, landscape featured in the horse racing, steeplechase and hunting pictures. Only at the beginning were such landscapes inspired by specific views of racecourses such as Longchamp, which served Paris. Increasingly, the racecourse scenes were dominated by the landscape of Lower Normandy at Ménil-Hubert, which in turn Degas related to English sporting prints by artists such as J. F. Herring, Henry Alken and J. F. Pollard. And even the ballet pictures were not exempt in so far as the painted stage scenery incorporated mountains, clouds, trees and water [191]. An early watercolour, for example, relates to *Portrait of Mlle Eugénie Fiocre: à propos the Ballet 'La Source'* [see 56] and shows the degree to which Degas was aware of Courbet's treatment of the landscape at Ornans [190]. From the 1880s, however, as Degas's style evolved, the backgrounds of his painted compositions, including those of the horseracing subjects, became more generalized and ultimately imaginary so that the horses with their jockeys seem almost lost among the hills and mountains.

The ambivalence in Degas towards landscape stemmed from his training. Ingres, too, had instilled in him the priority of studying the human figure and so Degas only discovered landscape at one remove by looking at the works of Delacroix and through him at Venetian Renaissance painters such as Titian and Paolo Veronese. There is a feeling, therefore, that when Degas examined a landscape he felt that he was playing truant, which is why he equated the confrontation of the landscape – both in theory and practice – with being on holiday. Given these strictures, it is highly paradoxical that the only one-man exhibition of Degas's work held in France during his lifetime was devoted to landscapes. The exhibition was held in 1892. It was organized by the dealer Paul Durand-Ruel in his gallery in the Rue Laffitte. There were about twenty-six works, all of which were colour monotypes, a technique closely related to drawing, which Degas took up in 1890 at Diénay with remarkably innovative results [185]. Previously, during the mid- and late 1870s, he had made monotypes in monochrome, often dramatically heightening them with pastel. These were mostly of urban scenes, but a few experimental monotypes of small dimensions were of landscape motifs. At Diénay, with Jeanniot acting as his assistant, Degas felt

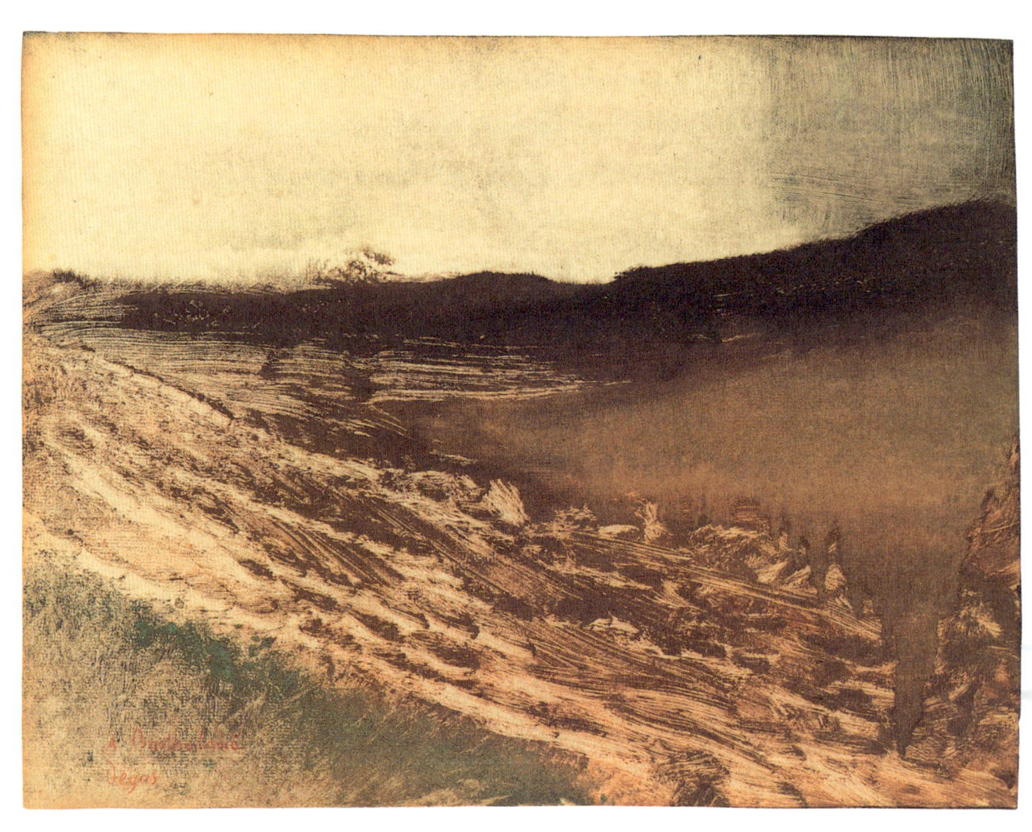

185. *Burgundy Landscape*, 1890.
Monotype, 30 × 40 cm (11¼ × 15¼ in.).
Musée d'Orsay, Paris

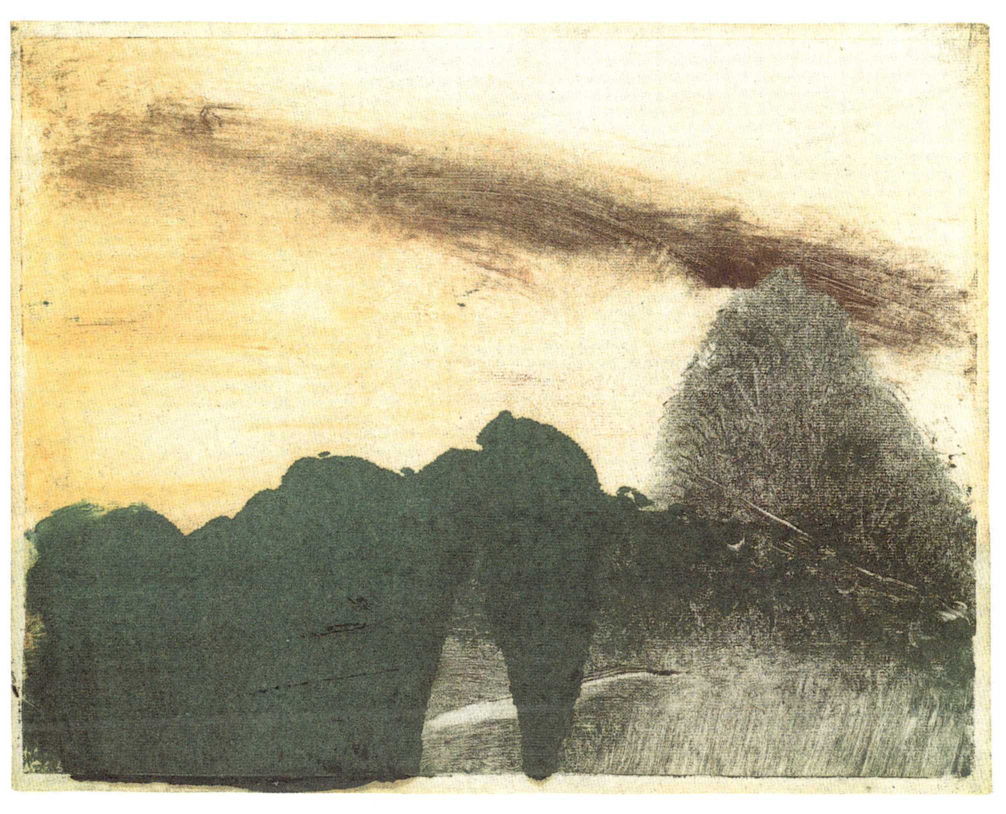

186. *Forest in the Mountains, c.* 1890.
Monotype, 30 × 40 cm (11¼ × 15¼ in.).
Museum of Modern Art, New York

liberated and for the first time made monotypes in colour, which he then
heightened with pastel according to whim [188, 189, 202].

Two years later, at Durand-Ruel's gallery where monotypes inspired
by trips to the Pyrenees and other parts of France were shown, in
addition to a few of those made at Diénay, Degas's mastery of the
medium was clearly evident for all to see [192–199]. The artist revelled
in the freedom of thinned down oil paint floating on the surface of a
metal plate, which he could then manipulate with pads, cloths, brushes,
fingers and thumbs – almost anything to hand. Contours and masses
could be transformed into different inchoate shapes and forms, some
of them on occasion alarmingly anthropomorphic, with additions in
pastel [193, 194]. The emphasis on colour was increased by the more
positive and robust use of pastel, not just as heightening but as part
of the process itself in conjunction with the thinned oil paint. The
compositions were the result of chance and accident owing to the
random dispersal of the medium at the time of printing [186]. Moreover,
the faded second impressions (only two were usually possible) could be
manipulated further after printing to form a cognate, or an 'echo', of
the first impression. In effect, these could seem like remarkably different
compositions and were probably hung as pairs at Durand-Ruel's gallery
[196 and 197, 198 and 199].

This sense of abandon in Degas's colour monotypes begs the
question as to whether they can legitimately be termed landscapes as
opposed to works of the imagination. It is known that Degas's eye
problems were worsening during the 1880s and 1890s and it is doubtful
that he could see all that much detail while passing through the
countryside at speed, either in a train or at the slower pace of a tilbury.
Of the monotypes made for exhibition at Durand-Ruel's gallery, Daniel
Halévy, the son of the artist's friend Ludovic Halévy, records Degas
saying: 'I would stand at the door of the coach and as the train went
along I would see things vaguely. That gave me the idea of doing the
landscapes.' It seems likely, therefore, that the colour monotypes were
basically done in the studio from memory after the journey was over.
Some of the views do have recognizable topographical features, but they
are generalized [188, 189, 192, 195]. Similarly, the colours are generic and
relate to different seasons, temporal conditions or times of day. There can
be no doubt that the colour monotypes as a group lack specificity. Degas
does not confront the scenery in a strictly topographical way so much
as reconstruct it in his mind. It is another example of how Degas could
depart so easily and so radically from a well-established tradition.

The works shown in Durand-Ruel's exhibition took everyone by
surprise. Degas himself reported to his sister Marguerite in an offhand

manner that the exhibition had been received 'rather favourably', but in fact it caught everyone off guard. An American visitor, Philip Hale, assessed the situation well:

> All these sketches represent the strangest, wildest country. They seem to have been done in some mountainous land of volcanic formation. Strange, fantastic-shaped peaks show sharply against the sky, and 'dreadful hollows' are at their base.

He goes on to describe an almost lunar landscape comprising such features as a glacier, a plain, a causeway, a lake, a tower, usually seen in isolation. Added to this are roads that lead over mountains to nowhere and islands that are set in limitless seas [202, 203]. These landscapes are deserted and seem becalmed or dormant. It is as though some terrible eruption or scene of chaos is about to take place or perhaps it is the world as it looked after the biblical floodwaters receded. Certainly it is imagery that is more redolent of Rodolphe Bresdin or Odilon Redon and diametrically opposed to anything that had appeared in Degas's work to this date.

Avant-garde critics such as Geoffroy recognized that in making such images Degas had liberated himself from Impressionism and was approaching Symbolism. He regarded the results as 'the passage of man across the scenery of things, and the wish to mark this passage by fixing the forms that so rapidly fade into the distance'. And he referred to their visual effect as comparable with 'precious sapphires in velvet jewellery boxes' and 'tapestries hung in secret boudoirs' with 'colours burnt by the light, disappearing in passages of greenish flame, falling into embers and pink ashes' – comparisons that resonate in Symbolist poetry. Degas's reaction to such analogies is not known, but when previously he was asked by Ludovic Halévy whether these 'vague things' reflected inner 'states of mind' the artist replied that they were more to do with 'states of eyes', thereby rather typically brushing aside any deep-seated philosophical connotations that his work might have – 'We do not use such pretentious language', Degas magisterially remarked.

187. *Sketch of a Landscape*, Notebook 18, p. 165, 1861.
Brown ink with wash, heightened with white,
25.4 × 19.2 cm (10 × 7½ in.).
Bibliothèque Nationale, Paris

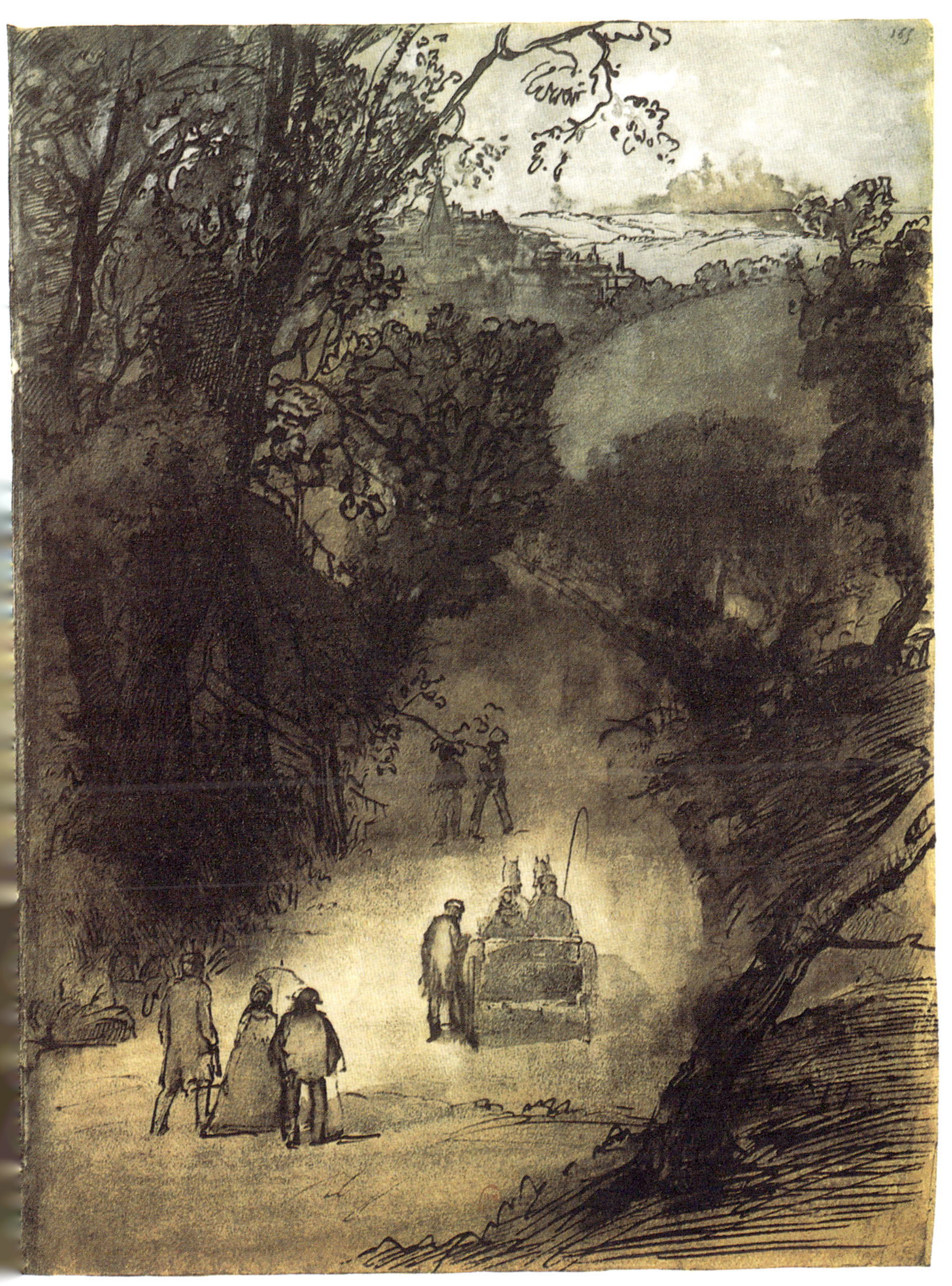

Landscape Drawings   253

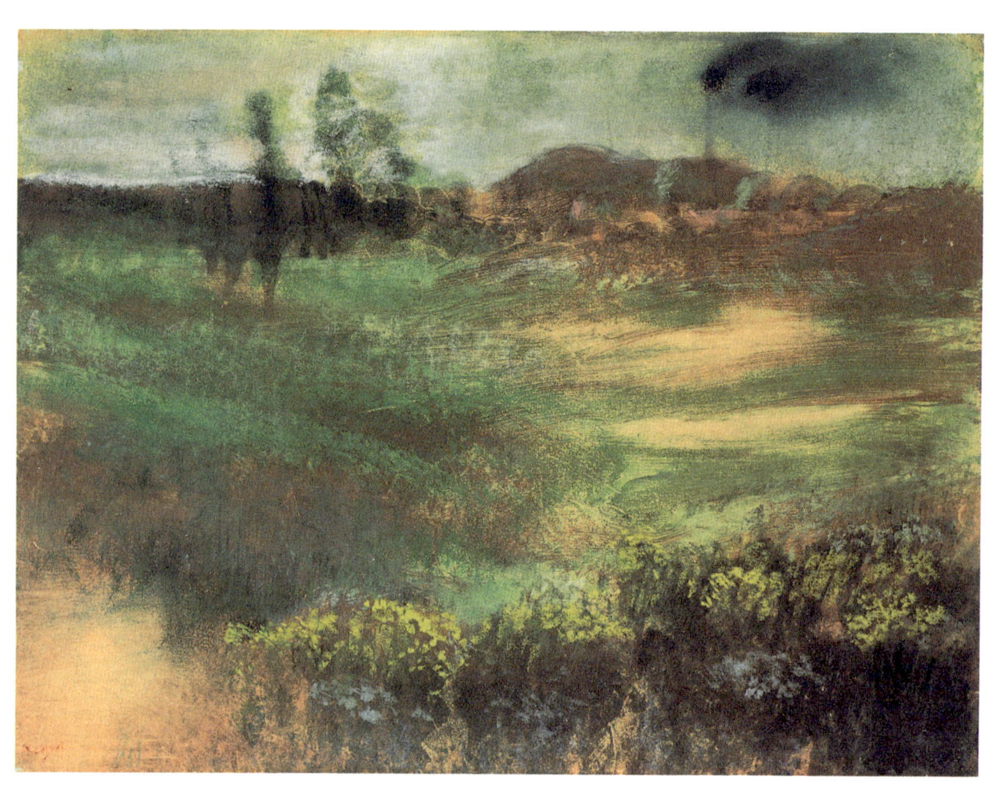

188. *Landscape with Smokestacks*, 1890.
Monotype and pastel, 31.7 × 41.6 cm (12½ × 16⅛ in.).
The Art Institute of Chicago

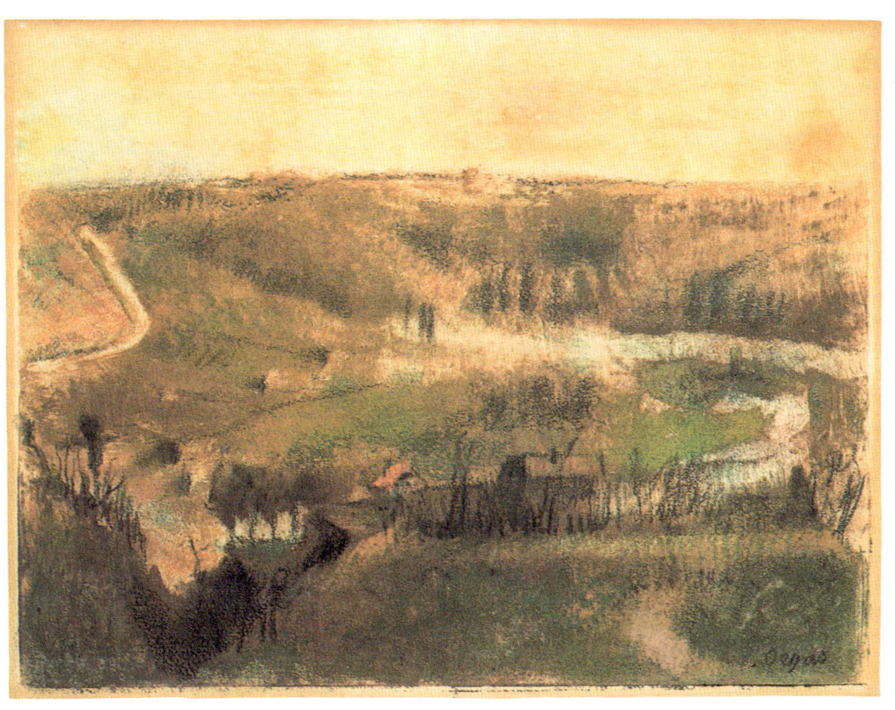

189. *Autumn Landscape*, 1890.
Monotype and pastel, 31.1 × 41.3 cm (12¼ × 16¼ in.).
Museum of Fine Arts, Boston

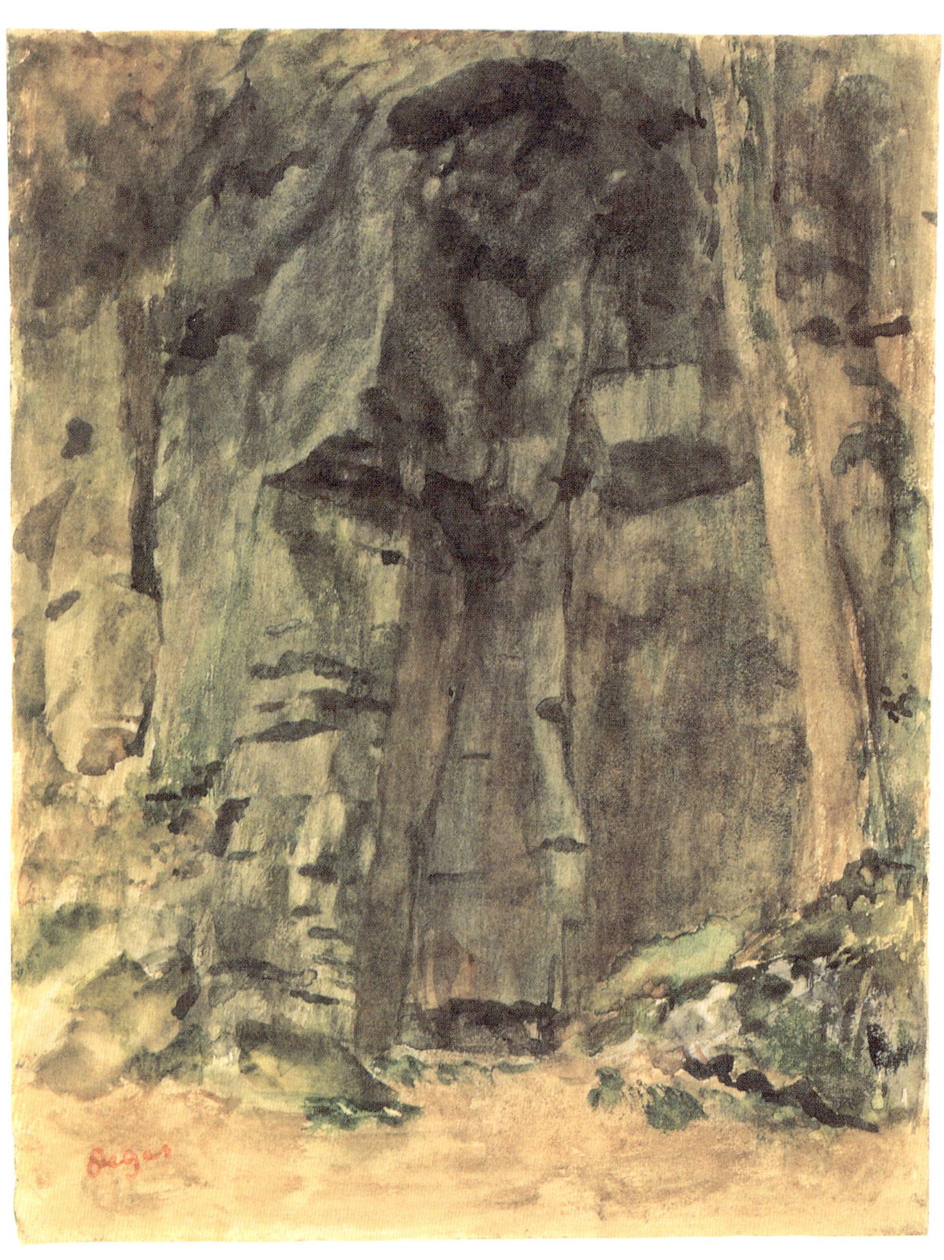

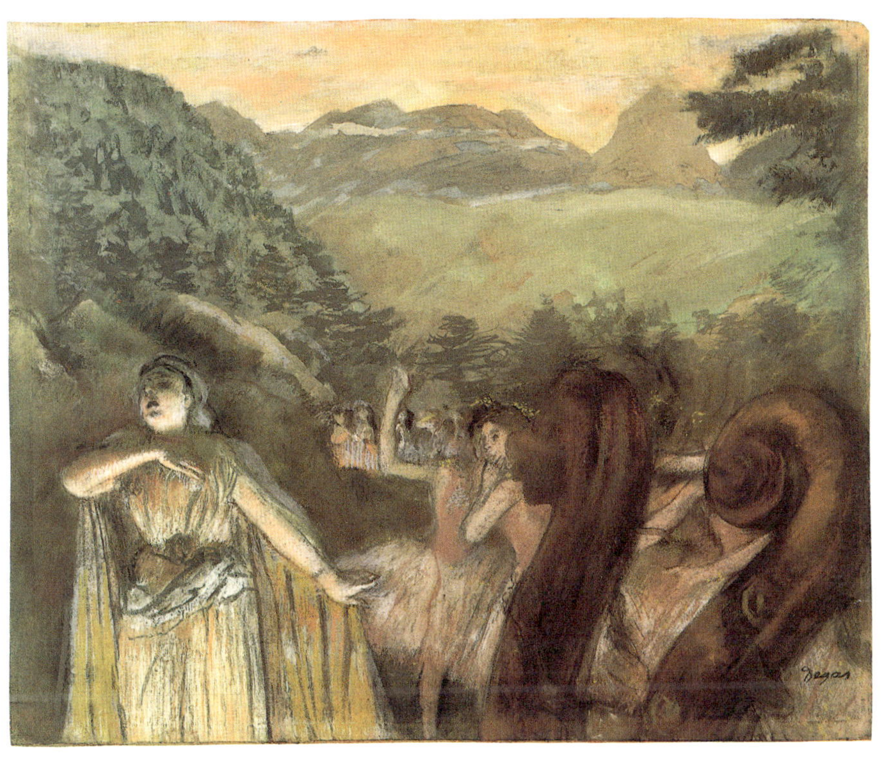

OPPOSITE
190. *Rocks and Trees at Bagnoles-de-l'Orne, c.* 1867.
Watercolour, 25.5 × 20.1 cm (10 × 7⅞ in.).
Fitzwilliam Museum, Cambridge

ABOVE
191. *Aria after the Ballet, c.* 1879.
Pastel with essence, 59.7 × 75 cm (23½ × 29½ in.).
Dallas Museum of Art

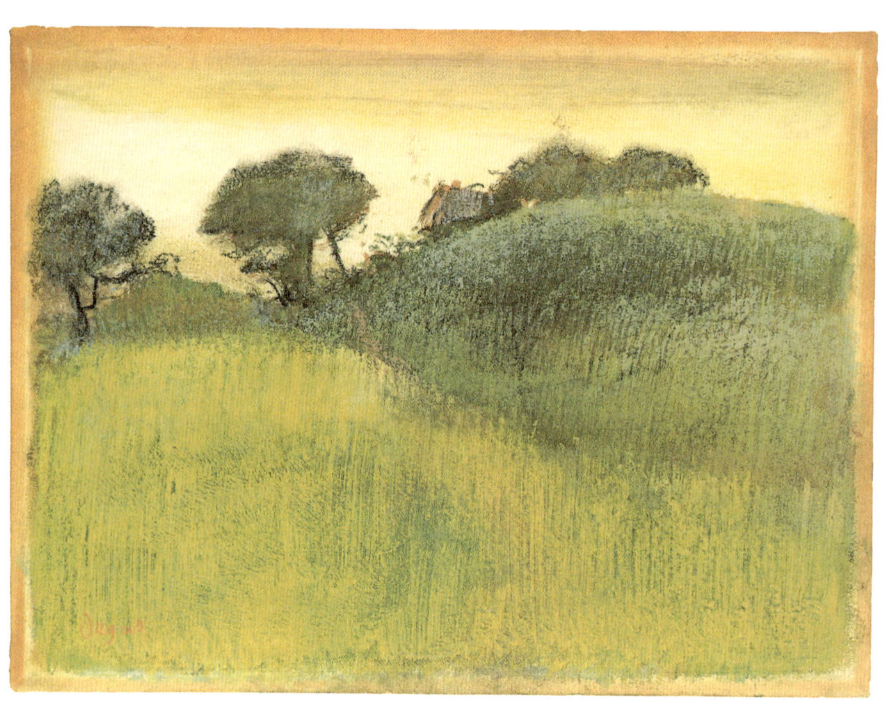

192. *Wheatfield and Green Hill*, 1892.
Monotype and pastel, 26 × 34 cm (10¼ × 13⅜ in.).
Norton Simon Art Foundation, Pasadena

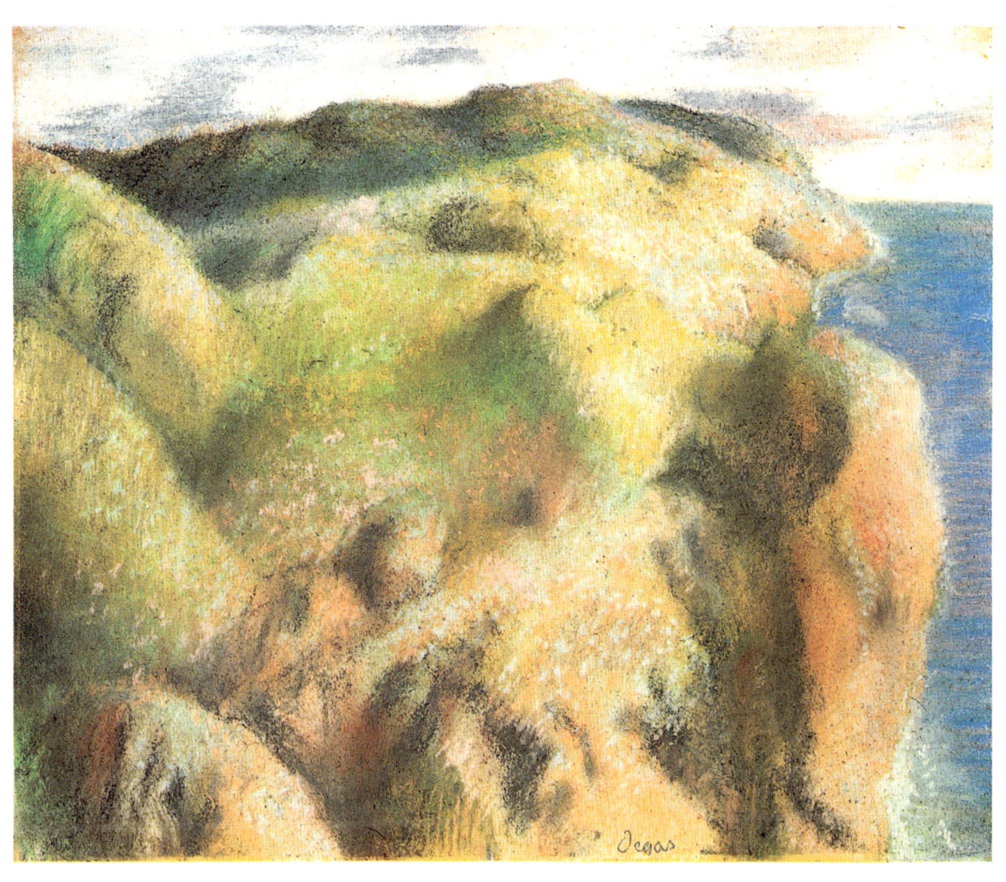

193. *Steep Coast, c.* 1890–92.
Pastel, 42 × 55 cm (16½ × 21⅝ in.).
Jan Krugier and Marie-Anne Krugier-
Poniatowski Collection, Geneva

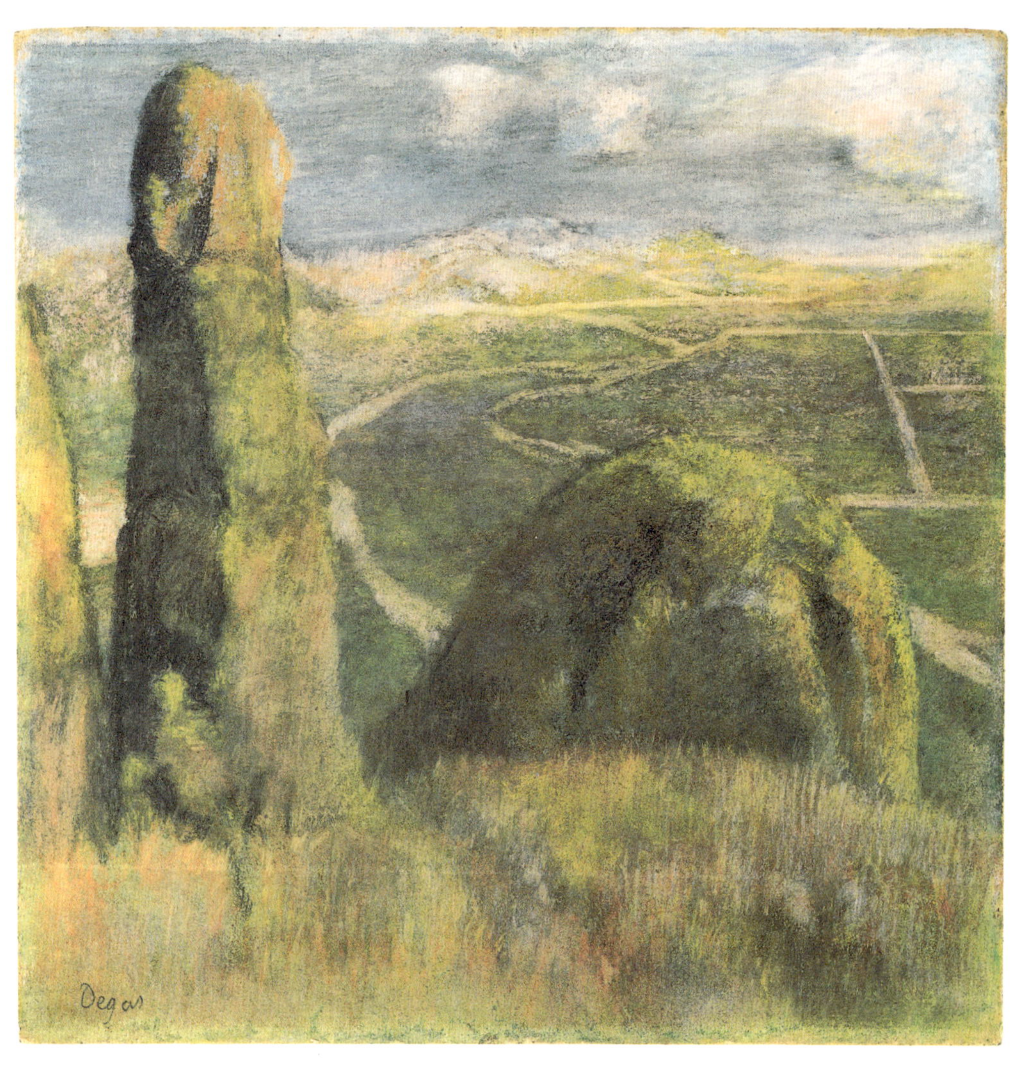

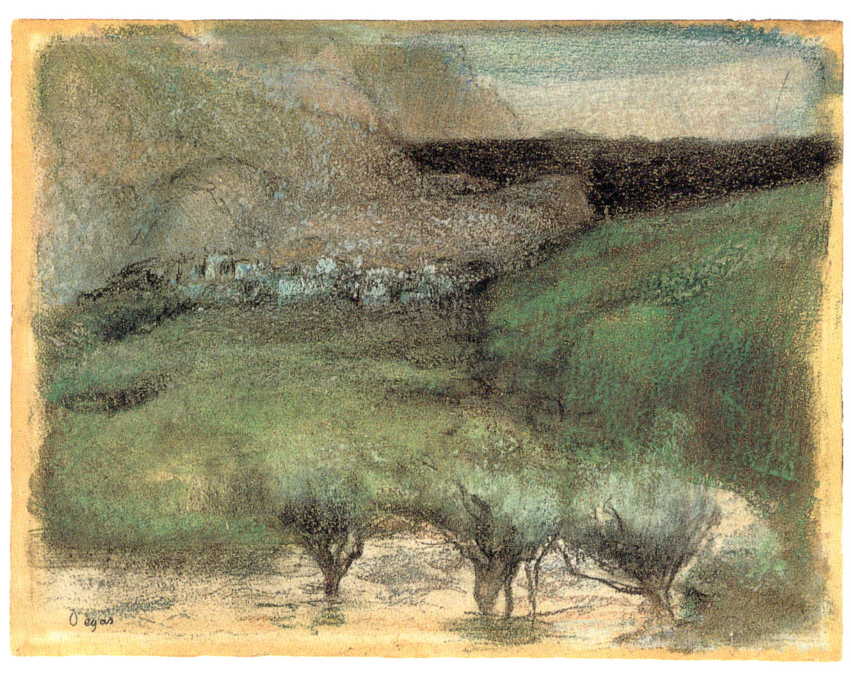

194. *Landscape, c.* 1890–92.
Pastel, 52 × 50 cm (20½ × 19⅝ in.).
Museum of Fine Arts, Houston

195. *Olive Trees against a Mountainous Background, c.* 1890–92.
Monotype and pastel, 25 × 34 cm (9⅞ × 13⅛ in.).
Norton Simon Art Foundation, Pasadena

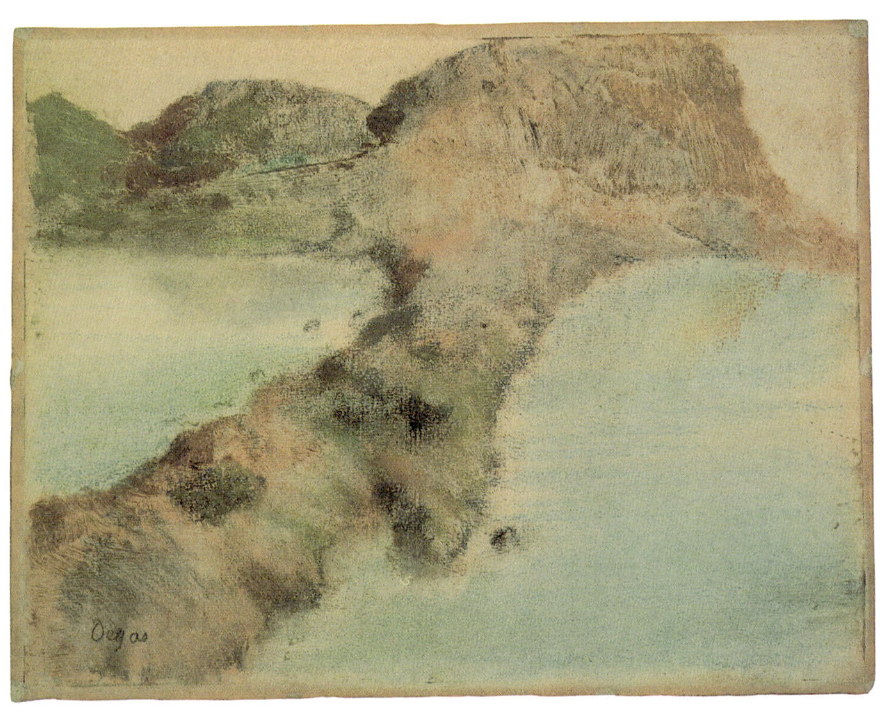

196. *Rocky Coast*, c. 1890–92.
Monotype and pastel, 31 × 42 cm (12¼ × 16½ in.).
Österreichische Galerie Belvedere, Vienna

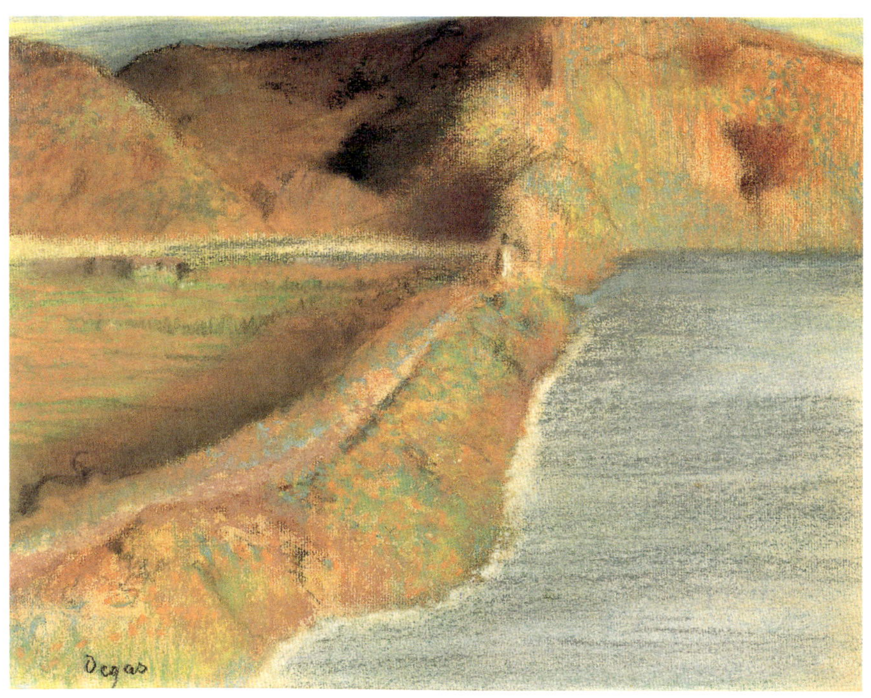

197. *Rocky Coast*, *c.* 1890–92.
Monotype and pastel, 30.5 × 40.9 cm (12 × 16⅛ in.).
Museum Ludwig, Cologne

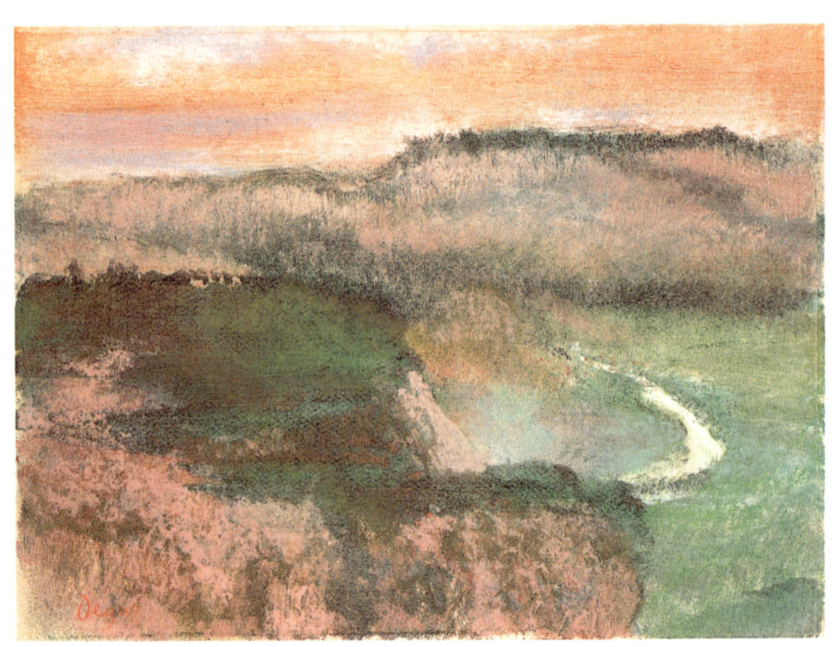

198. *Landscape*, 1892.
Monotype and pastel, 26.7 × 35.6 cm (10½ × 14 in.).
Museum of Fine Arts, Boston

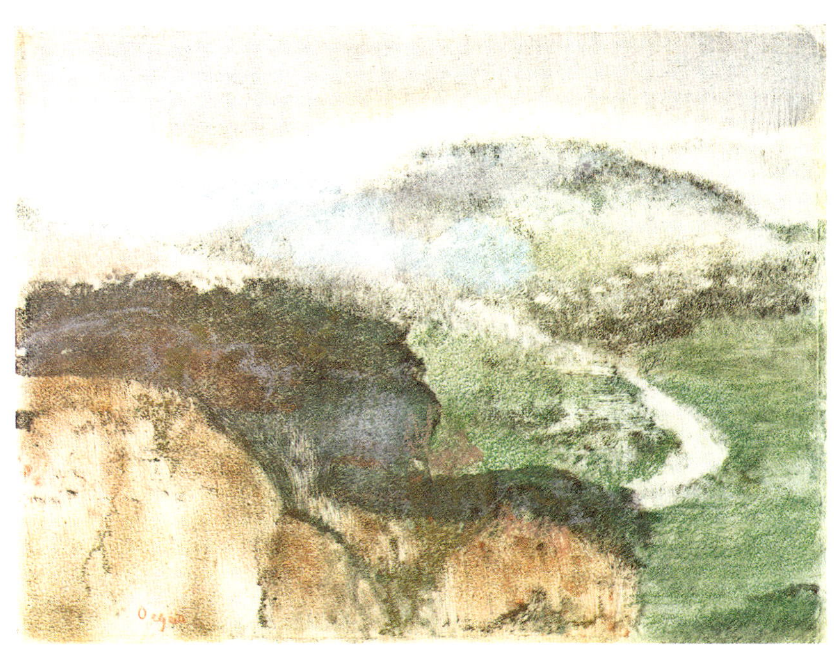

199. *Landscape*, 1892.
Monotype in oil colours and pastel, 25.4 × 34 cm (10 × 13⅜ in.).
Metropolitan Museum of Art, New York

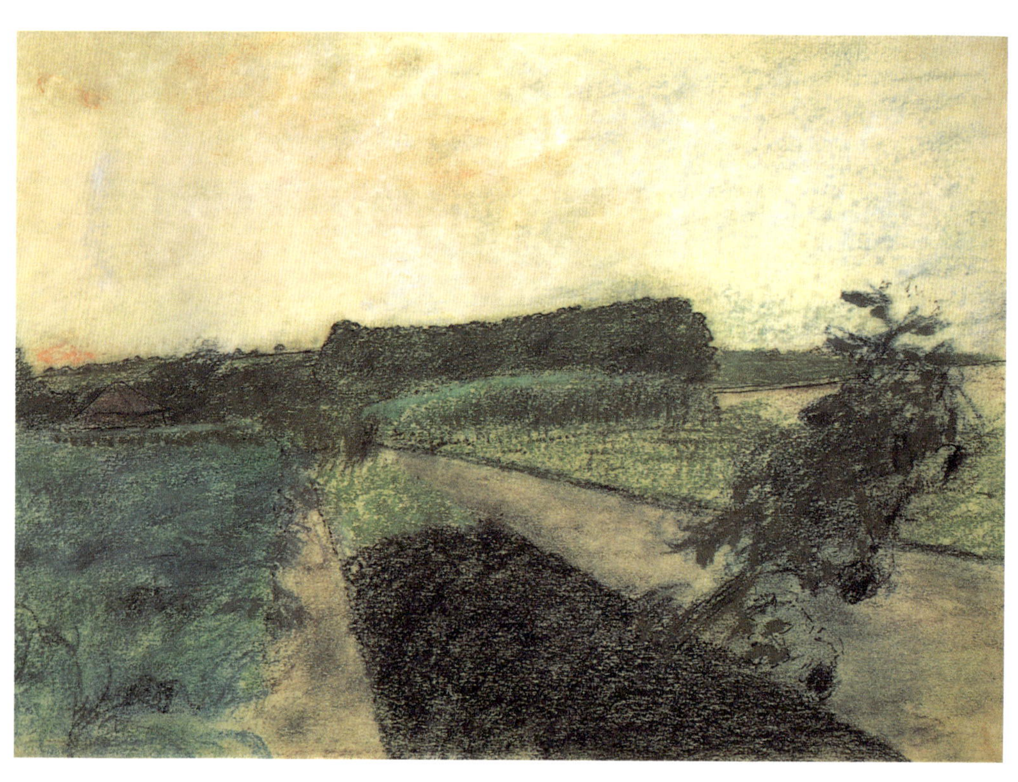

200. *Landscape in the Orne, c.* 1885.
Pastel, 27 × 41 cm (10⅝ × 16 in.).
Private collection

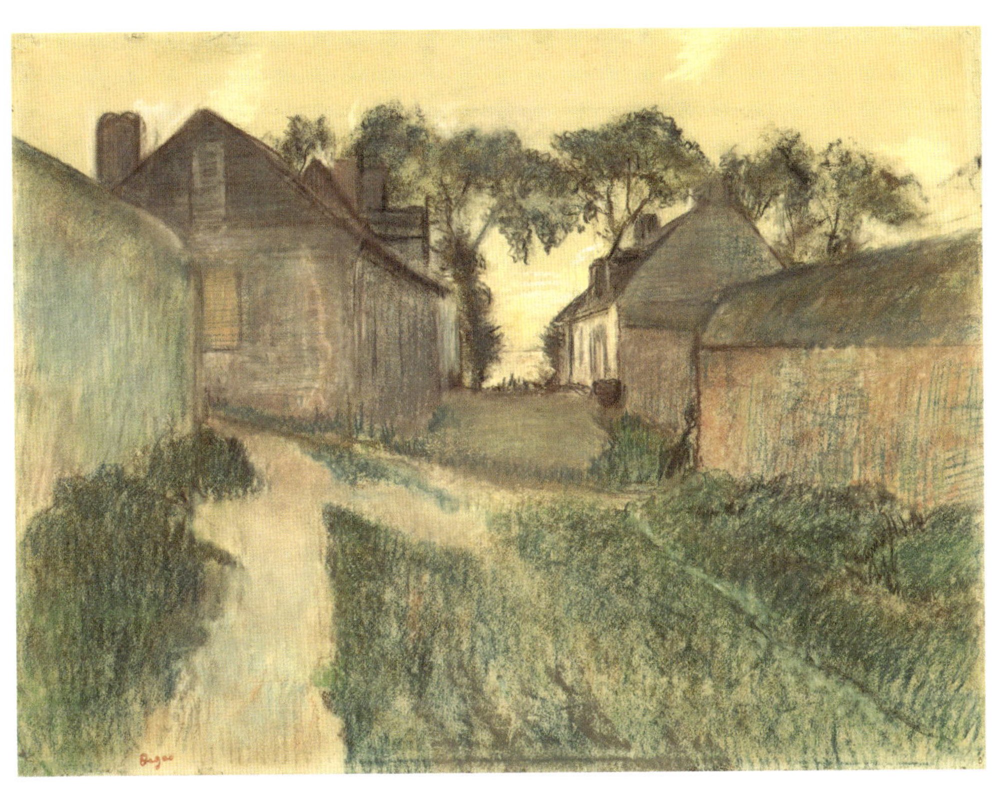

201. *La Rue de Quesnoy, Saint-Valéry-sur-Somme, c.* 1896–98.
Pastel, 48.9 × 65.1 cm (19 × 25⅝ in.).
Collection of Mr A. Alfred Taubman

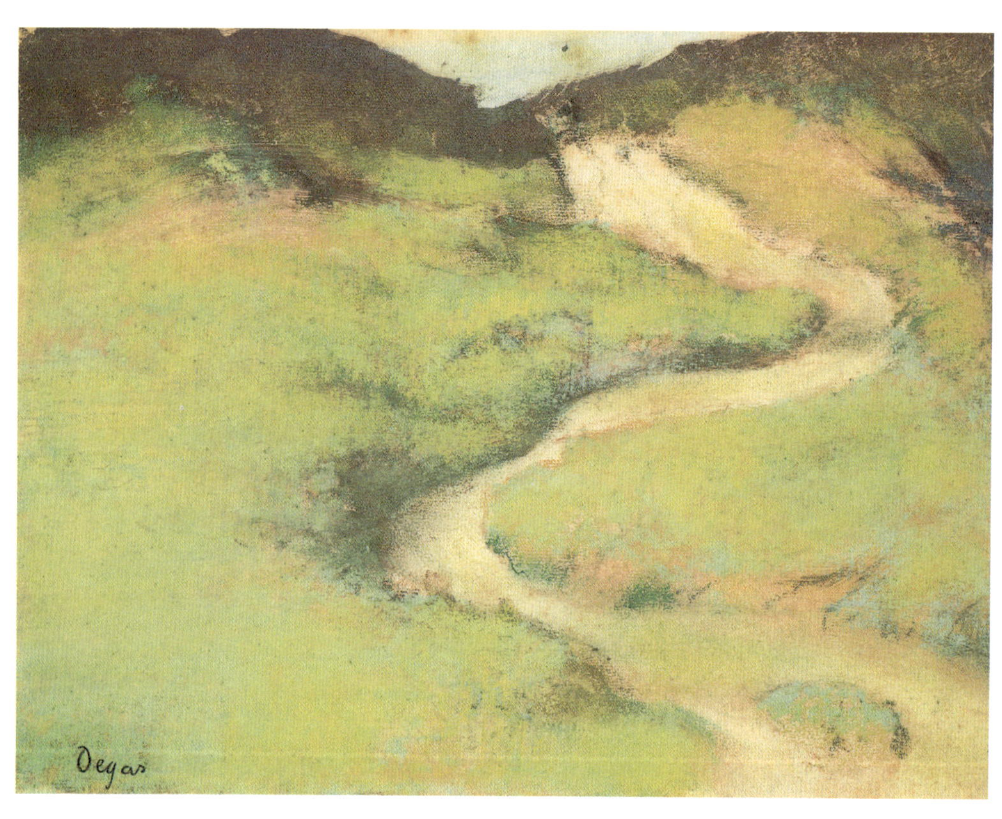

202. *Pathway in a Field*, 1890.
Monotype and pastel, 30 × 39.5 cm (11⅞ × 15½ in.).
Yale University Art Gallery, New Haven, Connecticut

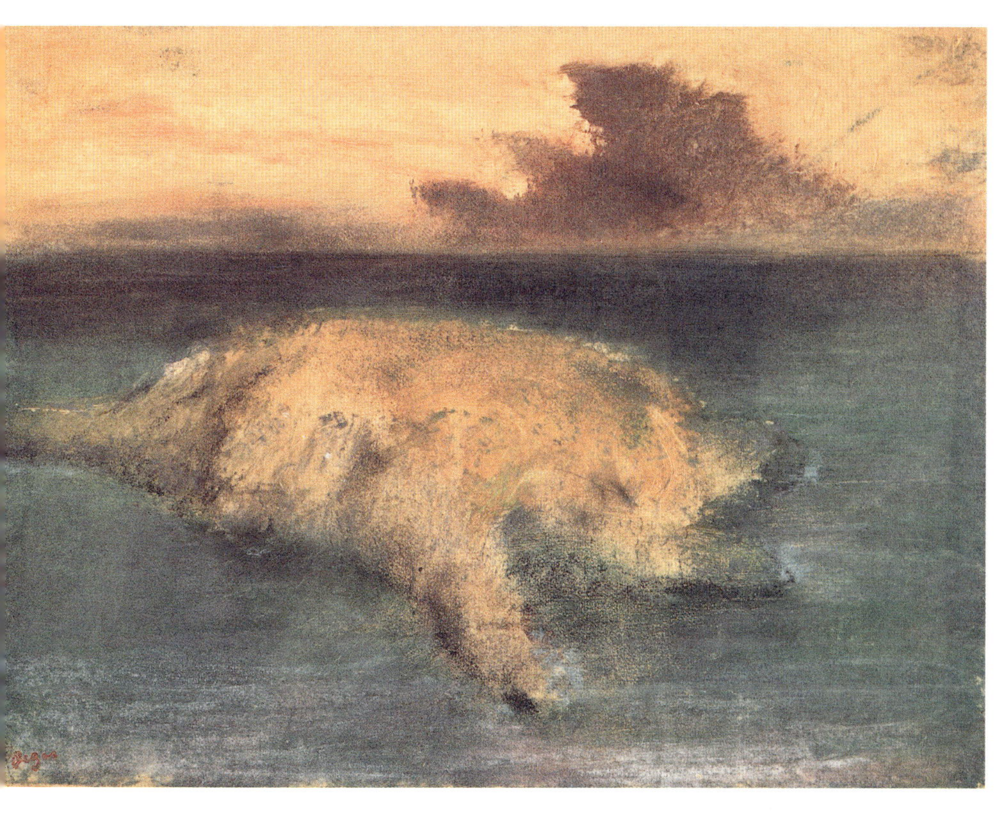

203. *An Island in the Sea*, *c.* 1890.
Pastel, 30 × 40 cm (11⅞ × 15¾ in.).
Musée d'Orsay, Paris

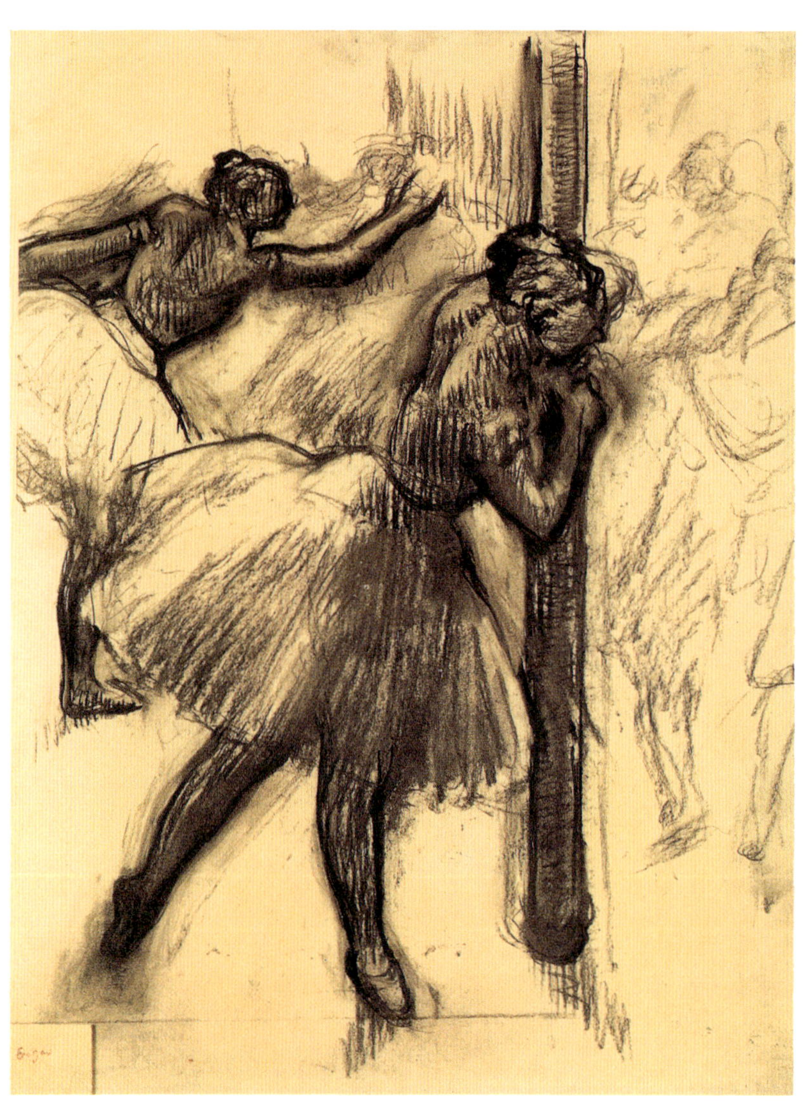

204. *Dancer Leaning on a Pillar*, c. 1895–98.
Charcoal, 69 × 53 cm (27⅛ × 20⅞ in.).
Folkwang Museum, Essen

CHAPTER EIGHT

'The Dying of the Light' 1890–c. 1912

*'Make a drawing, begin it again, trace it; begin it again,
and trace it again.'*

(Degas in Paul Lafond, *Degas*, 1, Paris, 1918, p. 20)

At the beginning of January 1890 Degas moved into his last studio at
37 Rue Victor-Massé on the slopes of Montmartre. It was an area he
knew well and where many artists lived and worked in close proximity
to one another. By the end of the 1890s the building at 37 Victor-Massé
had become his home in addition to a studio. It was divided into four
floors: Degas arranged his collection (referred to as his 'museum') on the
second level where he also slept; the third level was his proper apartment
– salons, dining room, kitchen – where he entertained; and the fourth
floor at the very top of the building was the studio. Presiding over the
household was a fierce housekeeper, Zoë Closier, who remained with
the artist until the very end [see 2]. The most important levels were the
second and the fourth: the 'museum' was sacrosanct and kept locked and
the fourth was strictly private where nothing could be touched except by
his housekeeper whose duties in this area were kept to the minimum. It
was in this dusty, cluttered, crepuscular space that Degas produced his
last works. Now, after a considerable lapse of time, these have deservedly
gained such respect that they exert a fascination comparable with that
accorded the final works of Titian, Rembrandt and Picasso.

Degas remained at 37 Rue Victor-Massé until the summer of 1912
when the threat of demolition forced him to make one last move to
6 Boulevard de Clichy. The distance was not great, but the symbolism of
the move was profound since it was at this point that the artist became
so demoralized that he stopped working altogether five years before
his death. The last decade of the nineteenth century and the first of
the twentieth, therefore, present another one of those paradoxes that
punctuated Degas's life. On a personal basis he sought seclusion to the
point of reclusiveness and his outlook on life and his political views

became markedly reactionary. Added to this, was the further deterioration of his eyesight. Photophobia had manifested itself as early as the late 1860s, but with age other visual impairments occurred so that he ended his working days in perpetual fear of blindness. Although at times querulous, taciturn and contrary, Degas had always been sociable and curious, frequenting ballet rehearsals, going to the opera, meeting people in cafés and restaurants, attending café-concerts and walking the streets of Paris. Such practices were part of his examination of modern life as advocated in 1876 by Duranty. Now he was less inclined to be adventurous and he assuaged his curiosity in different ways back in his studio.

The feeling of loneliness was exacerbated by the deaths of relatives, fellow artists and friends: Lépic died in 1890, Morisot in 1895, Stephane Mallarmé in 1898, Toulouse-Lautrec in 1901, Gauguin and Pissarro in 1903, and Cézanne in 1906. Of his closest friends, Paul Valpinçon died in 1894, Evariste de Valernes (a one-time pupil of Delacroix) in 1896 and Henri Rouart in 1912. From the family, his brother-in-law Edmondo Morbilli died in 1893, his sister Marguerite in 1895 in Buenos Aires and his other sister, Thérèse, in 1912 in Naples. Just as upsetting as these events was the severance at his own wish of his relationship with his close friends for many years, Ludovic and Louise Halévy. This occurred in 1897 over the unjust conviction for treason of the army officer Captain Alfred Dreyfus. Degas was anti-Semitic and an anti-Dreyfusard, which in his opinion ultimately made his relationship with the Halévys impossible.

There was also, unsurprisingly, a pronounced physical decline in Degas himself, to the extent that in 1913 Mary Cassatt could announce bluntly, 'Degas is nothing more than a wreck'. His brother René, to whom he was now reconciled, is more informative,

> Considering his age, his physical condition is certainly not all that bad; he eats well, suffers from no infirmity save deafness, which is getting worse and makes conversation very difficult…When he goes out, he cannot walk much past Place Pigalle; he spends an hour in a café, and it is all he can do to get back…His friends seldom come to see him because he hardly recognizes them…Sad, sad end! He is dying slowly but without suffering, without anxiety, well looked after by people devoted to him.

And yet, despite these personal misfortunes and infirmities, Degas continued to work with a strong sense of purpose and remained determinedly committed to the practice of his art. The financial rewards he was beginning to reap from sales of his work in Europe and America meant that he could extend his personal collection. He acquired works by El Greco, Ingres, Delacroix, Daumier and Corot – artists whom he had always admired. To these he added works by his immediate contemporaries, such as Cassatt, Cézanne, Jean-Louis Forain, Van Gogh, Gavarni, Gauguin, Pissarro, Sisley and Whistler. Artists were often represented in the collection by several examples in all media and Degas accumulated large numbers of prints by Daumier and Paul Gavarni in particular, not only because they were outstanding draughtsmen but also because their view of society coincided with his own. The collection, which he saw in terms of a museum project that he never completed, reflects Degas's own artistic predilections and, furthermore, it implies a line of descent which no doubt he was himself mindful of continuing in his own person. Already he had established a reputation with collectors through his participation in exhibitions and through dealers, but publications promoting him were beginning to appear. William Thornley issued a portfolio of fifteen lithographs after works by Degas (including drawings) in 1889 through the dealer Boussod, Valadon & Co.; in 1897 Michel Manzi oversaw another portfolio entitled *Degas:Vingt Dessins 1861–1896*; and Vollard was responsible in 1914 for *Quatre-vingt-dix-huit reproductions signées par Degas (peintures, pastels, dessins et estampes)*. The significance of these publications lies in the emphasis given to works on paper in addition to paintings.

An early biography was published in 1912 by Paul-André Lemoine, who then went on to compile the official catalogue raisonné (4 vols, 1946–49), while the artist's death triggered a host of reminiscences and memoirs published in one form or another. Many of these last were written by members of the younger generation with whom Degas kept in touch and whose friendship he encouraged: Julie Manet, the daughter of Berthe Morisot and Eugène Manet; Hélène and Ernest Rouart, two of the children of Henri Rouart; the writer Paul Valéry; and Daniel Halévy, one of the sons of Ludovic and Louise Halévy who kept in touch with Degas regardless of the manner in which the artist had forsaken his parents. In fact, the artist's enjoyment of the company of young people, particularly the children of his friends, was a reflection of his status as a bachelor.

Also notable is the amount of time that Degas spent with artists not of the first rank whom out of friendship he would encourage and advise – the sculptor Paul-Albert Bartholomé, the painters Suzanne Valadon and Louis Braquaval, and the printmaker Georges Jeanniot. It would seem, therefore, that even if Degas's increasing blindness caused some people to liken him to Homer and his curmudgeonly behaviour prompted others to compare him with King Lear, he was in fact not as remote as many assumed. His studio was perhaps more like Prospero's cell – or, less poetically, the laboratory of a forensic scientist.

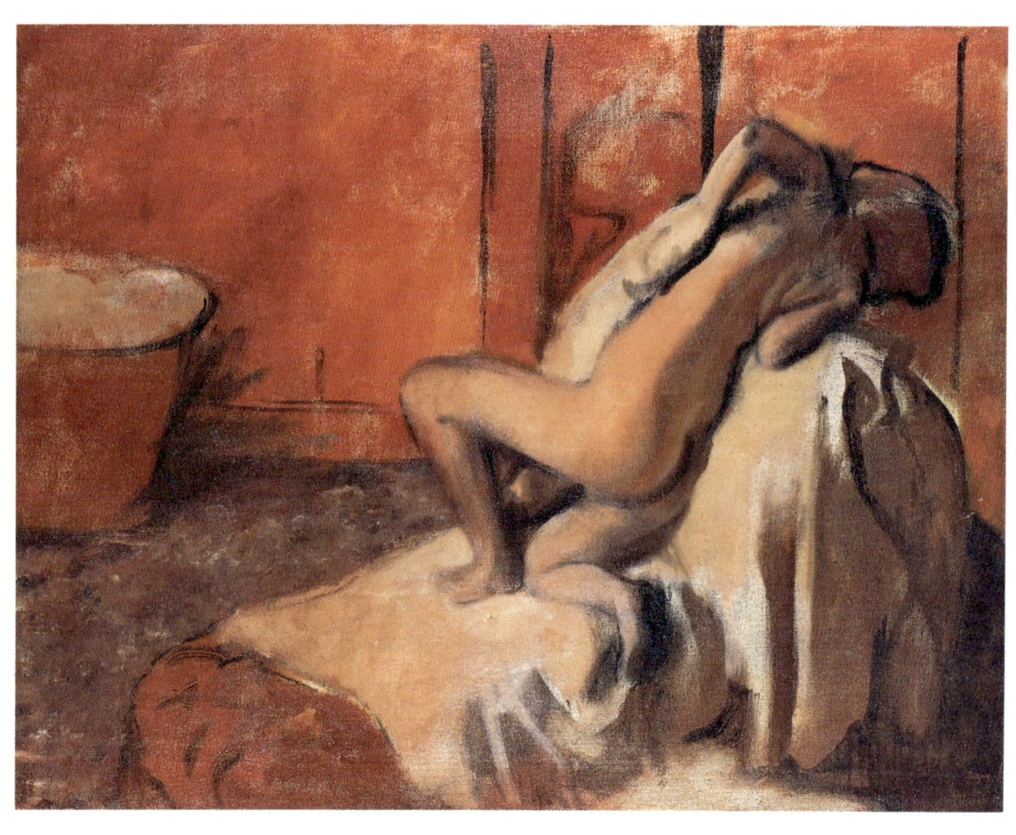

205. *After the Bath: Woman Drying Herself, c.* 1894–95.
Oil on canvas, 89.5 × 116.8 cm (35¼ × 46 in.).
Philadelphia Museum of Art

Meanwhile, Degas was also extending the boundaries of his own art. He continued to develop his printmaking skills; he took more photographs than before, firstly portraits of his friends and fellow artists and then of posed models in his studio in connection with the paintings and pastels he was working on; and he produced a great deal of sculpture – horses, dancers, bathers – more in fact than at any other time in his career. Degas modelled his sculptures in wax but he never saw them cast in bronze, which is how they are universally known today. He told the sculptor François Thiébault-Sisson,

> The only reason that I made wax figures of animals and humans was for my own satisfaction, not to take time off from painting and drawing, but in order to give my paintings and drawings greater expression, greater ardour and more life. They are exercises to get me going; documentary, preparatory motions, nothing more. None of this is intended for sale…What matters to me is to express nature in all its aspects, movement in its exact truth, to accentuate bone and muscle and the compact firmness of flesh.

For Degas, 'sculpture is an art which puts the artist under an obligation to neglect none of the essentials'.

A new and rather surprising departure in Degas's life was the writing of sonnets – about twenty altogether according to Valéry. The subjects mirror his art: dancers, horses, singers, the Opéra and the racecourse. As Valéry points out, the sonnet form complemented Degas's working methods as an artist:

> The poet's task, where it consists of a search, through successive approximations, for a final version which satisfies certain precise requirements, must have seemed to him akin to that of the draughtsman as he conceived it.

Against this background, Degas's late work can be seen as a reaffirmation and a recapitulation: it also reveals a process of consolidation ending in summation. There was no change of direction as far as subject matter is concerned and there was no loss of intensity. What was new was the single-mindedness of the approach and the determination in the execution. Retreating into his studio both concentrated his mind and hardened his resolve. Numerically, there was an increase in the output of pastels and it is the artist's preference for this medium over oil painting that really defines the final phase of his working life. Many of the oil paintings of this period are left unfinished or are heavily reworked with little attempt to disguise the heavy outlines that either betray the underdrawing or signal changes of mind (for example, *After the Bath: Woman Drying Herself* (c. 1894–95) [205];

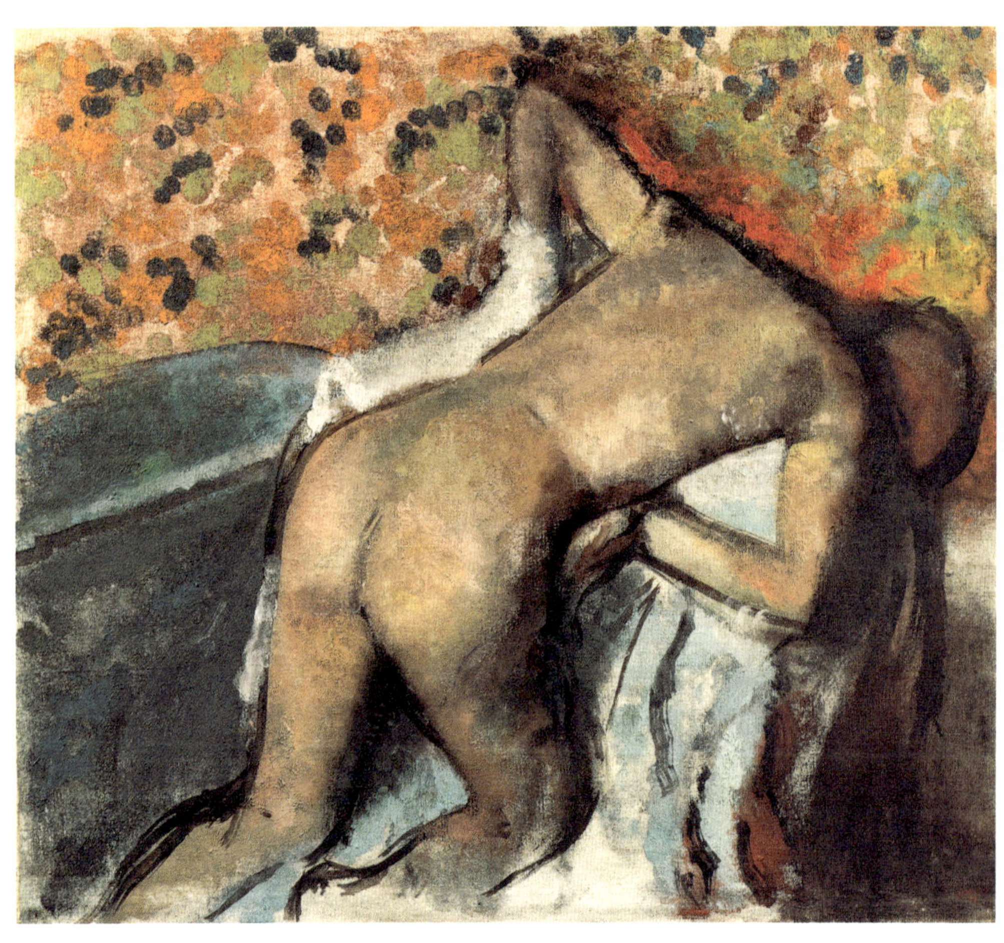

206. *After the Bath: Woman Drying Herself*, c. 1895.
Oil on canvas, 75.5 × 86 cm (29¼ × 33⅞ in.).
The Henry and Rose Pearlman Foundation on loan
to Princeton University Art Museum, New Jersey

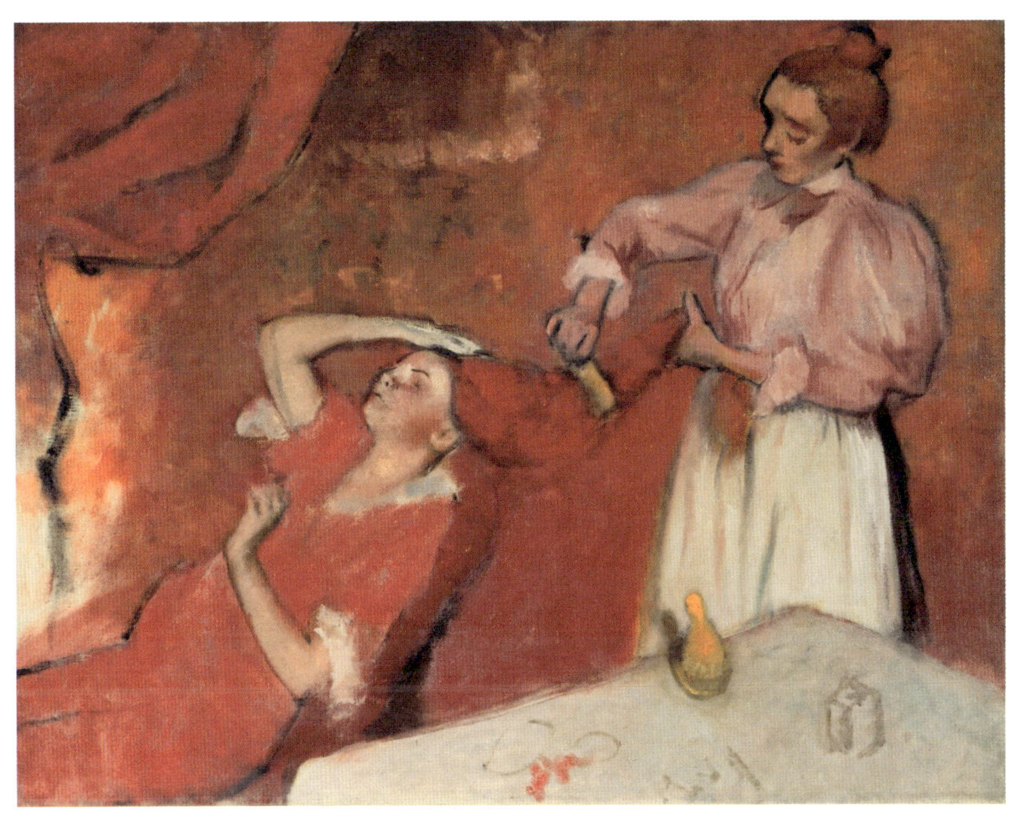

207. *Combing the Hair ('La Coiffure'), c. 1896.*
Oil on canvas, 114.3 × 146.7 cm (45 × 57¼ in.).
National Gallery, London

After the Bath: Woman Drying Herself (c. 1895) [206]; *Combing the Hair ('La Coiffure') (c.* 1896) [207], *Four Dancers (En attendant l'entrée en scène) (*1895–1900) [208]). The stylistic affinity that these and other such paintings have with pastels of the same date is striking, regardless of the difference in medium and methods of execution.

Pastel has an honourable place in the history of French art. A number of eighteenth-century practitioners produced works of the greatest distinction in this medium, usually portraits: J. S. Chardin, Maurice-Quentin de la Tour, Jean-Baptiste Perronneau. Perhaps no other work of art purveys the refinement of the eighteenth century quite as effectively as those pastel portraits shown to critical acclaim in great numbers at the Salon exhibitions. Pose, expression, dress were perfectly matched by nuanced touch and delicacy of colour, which one contemporary likened to 'l'eclat des fleurs' and another to 'the dust from butterflies' wings'. Interest in eighteenth-century art in France during the following century was mediated through the essays published by Edmond and Jules de Goncourt as *L'Art du Dix-huitième Siècle* between 1856 and 1875 where the pastels of de la Tour are described as having been 'blown from the face-powders of the period'. The Impressionists did not spurn pastel. Outstanding examples can be found in the *oeuvres* of Manet, Cassatt, Renoir, Pissarro, Caillebotte, Eva Gonzalès and Redon. But no one equalled Degas for the consistency and panache with which he allowed the medium to dominate his output from the mid-1880s.

The importance of pastel for Degas was that it was a means of drawing with colour. 'I am a colourist with line', he declared. In effect, the two basic elements of the art of painting – drawing and colouring – are combined as a single medium in pastel. The physical advantage of this for an ageing artist is obvious, but Degas seems to have satisfied himself that of all the media at his disposal pastel, in spite of its historical associations, was the best vehicle for the depiction of modern life. Indeed, given Degas's perverse nature, he probably derived a certain satisfaction from such a radical proposition, which pitted the rarefied elegance of life under the *ancien régime* against the harsh realities of nineteenth-century Paris.

Pastel is by definition chalk mixed with pigment. By the mid-nineteenth century artists could buy boxes of manufactured pastels with a wide range of hues. As a medium it was easily applied, but as a powder it was intensely friable, which explains the reports of the high dust levels in Degas's studio. Having already been alert to the advantages of softer media such as tempera and gouache from an early date, the temptation to test out pastel must have been great. Correspondingly, having experimented with thinning oil paint to produce *essence*, it was likely that Degas would also test out the properties of pastel to the full. Usually the medium was applied in its dry state, but Degas tried moistening the sticks and making a paste (*pastel à l'eau*) which he then applied with a brush. Strictly speaking, neither of these procedures was totally unknown to earlier pastellists, but for Degas they indicated ways by which the means of application could be extended. Where previously artists had seen pastel as a medium for limited use, Degas saw it as one freighted with new possibilities. The confidence he placed in it is reflected in the large scale of the pastels he made from the mid-1880s onwards, beginning with the 'Suite of Female Nudes' shown at the eighth Impressionist exhibition [see 169, 173, 178–180, 182]. For Degas there was no limit to the physical boundaries of a pastel while he was working on it. He frequently added extra pieces to the support in the form of strips attached to the edges so that the composition could be enlarged in an organic way, often investing the whole work with a kinetic energy of its own. As a result, Degas's pastels of the 1890s are comparable with paintings in terms of both scale and presentation.

This blurring of the traditional distinction between painting and drawing would have immense consequences for the development of art in the twentieth century. Parity meant that drawings were no longer perceived as having a secondary status as part of a deliberate and often laborious process leading to the ultimate goal of a finished painting. Instead, the elevation of drawing to a status equal to that of painting symbolized a breakdown in the hierarchical values in art imposed by the Renaissance. This created a greater freedom for those artists who wanted to define art on their own terms. The liberation of drawing presented them with new opportunities in the sense that a more open-minded approach to materials and working methods encouraged greater freedom of expression.

The role that Degas played in creating this freedom is nowhere more apparent than in his final works on paper, which he often made in series. His sequencing of images – bathers, jockeys, dancers – began with recollections of earlier compositions – no doubt with reference to the relevant drawings that he kept to hand – which were then re-examined with the aid of an endless stream of models in the studio. The power and abandon of the pastels and drawings that ensued demonstrates Degas's desire to move from the particular to the general. At this final stage he is less concerned to capture the fugitive than to search for the universal and make it a definitive statement. All his experience and technical knowledge were brought to bear on these drawings. Tracing paper, for example, was favoured both as a support and as a facilitator. If the drawing itself was made on tracing paper, then at a later stage it would be laid down on a firmer support by specialists working under the artist's instructions. The opportunity for tracing figures from one sheet of paper to another added greatly to Degas's armoury so that he could devise new compositions while remaining in his studio. Tracing paper allowed him to increase the number of his options so that poses could be transferred, reversed, modified, enlarged, transmuted or adapted. Consequently figures could be added or subtracted as required to form an infinite number of varied groupings. Many pastels and drawings could have a common origin but novel and sometimes surprising outcomes depending on the redeployment of the figures, the degree of finish or changes of coloration. As Degas declared, 'Art is the same word as artifice, that is to say something deceitful. It must succeed in giving the impression of nature by false means, but it has to look true.'

The late pastels have two distinctive technical features – the matt surface and the bright colour. Contrary to earlier practice in the eighteenth century, Degas built up the surface with several layers using hatching and cross-hatching of such opacity that he almost creates a three-dimensional effect. The powdery quality of the pastel itself, like the wax he used for sculpture, presented him with a tactile sense that was a useful point of reference for the quest to make permanent what was essentially fugitive. The irony is that Degas was attempting this with pastel, which, as his forerunners in the eighteenth century were all too aware, was no more than a composite made from particles of dust. This struggle was made even more personal with the use of fingers to smudge and blend the pastel. Also comparable with Degas's technique of painting, was the application of fixatives made of resin and casein, which he used like a glaze. This heightened the chromatic intensity of each layer of the pastel without causing discolouration or disturbing the texture. Many of these late pastels are heavily worked with forceful strokes added to the surface after the forms below have been defined. These strokes appear to have been made quite purposefully. They have their own independence and are sometimes in danger of overwhelming the figures [210, 212, 224]. The assertive and detached quality of these strokes anticipate the style of Abstract Expressionist painters such as Jackson Pollock and Willem de Kooning. It is in his pursuit of these technical advances that Degas is seen at his most innovative.

The range of colours in the pastels is also singular [213]. Admittedly, colour was by definition one of the main attributes of pastel, but it was the almost alchemical skill with which Degas blended his colours that produced such memorable results – rosy pinks, sparkling violets, almond greens, iridescent blues, vibrant oranges, striking yellows, russet reds, warm browns – all varying, sometimes saturated and often acidic, hues. 'To colour', Degas said, 'is to pursue drawing into greater depth.' Colour in late works by Degas has a language of its own anticipating the Nabis and the Fauves. As early as 1880, when reviewing the fifth Impressionist exhibition, Huysmans was alert to the singularity of Degas's sophisticated application of colour,

> No painter, since Delacroix whom he studied at great length and is his master, has understood, as Monsieur Degas has, the marriage and adultery of colours; none working today has a draughtsmanship as precise and as bold, a colour surface as delicate; none has, in a different art, the exquisiteness that the Goncourts put in their prose; none has captured as he has, in a delicate and personal style, the most ephemeral of sensations, the most fleeting of subtleties and shades.

The extent to which Degas perfected the subtlety of colour is apparent from comparing two of his pastels from the mid-1890s with similar titles: *The Morning Bath* (*c.* 1892–95) [216] and *The Morning Toilet* (1894) [217] where the strength of the morning light varies only fractionally but decisively and in so doing creates contrasting moods.

Testimony to Degas's continuing acuity with regard to colour lies in the series of fourteen or so pastels of Russian dancers dating from *c.* 1899 [218–219]. Reflecting the popularity of Russian culture in Paris at the turn of the century and his perennial interest in dance, Degas must have seen a performance of Russian folk dance and asked models to re-enact the scene in his studio. The kicking legs and flying elbows are brilliantly caught by the powerful outlines and rich colours of these animated pastels, which the artist described to Julie Manet as 'orgies of colour' – a phrase far removed from the eighteenth century and justifiably more in keeping with Igor Stravinsky's *Le Sacre du Printemps*, which had its premiere in Paris in 1913.

Apart from the Russian dancers, the subject matter in Degas's late work is more muted in tone. The compositions, although compelling, lack energy and are more static than in earlier decades. This much is to be expected for someone in Degas's state of mind. The bathers do not seem to leap in and out of their bathtubs with the same alacrity and prefer to dry themselves, comb their hair or receive the attentions of a maid [210, 220–223]. The jockeys seem less fretful and are depicted in landscapes that appear to be far removed from any racecourse [224, 225]. They gently walk their mounts or skilfully bring them under control, but are so self-contained that they are perhaps in danger of missing the start. The dancers seem more grounded, forming tighter groups enclosed by the stage scenery of distant landscapes [208]. They adjust their costumes or fiddle with accessories while waiting their cues [229]. They exercise

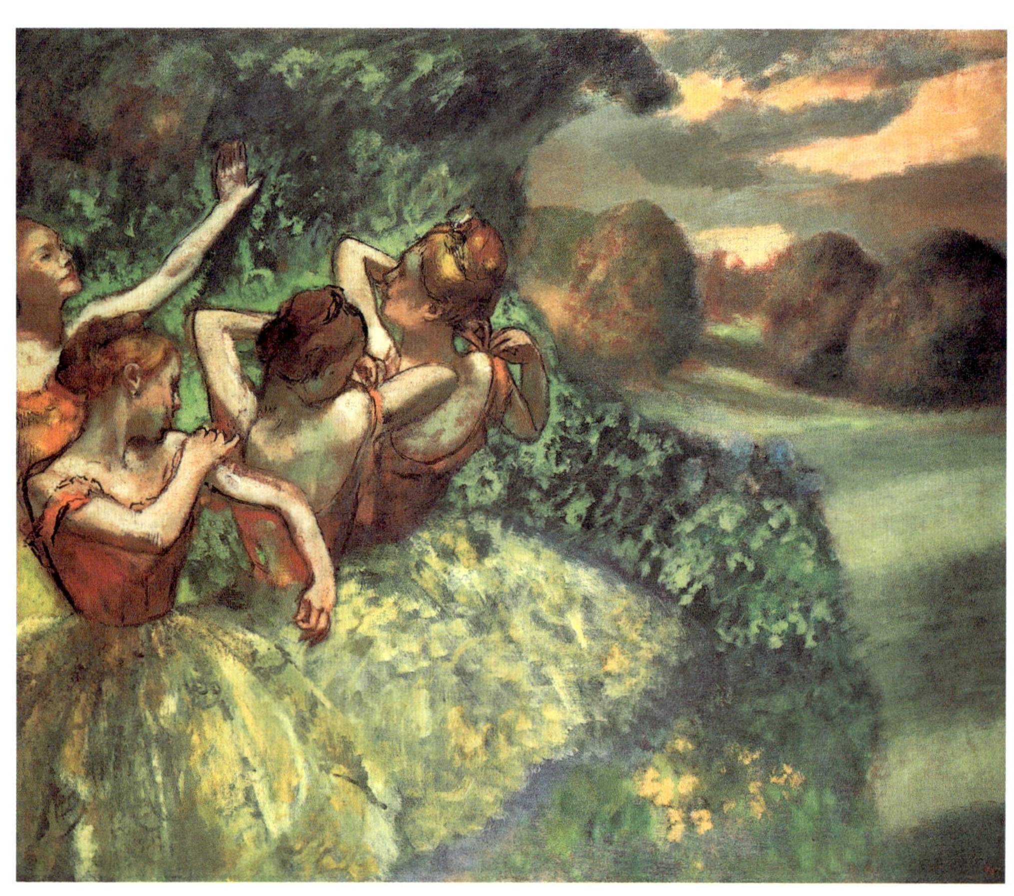

208. *Four Dancers (En attendant l'entrée en scène)*, 1895–1900.
Oil on canvas, 151.1 × 180.2 cm (59½ × 70⅞ in.).
National Gallery of Art, Washington, DC

and warm up in their own time, but without the promptings of a dance master. The narrative dimension in such scenes exists, but it is only implied. Degas is more interested in the figure itself – the monumentality of its form and the fragility of its existence [212–215].

The most moving drawings of these final years are the studies made in charcoal of female nudes [211, 232, 236, 237]. Broadly drawn and on a considerable scale, Degas chose charcoal to lay in the compositions and for making tracings, but he sometimes also heightened them with bursts of pastel thereby giving equal emphasis to both. These drawings are a link with the start of Degas's career and show his continuing concern to master the art of depicting the human figure. To compare the figure studies of the 1860s and 1870s with those dating from the 1890s is to appreciate the full extent of Degas's mastery as a draughtsman. The outlines are now as supple and as strong as anything drawn by Delacroix or Daumier. However fleeting, or, by contrast, however many times they have been redrawn and however heavily accented, they are utterly convincing. Their success can be gauged from the fact that they so vividly illustrate Degas's own aphorisms: 'Drawing is not what one sees but what one can make others see', or 'Drawing is not form, it is the sensation one has of it'.

The series of uncompromising drawings of bathers seen in the open air dating from *c.* 1896 are unresolved [234, 235]. It is possible that Degas planned to make a painting of this subject, but he probably realized that such an undertaking was unrealistic. The figures are awkwardly disposed by a stretch of water and assembled in a disjointed composition that lacks proper coherence. The women sprawl inelegantly and self-indulgently on the ground, undress, bathe, or comb their hair. Bathing scenes such as this were popular in nineteenth-century French art and of those by avant-garde painters Degas would have known compositions by Manet, Renoir, Gauguin and Cézanne. But in his unabashed and almost primitive rendering of the theme Degas points the way to Picasso, Matisse and Fernand Léger.

Another motif that absorbed Degas's attention until the last shows the extent to which the artist retained a respect for tradition while also challenging it. *Female Nude Drying her Neck* [237] originated with a small group of lithographs dating from *c.* 1891–92 showing a woman seen from the back drying her hips [209]. By the turn of the century this motif had changed to one of an identical figure drying her neck which was then explored further in other drawings and pastels. The drawings are mainly in charcoal on tracing paper, sometimes with additions in pastel. The example in Cambridge [237], which is in charcoal alone, has defining areas of shadow most obviously in the face, on the left hand

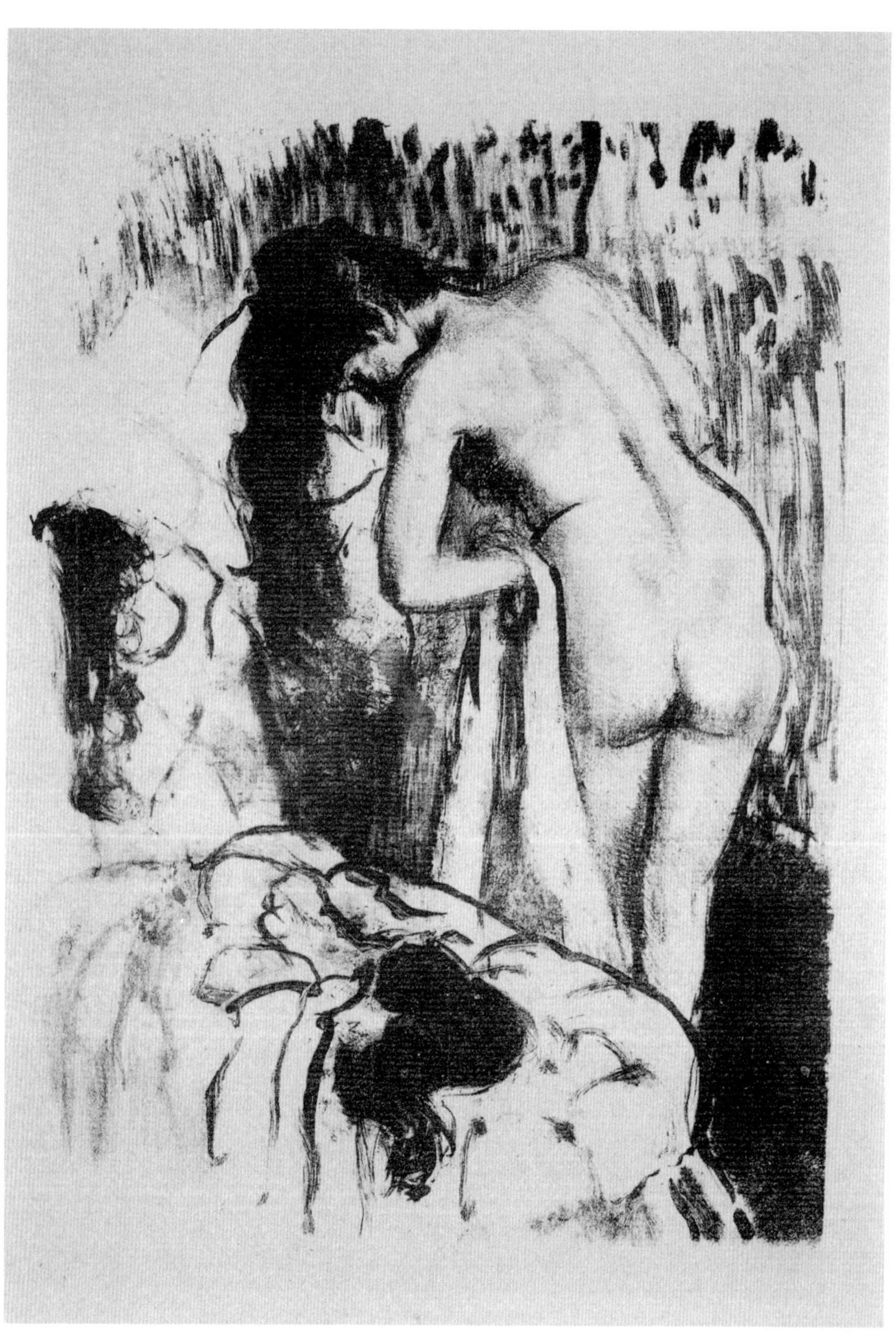

284   '*The Dying of the Light*' 1890–c. 1912

and down the right side of the back into the buttock. The contours have
been strongly reinforced and a flurry of movement is suggested by the
redrawing of the arms. The modelling is full of bravura with hatching
across the back, the right side and the upper part of the legs. The three-
quarters-length figure is compact; the form is monumental with the
solidity of a Renaissance bronze statuette; and the torsion in the body as
the model leans over to her left is balletic. Degas plays off the rounded
forms – pear-shaped buttocks, pendulant breast, inclined head – against
the more angular geometric shape suggested by the raised arms and
lowered head. Such studies made at this late date in his life testify to
Degas's total commitment to drawing and reveal the heights to which
he took it before the twentieth century engulfed him.

Valéry summed it all up in this way,

> A passionate pursuit of the one and only line that defines a form, a
> form seen in daily life, in the street, at the Opéra, at the modiste's
> (and even…elsewhere); and at the same time, taken unawares in
> its most characteristic attitude, at a particular moment, always a
> moment of action and expression: such, more or less, sums up my
> idea of Degas. He tried, he dared try to combine the snapshot with
> the endless labour of the studio, enshrining his impression of it in
> prolonged study – the instantaneous given enduring quality by the
> patience of intense meditation.

209. Nude Woman Standing Drying Herself,
c. 1891–92. Lithograph, transfer from monotype, crayon,
tusche and scraping, 33 × 24.5 cm (13 × 9⅝ in.).
Museum of Fine Arts, Boston

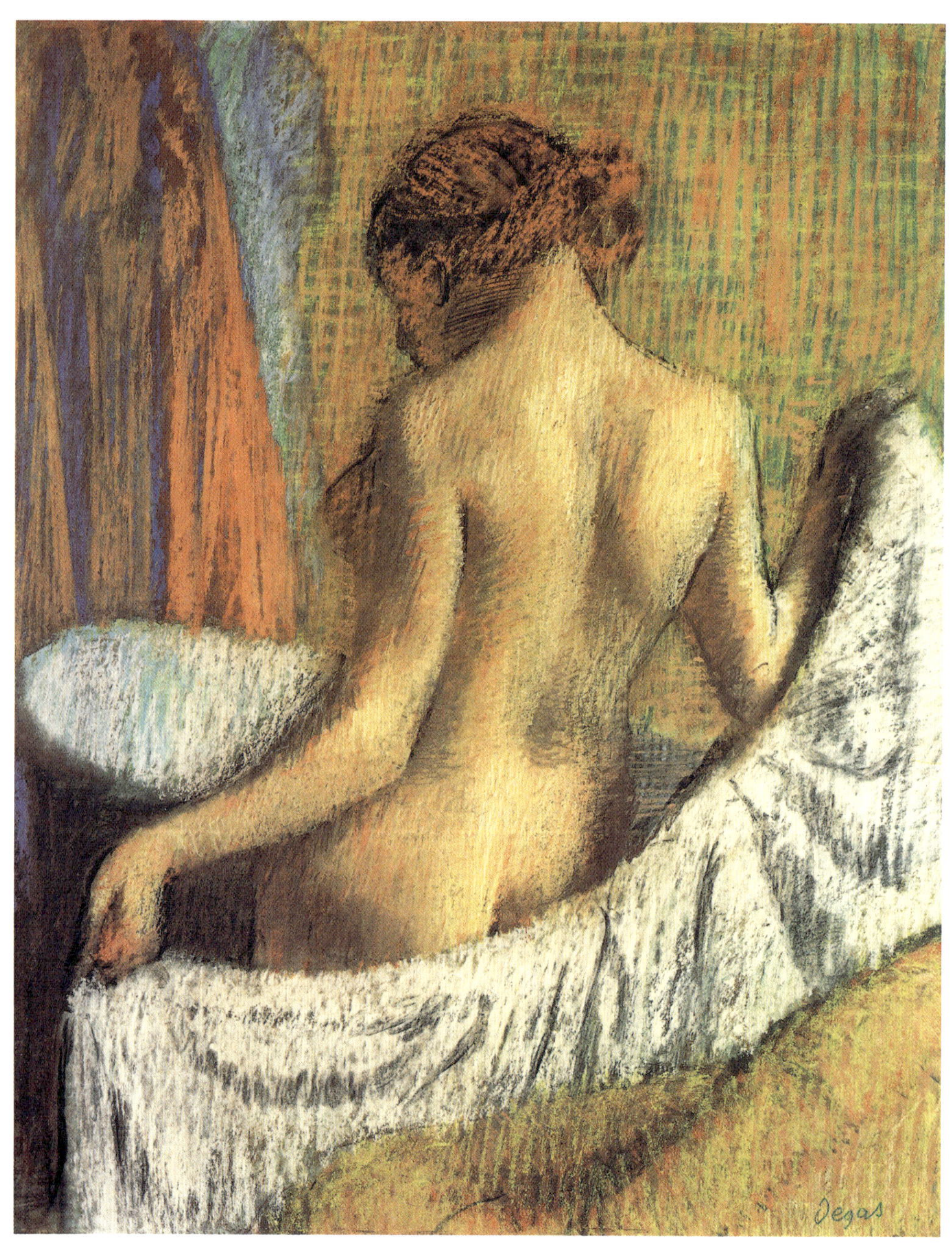

286   *'The Dying of the Light'* 1890–c. 1912

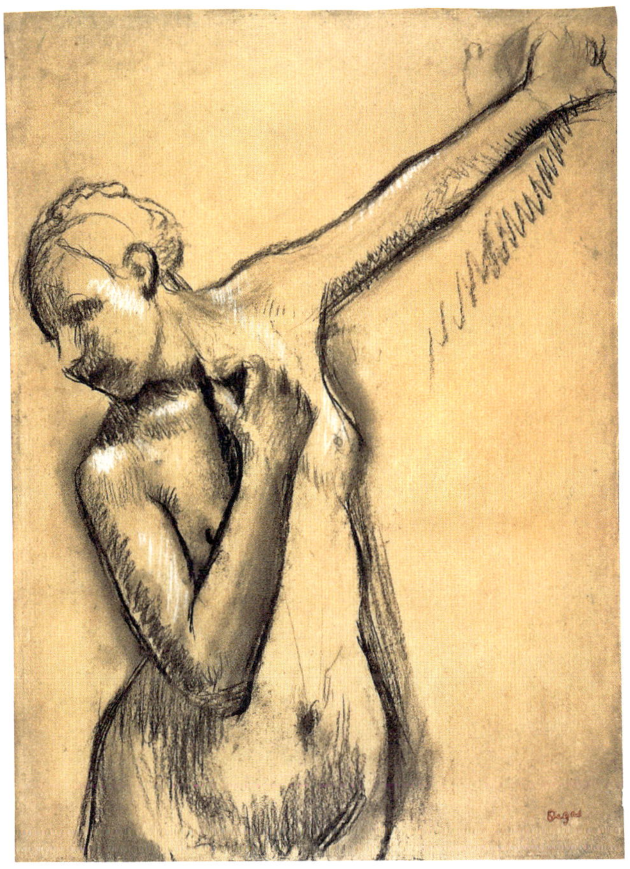

OPPOSITE
210. *After the Bath, Woman with a Towel*, c. 1893–97.
Pastel on blue-grey paper, 70.8 × 57.3 cm (27⅞ × 22½ in.).
Fogg Museum, Cambridge, Massachusetts

ABOVE
211. *Half-Length Nude Girl, Left Arm Uplifted*, c. 1898.
Charcoal heightened with white on tracing paper,
53.9 × 38.8 cm (21¼ × 15¼ in.).
Fitzwilliam Museum, Cambridge

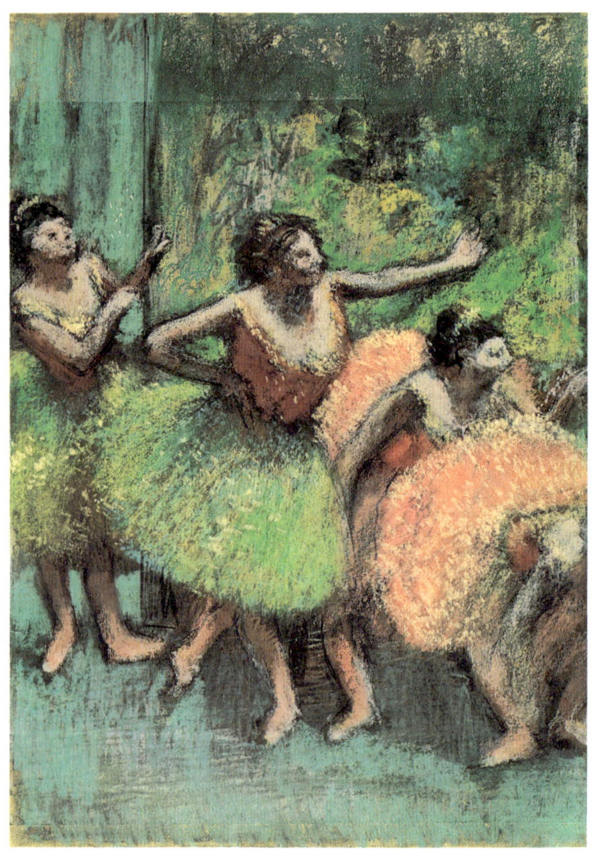

ABOVE
212. *Dancers in Green and Yellow, c. 1903.*
Pastel and charcoal on tracing paper, mounted on
board, 98.8 × 71.5 cm (38⅞ × 28⅛ in.).
Guggenheim Museum, New York

OPPOSITE
213. *Three Dancers in Violet Tutus, c. 1895–99.*
Pastel, 73.2 × 49 cm (28⅞ × 19¼ in.).
Private collection on loan to the National Gallery, London

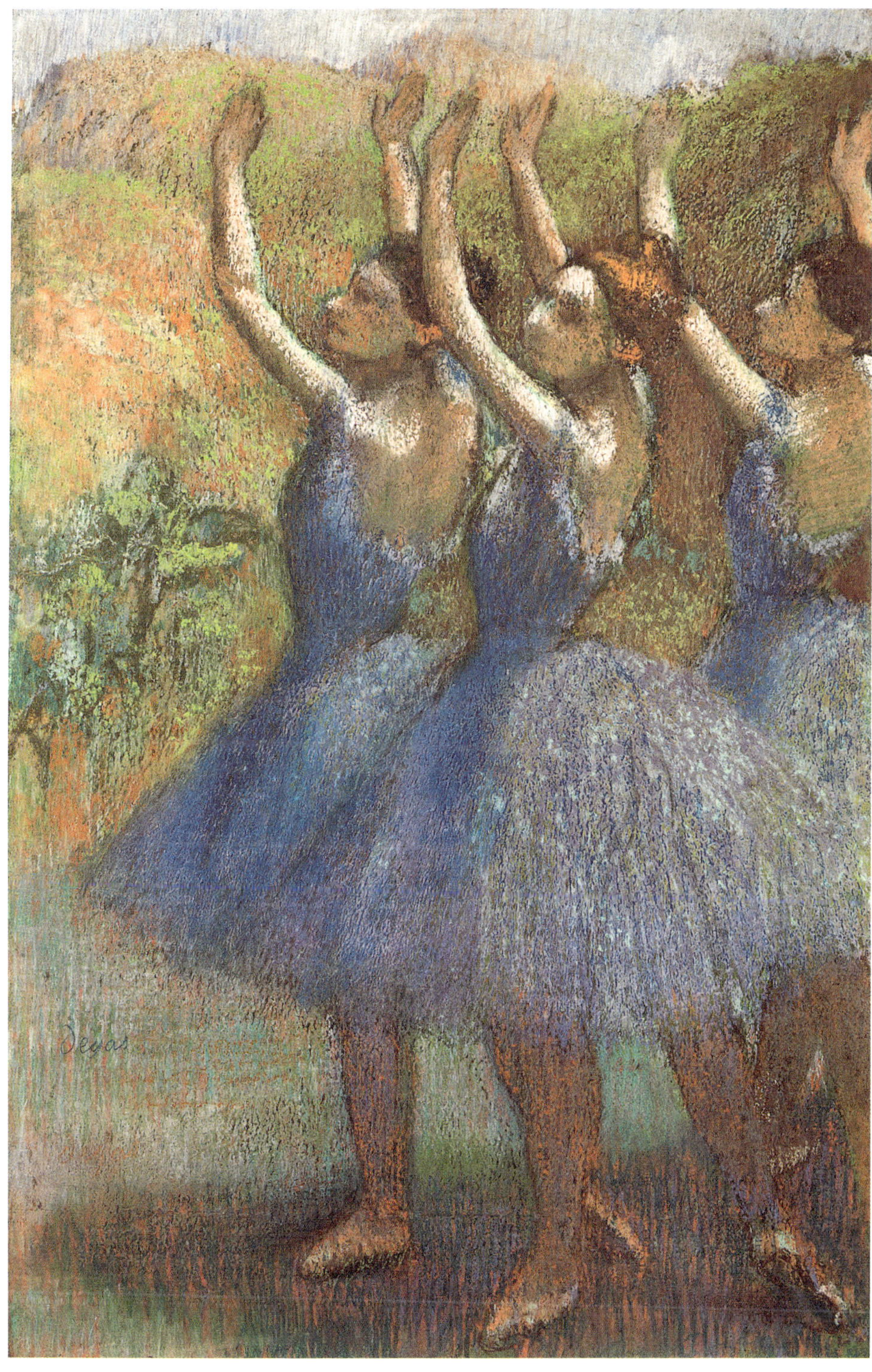

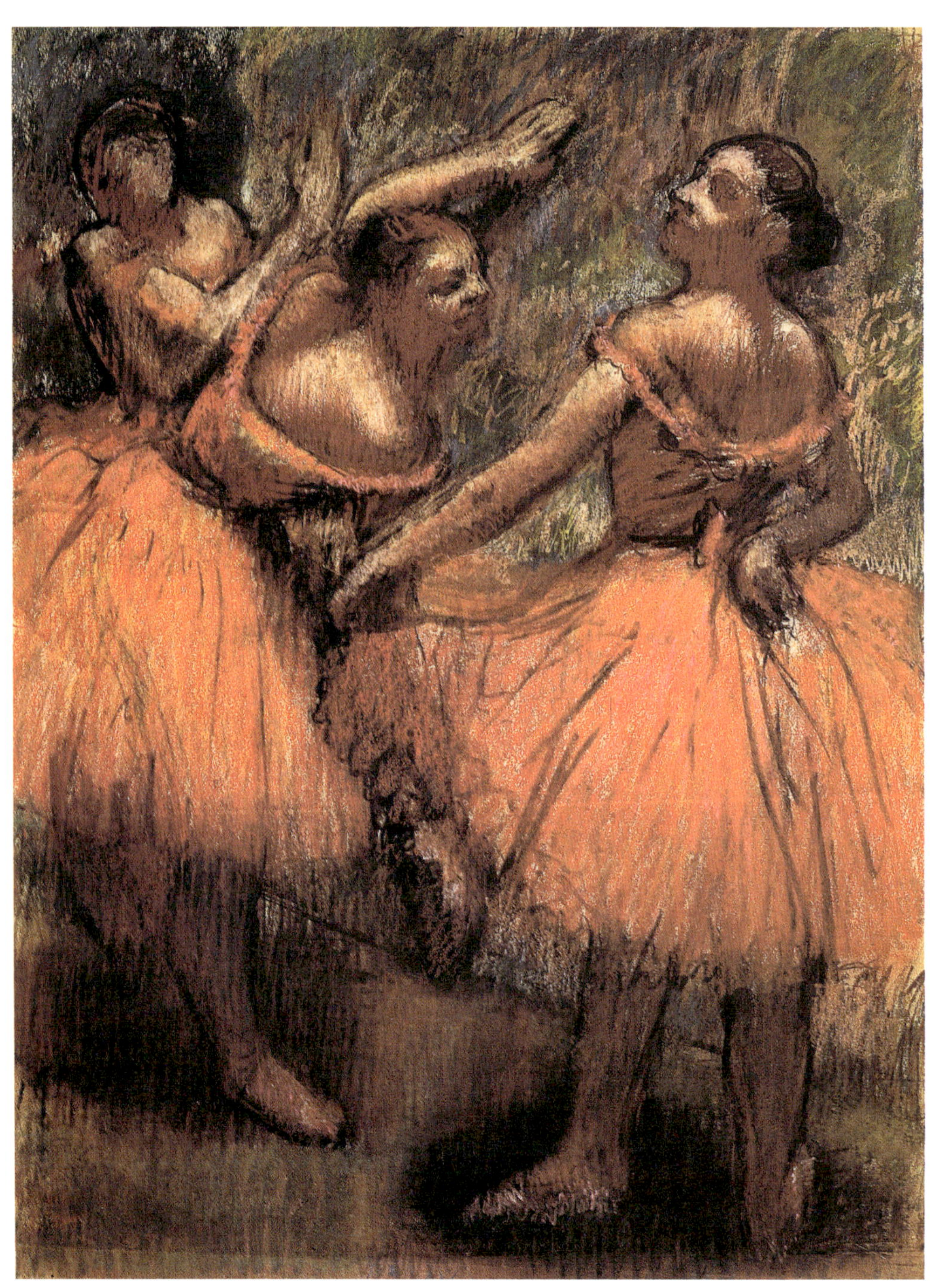

290   *'The Dying of the Light'* 1890–c. 1912

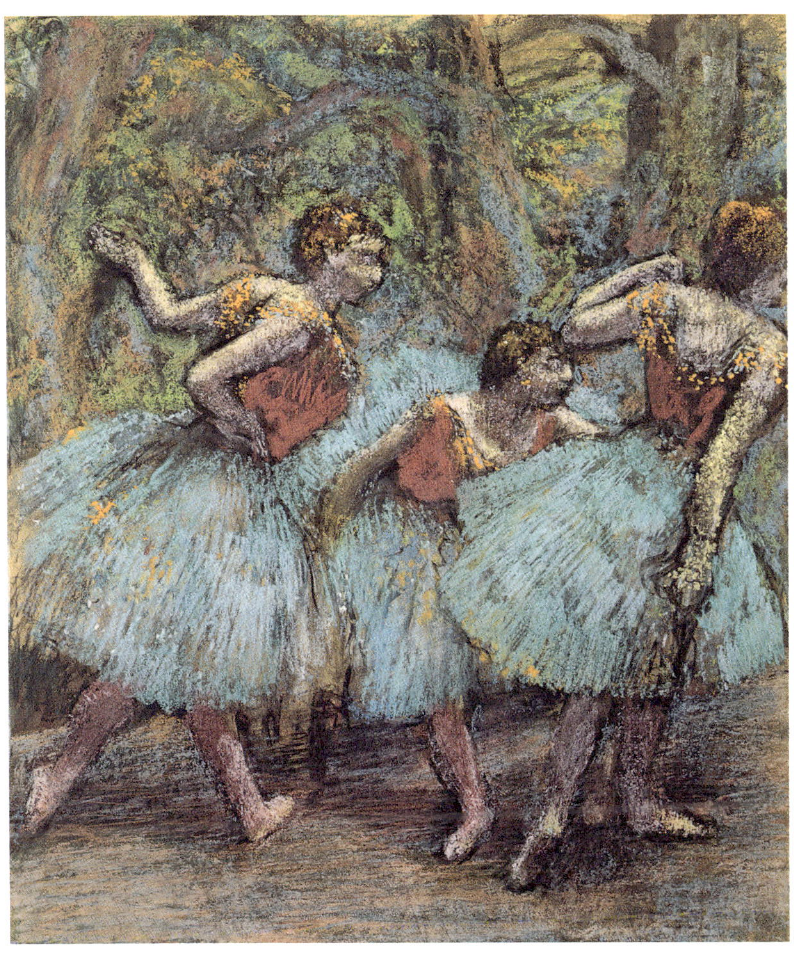

OPPOSITE
214. *Red Ballet Skirts*, *c.* 1897–1901.
Pastel on tracing paper, 81.3 × 62.2 cm (32 × 24½ in.).
Burrell Collection, Glasgow

ABOVE
215. *Three Dancers (Blue Skirts, Red Bodices)*, *c.* 1903.
Pastel on paper laid on card, 94 × 81 cm (37 × 31⅞ in.).
Fondation Beyeler, Riehen, Basel

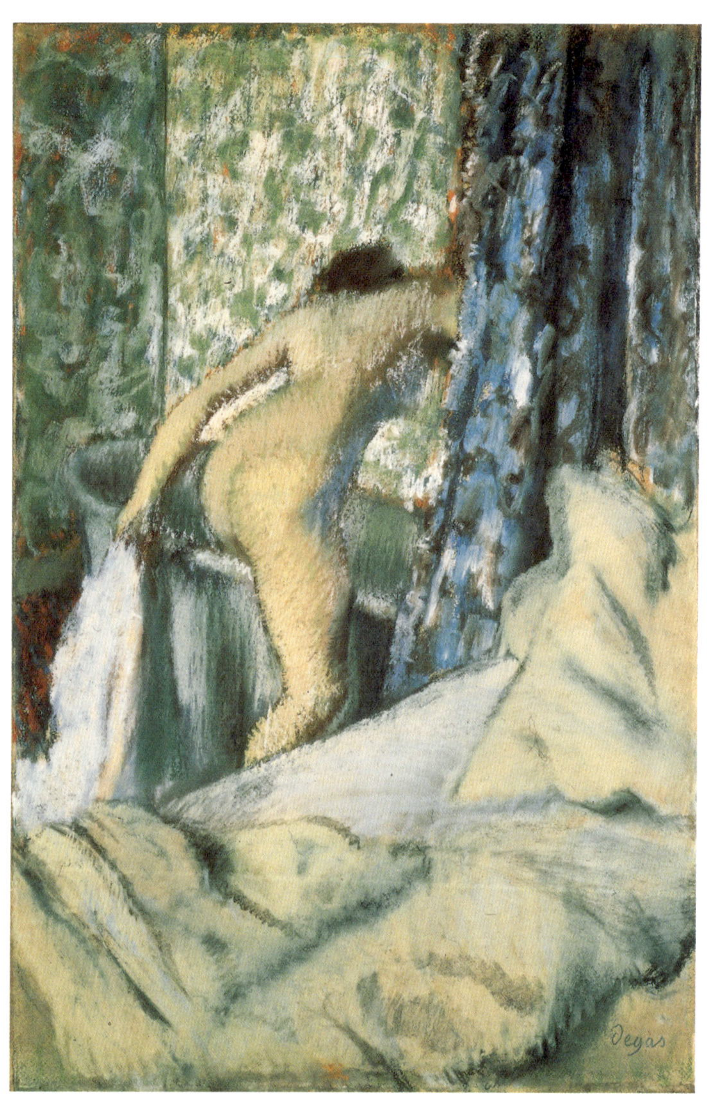

216. *The Morning Bath*, c. 1892–95.
Pastel, 70.6 × 43.3 cm (27¼ × 17 in.),
The Art Institute of Chicago

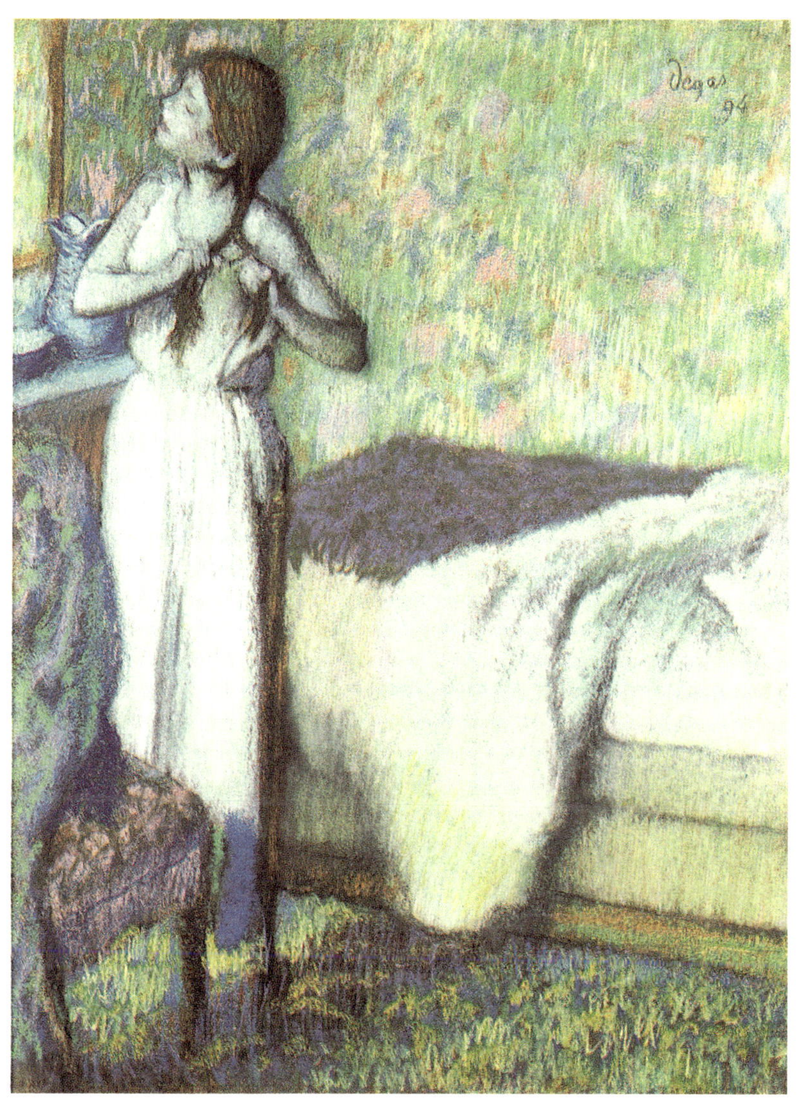

217. *The Morning Toilet*, 1894.
Pastel, 61 × 46 cm (24 × 18⅛ in.).
Private collection

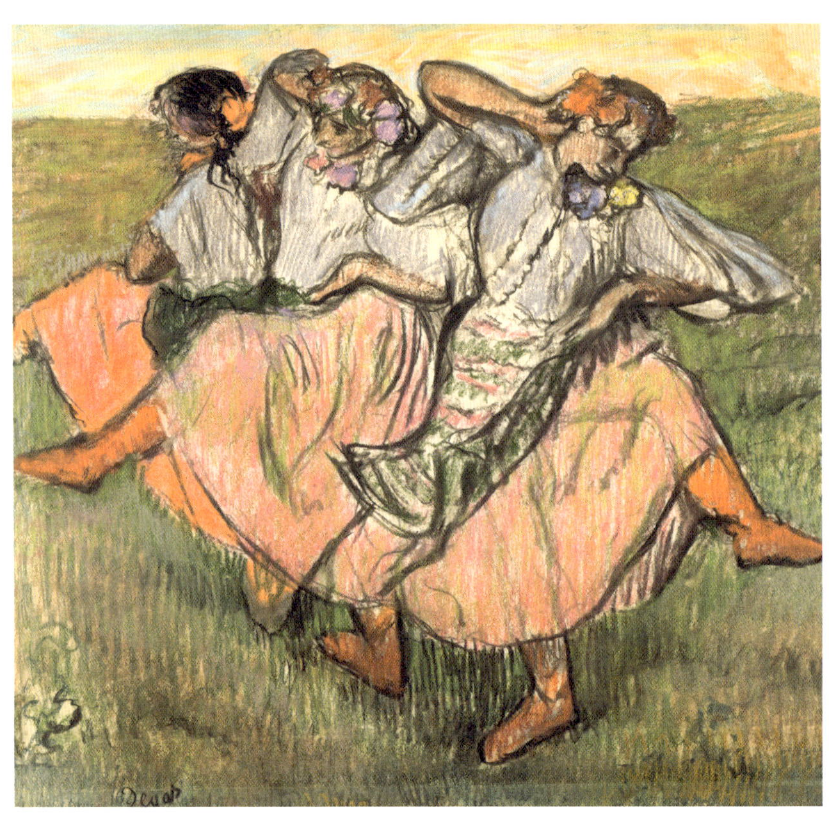

218. *Three Russian Dancers, c.* 1899.
Pastel and charcoal on tracing paper, 62 × 67 cm (24⅛ × 26⅛ in.).
Nationalmuseum, Stockholm

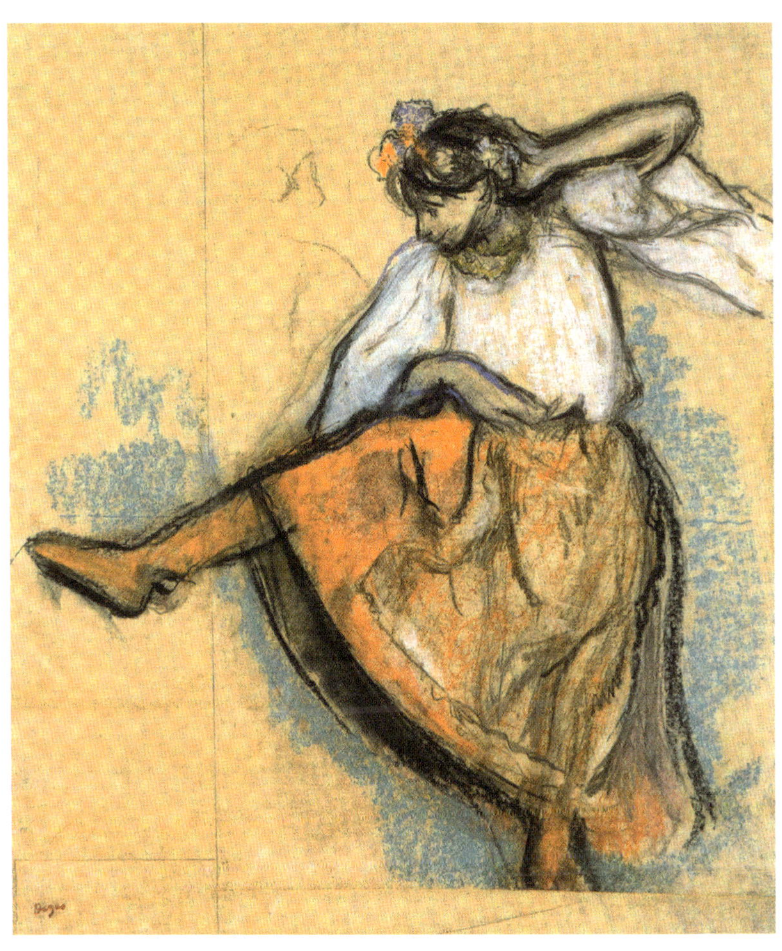

219. *Russian Dancer*, c. 1899.
Pastel and charcoal on tracing paper, 66.1 × 56.2 cm (26 × 22⅛ in.).
Museum of Fine Arts, Houston

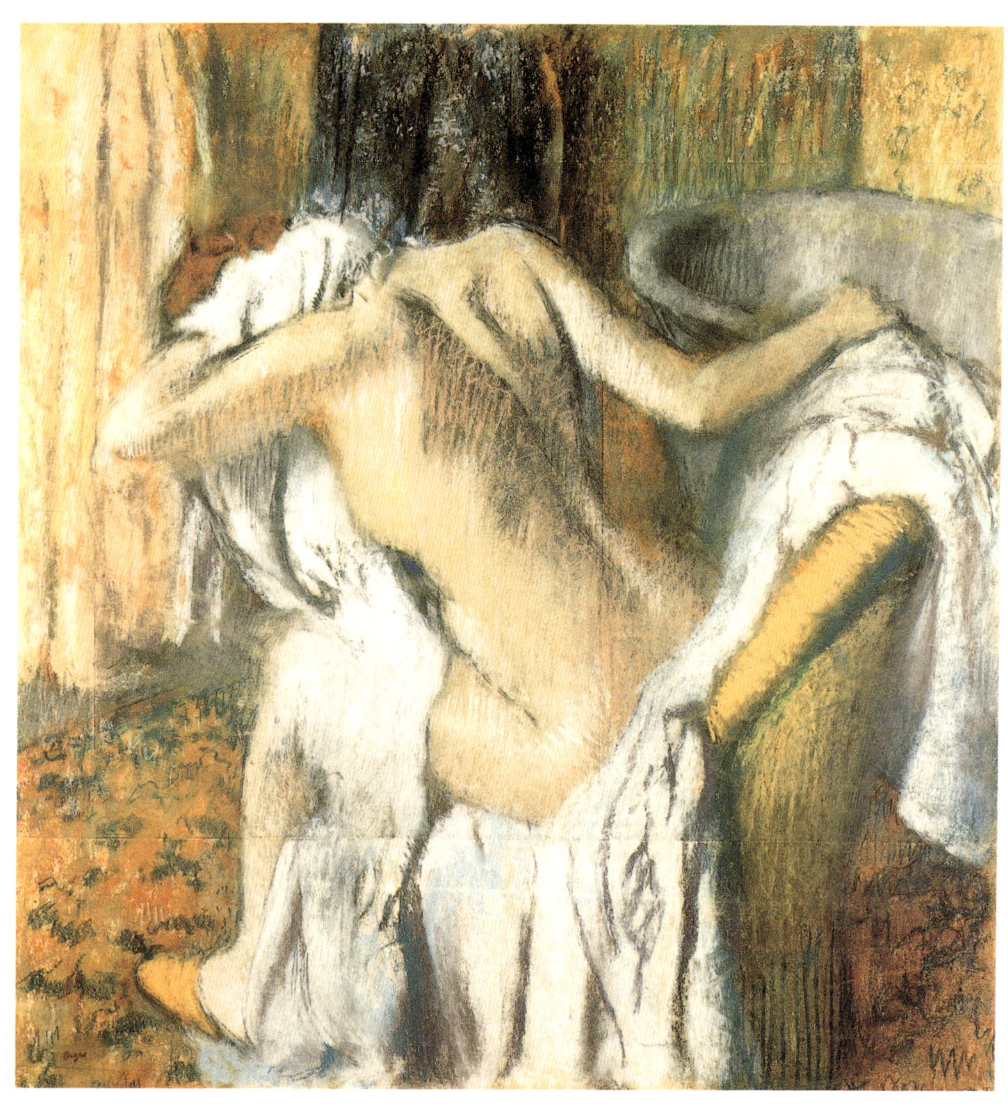

220. *After the Bath, Woman Drying Herself, c.* 1890–95.
Pastel on tracing paper, 103.8 × 98.4 cm (40⅞ × 38¼ in.).
National Gallery, London

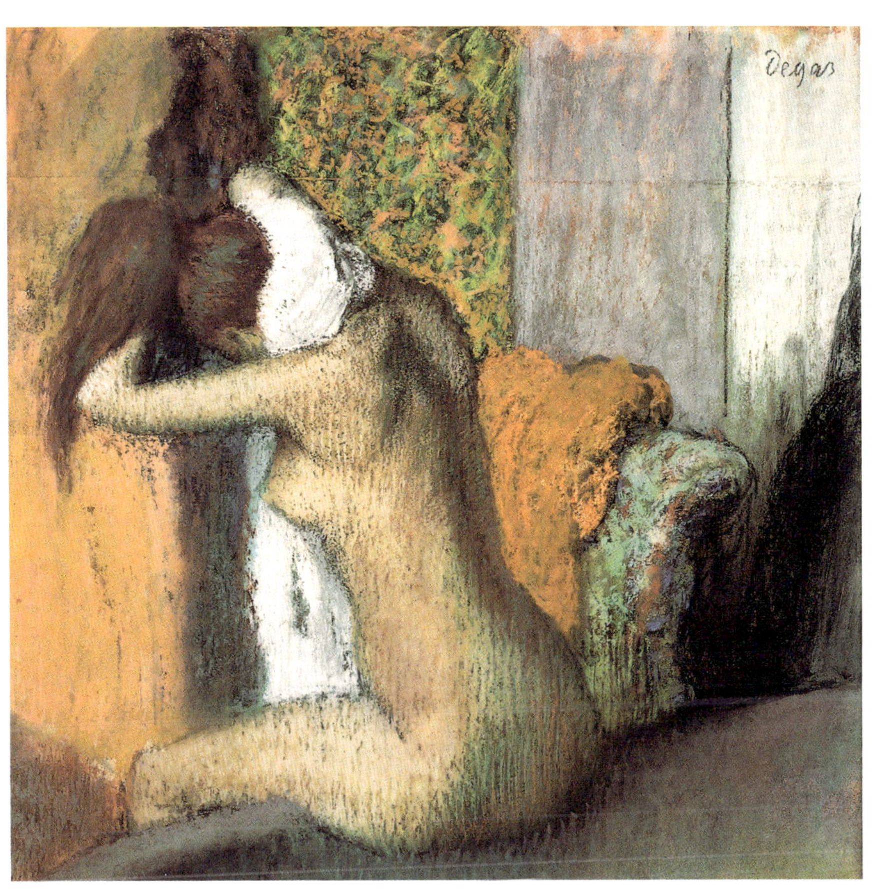

221. *After the Bath, Woman Drying Herself*, 1895–1900.
Pastel, 62.2 × 65 cm (24½ × 25⅝ in.).
Musée d'Orsay, Paris

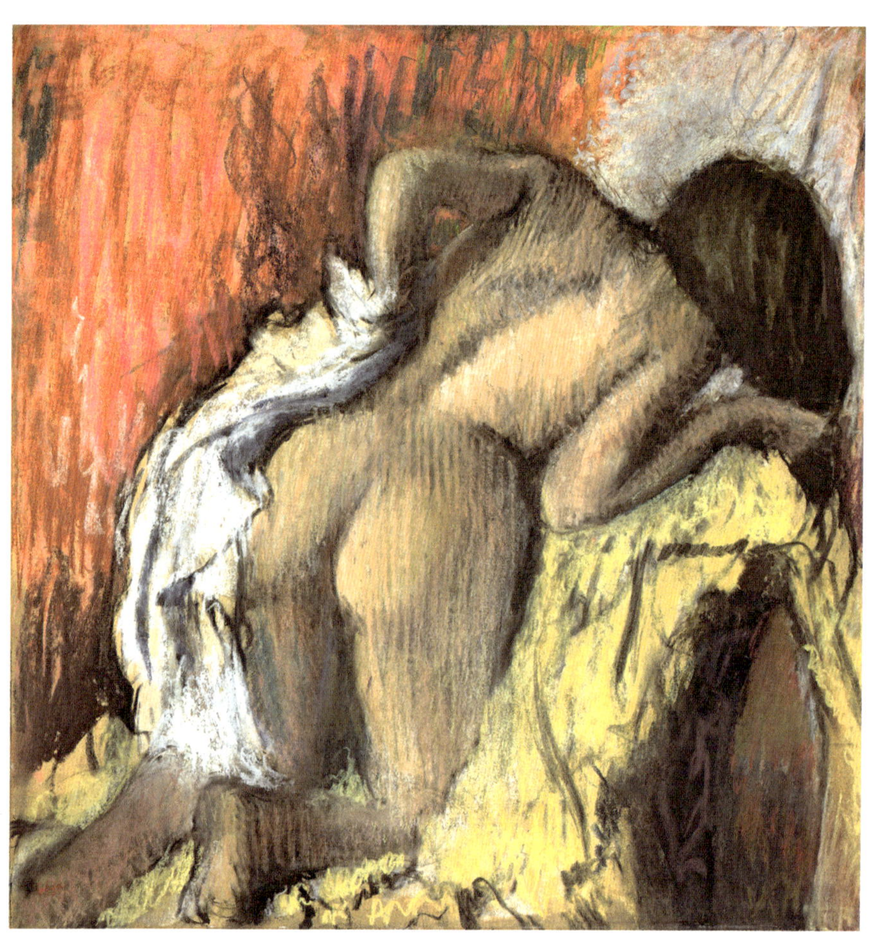

ABOVE
222. *Woman Drying Herself*, *c*. 1896–98.
Pastel on tracing paper, 64.8 × 63.5 cm (25½ × 25 in.).
National Gallery of Scotland, Edinburgh

OPPOSITE
223. *Breakfast after the Bath*, 1895–98.
Pastel, 121 × 92 cm (47⅝ × 36¼ in.).
Private collection

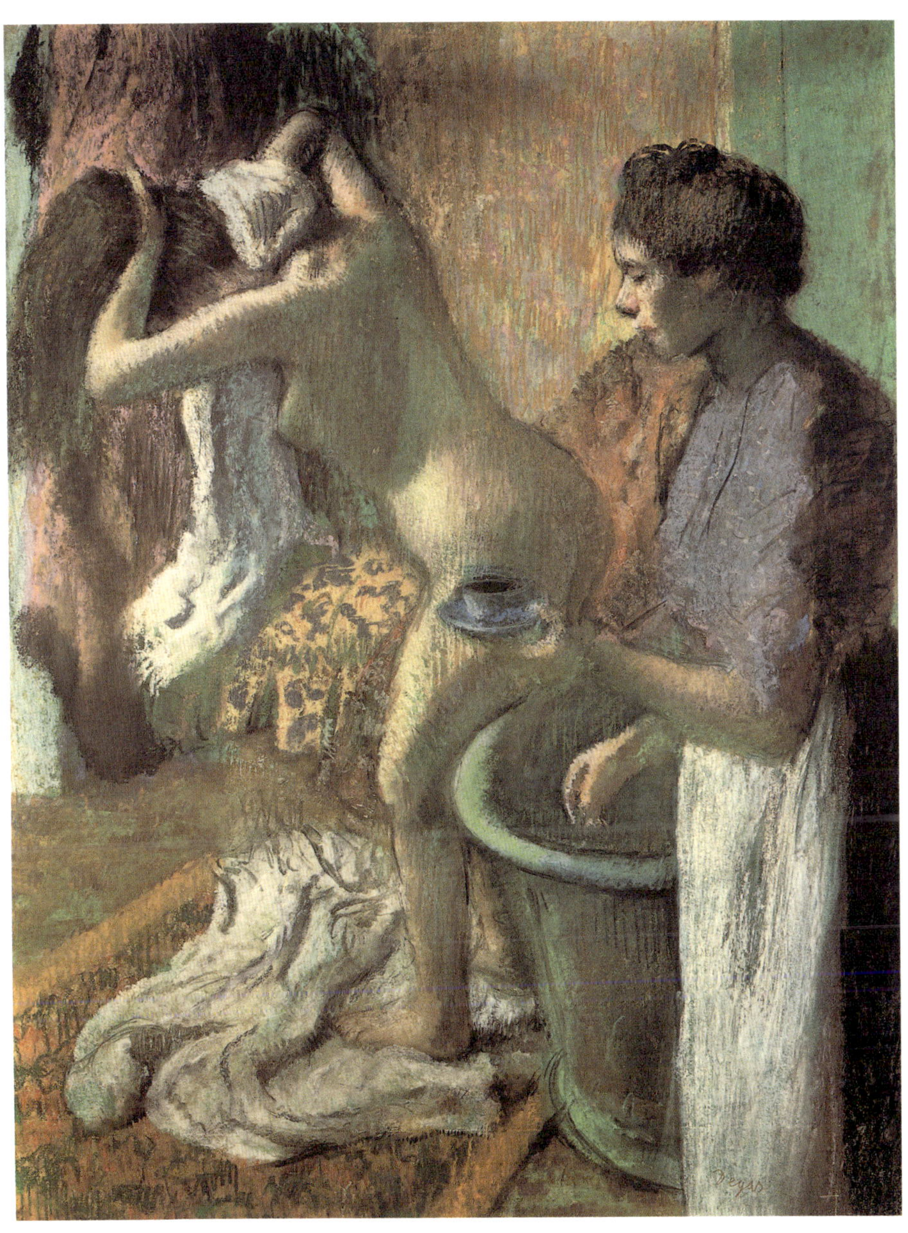

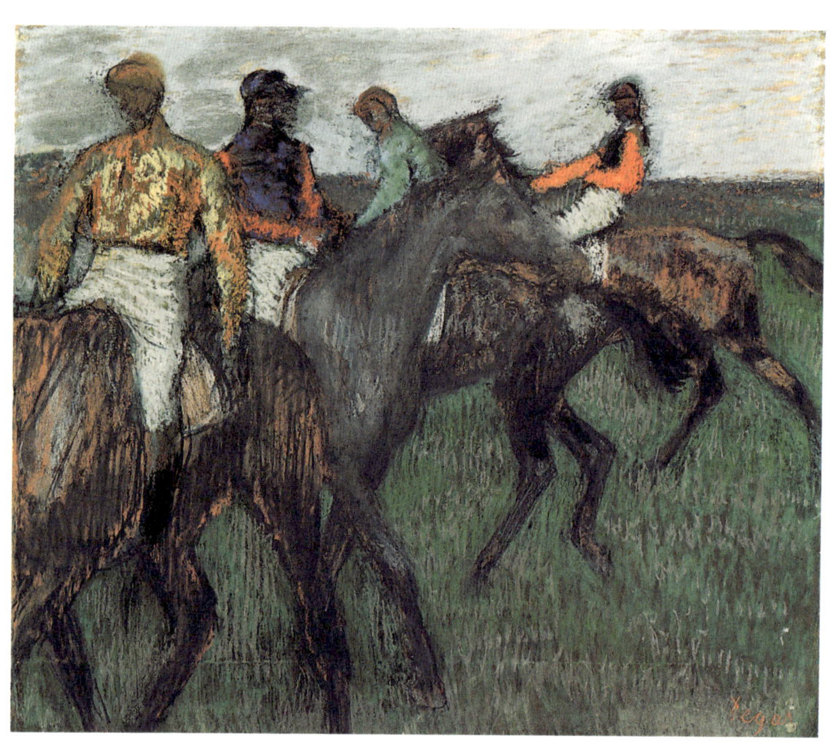

224. *Racehorses*, 1895–1900.
Pastel on tracing paper, 55.8 × 64.8 cm (22 × 25½ in.).
National Gallery of Canada, Ottawa

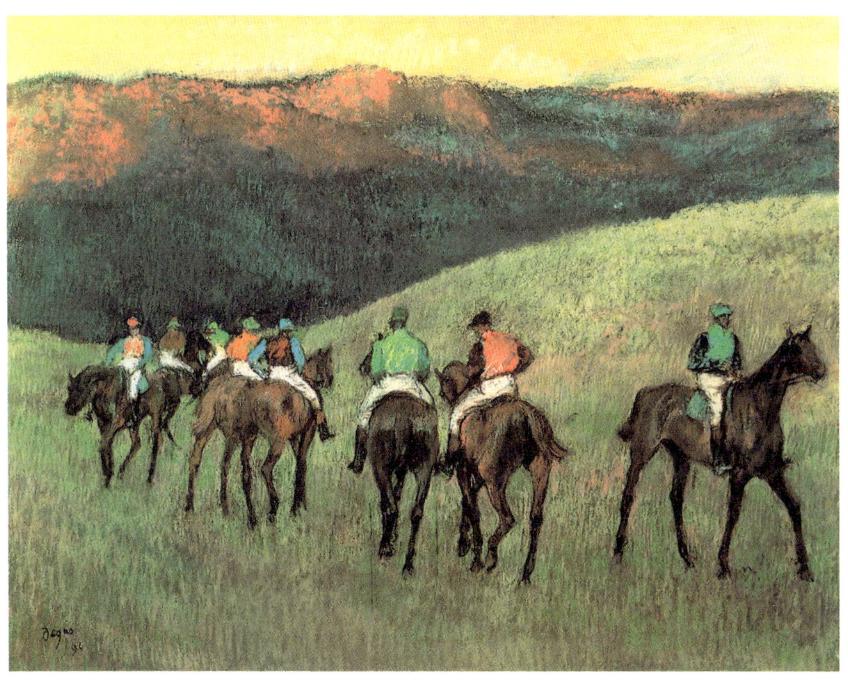

225. *Racehorses in a Landscape*, 1894.
Pastel, 47.9 × 62.9 cm (18⅞ × 25¼ in.).
Thyssen-Bornemisza Museum, Madrid

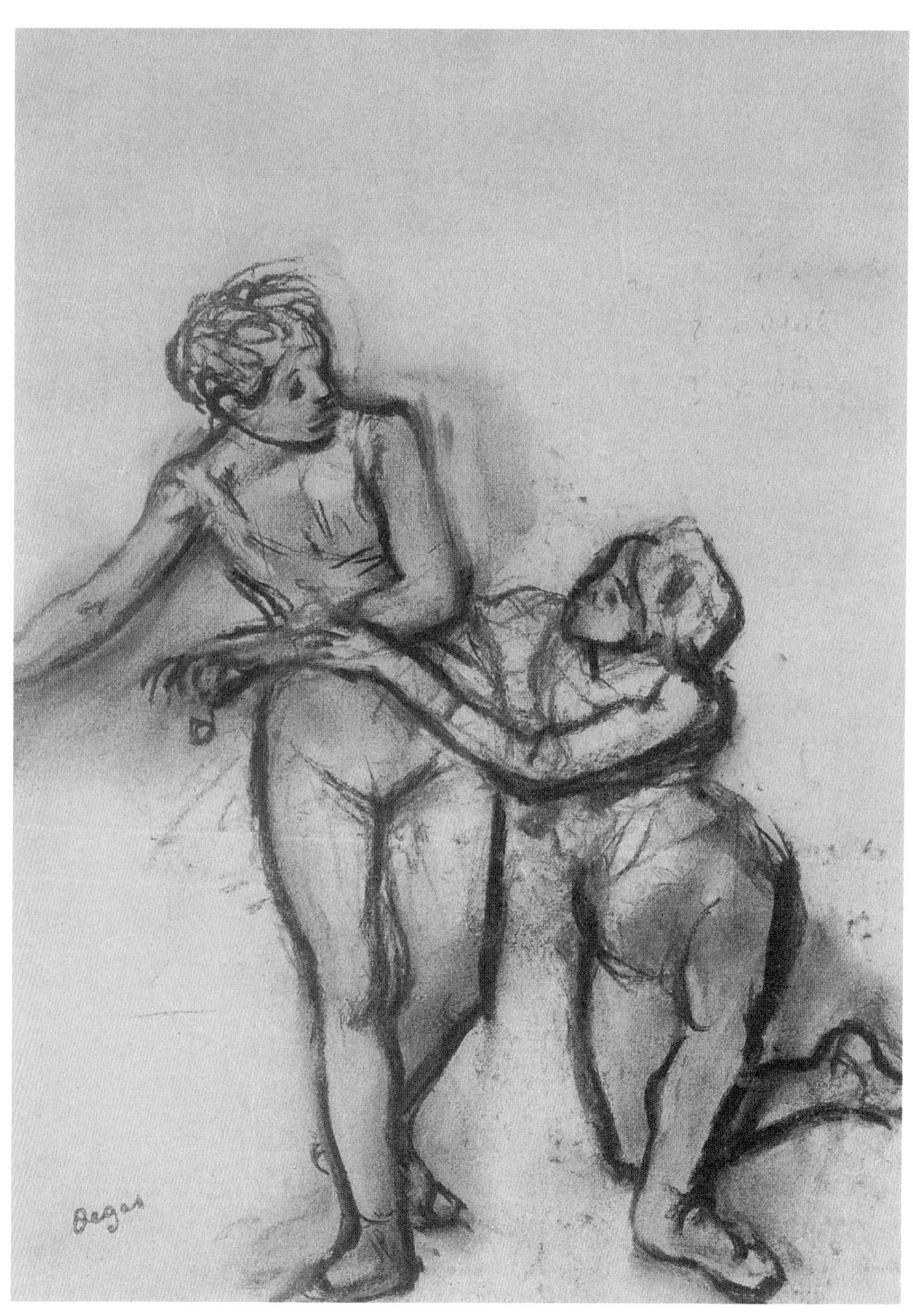

302   *'The Dying of the Light'* 1890–c. 1912

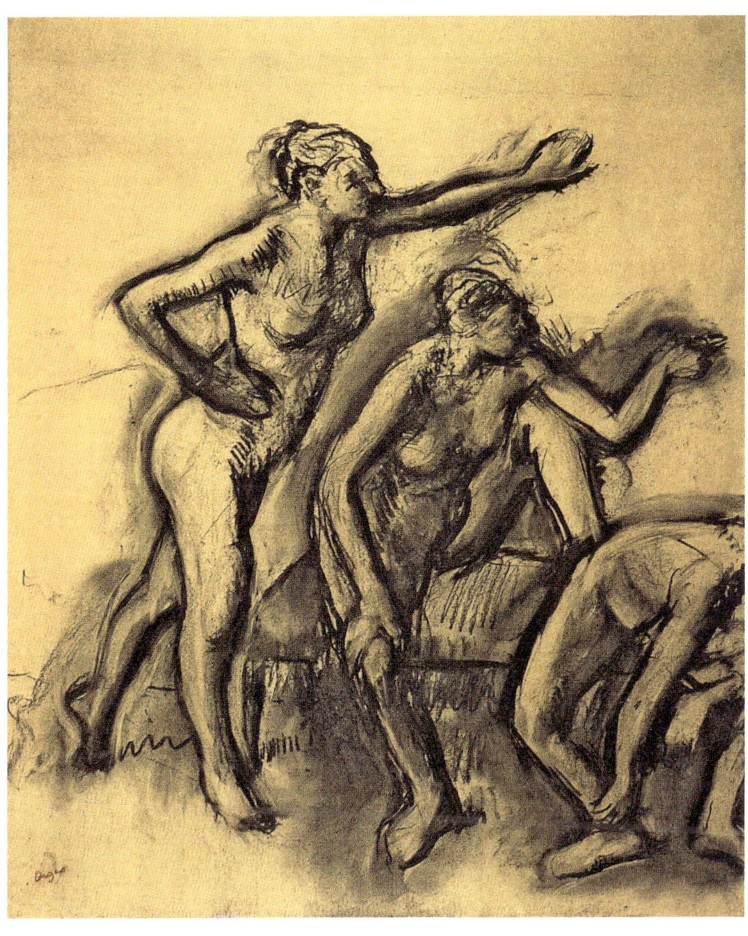

226. *Two Dancers, Harlequin and Colombine, c.* 1890–95.
Charcoal on tracing paper, 31.7 × 23.1 cm (12½ × 9 in.).
Boymans-van Beuningen Museum, Rotterdam

227. *Three Nude Dancers, c.* 1897–1901.
Charcoal on tracing paper, 77.2 × 63.2 cm (30⅜ × 24⅞ in.).
Arkansas Arts Center Foundation Collection, Little Rock

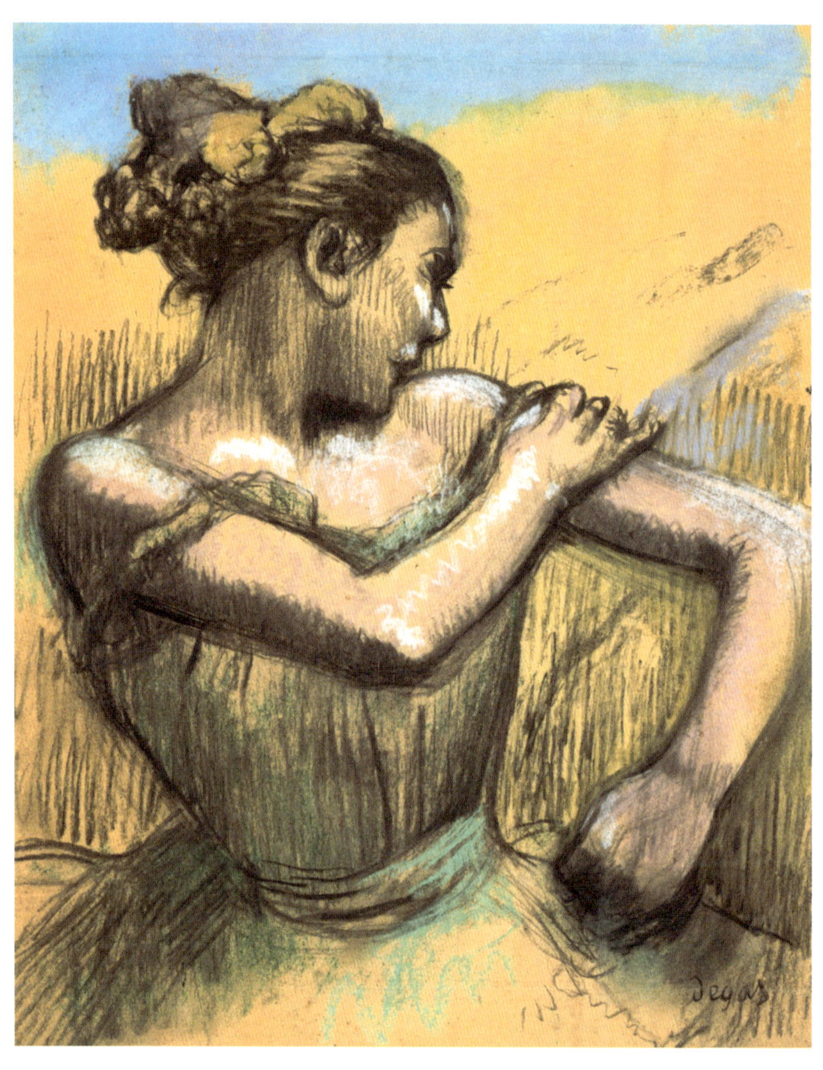

228. *Half-Length Dancer Adjusting her Shoulder Strap, c. 1895–99.*
Charcoal and pastel on tracing paper, 47.5 × 37 cm (18¾ × 14½ in.).
Kunsthalle Bremen

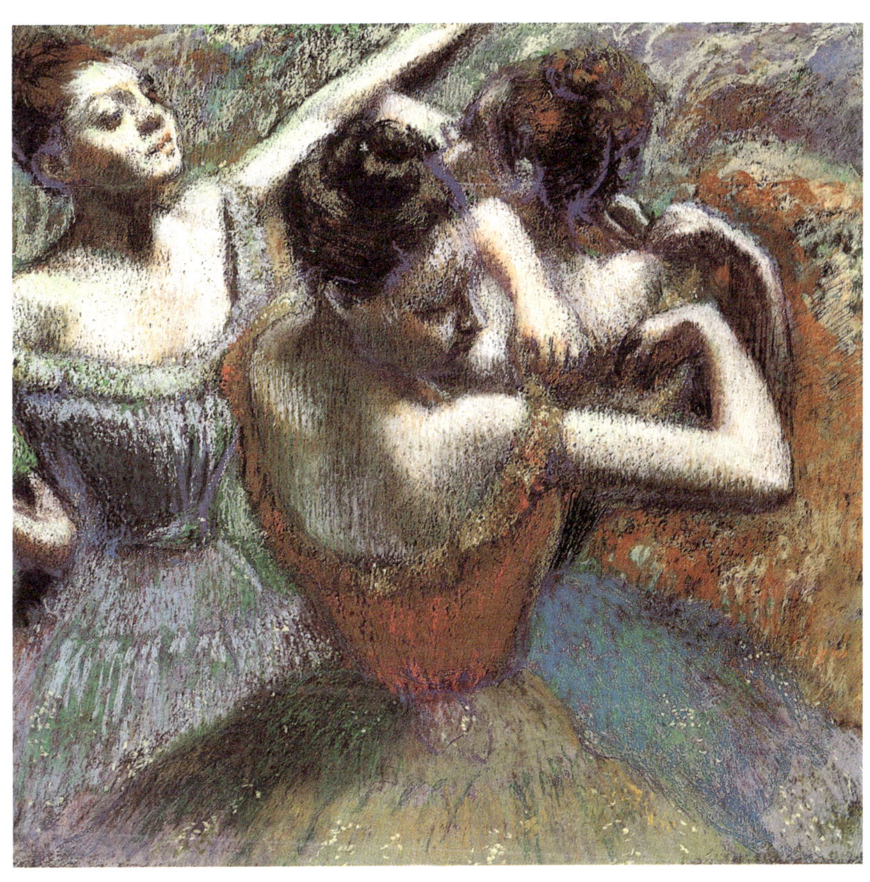

229. *The Dancers, c.* 1899.
Pastel, 62.2 × 64.8 cm (24½ × 25½ in.).
Toledo Museum of Art, Ohio

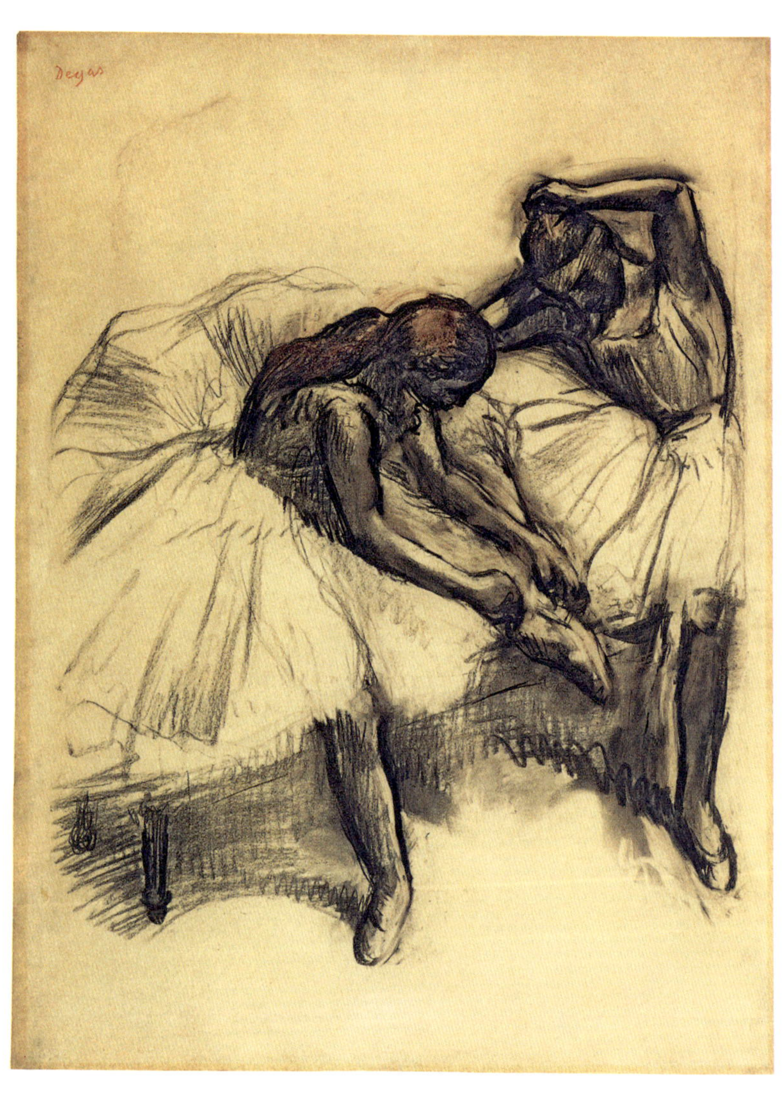

230. *Two Dancers*, *c.* 1900–05.
Charcoal and pastel on tracing paper,
109.3 × 81.2 cm (43 × 32 in.).
Museum of Modern Art, New York

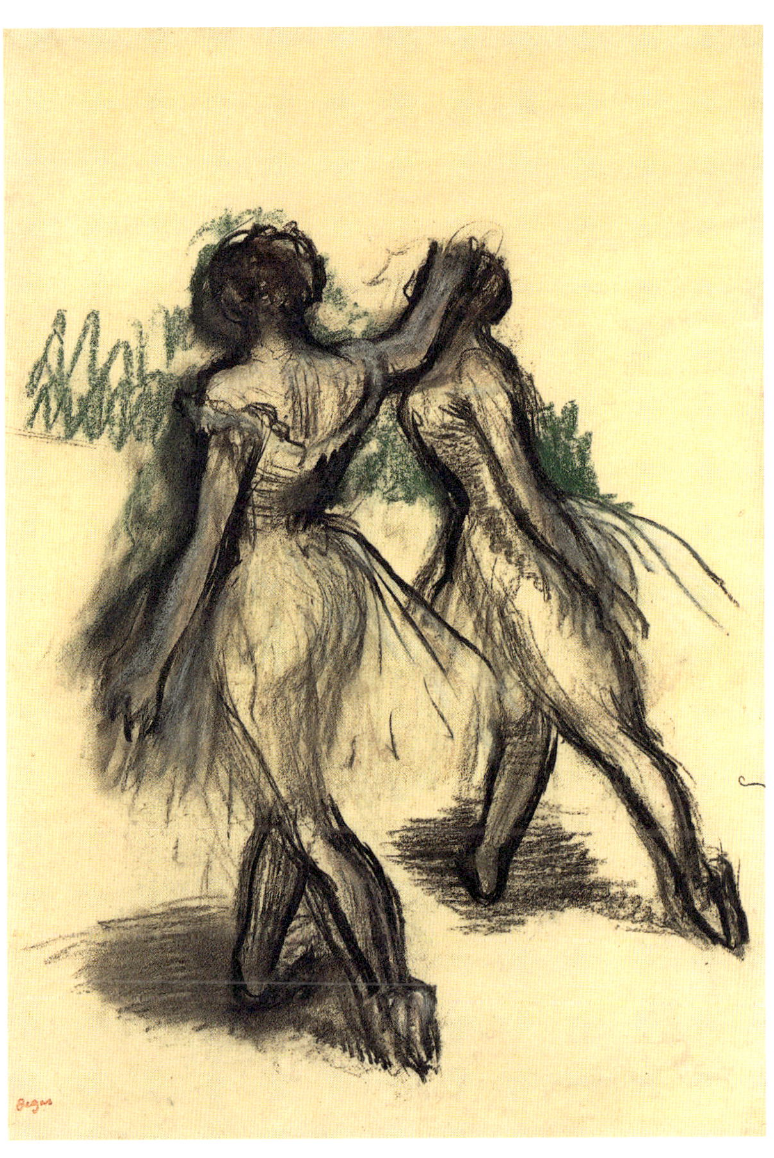

231. *Two Dancers, c. 1890–94.*
Charcoal and pastel, 58 × 41 cm (22⅞ × 16⅛ in.).
Private collection

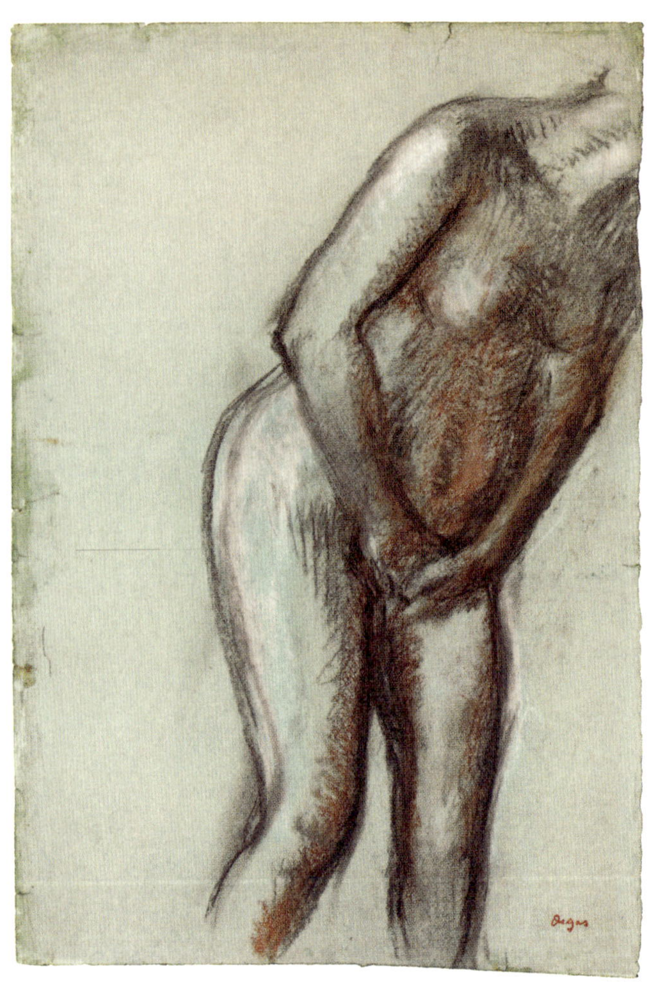

232. *Bather*, c. 1896.
Charcoal and pastel on blue paper, 47 × 32 cm (18½ × 12⅝ in.).
Princeton University Art Museum, New Jersey

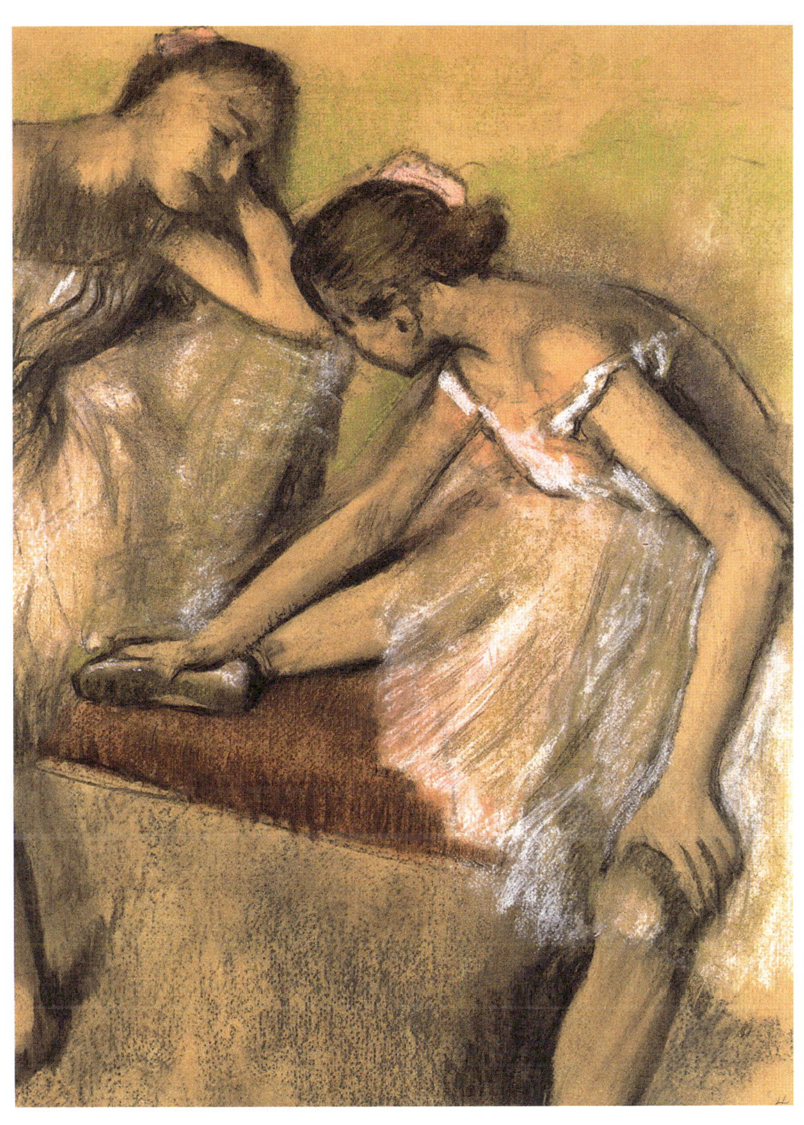

233. *Dancers in Repose, c. 1898.*
Pastel and charcoal, 57.1 × 42.8 cm (22½ × 16⅞ in.).
Detroit Institute of Arts

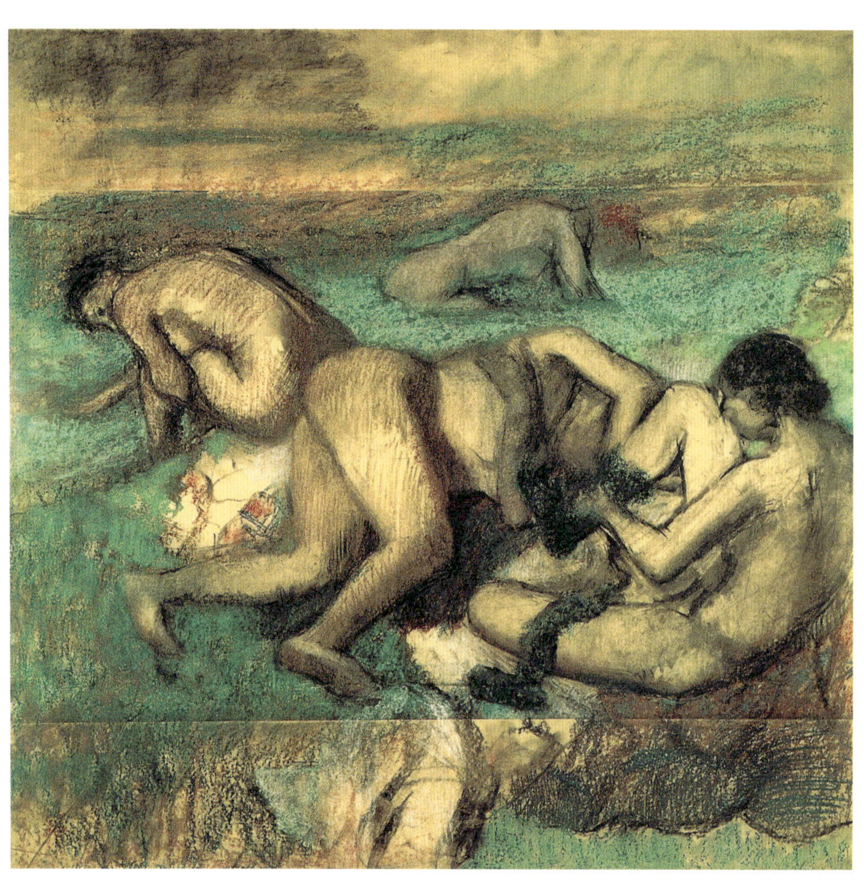

234. *The Bathers*, 1885–1905.
Pastel and charcoal on tracing paper mounted on
board, 113.4 × 115.7 cm (44⅝ × 45½ in.).
The Art Institute of Chicago

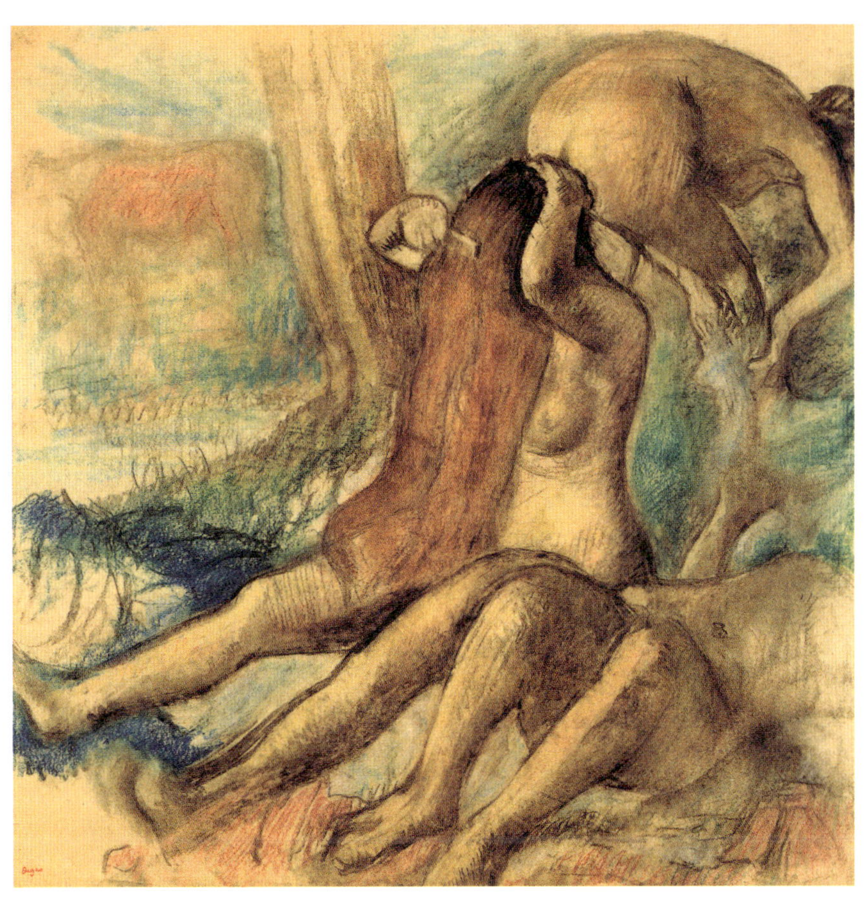

235. *The Bathers, c.* 1895–1900.
Pastel and charcoal on tracing paper,
108.9 × 111.1 cm (42⅞ × 43¾ in.).
Dallas Museum of Art

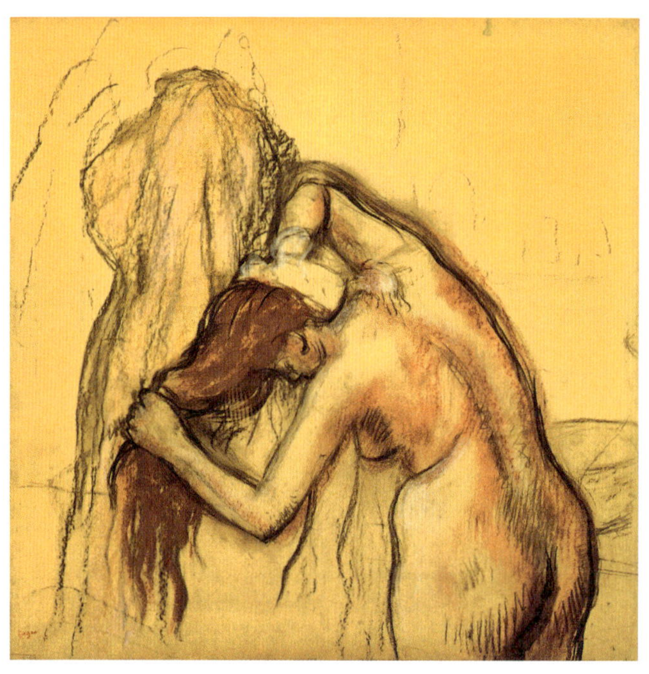

236. *Woman Drying Herself*, *c.* 1900–05.
Charcoal and pastel on tracing paper,
78.7 × 78.7 cm (31 × 31 in.).
Museum of Fine Arts, Houston

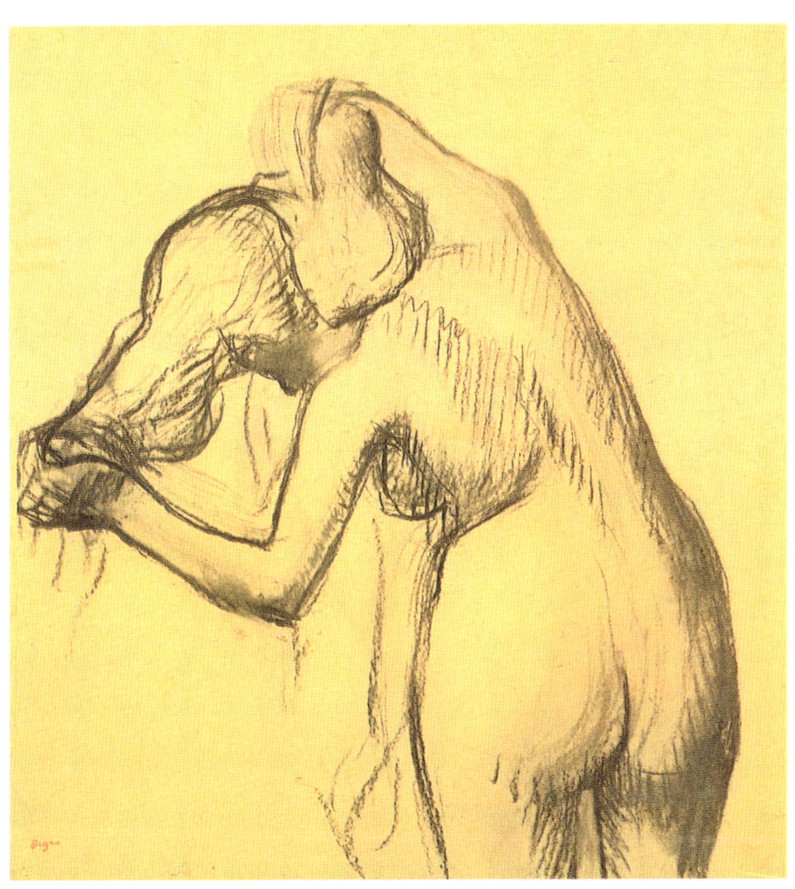

237. *Female Nude Drying her Neck*, *c.* 1900.
Charcoal, 79.3 × 76.2 cm (31¼ × 30 in.).
King's College, Cambridge (Keynes
Collection), on loan to the Fitzwilliam
Museum, Cambridge

Bibliography

The literature on Degas is extensive, but the following titles have been particularly useful in the preparation of this book. For exhibition catalogues, the location of the publisher has been given if the institution(s) hosting the exhibition did not publish the catalogue.

GENERAL

Adhémar, Jean and Françoise Cachin, *Degas: The Complete Etchings, Lithographs and Monotypes*, London, 1974, and New York, 1975

Berson, Ruth (ed.), *The New Painting. Impressionism 1874–1886. Documentation*, 2 vols, Fine Arts Museums of San Francisco, 1996

Boggs, Jean Sutherland et al., *Degas*, exh. cat., Galeries Nationales du Grand Palais, Paris, National Gallery of Canada, Ottawa, and Metropolitan Museum of Art, New York, 1988–89

Bomford, David et al., *Art in the Making: Degas*, exh. cat., National Gallery, London, 2004

Brettell, Richard and Suzanne Folds McCullagh, *Degas in The Art Institute of Chicago*, Chicago, 1984

Campbell, Sara et al., *Degas in the Norton Simon Museum, Nineteenth-Century Art*, Vol. 11, New Haven and London, 2009

Huysmans, Joris-Karl, *L'Art Moderne. Certains*, ed. H. Juin, Paris, 1976

Lemoisne, Paul-André, *Degas et son Oeuvre*, 4 vols, Paris, 1946–49, with *A Supplement* by Philippe Brame and Theodore Reff, Paris, London and New York, 1984

Kendall, Richard, *Degas: Beyond Impressionism*, exh. cat., National Gallery, London, and The Art Institute of Chicago, 1996–97

Lipton, Eunice, *Looking into Degas. Uneasy Images of Women and Modern Life*, Berkeley and London, 1986

Loyrette, Henri, *Degas*, Paris, 1991

Reff, Theodore, *The Notebooks of Edgar Degas: A Catalogue of the Thirty-Eight Notebooks in the Bibliothèque Nationale and Other Collections*, 2 vols, Oxford, 1976

—, *Degas: The Artist's Mind*, New York and London, 1976

Thomson, Richard, *The Private Degas*, exh. cat., Whitworth Art Gallery, Manchester, and Fitzwilliam Museum, Cambridge, 1987; London and New York, 1987

BALLET

DeVonyer, Jill and Richard Kendall, *Degas and the Dance*, exh. cat., Detroit Institute of Arts and Philadelphia Museum of Art, 2002–03; New York, 2002

—, *Degas and the Ballet: Picturing Movement*, exh. cat., Royal Academy of Arts, London, 2011

Kendall, Richard with Douglas Druick and Arthur Beale, *Degas and the Little Dancer*, exh. cat., Joslyn Art Museum, Omaha, Sterling and Francine Clark Art Institute, Williamstown, and Baltimore Museum of Art, 1998–99; New Haven and London, 1998

Shackelford, George, *Degas: The Dancers*, exh. cat., National Gallery of Art, Washington, DC, 1984–85

SCULPTURE

Millard, Charles W., *The Sculpture of Edgar Degas*, Princeton, 1979

PORTRAITS

Baumann, Felix and Marianne Karabelnik (eds), *Degas Portraits*, exh. cat., Kunsthaus, Zürich and Kunsthalle, Tübingen, 1994–95; London, 1994

ITALY

Loyrette, Henri, *Degas e l'Italia*, exh. cat., Villa Medici, Rome, 1984

THE NUDE

Shackelford, George and Xavier Rey, *Degas and The Nude*, exh. cat., Museum of Fine Arts, Boston, and Musée d'Orsay, Paris, 2011–12; Boston and London, 2011

Thomson, Richard, *Degas: The Nudes*, London, 1988

LANDSCAPE

Dumas, Ann et al., *Edgar Degas: The Late Landscapes*, exh. cat., Columbus Museum of Art and Ny Carlsberg Glyptotek, Copenhagen, 2006; London, 2006

Kendall, Richard, *Degas Landscapes*, exh. cat., Metropolitan Museum of Art, New York and Museum of Fine Arts, Houston, 1994; New Haven and London, 1993

HORSERACING

Boggs, Jean Sutherland with Shelley G. Sturman and Kimberly Jones, *Degas at the Races*, exh. cat., National Gallery of Art, Washington, DC, 1998; New Haven and London, 1998

MILLINERS

Groom, Gloria et al., *Impressionism, Fashion & Modernity*, exh. cat., Musée d'Orsay, Paris, Metropolitan Museum of Art, New York and The Art Institute of Chicago, 2012–13

DRAWINGS AND PASTELS

Adriani, Götz, *Edgar Degas: Pastelle, Ölskizzen, Zeichnungen*, exh. cat., Kunsthalle, Tübingen, and Nationalgalerie, Berlin, 1984; Cologne, 1984

Boggs, Jean Sutherland and Anne Maheux, *Degas Pastels*, London and New York, 1992

Lloyd, Christopher and Richard Thomson, *Impressionist Drawings from British Public and Private Collections*, exh. cat., Ashmolean Museum, Oxford, Manchester City Art Gallery, The Burrell Collection, Glasgow, 1986; Oxford, 1986

Lloyd, Christopher, *Impressionism: Pastels Watercolors Drawings*, exh. cat., Milwaukee Art Museum and the Albertina, Vienna, 2011–12; Milwaukee, 2011, and Vienna and Cologne, 2012

DEGAS'S COLLECTION

Dumas, Ann, *Degas as a Collector*, exh. cat., National Gallery, London, 1996

— et al., *The Private Collection of Edgar Degas*, Metropolitan Museum of Art, New York, 1997

MEMOIRS

Fèvre, Jeanne, *Mon Oncle Degas*, Geneva, 1949

Halévy, Daniel, *My Friend Degas*, trans. Mina Curtiss, London, 1966

Kendall, Richard, *Degas by Himself*, London, 1987

Valéry, Paul, *Degas Danse Dessin*, Paris, 1936; *Degas Manet Morisot*, Collected Works of Paul Valéry, vol. 12, trans. David Paul, New York, 1960

Vollard, Ambroise, *Degas. An Intimate Portrait*, trans. Randolph Weaver, London, 1927

—, *Recollections of a Picture Dealer*, trans. Violet MacDonald, London, 1936

Acknowledgments

In writing this survey of Degas as a draughtsman I am conscious of the huge debt I owe to the scholarship and expertise of the many scholars – past and present – who have worked on the artist (see Bibliography). Special thanks are due to Richard Kendall who has very kindly allowed me to use translations from two of his publications: *Degas by Himself* (1987) and *Degas Landscapes* (1993). As on previous occasions, my wife, Frances, has exercised her tutelary skills. It has been a pleasure to work with the team at Thames & Hudson, particularly Julia MacKenzie as editor and Lauren Necati as designer, who have nursed the book through the press and brought everything to a happy conclusion.

I would like to thank the following for quotations of copyright material: Richard Kendall, *Degas by Himself*, Macdonald Orbis, 1987; Richard Kendall, *Degas Landscapes*, © 1993 Richard Kendall. Reprinted by permission of Yale University Press; Paul Valéry, *Collected Works of Paul Valéry, Volume 12* © 1960 Princeton University Press, 1988 renewed. Reprinted by permission of Princeton University Press.

Picture Credits

Baltimore Museum of Art 27 (Cone Collection); Basel, Kunstmuseum, Öffentliche Kunstsammlungen 75 (inv. 1924); Birmingham, Barber Institute of Fine Arts, University of Birmingham 88 (Bridgeman Art Library), 93; Boston, Museum of Fine Arts 117 (58.1263), 160, 189, 198, 209; Bremen, Kunsthalle – Der Kunstverein in Bremen 10, 29 (inv. 57/98), 228 (Photo Lars Lohrisch, 04/1); Cambridge, Fitzwilliam Museum 18, 158 (PD 23-1978), 190, 211, 237 (on loan from the Keynes Collection, by permission of the Provost and Fellows of King's College, Cambridge); Cambridge (MA), Harvard Art Museums/Fogg Museum 7 (anonymous gift in memory of W. G. Russell Allen), 24, 58 (bequest of Meta and Paul J. Sachs, 1965.254), 101 (bequest of Meta and Paul J. Sachs, 1965.263), 125 (bequest of the collection of Maurice Wertheim, Class of 1906), 131 (bequest of Meta and Paul J. Sachs, 1965. 260), 210 (gift of Mrs J. Montgomery Sears, 1927.23); Chicago, Art Institute of Chicago 17 (Joseph and Helen Regenstein Foundation, 1961.792), 69 (1933.469), 134 (bequest of Adele R. Levy, 1962.703), 171 (bequest of Mrs Sterling Morton, 1969.331), 188 (purchased from the collection of Friedrich and Louise Gutmann, and gift of Daniel C. Searle), 216 (Mr and Mrs Potter Palmer Collection, 1922.422), 234 (gift of Nathan Cummings, 1955.495); Cincinnati Art Museum 114 (bequest of Mary Hanna, 1956. 114); Cleveland Museum of Art 25 (John L. Severance Fund), 59 (Bridgeman Art Library. Mr and Mrs Lewis B. Williams Collection, 1951.483); Cologne, Museum Ludwig 197; Dallas Museum of Art 152 (1986.277), 191 (Reves Collection), 235 (Reves Collection, 1985,R.24); Denver Art Museum 107 (1941.6), 145 (1973.234); Detroit Institute of Arts 100 (bequest of John S. Newberry, 65.145), 233 (gift of Edward E. Rothman, 72.441); Edinburgh, National Gallery of Scotland 222 (Bridgeman Art Library); Essen, Folkwang Museum 204; Farmington (CT), Hill-Stead Museum 175; Fort Worth, Kimbell Art Museum 161; Geneva, Jan Krugier and Marie-Anne Krugier-Poniatowski Collection 193; Glasgow, Burrell Collection 73 (Art Gallery and Museum, Kelvingrove/Bridgeman Art Library), 85, 91, 166, 182 (35.235), 214; Glen Falls (NY), The Hyde Collection 154; Hamburg, Kunsthalle 146; Houston, Museum of Fine Arts 194, 219 (gift of the Sara Lee Corporation, inv. 1193), 236 (gift of Sarah Campbell Blaffer); Kansas City, Nelson-Atkins Museum of Art 115 (F 73.30), 149 (F 79.34); Karlsruhe, Staatliche Kunsthalle Kupferstichkabinett 108 (1980.12, 2013 Photo A. Fischer/H. Kohler); Little Rock, Arkansas Arts Center Foundation Collection 227; London, British Museum 72 (1968.2.10.26), 105 (1968.2.10.25); London, National Gallery 34, 87 (NG4121), 122 (on loan from Tate, presented by the Art Fund 1916), 207 (NG4865), 220; London, Tate 173 (TO 3563); Los Angeles, J. Paul Getty Museum 104 (95. GD. 35.13), 139 (owned jointly with the Norton Simon Art Foundation, Pasadena, M. 1983.1); Lyon, Musée des Beaux-Arts 123; Madrid, Thyssen-Bornemisza Museum 112, 150, 225; Memphis, Dixon Gallery and Gardens 156 (bequest of Mr and Mrs Hugo N. Dixon, 1959.2); Minneapolis Institute of Arts 102 (gift of Julius Boehler, 26.10); New Haven (CT), Yale University Art Gallery 202; New York, Brooklyn Museum 56 (gift of James H. Post, A. Augustus Healy, and John T. Underwood, 21.111); New York, Guggenheim Museum; 212 (Justin K. Thannhauser Collection); New York, Metropolitan Museum of Art 40 (Lehman Collection, inv. 1975.1.609), 57 (1918.19.51.7), 76 (1976.201.8), 98 (H. O. Havemeyer Collection, bequest of Mrs H. O. Havemeyer, 1929, 29.100.941), 103 (29.100.943), 113 (H. O. Havemeyer Collection, bequest of Mrs H. O. Havemeyer, 1929, 29.100.39), 118 (19. 51.1), 121 (H. O. Havemeyer Collection, bequest of Mrs H. O. Havemeyer, 1929, 29.100.185), 147 (H. O. Havemeyer Collection, bequest of Mrs H. O. Havemeyer, 1929, 29.100.38), 162 (bequest of Stephen C. Clark, 1960, 61.101.7), 170 (H. O. Havemeyer Collection, bequest of Mrs H. O. Havemeyer, 1929, 29.100.35), 177 (gift of Mr and Mrs Nate B. Spingold, 1956, 56.231), 180 (29. 100. 41), 199; New York, Museum of Modern Art 148 (gift of Mrs. David M. Levy), 186 (Louise Reinhardt Smith bequests), 230; New York, Pierpont Morgan Library (Thaw Collection) 60, 65, 126, 127; Northampton (MA), Smith College Museum of Art 36; Ottawa, National Gallery of Canada 224; Oxford, Ashmolean Museum 6, 12, 119, 167 (all The Art Archive); Paris, Bibliothèque Nationale 1, 2, 3, 4, 5, 14 (Notebook 2, p. 53), 31 (Notebook 1, p. 17), 32 (Notebook 19, p. 11), 38 (Notebook 18, p. 79), 183 (Notebook 18, p. 163), 184 (Notebook 18, p. 127), 187 (Notebook 18, p. 165); Paris, Musée du Louvre 143 (Album Gauguin 4 f.3 verso, page 6, RF 30273.7), 144; Paris, Musée d'Orsay 11 (RF41640), 16 (L79), 20 (RF16585), 22 (RF11689), 33 (RF15502), 35 (RF2207), 37 (RF15530), 39 (Lemoisne 126), 41 (RF11691), 42 (RF15488), 43 (RF22615), 44 (RF15515), 45 (RF15481), 46 (RF12265), 47 (RF12261), 48 (RF15505), 49 (RF15517), 50 (RF15522), 51 (RF15506), 52 (RF15519), 53 (RF12274), 55 (Isaac de Camondo bequest, 1911), 67, 70, 79 (RF31201), 80 (RF31202), 82 (RF30263), 83 (Isaac de Camondo bequest, 1911), 84 (RF1977), 92 (RF31140), 96 (RF16723), 97 (RF4038), 99 (RF4645), 109 (RF4039), 120, 130 (RG12257), 138 (RF5605), 159 (RF30015), 163 (RF4534), 169 (RF4046), 176 (RF4045), 181 (REC50), 185, 203, 221 (RF4044); Paris, Musée Picasso 142; Paris, Prat Collection 21; Pasadena, Norton Simon Art Foundation 110 (F.1969.40), 111 (M.1977.6), 128 (M.1978.26), 129 (F.1978.4), 192, 195; Pau, Musée des Beaux-Arts 19 (L320); Philadelphia Museum of Art; 89 (The Henry P. McIlhenny Collection in memory of Frances P. McIlhenny, 1986), 116 (The Henry P. McIlhenny Collection in memory of Frances P. McIlhenny, 1986, 1986.26.15), 151 (John G. Johnson Collection, 1917, inv. 969), 205 (Purchased with funds from the estate of George D. Widener, 1980, 1980-6-1); Princeton (NJ), Princeton University Art Museum 179 (on long term loan from The Henry and Rose Pearlman Foundation), 206 (on long term loan from The Henry and Rose Pearlman Foundation), 232; Private collections 13 (Walter Feilchenfeldt, Zurich), 15 (Walter Feilchenfeldt, Zurich), 68, 71, 74, 77, 78 (Marlborough Fine Art Ltd, London), 94 (Thomas Gibson Fine Art, London), 95, 106, 132, 133 (Walter Feilchenfeldt, Zurich), 135 (Thomas Gibson Fine Art, London), 136, 137 (Eberhard W. Kornfeld, Berne), 155, 157 (Lefevre Gallery, London), 172 (formerly Thomas Gibson Fine Art, London), 200 (Artemis Gallery, London), 201 (Collection of Mr A. Alfred Taubman), 213 (on loan to the National Gallery, London), 217, 223, 231 (Galerie Schmit, Paris); Providence, Rhode Island School of Design 164 (Gift of Mrs Murray S. Danforth, 57.233); Riehen, Basel, Fondation Beyeler 215; Rotterdam, Boymans-van Beuningen Museum 64 (F.11.127), 141 (F.11.22), 168 (F.11.129), 226 (F.11.217); Shelburne (VT), The Shelburne Museum 86; St Petersburg, State Hermitage Museum 174; Stockholm, Nationalmuseum 218 (Bridgeman Art Library); Toledo (OH), Toledo Museum of Art 229; Vienna, Österreichische Galerie Belvedere 196; Washington, DC, Corcoran Art Gallery 124; Washington, DC, Dumbarton Oaks, House Collection 23 (HC.P. 1937.12. E); Washington, DC, National Gallery of Art 54 (collection of Mr and Mrs Paul Mellon, 1999.79.10), 61 (1999.79.11), 90 (collection of Mr and Mrs Paul Mellon, 1999.80.28), 178 (gift of the W. Averell Harriman Foundation in memory of Marie N. Harriman, 1972.9.9), 208 (Chester Dale Collection, 1963.10.122); Williamstown (MA), Sterling and Francine Clark Art Institute frontispiece, 8, 9 (Bridgeman Art Library), 26, 28, 62, 63, 66, 140 (Bridgeman Art Library), 153 (1955.559); Wuppertal, Von der Heydt Museum 30 (inv. KK 1060/165), 81 (inv. G 960); Zurich, Kunsthaus 165

Index

Page numbers in *italics* refer to illustrations.

Ingres, Jean-Auguste-Dominique 8, 19, 84, 185, 246, 272; influence on ED 10–11, 22, 53–5, 81, 247; *Roger Freeing Angelica* 29
Italy, ED's travels in 10, 31–7, 243–4, 245

Japanese prints 190
Jeanniot, Georges 15, 244–5, 247, 273; *Memories of Degas* 53, 193, 197–8
Jephthah 58–9, *58*
Jour et la Nuit, Le (proposed publication) 128

Kollwitz, Käthe 63

Lafond, Paul, *Degas* 271
Lamothe, Louis 19, 22, 80
laundresses 118–19, 124, 187
Lecoq de Boisbaudron, Horace 192–3
Léger, Fernand 283
Lemoine, Paul-André 273
Leonardo da Vinci 7, 20, 34, 43
Lépic, Count Ludovic 122, 272
lithographs 273, 283, 284
Longchamp (racecourse) 17, 247
Lorrain, Claude 243–4
Lycurgus 55
Lyon 22

Mallarmé, Stephane 272
Malo, Mlle (dancer) *135*
Manet, Edouard 7, 79–80, 86, 116, 132, 193, 278, 283; sketchbooks 12; *Déjeuner sur l'herbe* 79; *Olympia* 79
Manet, Eugène 273
Manet, Julie 273, 281
Manet, Suzanne 80
Mantegna, Andrea 20, 21, 23, 27, 59
Manzi, Michel 273
Marey, Etienne Jules 192
Matisse, Henri 8, 193, 194, 283
Maupassant, Guy de 117
Ménil-Hubert 16, 79, 244, 247
Michelangelo 7, 28, 34
milliners 186–8
Minkus, Ludwig 84
Mirbeau, Octave 185, 194, 198
Miss La La (circus performer) 124–5, *126*, *127*
Monet, Claude 83, 115, 116, 185, 187, 243, 244, 245, 247, 250
monotypes 15, 125, 131–2, 194, 245
Montauban 246
Montefiascone 36
Moore, George 15, 63, 198
Morbilli, Edmondo 33, 272

Morbilli, Giuseppe, Duke of Sant'Angelo a Frosolone 31–2
Morbilli, Rosa, Duchess of Sant'Angelo a Frosolone (*née* Degas) 31–2
Morbilli, Thérèse (*née* Degas) 33, 34, 83, *107*, 272
Moreau, Gustave 35, 53, 56, 62
Morisot, Berthe 80, 116, 272, 273
Mulready, William 244
Musson, Célestine (ED's mother) 7, 33
Musson, Estelle 33
Muybridge, Eadweard 192

Nabis, Les 8, 281
Naples 7, 31, 34, 37, 51, 244; Palazzo Pignatelli di Monteleone 31
Napoleon III, Emperor 116
Naturalism 115, 132
Neo-Impressionism 8
New Orleans 7, 33–4, 59
Normandy, ED visits 79, 80, 83, 244, 247
North Africa, ED visits 245

Orléans 31, 59
Ornans 247
Orvieto 34, 36–7

Paris: Bibliothèque Nationale 19; Ecole des Beaux-Arts 10, 19–20; ED's studios 14, 271; Lycée Louis-le-Grand 8, 19; Musée du Louvre 19, 20, 56, 79, 128; Opéra 84, 119–22, 123, 189
Paris Salon 10, 53, 79, 115–16, 278; (1861) 62; (1865) 59; (1866) 79; (1867) 32, 79; (1869) 79; (1870) 79
Pellegrini, Carlo *165*
Perronneau, Jean-Baptiste 278
Perrot, Jules 123, *159*
Perugia 34
Petit, Georges 7, 117
photography 9, 14, 190, 192, 275
Picasso, Pablo 8, 125, 194, 271, 283
Piero della Francesca 56
Pintoricchio 34
Pisa 34
Pissarro, Camille 7, 115, 116, 128, 185, 193, 243, 272, 273, 278; fans *131*; sketchbooks 12
Plutarch 55
Pollard, James 247
Pollock, Jackson 280
Post-Impressionism 185–6
Poussin, Nicolas 20, 244
Primicile, Gioacchino, Duke of Montejasi 31–2